ﺡ ﺻ -

A HISTORY

OF THE

LITERATURE OF ANCIENT ISRAEL

THE MACMILLAN COMPANY
NEW YORK · BOSTON · CHICAGO
DALLAS · SAN FRANCISCO

MACMILLAN & CO., LIMITED
LONDON · BOMBAY · CALCUTTA
MELBOURNE

THE MACMILLAN CO. OF CANADA, LTD.
TORONTO

A HISTORY

OF THE

LITERATURE OF ANCIENT ISRAEL

FROM THE EARLIEST TIMES TO 135 B.C.

BY

HENRY THATCHER FOWLER, Ph.D.

PROFESSOR OF BIBLICAL LITERATURE AND HISTORY
IN BROWN UNIVERSITY

New York

THE MACMILLAN COMPANY

1922

All rights reserved

PRINTED IN THE UNITED STATES OF AMERICA

The Bible Text used in this volume is taken from the American Standard Edition of the Revised Bible, copyright 1901 by Thomas Nelson and Sons, and is used by permission.

COPYRIGHT, 1912,

BY THE MACMILLAN COMPANY.

Set up and electrotyped. Published September, 1912.

Norwood Press
J. S. Cushing Co. — Berwick & Smith Co.
Norwood, Mass., U.S.A.

220.6
F 786 L
c. 3

TO

HARRIET NESMITH FOWLER

STUDENT OF LITERATURE, KEEN CRITIC

WISE COUNSELLOR

PREFACE

In recent years, many have written general histories of Israel and more have discussed her writings; but, thus far, little attempt has been made to tell the connected story of the growth of Israel's thought in its changing forms of expression and in relation to other aspects of her history. It is now possible to arrange the writings of ancient Israel in their historical connections with more of detail and certainty than in the case of most early literatures, and the time seems ripe for writing a history of the literature of this nation similar to those written for ancient Greece, Rome, India, Persia, Arabia, and more modern peoples.

Some excuse for the undertaking of this high task by the present writer may be found in the fact that he has waited a dozen years since it first seemed to him full time for the history, and has not ventured to write this volume before proving, in university and general lectures, that such treatment of Israel's literature can be made intelligible and helpful to constructive thinking.

Confidence is felt that the historical order set forth rests upon a firm basis, since it varies in only a few particulars from that presented in "Outlines for the Study of Biblical History and Literature," published nearly six years ago by F. K. Sanders and H. T. Fowler. Constant reëxamination of the Hebrew writings themselves and consideration of the critical discussions published in the intervening years indicate few and slight changes in the outline of Israel's literary history, then assumed as presenting the consensus of scholarship.

Special acknowledgment of indebtedness is due to Rabbi Nathan Stern, Ph.D., who has read and criticised the present work; to Hon. John C. Rose, of the Federal Bench, for similar service in the portions that treat of the eighth century reformers and the law books Deuteronomy and Leviticus; and to Professor Morris Jastrow, Jr., Ph.D., for a thorough revision, almost a new translation, of his version of the Babylonian Deluge narrative, made expressly for this work and most generously placed at the service of the author. Indebtedness is cordially acknowledged also to Thomas Nelson and Sons for permission to quote The American Standard Version of the Bible at length, and to the Delegates and Syndics of the University Presses of Oxford and Cambridge for similar permission to use the Revised Version of a portion of the Apocrypha; to Charles Scribner's Sons, Lemcke and Buechner, Luzac and Company, Dodd, Mead, and Company, and the George H. Doran Company for permission to print certain translations of Hebrew and other Semitic literature published by them.

The author alone is to be held responsible for any errors in the statement of facts or in the copying of translations which may appear in the present volume.

HENRY THATCHER FOWLER.

BROWN UNIVERSITY,
17 June, 1912.

NOTE ON BOOKS OF REFERENCE

In "Outlines for the Study of Biblical History and Literature," F. K. Sanders and H. T. Fowler (New York: Charles Scribner's Sons. $1.25), the writings of ancient Israel are analyzed and arranged in their historical connections with explicit references to the best critical literature.

Dr. Karl Budd in his "Geschichte der althebräischen Litteratur" (Leipzig: C. F. Amelang, m. 8.50) discusses the writings of ancient Israel in their general chronological order, though grouping topically more than the present work. Dr. Alfred Bertholet contributes the chapter on the Apocrypha in this volume.

The volumes of "The Student's Old Testament," C. F. Kent, offer a new critical translation of the books, analyzed into their component documents, with historical introductions and copious notes and bibliographies. The arrangement is in part chronological and in part topical. The successive volumes are: "Narratives of the Beginnings of Hebrew History"; "Israel's Historical and Biographical Narratives"; "Sermons, Epistles, and Apocalypses of Israel's Prophets"; "Israel's Laws and Traditional Precedents"; "Songs, Psalms, and Prayers"; "Proverbial and Didactic Poems" (New York: Charles Scribner's Sons. $2.75 per volume).

The standard Old Testament "Introductions" discuss the literary history of each book, but do not arrange the books and documents in historical order The best of these include: "An Introduction to the Literature of the Old Testament," S. R. Driver (New York: Charles Scribner's Sons. $2.50); "Introduction to the Canonical Books of the Old Testament," C. H. Cornhill (New York: G. P. Putnam's Sons. London: Williams and Norgate. $3); "A Biblical Introduction," W. H. Bennett and W. F. Adeney (New York: Thomas Whittaker. $2); "Introduction to the Old Testament," J. E. McFadyen (New York: A. C. Armstrong and Son. London: Hodder and Stoughton. $1.75).

Thorough articles on each Old Testament book are given in: "Encyclopædia Biblica" (New York and London: Macmillan and Company. 4 vols. $5 each); "A Dictionary of the Bible," James Hastings (New York: Charles Scribner's Sons. Edinburgh: T. and T. Clark. 5 vols. $6 each). Briefer, but excellent, articles are given in the Hastings "One Volume Bible Dictionary" (New York: Charles Scribner's Sons. $5); "The Standard Bible Dictionary" (New York: Funk and Wagnalls. $6); "The Encyclopædia Britannica."

Recent commentaries, such as "The Bible for Home and School" (New York: Macmillan and Company); "The International Critical Commentary" (New York: Charles Scribner's Sons); "Westminster Commentaries" (New York: Edwin S. Gorham. London: Methuen and Company); "Göttinger Handkommentar zum Alten Testament," W. Nowack (Göttingen: Vandenhoeck and Ruprecht); "Kurzer Hand-Commentar zum Alten Testament," K. H. C. Marti (Tubingen: J. C. B. Mohr), treat the literary history of the books in the introductions of the several volumes.

Various aspects of the English Bible as literature are discussed in "Life and Literature of the Ancient Hebrews," Lyman Abbott (Boston: Houghton, Mifflin and Company. $2); "The Bible as English Literature," J. H. Gardiner (New York: Charles Scribner's Sons. $1.50); "The Literary Study of the Bible," R. G. Moulton (Boston: D. C. Heath and Company. $2); "A Short Introduction to the Literature of the Bible," R. G. Moulton (Boston: D. C. Heath and Company. $1); "Hebrew Life and Thought," L. S. Houghton (Chicago: The University of Chicago Press. $1.50).

CONTENTS

xi

CHAPTER VIII

CHAPTER IX

CHAPTER X

CHAPTER XI

CHAPTER XII

CHAPTER XIII

CHAPTER XIV

CHAPTER XV

CHAPTER XVI

CHAPTER XVII

CHAPTER XVIII

CHAPTER XIX

CHAPTER XX

CHAPTER XXI

CHAPTER XXII

CHAPTER XXIII

CHAPTER XXIV

CHAPTER XXV

CHAPTER XXVI

A HISTORY

OF THE

LITERATURE OF ANCIENT ISRAEL

A HISTORY OF THE LITERATURE OF ANCIENT ISRAEL

CHAPTER I

ISRAEL IN THE ANCIENT SEMITIC WORLD

WHEN the Hebrews became a nation, the history of Semitic civilization in Babylonia already spanned a period as long as that from the opening of the Christian era to the present century.[1]   The most ancient records found in the Tigris-Euphrates valley indicate that the Semites had conquered and settled among earlier inhabitants of another race, who had developed a high degree of civilization before their conquerors came into the region.   When the earliest written records begin, two races are intermingled, with the Semites dominant, and two languages exist side by side, the one an agglutinative tongue, the other Semitic.   Both languages are written in the cuneiform characters which had evidently been borrowed by the Semites.   Civilization was far removed from savage or pastoral conditions; a pure agricultural stage had been

[1] A few years ago most students of Babylonian history were agreed that our knowledge of it extended back at least as far as 4500 or 5000 B.C., and that the culture then existing testified to a long period of development far removed from anything that could be styled a state of savagery. — See Goodspeed, *A History of the Babylonians and Assyrians;* Rogers, *History of Babylonia and Assyria;* Sanders and Fowler, *Outlines of Biblical History and Literature;* etc.   More recent discoveries, however, indicating that some of the later Babylonian dynasties overlapped, have made it probable that our earliest actual historical knowledge of Babylonia does not greatly antedate 3000 B.C., although it is true that the civilization then existing clearly indicates a long period of previous development.   See Winckler, *History of Babylonia and Assyria;* King, *History of Sumer and Akkad.*

reached, with walled cities inhabited by people familiar with many of the arts. The prevalent type of government was that of the city state; but a tendency toward consolidation through conquest was soon manifest, resulting in the formation of more or less extensive kingdoms.

Most investigators of the subject believe that the Arabian peninsula was the region whence the conquerors came into the fertile valley. It has recently been contended that, whatever may have been the earlier home of the common Semitic stock, the conquerors of Babylonia moved down from the northwest, from a great centre of Semitic civilization in Syria which antedated that in Babylonia.[1] The arguments adduced hardly prove the thesis, but under either hypothesis, early in the third millennium B.C., civilized Semites controlled the entire fertile crescent of territory extending from the Persian Gulf to the borders of Egypt, northward of the plateau of Arabia.

Southern Semites occupied the great interior of Arabia and developed civilized states on its southern shores, many centuries before the Christian era. Thence some, at an early date, crossed the lower end of the Red Sea and settled in that part of Africa which we call Abyssinia. These may be passed by with brief mention, for it is with the northern Semites that the student of Hebrew history is concerned.

According to the view usually held, a second irresistible wave of expanding population brought new hordes from Arabia into the region about its northern end during the third millennium. To this so-called Amorite migration is ascribed the coming of the early Canaanites and Phœnicians into the regions which they secured and so long held. Here they displaced a non-Semitic, cave-dwelling people.[2]

At an early date Egypt was influenced by Semitic culture, and, in turn, Egyptian influence greatly affected Canaan. About 1675 B.C. an Asiatic dynasty, known as the Hyksos, ruled in Egypt, and when the native Egyptians succeeded in expelling the foreigners, a century later, the impulse of the movement carried the conquering Egyptian armies into Canaan and brought the land

[1] *Amurru, the Home of the Northern Semites*, Albert T. Clay.
[2] *Canaan d'après l'exploration récente*, H. Vincent, pp. 373–426.

under the sway of the Pharaoh.   Before 1450 B.C. Egypt's power
extended as far as the Euphrates, or even into Mesopotamia.

The discovery at Tell-el-Amarna in Egypt (1887–1888) of a
large collection of letters and despatches to the Egyptian kings,
Amenophis III and IV, has given a vivid picture of conditions in
Canaan at the opening of the fourteenth century.[1]   It appears
that the land was under local governors responsible to the Pharaoh ;
these officers were at feud with one another, and the Egyptian power
in the land was evidently weakening.   Some of the letters are
frantic appeals from the various governors for the king to send
troops, before the land and cities are entirely lost to Egypt.   One
of the Jerusalem letters will serve as an example.

"To my lord, the king : — Abd-hiba, your servant.   At the feet of my
lord, the king, seven and seven times, I fall.   What have I done against
my lord, the king ?   Some one has slandered me before my lord, the king,
(saying) : 'Abd-hiba has revolted from his lord, the king.'   Behold,
neither my father nor my mother appointed me in this place.   The strong
arm of the king inaugurated me in my father's territory.   Why should I
commit an offense against my lord, the king ?   True as the king lives,
because I said to my lord, the king's officer : — Why are you favorable
to the Habiri and unfavorable to the (native feudal) princes, for this reason
they slander me before my lord, the king.   Because I say : — The territory
of my lord, the king, will be ruined, for this reason they slander me before
my lord, the king.

" Let my lord, the king, know that my lord, the king, had stationed a
garrison, but Janhamu has taken (it) ... Egypt ... my lord, the king ...
there is no garrison there.   Let the king care for his land, and [pay some
heed] to his land ; the cities of my lord, the king, belonging to Ili-milki, have
fallen away, and the whole territory of the king will be lost.   Let my lord,
the king, therefore, care for his land.   I think I will go to the court to my
lord, the king, and see the tears [2] of my lord, the king, but the enemies are
powerful against me, and I am not able to go to court, to my lord, the king.
May it seem good therefore to my lord, the king, to send a garrison, in
order that I may go to court and see the tears [2] of my lord, the king.   As
long as my lord, the king, lives [3] when an officer goes forth, I (always)

[1] The letters include diplomatic correspondence between the kings of
Babylonia and Mesopotamia and the Pharaoh, messages from subject
rulers of Phœnicia and northern Syria, as well as from various cities of
Palestine, — Jerusalem, Ashkelon, Gezer, Lachish.

[2] Perhaps an error for "face."   [3] Oath = by the life of the king.

say : — The land of the king is going to ruin. If you do not listen to me, all the dependent princes will be lost, and my lord, the king, will have no more dependent princes. Let the king therefore turn his attention to the princes, and let my lord, the king, send troops. The king has no longer any territory, the Habiri have devastated all the king's territory. If troops come in this year, the territory will remain my lord, the king's, but if no troops come, the territory of my lord, the king, is lost. To the scribe of my lord, the king : — Abd-hiba, your servant. Bring plainly (aloud) before my lord, the king, (these) words : 'The whole territory of my lord, the king, is going to ruin.'" [1]

Frequent mention is made of a people called Habiri who are rapidly getting a foothold in the land. In these we may possibly be justified in finding the forerunners of the Hebraic migration.

The language used, even when a local governor of Syria or Canaan is writing to Egypt, is the Semitic Babylonian, and the script is the cuneiform. Whatever may have been the course of the early migrations and settlement, it is clear that the language and mode of writing of the Babylonians had spread throughout the entire region from the lower Euphrates valley to the borders of Egypt. Recent discoveries at the old Hittite capital in Asia Minor show that the same mode of writing was familiar there, even though the Hittites had their own written language.

At the time of the Egyptian conquest of Syria, the political power of Babylonia had waned. The next three centuries saw the north Semitic world in much confusion. A people styled the Mitanni ruled in Mesopotamia, and the Hittites moved down into Syria. While these two seem to have been kindred peoples, they were mutually hostile. Spreading from an original centre on the east side of the upper Tigris, the new Semitic kingdom of Assyria extended itself into Mesopotamia and waged bitter war with the Babylonians on its south. The Hittites forced Egypt out of northern Syria and limited her Asiatic territory to the region south of the Lebanons.

During these centuries of confusion, there seems to have come another overflow from Arabia, styled the Aramean migration. By 1300 B.C. the Arameans were moving up the Euphrates valley and westward. It was probably this movement which brought

---

[1] Winckler, *The Tell-el-Amarna Letters*, pp. 303–305.

the progenitors of the Hebraic peoples from Mesopotamia to the borders of Palestine.[1] Here in the region east of the Jordan and Dead Sea, a part of the migrating people obtained settlement and became the nations of Ammon and Moab. The others passed to the south of the Dead Sea, where a part found a permanent home in the mountainous district, becoming the people known as Edom. Still others continued in a somewhat wandering state on the high steppe land at the south of Canaan, until a part of them entered the Delta region of Egypt. The fertility of this district has ever attracted those who dwell on the borders of the desert. It seems probable that only a small part of the tribes eventually amalgamated into the Hebrew people actually entered Egypt. Possibly only two closely allied tribes knew Egyptian bondage; there is indication that others remained in the region southward of Beersheba, and that still others were assimilated after entrance into Canaan.

It was not far from 1200 B.C. that the tribes which had settled in Egypt made their escape, after they had been for a time subjected to task work by Ramses II. In the wilderness south of Palestine they became closely affiliated with the kindred tribes that had continued in that region, and entered into covenant relation with the God Yahweh.[2] After a somewhat prolonged sojourn in this

---

[1] Cf. Deuteronomy 26 [5].

[2] The form Jehovah, the use of which has not been noted earlier than the fourteenth century A.D. (see Moore, *Am. Jour. Theol.*, January, 1908), was certainly not the name of the God of ancient Israel. Jehovah is, however, generally used in the present volume to avoid the interruption of thought occasioned to most readers by meeting the name in an unfamiliar form. The chief exceptions are in translations of poetry when "Jehovah" sadly breaks the metre. The Hebrew name was written Yhwh, and long before the vowel signs were invented, the Jews had come to regard "the name" as too sacred for utterance. In its place, they read usually Lord, sometimes God. When the vowels were inserted in the Hebrew text, those of Lord or God were written. The vowels of the Hebrew word for Lord, with the four consonants of the proper name of Israel's God came finally to be represented in English as Jehovah, though the English versions, prior to the American Revision, generally followed the practice of using the title Lord instead of the proper name, indicating the places where it represented the proper name by printing in capital letters. The vowel sounds were probably originally *a* and *e*. The name Yahweh, from

district, movements east of the Jordan offered an opportunity to secure a more settled abode. A king from the region to the northeast of the Sea of Galilee had recently moved down and driven Ammon back to the borders of the Arabian desert. The confederated tribes, making a long detour to the south of Edom and east of Moab, swept down upon the Jordan valley at the northern border of Moab and effectually dislodged the new Amorite settlers.

From the vantage ground of the east Jordan district, favorable opportunity was soon found for the passage of the river and for the gradual occupation of the central ridge of Canaan, which runs from north to south on the west of the Jordan valley. The older portions of Israel's historical narratives, supported by the facts of later conditions, show that this occupation was indeed very gradual and that the newcomers were forced to live for generations in the midst of the older population which continued to hold many of the walled towns and the more fertile valleys.[1]

Before the close of the twelfth century B.C., the major part of the federated tribes which acknowledged Jehovah as their covenant God had crossed to Palestine proper, although some had found permanent settlement east of the Jordan and north of Moab. A reference on an Egyptian monument seems to make it clear that Asher was settled in Canaan before the exodus from Egypt, and the theory is plausible that the other three concubine tribes[2] were late members of the confederation, perhaps affiliated only after the settlement in Canaan.

We do not know how far the invading tribes may have been familiar with the arts and usages of settled agricultural life when they entered Canaan, nor how much they already possessed of the customs, laws, and traditional lore of their race. Haran in Mesopotamia, whence the Hebraic migration apparently moved down, was an ancient seat of Semitic religion and culture. It may be that the tribes which ultimately became the people of Israel brought from their temporary Mesopotamian home, and

a root meaning *to become*, may signify either *He who is*, absolutely, or *He who brings into being.*

[1] See, *e.g.*, Judges 1 [20, 21, 27-36].

[2] Dan, Naphtali, Gad, Genesis 30.

preserved through all their nomad days, more of the traditions of the civilized Semites than pure nomads would naturally possess. It may be that the influential portion of the tribes which sojourned in Egypt absorbed and carried away some elements of Egyptian culture. It will never be possible to determine how much Israel brought with her into Palestine, for she settled in the midst of the highly civilized Semites of Canaan and gradually absorbed their ancient culture. The close kinship of the Canaanite culture with that of Babylonia and the long rule of Egypt in Palestine have already been noted. It is, therefore, impossible to discriminate between Babylonian and Egyptian ideas which Israel brought into Canaan and those which she gained from the earlier inhabitants of the land.

Israel's prehistoric traditions have been subjected to the most searching analysis in the effort to determine their ultimate origin. Some bear on their face evidence of their rise in the Tigris-Euphrates district; such are the story of the Garden of Eden and of the Tower of Babel. Some seem to be of Canaanite origin; many of these centre about Hebron or Bethel. Still others indicate something of Egyptian influence. While it is possible thus to determine with much certainty the original habitat of many of Israel's stories, such analysis does not necessarily indicate when the various elements became the possession of Israel. To the sources of uncertainty on this point that have already been indicated, we must add the facts that direct intercourse with Egypt continued throughout all periods of Hebrew history, and, from the middle of the ninth century on, Israel came into contact, first, with Assyria and then, with the new Babylonian kingdom. Assyria conquered and absorbed northern Israel in the eighth century, and later, Babylon subdued Judah and carried into exile the more cultured portion of the people. Of these the greater part never returned to Palestine, and the Babylonian Jews dominated the life and literature of Palestinian Judaism for centuries. These facts may suffice to indicate the difficulty of determining the exact historical relation between Israel's thought and that of the Babylonians, Assyrians, Canaanites, and Egyptians, and also to suggest that all periods of Hebrew literature will show influences from one or several of these sources.

It is possible to distinguish, in large measure, those elements of Israel's literature, both of form and substance, which are a part of her heritage as a division of the great Semitic race and those which are due to her own peculiar genius and national history.[1] Such discrimination will reveal the fact that the literature of ancient Israel has preserved and transmitted to the modern world the rich deposit of whole millenniums of cultural development, so that through it the Christian nations have become heirs to a great Semitic heritage. Yet such discrimination will make it equally clear that the notion of Israel's literature as little more than the retort in which the fine metal was precipitated is quite inadequate.

The study of pre-classical history is making it more and more clear that Greek civilization was not born Athene-like, but that the Hellenes absorbed vast stores of culture, intellectual, moral, artistic, from the nations that had gone before. Greece was heir of Egypt and Babylonia. Greek architecture, law, letters, philosophy, all show the influence of these earlier civilizations; yet a Greek temple is not simply an Egyptian temple, despite its manifest kinship, and Greek stoicism is not simply a Semitic philosophy, though its founder was a Semite. According to their peculiar genius, the Greeks transformed, perfected, and

---

[1] If we agree with the Panbabylonists that "it is evident to the simplest reflection on the nature and origin of human thoughts that the ideas which conquered the old civilized world did not spring up in some remote corner," we may be forced to admit that among the Babylonians "Judaism must have received not only its impulse, but also its entire system," and we may even assent to the sweeping generalization "that the origins of the fundamental teachings of Judaism, not yet discovered in cuneiform literature, shall yet be found there." See Winckler, *History of Babylonia and Assyria*, Eng. trans., pp. 157–158. Most of us, however, will hardly feel justified in coming to conclusions that leave mere facts so far behind, resting on assumed invariable, historical law that is itself hardly established; if, indeed, it be not contrary to known facts of history. The discussion of the literary history of Israel in the following pages will proceed along the lines already indicated in the text, recognizing that Israel inherited or absorbed much from the closely interrelated world of which she was a part, but that her own national genius is entitled to the credit for those elements of spirit and thought in her literature which have no parallel or close analogy in the writings of other peoples.

made a new creation all that they adopted from preceding ages. Quite as distinctly in certain directions, Israel made her heritage a new creation. Her literature is not only the deposit of millenniums of Semitic history, but something unique in itself — inadequately symbolized by the fine metal — rather the finest flowering of the whole Semitic race.

CHAPTER II

THE BEGINNINGS OF HEBREW LITERATURE

(Before 1040 B.C.)

THE Tell-el-Amarna tablets and some recent discoveries in Palestine itself have shown that in the fifteenth century B.C. the written language of Canaan was cuneiform Babylonian.[1] Just when the alphabetic writing of the people of Canaan superseded this mode of expression is, as yet, undetermined; though it must have been between 1400 and 1000 or 900 B.C. The Moabite Stone, a few Hebrew inscriptions from the age of the monarchy, Phœnician and Aramaic inscriptions, show that from the ninth century and probably indicate that from at least 1000 B.C. the peoples of Canaan employed essentially one language and one alphabetic mode of writing. This was already so perfected by the ninth century as to suggest long usage.[2]

Indications as to the dates of the oldest documents into which the Hebrew histories may be analyzed carry us back to about the same point as the inscriptions. Our earliest Hebrew book (Amos) dates only from the eighth century; but critical analysis of the books of Samuel yields connected prose narratives which must have assumed written form at least a century earlier, and it may be as early as the latter part of the tenth century. Such facts limit the time for the transition from the Babylonian cunei-

[1] See p. 4.

[2] Some date the earliest Phœnician inscription at about 1000 B.C. See *Standard Bib. Dict.*, § Alphabet; *Ency. Brit.* (11th ed.), § Alphabet. The Moabite Stone, set up by Mesha, king of Moab, to commemorate his deliverance from Hebrew oppression soon after Ahab's reign, dates from about 845 B.C. The bits of inscribed pottery, found in the supposed palace of Omri and Ahab by the Harvard expedition in 1910, indicate that in the first half of the ninth century B.C. Israel used alphabetic writing with the ease and grace of long custom. See *Harvard Theological Review*, January, 1911.

form to Canaanite alphabetic writing to a period of four or five centuries.[1] This extends from two centuries before the exodus[2] to the time of David or the early years of the divided kingdom, soon after Solomon's death.

Some poems and many historical traditions concerning the exodus and settlement in Canaan have come down from this period; but we cannot say whether any of these were committed to writing earlier than the time of David or Solomon. We know that some of them were already written and even gathered into books before they were embodied by the historians of the ninth and eighth centuries in their writings; but if they were not written down till a short time before this, none of the extant Hebrew poetry would indicate a period of oral transmission longer than that established for some of the pre-Islamic, Arabic poems — the latter were preserved by oral tradition for at least three or four hundred years.[3] We can only say that a few poetic bits, preserved to us, probably assumed fixed form before the entrance into Canaan, and that several short poems and one of some ninety lines have existed in substantially their original form since the early years of struggle for possession of Palestine.

Among the fragments that may have been composed in the wilderness period, the song commemorating the unexpected escape at the Red Sea naturally comes to mind at the outset. In its present form this elaborate poem shows unmistakable acquaintance with later events.

> Then were the chiefs of Edom dismayed:
> The mighty men of Moab, trembling taketh hold upon them:
> All the inhabitants of Canaan are melted away.[4]

These lines presuppose events at the close of the wilderness sojourn, while

[1] The significance of the origin of this "Semitic alphabet" is appreciated when one realizes that from it came the Greek and other European alphabets.

[2] Present knowledge of Egyptian history and of Egyptian control over Palestine makes it clear that the exodus could not have occurred till about 1200 B.C. See *Outlines Biblical Hist. and Lit.*, Sanders and Fowler, pp. 28–29, where references are given to recent literature.

[3] R. A. Nicholson, *Literary History of Arabs*, pp. xxii, 131.

[4] Exodus 15 [15].

> the mountain of thine inheritance,
> The place, O Yahweh, which thou hast made for thee to dwell in,
> The sanctuary, O Lord, which thy hands have established,

clearly carry us down at least to the time of Solomon, more than two centuries later than the deliverance at the Sea. There is, however, no reason why the nucleus of this poem may not have been composed at the time of the event commemorated. How far this nucleus extended beyond the couplet —

> Sing ye to Yahweh, for in triumph he rose;
> Horse and chariot he cast to the sea[1] —

it is impossible to say.[2]

In the traditions of the Exodus period, the north Arabian tribe of the Kenites is prominent. In their district was the sacred mountain where Moses had his vision of Jehovah and where, after the escape from Egypt, the tribes entered into covenant with the God who revealed himself in thunder clouds, on the mountain's summit. Without committing ourselves to the theory that this was Israel's first contact with Jehovah and that the covenant was simply an adoption of the Kenite God, we may fully recognize that the Kenites became a part of the confederation which ultimately developed into the Hebrew nation, and that their traditional lore became a portion of Israel's heritage. One trace of this

---

[1] Adopting with Cornill (*Intro. Canonical Bks.*, *O. T.*, pp. 118–119) the form of v. 21, "Sing ye," rather than "I sing." Usually where the translations of Hebrew poetry given in this book vary from those of the *American Standard Version* without special note, it is due to the present author's attempt to approach more nearly to the terseness and rhythm of the original; these qualities cannot be adequately reproduced in a translation. For example, in the second line of the above couplet, the Hebrew has only four words, of seven full syllables in all. The usual English version (both A. V. and R. V.) has thirteen syllables; the above translation has reduced the number to ten and has tried to suggest in each line the four beats of the Hebrew metre. By a slight change of the late vowel points, one may read chariot rather than rider or charioteer. See McNeile, *Exodus, Westminster Com.*, *in loc.*

[2] Consideration of the poem in its relation to the parallel prose narrative of ch. 14, and to the general development of Hebrew language and literature, leads to the conclusion that it was composed, as a whole, not earlier than the Babylonian Exile and perhaps even later. See McNeile, *op. cit.*, p. 88 f. Baentsch in Nowack's *Handkommentar*, I, 2, p. 128 f.

latter fact we may find in "The Song of the Sword."[1] The context
suggests the theory that the song utters the fierce joy incident to
the discovery of the advantage of sharp-edged weapons of metal.
Although there is no adequate ground for believing that these lines
took shape in any such remote past as the time when the Kenite ancestors first made this discovery, the song does sound "an echo from
the old times of the Bedouins"[2] and may give us a true type of the
boastful speech of a nomad tribe, a report from the beginning of
poetic art.[3] Perhaps the shout "Cain shall be avenged sevenfold"
was an old Kenite tribal cry.[4] The poem is now commonly interpreted as an expression of the law of blood revenge, so dominant
among the Bedouin of to-day and constantly presupposed in
Hebrew law and literature. Marti, however, finds in it the voice
of an age when "the strict law of the *Jus talionis* was as yet unknown, when vengeance still had free play."[5] The poem consists
of six lines : —

> Adah and Zillah, hear my saying,
> Wives of Lamech listen my speaking :
> For a man have I slain for my wounding,
> And a youth for my striking.
> If sevenfold Cain shall sure be avenged,
> Then Lamech seventy and seven.[6]

One would like to feel certain that the charming little "Song
of the Well"[7] can rightly be ascribed to the same early era of

---

[1] Genesis 4 23.

[2] Marti, *Religion of Old Testament*, p. 46.

[3] Budde, *Geschichte der Althebräischen Litteratur*, p. 14.

[4] See Gordon, *Early Traditions of Genesis*, pp. 188–191.

[5] Marti, *op. cit.*

[6] This translation seeks to indicate the uniform ending of the first four
lines and also the shortening from four to three beats in the second
members of the second and third couplets. In the Hebrew each line
ends in *i*. A similar effect has been well brought out in the German by
Budde (*Gesch. Alth. Lit.*, p. 14).

> Ada und Zillah, hört meine Stimme,
> Ihr Weiber Lamechs, lauscht meiner Rede :
> Einen Mann erschlag ich für meine Wunde,
> Und ein Kind für meine Strieme.

[7] Numbers 21 17–18.

the wilderness sojourn. The Negeb,[1] with its traditions of ancient wells on which the possibility of life depended,[2] may easily have been its birthplace, but whether it comes from the days of the nomad life or later, it is a true bit of early folksong with idyllic flavor; it has the typical folksong form, a single strophe of four lines complete in itself.[3]   Budde may be right in finding in it reference to a custom known among later Arabs of lightly covering a well that has been discovered and later formally reopening and declaring it clan property.   In this ceremony, symbolic action is performed with the sceptre-like staffs of the Sheiks.[4] Ewald thought of it as belonging to the class "of popular songs accompanying the alternate strokes of hard labor."[5]   Such songs of work are known to us from the fourth millennium B.C. in Egypt; such are still the delight of the fellahin as they work their water-wheels.[6] It is noticeable in this folksong that the well is not conceived as the abode of some spirit; at first the opening seems like an example of personification; but, more probably, as Robertson Smith held, the fountain itself was thought of and addressed as a supernatural being; "of all inanimate things that which has the best marked supernatural associations among the Semites is flowing or, as the Hebrews say, 'living' water."[7]   The lines are:—

> Spring up, O well! Sing to it!
> Well that the princes dug,
> That the nobles of the people delved,
> With sceptre, with their staffs.[8]

[1] The regions south of Judah, approximately from the hills south of Hebron to Kadesh.

[2] Genesis 21 [22 ff] ., 26 [15 ff] .; Judges 1 [15]; Joshua 15 [19].

[3] See Gummere, *The Beginnings of Poetry*, p. 417.

[4] *New World* (March, 1895), pp. 136–144; *Preussische Jahrbücher*, 1895, pp. 491–580, referred to by Gray, *Numbers, Int. Crit. Com.*

[5] Ewald, *Hist. Isr.* (Eng.), II, 203, n. 3.

[6] See Erman, *Life in Ancient Egypt* (Eng.), p. 385.

[7] See Smith, *Religion of the Semites*, pp. 127, 167. For criticism of the last interpretation, and for general discussion of the entire subject with additional references, see Gray, *Numbers, Int. Crit. Com.*, pp. 288 ff.

[8] In the Hebrew, the last couplet rimes. One might try to reproduce **very** freely in English

> Well that the nobles may now quaff.
> Opened with their sceptre and their staff.

Another possible specimen of the songs of this period is introduced in Numbers[1] as commemorating the conquest of the east Jordan territory before the entrance into Canaan. Strong arguments have been adduced for believing that the poem grew rather out of Omri's victories over Moab, after 900 B.C., and was modified to fit the earlier period. If such is really the case, it belongs to a later time than that now under consideration.[2]

> Come ye to Heshbon! Let it be built!
> And let Sihon's city be established!
> When fire went out from Heshbon,
> Flame from Sihon's burgh:
> It devoured Ar of Moab;
> It consumed the heights of Arnon.
> Woe to thee, Moab!
> Perished, O folk of Kemosh!
> He hath given his sons as fugitives,
> And his daughters into captivity,
> To an Amorite King, Sihon.[3]

The introduction preceding this song, "They that speak in proverbs say," indicates the existence of a recognized class of composers and reciters of such poems. Their presence would facilitate long oral transmission, as it did, many centuries later, among the Arabian Semites. This song of triumph exhibits something of the character of ancient taunt songs so widely found among primitive peoples.[4] From the days of the Judges, before the rise of the monarchy, comes, quite surely, Jotham's striking fable concerning the trees that went forth to anoint a king over them.[5] In its artistic, elaborate structure, it testifies to a long

---

[1] 21 27-30.

[2] For discussion of occasion, see Gray, *Numbers, Int. Crit. Com.*, pp. 300 f.; Baentsch, Norwack's *Handkommentar*, I, 2, pp. 184 f.; Schmidt, *Messages of the Poets*, pp. 326 f.

[3] The last couplet is omitted, for the text and translation are utterly uncertain.

[4] The Fescennine verses of the early Romans, with their personal raillery and satirical comment, may be compared. See Duff, *Literary History of Rome*. Mr. H. E. Krehbiel in his lecture on *American Folksong* gives an interesting example from the West Indian negroes.

[5] Judges 9 8-15.

previous development of the type. To the same age, Samson's
riddles are to be assigned. The first of these that we meet,

> From the eater came forth food
> And from the fierce came something sweet,[1]

is a "riddle" quite insoluble without knowledge of a particular
fact. When the needed information has been obtained through
Samson's wife, the answer is given in a corresponding couplet : —

> What is sweeter than honey?
> And what is fiercer than a lion?[2]

Samson's reply forms a rimed couplet : —

> If with my heifer you did not plow,
> You had not solved my riddle now.[3]

The lines celebrating the slaughter of the Philistines contain a
pun, the same Hebrew word being used for both ass and heap or
mass.

> With the jawbone of an ass
> Mass upon mass,
> With the jawbone of an ass
> Have I slain a thousand men.[4]

These examples of bucolic rime and humor give us a glimpse of
that early age when each man did that which was "right in his
own eyes," in the field of poetic composition as in other activities.
In the use of paronomasia, however, they were not anomalous.
The Egyptians, of ancient culture, took great delight in puns,[5] and
later Hebrew literature is full of curious plays upon words, sometimes in the most solemn passages of warning or denunciation.

[1] Judges 14 14.

[2] Judges 14 18.

[3] Adopting translation of Kent, *Student's O. T.*, I, 343. The final
words of the two lines are *eglathi* and *hidathi*.

[4] Judges 15 16.

[5] Erman attempts to reproduce the effect of some of their lines, declaring
the English puns no more far-fetched in sound than the original.

> The *wheels* of thy chariot
> Thou *wieldest* thy battle axe.
> The *scythe* of thy chariot
> Draws *sighs* from all nations.
> — *Life in Ancient Egypt*, p. 396.

From the Samson bits, which a rude age thought worth preserving, we may turn to the prayer at the taking up of the sacred ark. If this did not come from the period of the wilderness sojourn, it must at least have been formulated before the ark was brought to its permanent resting place on Mount Zion. The prayer would be appropriate in connection with sending forth the ark as a palladium in battle, as in the instance narrated in 1 Samuel 4.

> Rise up, O Yahweh,
> And make thine enemies to flee,
> And let them fly who hate thee.[1]

The corresponding lines for the safe return of the ark to its resting-place may be rendered : —

> Return, O Yahweh,
> And bless the myriads
> Of Israel's clans.[2]

Aside from these interesting relics, most of the poems included in the narratives from Genesis to Judges bear their own internal testimony to their origin under the monarchy, rather than in the earlier times with which their settings associate them. Whatever of uncertainty may attach to the effort to assign many specific poems to the pre-monarchical period, the one great literary monument of this age, the Deborah Song,[3] is in itself evident proof that already, in the days of the early tribal struggles for possession of the land, the poet's art had reached great power and some refinement.

This victory ode has suffered sadly in its long transmission, so that many lines are no longer fully intelligible, especially in the central portion of the poem (vv. 8–15). Yet enough remains clear to give us a priceless memorial of Israel's history and literature. From the historians' point of view this song is the

[1] Numbers 10 35. With the Septuagint the last word is omitted; this does not affect the rime of the second and third lines, since the added word ends with the same sound as the preceding, *eka*. The final words become *oyebheka* and *mesaneka*.

[2] Numbers 10 36. The above translation rests upon a fairly probable emendation of the text. See Kittel, *Bib. Heb., in loc.;* Baentsch, *Handkommentar, in loc.*

[3] Judges 5.

most important document for the formative period of Israel. It
gives a fleeting, yet sharply drawn picture of the conditions in
Palestine after the Hebrew tribes had obtained possession of much
of the central mountain ridge, and the fertile valley still remained
in the hands of the earlier inhabitants.[1] A Canaanite king, whom
they had been unable to overcome, had reduced the immigrant
tribes almost to despair. They were disunited and disheartened.

> In the days of Shamgar ben Anath, caravans ceased,
> And travellers of the road journeyed in crooked by-paths.
> Was there seen a shield or a spear
> Among forty thousand in Israel?[2]

In this crisis, when the greatest possible effort to rally the tribes
was made, the Joseph tribes, Ephraim, Benjamin, Manasseh,[3]
which had settled on the hills to the south of Esdraelon, with
Zebulun, Issachar, and Naphtali from the Galilean hills to the
north, responded. The eastern tribes as a whole abode beyond
the Jordan — sat "among the village refuse heaps"[4]

> To hear the calling of the flocks.

The northernmost tribes, Asher and Dan, remained amongst their
Phœnician neighbors, and they too had no part in the supreme
effort which was to give Israel a new strength in the land and to
advance the tribes far toward a national consciousness. The
Hebrews who lay to the south of the hill country of Ephraim, cut
off from their northern kindred by the ancient stronghold of
Jebus, are not even mentioned for reproach; that Judah and
Simeon should come to a fight in the north was not conceivable at
the time. Any real union between the southern and northern
tribes was a later matter and never became permanent. The
battle cannot be followed in all its details; the verses which
describe the muster (last line of v. 11 through first three lines
of 15) are in the portion of the poem which has suffered most.
The first line of this part,

---

[1] See p. 6.

[2] Judges 5 ⁶.

[3] Machir (v. 14) seems to be used here for Manasseh, "of which tribe
it was the principal branch." See Moore, *Judges, Int. Crit. Com.;* Barton,
§ Israel, Hastings (1 vol.), *Bible Dictionary.*

[4] See Moore, *Judges, Int. Crit. Com., in loc.,* and B. D. B., *Heb. Lex.*

Then went down to the gates the people of Yahweh,

apparently anticipates the lines that follow, in which the coming down from the hills of the chieftains with the various tribes seems to have been recounted.   The last line of the section describes the descent of the Galilean tribes into the plain as an impetuous rush of the chieftains upon the heels of Deborah and Barak.   Then follow vituperations upon those who sat at home, with two lines that suggest in contrast the desperate courage with which Zebulun and Naphtali drove the enemies from the higher ground on which they tried to make a stand.

> Zebulun a people that scorned[1] its life to the death,
> Naphtali too upon the heights of the open field.

The song turns to describe briefly the muster of the Canaanite kings at Tanaach, on the southern border of the great plain, near the upper course of the river Kishon.   It is not clear whether the light-armed peasants of the hills, through some clever strategy, led the Canaanites, with their heavy chariots, into the hopeless mire on the borders of the stream swollen by winter rains, even compelling them to enter the river so that

> Torrent Kishon swept them off,

or whether a sudden downpour turned the plain to mire and so the defeat of the heavy-armed Canaanites became easy.   This latter has been the usual interpretation from ancient times. Josephus, writing in the first century A.D., is able to tell exactly how it happened.   "There came down from heaven a great storm with a vast quantity of rain and hail, and the wind blew the rain full in the face of the Canaanites, and so darkened their eyes that their arrows and slings were of little or no advantage to them, nor would the coldness of the air permit the soldiers to make use of their swords; (!) while this storm did not so much incommode the Israelites because it came at their backs."[2]

The prose version of the story (Judges 4) was preserved in an eighth-century document of northern Israel.   It leaves out all explicit reference to the part played by the forces of nature in the battle: Jehovah discomfited Sisera, and all his chariots, and all

---

[1] Literally, reproached or taunted.
[2] *Antiquities*, V, 5, 4.

his host, with the edge of the sword before Barak, is its barren account.[1]   In the poem, the inhabitants of an otherwise unknown village, Meroz, past which presumably the fleeing Sisera made his escape, are bitterly cursed.   Alone, the fugitive at length came to a Bedouin tent, where he fell by a woman's blow, when he buried his face in the large bowl of curdled milk which she gave him in place of the water he asked.

The prose account, while it may in part rest upon tradition independent of the poem, contains many inconsistencies and in general must be counted as an historical source far inferior.   The poem, in spite of the obscurity of many of its lines, gives a remarkably consistent picture, or rather series of pictures.[2]

To the student of literature, the comparison of chapters 4 and 5 is of especial interest as an early example of the inherent differences between prose and poetry.   The poem gives the really vital points in luminous pictures — the desperate condition of Israel, the one cry that could unite the tribes in uttermost endeavor, the part played in the battle by the forces of nature, the wretched death of Sisera, in contrast to the expected victory and booty. These are the elements of universal human interest.   Even the almost detailed description of the muster has its significance ; the modern poet of action understood this: —

> Fast as the fatal symbol flies,
> In arms the tents and hamlets rise.[3]

Few parts of Sir Walter's song kindle the imagination and cling to the memory more effectively than "The Gathering."

The prose narrator is constrained to give the heroine formal introduction with full statement of her recognized standing in

---

[1] Judges 4 [15].

[2] Moore (*Int. Crit. Com.*) inclines to the view "that the basis of chapter 4 is an old prose story of Sisera."   McFadyen (*Intro. O. T.*) favors the theory, now often met, that Israel's prose narratives of the earlier centuries were originally in poetic form.   He remarks, *à propos* of the difference in the account of Sisera's death in the prose and poetic forms, that "we see the risks which the ballads ran when turned into prose," and further says it is "natural to suppose that other stories in the book of Judges may have similarly originated in war ballads."   See also Kent, *Beginnings Heb. Hist.*, pp. 15 f.

[3] *Lady of the Lake*, III, xiv.

Israel, to set forth the preliminary negotiations with Barak, to tell how it came about that Heber had his tent in the road of Sisera's flight, and why Sisera turned in to that particular tent. The story of the assassination was quite too simple and brief for him; it was necessary to have the victim enter and make arrangements for concealment from his pursuers. Yet the details are elaborate only in comparison with the poem; the prose account is itself ancient and so objective; there is no analysis of Jael's motives, no picturing of a conflict in her soul.

That which Professor Moulton styles the "lyric device of interruption" is also conspicuous in the poem, in contrast to the chronological movement of the prose. A refrain, a prelude, "and a long apostrophe are interposed before the narrative even commences." [1]

While we cannot find any rigid structure in this early victory ode, we may trace the general divisions of the song, with their dramatic contrasts and sudden and effective changes of rhythm. The ode begins: —

> For the leading of the leaders in Israel,
> For that the people offered themselves,
> Bless ye Yahweh.
>
> Hear, ye kings; give ear, ye rulers:
> I, to Yahweh, I will sing,
> Sing praise to Yahweh God of Israel.

This is followed by a splendid theophany, the type of many similar descriptions of the majestic approach of Him who revealed himself in the storm clouds; who ever came for the deliverance of his people, from the wilderness where they had covenanted together. [2]

[1] *Literary Study of Bible*, p. 131. For Professor Moulton's full discussion, see pp. 130 ff. His division of the poem into strophe and antistrophe for antiphonal performance by male and female choruses, led respectively by Barak and Deborah, does not commend itself. The historian of Semitic literature must often dissent from the tendency among students of late literature to attribute elaborate, rigid structure, characteristic of classical and modern poetry, to ancient Semitic song. The ancient culture peoples did indeed develop rigid conventions, but they were their own.

[2] It was a century after Solomon built his splendid house for Jehovah to dwell in that, at the hour of his loneliness and desolation, the great

In our poem, six lines suffice for the picture: —

> Yahweh, in thy going forth from Seir,
> In thy march from the field of Edom,
> Earth shook and heavens poured down,
> Yea clouds poured down water.
> Mountain torrents flowed before Yahweh,
> Before Yahweh God of Israel.

The words and metre in the Hebrew strike short and sharp, a quick but crashing step, for the march of the strong deliverer from Edom. Then the measure changes from lines of three and four beats to the long five-beat rhythm, with the suggestion of the division of the long line into parts of three and two beats. At a later era this type of line will be used in the finished elegy. The scene is of the silence of death; the highways are deserted; the only travellers skulk noiselessly through the by-paths.

> In the days of Shamgar ben-Anath, caravans ceased,
> And travellers of the road journeyed in crooked by-paths.
> Hamlets ceased in Israel, they ceased.[1]

The dirge-like tone is quickly interrupted by sharp trimeters

> Until thou arose, O Deborah,
> Thou arose, a matron in Israel.[2]

The next two lines are very uncertain, but the following couplet shows that they must have continued the description of Israel's sad estate before the great battle. The text of the next nine lines has suffered so severely that discussion is fruitless. The section seems to close, as the poem opened, with a summons to serve Jehovah. The fine muster scene follows with its praise and scorn; then the battle. The measure becomes short and sharp, somewhat as in the earlier description of Jehovah's advance.

Elijah went, not to the temple, but the long journey back to Horeb, to meet God in his ancient mountain. Long after that, when the temple had become fully established as the dwelling-place of Jehovah, the poets continued to picture him as coming from Sinai in the glory of the mountain-bred storm.

[1] Moore's translation of the last line.

[2] It seems preferable to translate these verbs as second rather than first person; the Hebrew permits, and the lines are thus brought into accord with v. 12. See Moore, *Judges, Int. Crit. Com., in loc.*

> Kings came, they fought,
> Then the Kings of Canaan fought;
> In Tanaak by Megiddo's waters.
> Prey of silver they took not.

After this last line with its unexpected "sarcastic meiosis," the thought turns to the heavenly bodies that contended against Sisera: the staccato movement of the verse is varied by two polysyllabic lines:—

> From heaven the planets engaged in battle,
> From their courses engaged in battle with Sisera.

From these lines of eleven syllables, in the original, we come down to the quick action of the field. A six-syllable line tells how

> Torrent Kishon swept them off.

The next two lines are in part doubtful. When we catch the full meaning again, we hear the retreating hoof-beats of such of the horses as have brought their Canaanite masters through to the hard plain.

> Then smote horse hoof-beats,
> From the gallop, galloping of his steeds.[1]

The last line seems to be onomatopoetic in its repetition *daharoth, daharoth.* Certainly later Hebrew writers were only less skilful in sound imitation than Homer himself, and we may find a suggestion of it in the earliest great poem of Israel.[2]

Apparently the retreat leads past the hamlet of Meroz, for now the sound of the galloping horses is drowned in the poet's curse of the coward town.

> Curse ye Meroz, saith the messenger of Yahweh;
> Curse with a curse its inhabitants.
> For they came not to the help of Yahweh,
> To the help of Yahweh among the brave.

With a contrasted blessing upon Jael, the poem passes quickly to the scene at the tent-door where Sisera meets his death.

[1] Adopting Moore's happy translation of the last line.

[2] The word translated gallop is used only once elsewhere, and then it is in Nahum's wonderful description of the utter confusion in Nineveh's last siege.

> Sound of whip, and sound of rattling wheel,
> And galloping horse, and bounding chariot.

Most blessed of women be Jael,
Most blessed of nomad women be.[1]
Water he asked, milk she gave;
She brought him leban in a royal dish.
Her hand to the helve she reaches out,
Her right hand to the heavy hammer.[2]
Yea she strikes, crushes his head;
She smites, strikes through his temple.
Between her feet he bowed, he fell, lay prone,
Where he bowed, there he fell, slain.

The last scene changes from the lonely tent to the lonelier palace
that was Sisera's.

Through the window she looked and strident cried,
The mother of Sisera, through the lattice.
Why delays his chariotry in coming?
Why tarry the hoof-beats of his chariots?
Her prudent princesses answer her,
Yea she returns answer to herself:
Are they not finding, dividing spoil?
A damsel, two damsels to every man,
A spoil of dyed stuffs for Sisera,
A spoil of dyed stuffs embroidered.[3]
So shall all thine enemies perish, O Yahweh,
But his friends be as the rising sun in his strength.

Had we the *Book of the Wars of Yahweh*, to which reference
is made in Numbers 21, it may be that we should have many early
songs comparable to this; but we count ourselves fortunate that
this one has been preserved from these early days of fierce struggle
for the possession of Canaan's fertile plain and hill, when the clans
united in Jehovah's name.[4]

---

[1] For the omission of "the wife of Heber the Kenite," see Kittel, *Bib.
Heb.*, *in loc.*; Moore, *Judges*, *in loc.*

[2] The parallelism and the possibility of the action described make it
highly probable that the "pin" and the instrument named in the next
line stand for one and the same tool or weapon; hammer is as plausible
a translation as any. "Heavy" is adopted as the possible meaning, by a
metonomy which Moore suggests, but does not himself adopt. For discussion of the great difficulties of the passage, see Moore, *Judges*, *in loc.*

[3] Next line uncertain.

[4] Aside from Beowulf, fifty lines of Finnsburh, and two shorter frag-

Note on the Form of Hebrew Poetry

In the foregoing discussion, references have been made to the changing harmony of sound and thought in these brief remains of early Hebrew song. That the Hebrew language itself is peculiarly adapted to express the "action, imagery, and passion" of poetry was effectively maintained in the eighteenth century by the poet Herder.[1] Quoting Lessing's words concerning Homer, that "in him all is bustle, motion, action," Herder emphasized the prominence of verbs in the Hebrew and the fact that the nouns, remaining very nearly related to them, "are still active agents and exhibit a continual personification." In the lack of true adjectives he found the qualities of a subject assuming the form of distinct individual agents; the very objects themselves are seized upon and almost always with some mark of emotion or passion. The sensuous form and the sensation or sentiment that it produces are combined. Herder even found poetic advantage in the absence of a tense system, since to poetry all is present. Certainly it is true that the poetic advantages possessed by relatively simple and primitive languages are very manifest in the Hebrew; abstract terms it hardly knows, and few words have gone far from their root meanings. When such meanings have been extended, it is often through some quaint and childlike association of ideas by which the picturesque qualities of the words are enhanced rather than lost.

How far the Hebrew poetry was characterized by what would seem to us true musical rhythm is a subject long discussed and, in recent years, more keenly than ever. The Jews themselves have preserved no reliable tradition of metres. Josephus, it is true, spoke of the Miriam song (Exodus 15) as composed in "hexameter verse," of the "Blessing of Moses" (Deuteronomy 32) as a "hexameter poem," and made the general statement that David "composed songs and hymns to God of several sorts of metre," some "trimeters," some "pentameters."[2] Even if these

---

ments of Waldhere, the early national epic poetry of England is gone. See *Cambridge Hist. Eng. Lit.*, I, p. 34.

[1] J. G. Herder, *Spirit of Hebrew Poetry*, first published 1782.

[2] *Antiquities*, II, xvi, 4 ; IV, viii, 44 ; VII, xii, 3.

remarks should be accepted as representing a living tradition in the first century A.D., this was lost before the time of our earliest Hebrew manuscript, and it is impossible to determine to-day what Josephus meant by these metres as applicable to Hebrew poetry. We suspect that he would have been hard put to it to explain. He was writing in Greek and seeking to make the ancient culture of his people intelligible and respected in the Græco-Roman world. Probably he meant Greek hexametres and not any true Semitic metre. His views may have had as firm a basis in facts as Philo's statements that Moses was instructed by Greek tutors and learned "the whole science of rhythm and harmony and metre." [1]

In the early Middle Ages, Jewish students invented a highly elaborate system of vocalizing, accenting, and punctuating their ancient language, which had hitherto been written in a consonantal text. How nearly the pronunciation, which thus became artificially fixed about 600 A.D., resembled that of the centuries when Hebrew was a living language, it is impossible to decide. Long ere this time the Jewish people had ceased to think of their ancient writings as literature, and the indication of the pronunciation was for use in the synagogue services.

The tradition of the text has preserved a few traces of the stichometric structure of the ancient poetry; a few poems occurring in the prose books are written in distinct lines separated by spaces.[2] The text itself attests more clearly the division of poetry into lines in the case of the alphabetic poems, of which a number exist. Lamentations 3 is a particularly exact specimen — each of the first three lines begins with Aleph, of the next three with Beth, and so throughout the sixty-six lines and twenty-two letters of the Hebrew alphabet. In Lamentations 1 and 2 every third line is thus marked, and in 4, every second line.

---

[1] *Life of Moses*, I, 5. Distinct metre is not found in Hebrew poetry before the mediæval Jewish poets of North Africa, Italy, Spain, and France.

[2] Exodus 15 [1-19], Deuteronomy 32 [1-43], 2 Samuel 22 and its duplicate Psalm 18. The different mode of chanting these poetic sections in the orthodox synagogues from the usual chant of prose affords further traditional evidence.

Psalm 119 is printed in the Revised Version in twenty-two groups of eight distichs each, with a letter of the alphabet at the head of each group. In the Hebrew, each couplet of the group begins with the letter thus indicated. These and other alphabetic poems give a starting-point for a study of the structure of Hebrew verse. Rime, of which examples have been noted, does not occur with sufficient regularity to offer much aid in determining the lines, but the stichometric structure is clearly established by the means already noted. Correspondence of grammatical structure with these occasional indications gives confirmation, if any were needed, and serves to indicate unmistakable division where other criteria are lacking. Each line of Hebrew poetry is regularly a logical unity with a distinct break in the thought at its end; "run over lines," not uncommon in poetry that has clear divisions into bars or feet, were not in vogue in the poetry of ancient Israel. In the King James version, no attempt was made to divide into lines, yet the English frequently shows a semicolon or stronger punctuation at the end of each Hebrew line.

A logical relation between adjacent lines had been recognized, but not commonly emphasized until Bishop Lowth delivered and published his Oxford lectures *De sacra poesi Hebræorum* in the middle of the eighteenth century. He used the happy term *parallelismus membrorum* to express the relationship which has since been generally recognized as the most characteristic element of the form of Hebrew poetry. The lines concerning Heshbon and Moab may serve to illustrate rigid and simple parallelism. There are five couplets, each made up of synonymous lines : —

> Come ye to Heshbon ! Let it be built !
> And let Sihon's city be established !
> When fire went out from Heshbon,
> Flame from Sihon's burgh :
> It devoured Ar of Moab ;
> It consumed the heights of Arnon, etc.

As Professor Moulton has suggested,[1] the rhythmical effect of parallelism may be appreciated by reading, in contrast, the lines with the alternating parallel lines omitted.

[1] *Literary Study of the Bible*, p. 47.

Balancing of clauses is a familiar device of oratory, and parallelism appears sporadically in various poetry, but as a distinctive poetic form, it is known only among the closely interrelated peoples of southwestern Asia and northeastern Africa. Examples are numerous in the literature of Egypt and Babylonia. One of the most famous of Egyptian songs will illustrate: [1] —

> How beautiful is this righteous prince!
> The beautiful destiny is fulfilled.
> The bodies pass away since the time of Rê,
> And the younger ones step into their places.
> The sun reappears each morning,
> And the evening sun sets in the west.
> Men are begetting, women are conceiving,
> Every nostril breathes the breath of the morning.
> But those who are born there, all together,
> They go to the place, which is ordained for them.
> Celebrate a joyful day, O priest!
> Place oils and sweet odors for thy nostril.
> Wreaths of lotus flowers for the limbs,
> For the body of thy sister, who dwells in thy heart,
> Who sits beside thee.
> Let there be music and singing before thee,
> Cast behind thee all cares, and mind thee of joy.

In the Babylonian penitential psalms, repetition of parallel lines, with little or no progress of thought, is carried to great weariness: —

> The lord has looked upon me in the rage of his heart,
> A god has visited me in his wrath,
> A goddess has become angry with me and brought me into pain,
> A known or unknown god has oppressed me,
> A known or unknown goddess has brought sorrow upon me.
> I seek for help, but no one takes my hand.
> I weep, but no one approaches me.
> I call aloud, but no one hears me.
> Full of woe, I grovel in the dust without looking up.
> To my merciful god I turn, speaking with sighs.
> The feet of my goddess I kiss imploringly (?),

[1] This version is taken from the tomb of the priest Neferhôtep. Erman, *Life in Ancient Egypt*, p. 387.

To the known or unknown god do I speak with sighs,
To the known or unknown goddess do I speak with sighs.
O lord, look upon me, accept my lament,
O goddess, look upon me, accept my lament.
O known or unknown goddess, look upon me, accept my lament![1]

In the Babylonian Creation Epic the tendency to parallelism
may be seen : —

When in the height, heaven was not yet named,
And the earth beneath bore no name;
While still the primeval Apsu, who begot them,
And raging Tiamat, who brought forth both,
Mingled their waters together;
When no field was yet found, no marsh was seen;
When none of the gods had yet been called into being,
No name mentioned, no fate determined,
Then were the gods created.[2]

Lowth distinguished three forms of parallelism — synonymous,
antithetic, and synthetic. If one insists on finding strict relationship among all the lines in Hebrew poetry, he will be forced to
stretch the last category very wide. At best in "synthetic"
parallelism, in which the second member is required to complete
the sense of the first, the harmony extends hardly beyond
grammatical structure, and frequently even this relation is not
discoverable. Often "a comparison, a reason, a consequence,
a motive, constitutes one of the lines in a synthetic parallelism.[3]

At least one other distinguishable form is so frequently met and
so effective that it should be noted. This Driver calls "climactic,"
and others have styled "ascending rhythm."[4] In this form of
parallelism, which is especially suited to the most elevated themes,
the second line catches up and repeats a part of the preceding, and
then adds to it. We have had an example in the description of
Jehovah's approach in the Deborah Song : —

Earth shook and heavens dropped,
Yea, clouds dropped water.

[1] Jastrow, *Religion of Babylonia and Assyria*, **p. 321.**
[2] Kent, *Beginnings Heb. Hist.*, p. 363.
[3] Driver, *Intro. Lit. O. T.*, p. 363.
[4] Driver, *op. cit.*, p. 363.

> Mountain torrents flowed before Yahweh,
> Before Yahweh, God of Israel.[1]

Where rigid structure at first sight seems lacking, the parallelism sometimes proves to be of a highly complicated form, alternating, introverted, etc.   Unlike true metre, this "thought rhythm," as it is often called, is not entirely lost in translation, though the similarity of the length of lines in the original is often quite obscured; one Hebrew word may require three or four English words for its translation.   As Gardiner says, speaking of the King James version, "The men who made our translation did not attempt to arrange the lines in a different form from the prose of the rest of the book.   The result has been in English to produce a kind of writing unique in our literature, since it is neither regular prose nor regular poetry, but shares the power of both.   It has the strong balance and regularity which result from this underlying parallel structure of the Hebrew, and at the same time all the freedom and naturalness of prose."[2]   This quality is certainly most excellent in poetry which hundreds must read in translation for each individual who reads it in the original.   Not all of us will be ready to go on and declare it in fact a thoroughly satisfactory poetic form, in comparison with true metre.   Professor McFadyen seems rather enthusiastic when he says of parallelism: "It suggests a rhythm profounder than the sound of any words — the response of thought to thought, the calling of deep to deep, the solemn harmonies that run through the universe."[3]

Perhaps Josephus was too much influenced by Greek poetic forms in his ascription of metre to Hebrew poetry; yet there have been many in recent centuries who have not rested satisfied with "thought rhythm" and have persistently tried to find a system of true metre in the Hebrew and kindred poetry.

The earlier efforts to recover Hebrew metre, in the seventeenth and early eighteenth centuries, were chiefly based on classical models.[4]   Lowth saw their unsatisfactoriness and thought it unpractical to work out any definite system, because of our lack

---

[1] Cf. Psalm 29 [1, 8]; Exodus 15 [16b].
[2] Gardiner, *The Bible as English Literature*, p. 109.
[3] McFadyen, *Intro. to O. T.*, p. 238.
[4] Briggs, *Int. Crit. Com., Psalms* I, pp. xxxviii–xxxix.

of knowledge of the original pronunciation.[1] In the latter part of the eighteenth century (1776) the rules of Arabic metre, which, like the classical, is quantitative, were applied to Hebrew poetry. At the same time in publications on Hebrew metre (1770) and the Psalms (1780), C. G. Anton made accent the determining principle of measurement. In other respects few would follow him to-day, but in this vital point his "conjecture," as he called it,[2] seems in accord with the character of the Hebrew. Accent is dominant, as the language is known to us; a short vowel cannot stand in an unaccented open syllable, while a long vowel in an open syllable, by the shifting of the tone, may become a mere half vowel, barely pronounced.

No real advance over the eighteenth century was made until the latter part of the nineteenth, when various students took up the problem of Hebrew metre with new energy and equipment. One tried to apply the principle of Syriac poetry, in which the metrical system is determined by the counting of the syllables.[3] In his view, there was a constant alternation of rise and fall, so that only iambic and trochaic feet were possible. The comparison with Syriac, like that with Arabic poetry, has the advantage of keeping within the same family of languages as the Hebrew, but both Syriac and Arabic poetry are post-Christian, and it has recently been "shown that the earliest even of the Syriac poetry did not measure by number of syllables."[4] More recently, Sievers, who has done much on Teutonic metres, working from the point of view of the laws of speech and song, rather than from a knowledge of Semitic languages, has wrought out an astonishing system, finding everywhere a sort of anapestic foot, two unaccented syllables of any length followed by a long accented. This system involves both quantity and accent, but it is forced to reject the traditional pronunciation and to invent a new one devised to fit the scheme. Even so, as Cornill points out, Sievers gets no orderly system in the number of verse feet in successive lines.

[1] Lowth, *Sacred Poetry of the Hebrews*, p, 33.

[2] *Conjectura de metro Hebræorum*, 1770, *Specimen editionis Psalmorum*, 1780.

[3] G. Bickell, various publications, 1879–1884.

[4] Briggs, *Int. Crit. Com.*, Psalms I, p. xxxix.

Follow him, and one may prove any prose narrative poetry, as Sievers's own publications indicate.[1] Very few Semitic scholars have found his arguments convincing.

In the same period the now generally dominant theory has been developed by a succession of workers. In a series of publications extending from 1866 to 1887, Julius Ley revived Anton's view that accent was the determining principle in Hebrew metre. He maintained that the number of unaccented syllables did not count and that the metre was determined solely by the number of *ictus*. In 1882 Karl Budde published[2] a careful study of the Hebrew Qina or elegiac verse.[3] He showed that wherever there is a song of lamentation[4] there is a tendency to a verse form made up of a longer followed by a shorter member. Commonly the first member has three accents and the second two; and between the members there is a decided cæsura. The number of unaccented syllables in these comparatively regular units is exceedingly variable. This evidence points strongly toward the contention of Ley that only stresses counted in the metrical system. More recently it has been strongly argued by Zimmern and Gunkel that Old Babylonian poetry possessed an accentuating metrical system based on the equal value of the accentual rises. The same seems to have been true in the case of the Egyptian poetry.

A theory of *moræ* published in 1896–1897[5] arrived at a more exact quantitative law, but was forced to distinguish syllables of the values of 4, 3, and 2 *moræ*. Like Sievers's even more recent theory, this seems too artificial, and the vast majority of students to-day rest in the conviction that in ancient Hebrew poetry the accents alone counted. As the poetry has come down to us often imperfectly preserved, even these are so irregular that frequently the text must be emended, or we must say we can discover only a tendency toward regular arrangements of the number of ictus.

---

[1] E. Sievers, *Studien zur hebräischen Metrik*, 1901, etc.

[2] *Zeitschrift für Altetestamentliche Wissenschaft.*

[3] A general statement of Budde's views is given in § Poetry, in Hastings, *Dict. of the Bible*, Vol. III.

[4] Hebrew *Qina.*

[5] H. Grimme in Z. D. M. G., L, pp. 529 ff., LI, pp. 683 ff.

If the actual pronunciation of the living Hebrew was as free in its variations of time as Sidney Lanier holds English to be, and if poetry must be divisible into feet of exact time equivalence, then we may suppose that the accents were made to fall at regular time intervals in the pronunciation of Hebrew poetry. In that case the discrimination of half vowels, full short vowels, and long vowels made in our Hebrew text must be far indeed from representing true time relations in the original pronunciation of the poetry.[1] Probably, too, other syllables than those now accented must have received the tone, but one may well remember in this connection, that our knowledge of many of the long vowels goes back into the consonantal text of the Hebrew, and so is early.

In its parallelism, Hebrew poetry followed, as we have noted, a form already long used in Babylon and Egypt, which countries had successively dominated Syria for many centuries before Israel found settlement among the Canaanites. The evidence thus far attainable seems to show that in metrical structure, too, the poetry of the three was similar. More elaborate systems of Hebrew metre, such as those of Sievers or Grimme, involving as they do disregard of the earliest pronunciation of the language which we possess, will probably continue to be rejected by most students of Semitic literature and to commend themselves only to those who approach the subject with fixed convictions based upon later forms of poetry and music.[2]

[1] It is true that in the later Jewish poetry, which had adopted metrical form, half vowels were often counted as forming full syllables.

[2] It is generally held that Anglo-Saxon poetry and the ancient German two-membered alliterative verse were measured by the number of accented syllables, without regard to the unaccented. The ancient Latin Saturnian metre may have been of the same form. Until it can be shown that these later verse forms had a more exact metrical structure, it is not to be expected that this will be established in the case of ancient Semitic poetry.

For Anglo-Saxon see Saintsbury, *History of English Prosody;* for the German, Budde, § Poetry, Hastings, *Dict. Bible;* for this theory of Latin, Duff, *Literary History of Rome*, pp. 74–75.

D

CHAPTER III

(*About 1040 to 940 B.C.*)

AFTER the Deborah song, no contemporary poem that connects itself with definite historical events embodies Israel's experience until generations have passed. The succeeding years witnessed harassing struggles between the Hebrew tribes and others who desired to possess Canaan, or to plunder its inhabitants; but the next life-and-death struggle was with a people which had settled on the western coast plain at almost the same time that Israel crossed the Jordan and overran the central mountains. This people, the Philistines, left its name on the country which we call Palestine. In the days of Amos, about 750 B.C., the Philistines were still counted an immigrant people, come from Caphtor.[1] They are supposed to have been a part of the peoples from the northern shores and islands of the Mediterranean who pushed southward, on land and water, during the twelfth century B.C., pressed from behind by those great movements in Europe that brought the Dorians into Greece. They sought foothold in the Egyptian Delta, but were driven back by the Pharaoh, and a part of the receding wave found settlement on the coast plain of Canaan.

The Philistines have left no written records to tell through what struggles and defeats they learned the vital lesson of united action. From Israel's experience with them, it would seem that they were ever able to act together effectively, though they dwelt in separate city states, with different kings. Whether this be true or not, it is evident from the earliest strand of narrative preserved in Samuel [2] that they eventually succeeded in reducing the disunited tribes of Israel to a state of subjection similar to that of the days of

---

[1] Crete? Amos 9 [7].

[2] For the contents and character of this strand, see below, ch. IV.

Shamgar-ben-Anath. Now, however, Israel had the precious memory of a day when her clans had united in Jehovah's name, and thrown off the oppressor's yoke.

About the middle of the eleventh century there appeared in the land bands of religious enthusiasts going about with music and song and, in sympathetic connection with them, a seer whose keen eyes had perceived that the time was ripening for a great struggle for independence. This one was evidently watching for the born leader about whom the enthusiasm of the hour might crystallize into effective action. One day there came to his door a man of giant stature and simple heart, searching with persistent zeal for his father's lost asses. In the unawakened soul there was slumbering power — capacity for new and consuming enthusiasm and for instantaneous action. Samuel the seer recognized his man in Saul-ben-Kish. There must be the awakening; dogged devotion to the home interests must be turned into larger channels. The conspicuous honor showed at the village sacrificial feast, where the seer presided, the secret anointing in the name of Jehovah, the charge to do as occasion should serve, the predicted meetings, culminating in the meeting with a company of the religio-patriotic enthusiasts, the strange ecstasy so exciting the wonder of those who had known the unassuming giant, that the question, "Is Saul also among the prophets," became a proverb — all these experiences accomplished the inward change which the seer desired. Saul went home and kept his own counsel till the news of the terrible straits of the Israelites in Jabesh Gilead, across the Jordan, reached him, as he came following the oxen out of the field. At last the insight and patience of Samuel were justified; Saul hewed to pieces a yoke of the oxen and sent the bloody tokens throughout the land with bitter threat for every coward laggard. The clans gathered at the summons of a determined leader, the siege of Jabesh was raised, and Israel saw once more what she could accomplish when united; yet the dread of Philistia soon sent the more part of the warriors slinking to cover till Jonathan's strange and gallant exploit at the pass of Michmash and the Philistine rout following gave new courage.

Saul was the man for the hour, but was not the statesman who could secure a permanently united Israel. The impulsiveness that gained the first successes nearly cost the nation the life of the gallant Jonathan. The first enthusiasm past, strange moods came upon the leader that could be dissipated only by music. The young musician David, hence brought into Saul's personal service, soon proved a man of military genius whose success called forth from the dancing women an antiphonal couplet : —

> Smitten hath Saul his thousands now,
> And David his myriads, I trow.[1]

Quick jealousy followed fond affection and developed, till Saul seemed almost more eager to be rid of David than of the Philistines. David, when forced to flee, became the leader of an outlaw band and then a vassal of one of the Philistine kings. David's own tribe of Judah and the affiliated clans to the south, which had been brought into union with the northern tribes, were now secretly sympathetic with the outlaw. The Philistines, encouraged, it may be, by the internal feud and the loss to Saul of his brilliant officer, united for a great invasion of Israel's territory. They marched up the coast plain, crossed the ridge of Carmel, and came into the Kishon valley, where the fateful battle had been fought in Deborah's day. Mustering on the northern side of the valley of Jezreel near Shunem, they faced Saul's forces on the southern side. The battle was fought on the slope of Gilboa. In the defeat of Israel, Saul and Jonathan, with two other sons of the king, met their death.

To David the death of Saul meant the possibility of escape from an intolerable position of double-faced conduct which could not long be maintained, and possible succession to the throne. But it meant also the humiliation of his people, with their land once more open to the plundering armies of Philistia, the death of the anointed king and of his son whose soul was knit to David's.

There is no reason to question the Davidic authorship of the wonderful dirge commemorating the death of Saul and Jonathan on Gilboa[2]; nor is there any reason to doubt the sincerity

---

[1] 1 Samuel 18 [7]. The above free representation of the lines finds its only excuse in its effort to reproduce the assonant endings and in its preservation of the relative length of the lines. The final words of the two lines end in *phaw* and *thaw*.

[2] For a brief but adequate argument, see H. P. Smith, *Samuel, Int. Crit. Com.*, p. 258.

of David's respect for Saul and his deep sense of the nation's loss. It was to David's interest, it is true, to show all respect to the fallen king, but all the traditions are unanimous in representing David as most sincerely devoted to Saul, and this contemporary poem rings true. One argument for the genuineness of the poem is that an imitator would almost inevitably give "at least a veiled allusion to David's experience at the court of Saul and during his forced exile." [1] We have, then, in David's lament over Saul and Jonathan, a valuable contemporary historical monument, a genuine production of one of Israel's most versatile geniuses to whom later generations assigned many songs, and the earliest example of the dirge in Hebrew literature.

That David was a musician is attested in the earliest prose narrative of his relations with Saul. This narrative was perhaps the earliest connected prose of Israel and was certainly written not much later than Solomon's time.[2] About two centuries after David's death the prophet Amos speaks of those who devise musical instruments like David.[3] Poet and musician were one in antiquity, and David may have composed many songs, though it is impossible to say how many of these are preserved, or with certainty to assign any specific ones to him, except this lament and that for Abner.

The spirit of the dirge for Saul and Jonathan is national first, then personal. It affords an example of magnanimity, of freedom from petty feelings of revenge that would do credit to a Christian statesman; but it is quite without any definitely religious thought. In this last fact, we have another proof of genuineness, since the latter ages, which made David such a religious hero, could hardly have failed to include some mention of Jehovah in a pseudo-Davidic poem composed to fit an occasion like the death of Saul. This early elegy certainly implies in its artistic adequacy a considerable development of this type, although the characteristic elegiac metre appears very little, if at all. In the much earlier Deborah song there seemed to be genuine examples of the metre.[4]

[1] H. P. Smith, *op. cit.*
[2] This document will be discussed in Chapter IV.
[3] Amos 6 [5].
[4] See p. 22.

In David's lament, lines of two and four beats prevail and are
sometimes arranged quite effectively in groups that begin with
short lines and culminate in lines of four beats. Of the few
five-beat lines in the poem, the one which gives the refrain,
with an addition, seems most like the typical elegiac line : —

> How are the mighty fallen, in battle's midst.

Even here, however, there is no considerable logical pause between
the third and fourth accents, and it is doubtful whether any line
of the poem is properly to be classed as one of the Qina rhythm.
The absence of the elegaic verse-form is an argument against
calling the measure elegiac; but its frequency of occurrence in
later elegies and its appropriateness to the expression of the
emotion of grief justifies the name. Like the Deborah song, the
text of David's elegy has suffered in transmission, and it may be
that its metre was originally much more regular than its present
form indicates. In the varied measures of the lines as we have
them (two, three, four, five beats), there is discoverable no such
adapting of rhythm to thought and feeling as was manifest in the
earlier great poem. On the other hand, the parallelism is notably
symmetrical; except for the addition of the last two lines, the
poem divides itself naturally into six groups of four lines each.
In general, these groups are made up of couplets in which the
parallelism is very distinct, while the second couplet stands in
synthetic relation with the first. This becomes evident, if the
first and third lines of each quatrain are read consecutively.
These uniformly show a true synthetic parallelism, and the second
and fourth lines usually stand in the same relation. The translation which follows is based upon a Hebrew text considerably
revised and sometimes of doubtful conjecture:[1] —

> Wail, O Judah !
> Grieve, O Israel !
> The slain are on thy heights.
> How are the mighty fallen !

[1] Commonly the textual emendations adopted by Dr. H. P. Smith in
the *International Critical Commentary* have commended themselves to the
present writer, although, in some cases, other readings have been pre-
ferred. As in the previous translations of this volume, effort has been
made to approximate the accentual character of the original lines.

Tell it not in Gath,
Publish it not in the streets of Ashkelon;
Lest the Philistine daughters rejoice,
Lest the foreigners' daughters triumph.

Mountains of Gilboa, may no dew descend,
Nor rain upon you, fields of death!
For there the shield of heroes was defiled,
The shield of Saul, weapon of the anointed.

Saul and Jonathan, the beloved and the lovely,
In life and death they were not divided,
Than vultures were swifter,
Than lions were stronger.

Daughters of Israel, weep over Saul,
Who made you scarlet wear, with luxuries,[1]
Who put adornments of gold upon your raiment.
How are the mighty fallen, in battle's midst!

Jonathan, by thy death am I pierced,[2]
I am distressed for thee, my brother Jonathan.
Thou wert delightsome to me, exceeding wonderful!
More than women's love was thine to me.

How are the mighty fallen,
And perished the weapons of war!

Two of the most beautiful aspects of David's life were his attitude toward Saul as king and his friendship with Jonathan.   The poem seems to end with the line: —

How are the mighty fallen, in battle's midst!

The note of public loss has been dominant to this point; Saul and Jonathan have been thought of as mighty warriors, the defenders and enrichers of Israel; then the poet's personal grief bursts forth in four unsurpassed lines of lament.

After the death of Saul and his three sons on Gilboa, the people of Judah chose David as their king, while the northern tribes were

---

[1] Possibly fine linen.   See H. P. Smith after Graetz.
[2] Following emendation suggested in Kittel, *Biblia Hebraica*.
[3] 2 Samuel 1 19-27.

loyal to Saul's line in the person of his son Ishbaal.[1] Though himself incompetent, the ability of his father's old general, Abner, and the loyalty of the people made it possible for Ishbaal to maintain himself in guerilla warfare with David's uncle and general, Joab. Joab was a ruthless man, and when at length Abner, incensed at Ishbaal, sought terms with David, Joab, gaining opportunity through guile, struck him down. The assigned reason was blood vengeance for the death of Joab's brother, but jealous fear lest Abner should become David's commander may have added venom to the blow. It was a deed fraught with grave danger for David's ambitious plans of uniting the northern tribes with Judah. By custom that had come down from the days of the desert life, Joab was justified, and David could not punish if he would. Joab was, too, a general whose services David could not spare, and he continued in a dominant position throughout David's long reign, though at times the king strove to rid himself of the brutal warrior. David had occasion to regret Abner's untimely death and to disavow the deed; we have no reason to suppose that he had any personal affection for Saul's general, who for years had been the chief obstacle to his advancement over all Israel. So far as David's brief lament for Abner goes, it shows no very great emotion, unless toward the slayer, and herein it accords well with the circumstances. The inappropriateness of Abner's death seems the dominant sentiment;[2] to meet death thus was to the Hebrew mind, with its belief in the reward of character by long and prosperous life, a mark of divine displeasure or an incomprehensible experience.

> As die the base, must Abner die?
> Thy hands were not bound,

[1] Ishbaal (man of Baal), the original form of the name of Saul's son, was changed by later generations by substituting *bosheth* (shame) for Baal. The same is true of the name of Jonathan's son Meribbaal. Evidently in the days of Saul names compounded of Baal gave no offence in Israel. The ostraca discovered by the Harvard expedition at Samaria indicate that "Baal" continued to be used in the same way at least as late as Ahab's time.

[2] The thought cannot be fully translated. The word translated as *base*, usually *fool*, hardly has an English equivalent. While it means *senseless*, this to the Hebrew way of thinking is more moral than intellectual blindness.

> Nor thy feet in fetters placed.
> As one falls before the wicked, fellest thou.[1]

In our first English poetry, the dirge for the fallen hero is more prevalent than the victory ode. An interesting example for comparison with David's great elegy is the old Gaelic lament on the death of Oscar, beginning:—

> "Say, Bard of the Feinn of Erin,
> How fared the fight, Fergus, my son,
> In Gabhra's fierce battle day? Say!"

> "The fight fared not well, son of Cumhaill,
> From Gabhra come tidings of ruin,
> For Oscar the fearless is slain.
> The sons of Caeilte were seven;
> They fell with the Feinn of Alban.
> The youth of the Feinn are fallen,
> Are dead in their battle array.
> And dead on the field lies MacLuy,
> With six of the sons of thy sire.
> The young men of Alban are fallen;
> The Feinn of Breatan are fallen.
> And dead is the king's son of Lochlan,
> Who hastened to war for our right —
> The king's son with a heart ever open,
> And arm ever strong in the fight."[2]

At an early date in Israel, it became customary to compose oracles in verse. In the form that these have come down to us, it is clear that they are prophecies *ex eventu;* it was a popular literary device to put into the mouth of some ancient hero a poetic blessing or curse in which events already historical were pictured as foreshadowed by him. Thus we have in Genesis 49 the so-called Blessing of Jacob, the subsequent situation, character, and fate of the tribes of Israel pictured as predictively declared to the twelve sons, just before the death of Jacob. In its present form, the poem is to be ascribed to the time of the early monarchy, and it represents the history as then known. This oracle is important

---

[1] 2 Samuel 3 [33].
[2] Henry Morley, *English Writers*, Vol. I, p. 194 f.

as an ancient historical monument, but it is not very attractive as
a poem.   One of its most interesting literary features is its play
upon words, of which we have seen examples in early poetry;
there seems no very good reason, for example, why Dan should be
singled out as judging his people, except that the Hebrew word
for judging resembles the name Dan in sound.

The Balaam oracles have far more of freedom and charm.   As
they appear in Numbers 23 [7-10], [18-24], and 24 [3-9], [15-17], we have
approximately the form which they had assumed in the early days
of the monarchy.   The poems as given in chapter 24 suggest
the frenzy characteristic of early prophets in contrast to the later
prophets of Israel.   A vivid picture of the customs of the prophets
of Baal is given in 1 Kings 18 [26-29], the description of the Carmel
scene where, in their frenzied zeal, they had leaped upon the altar,
gashed their flesh, and cried aloud to their god.   The condition
in which Balaam is pictured as receiving his vision when fallen
down is not out of accord with the wild free note of the oracles.[1]
The poems do not naturally fall into any strophic form, as in the
case of David's lament, nor do they exhibit any such well-arranged
series of dramatic pictures as the Deborah song.   The figures are
constantly changing in response to the intensity of feeling; all is
spontaneous and at the farthest remove from artificiality or rigidity.
The poems of chapter 23 partake less of the wild, free spirit of the
desert and show more of the influence of religious ideas which
are becoming traditional and stereotyped.   This is in harmony
with the fact that chapter 23 [1-24] comes from a document which
is somewhat later and more developed in its theological ideas than
that from which 24 [1-19] was taken by the compiler of the narrative.[2]
In chapter 24, we probably have the form in which the oracles
were preserved in Judah, and in 23, their Ephraimite, or northern
Israelitish form.

Before concluding our survey of the poetry of the United Kingdom, we may note that it was very possibly during this century
that the *Book of the Wars of Jehovah*, to which allusion was
made in the preceding chapter, was compiled.   In the years of

---

[1] Interesting comparisons with the habits of modern Dervishes are often
suggested.

[2] For discussion of the two documents, see below, Chapters V and VII.

conquest and struggle for the possession of the land, Jehovah was chiefly the Lord of Hosts, the great leader of Israel's armies. When, in later centuries, Israel had learned to view her God in other and higher aspects, her warlike cousins, the Assyrians, still thought of their god Ashur mainly as the giver of victory in wars of conquest; the phrase "my god Ashur giving me the victory" recurs with monotonous uniformity in the records of the Assyrian kings.

The other book of early poems, to which allusion is made in Hebrew literature, certainly was not completed before David's time, since it contained his great elegy — "behold it is written in the book of Jashar.[1]" The name Jashar seems to be used as a synonym for Israel[2]; and this too was evidently a book of national songs. Our tantalizing glimpses of these early collections of songs lift the veil a little from the real Israel in lusty youth. When one compares these national song books that lie back of the Bible with the great national song book that has been preserved (Psalms), the distance that Israel travelled between the days of the Judges or early monarchy and the latest pre-Christian centuries becomes palpable.

Even within individual Psalms the sharpest contrasts between the spirit of early Israel and the post-exilic age may be felt. In 24, for example, verses 7–10 may very well come from David's time, celebrating the entrance of the ark into Jerusalem; these lines by themselves give only the warlike God of Deborah.

> Lift up your heads, O ye gates;
> And be ye lifted up, ye everlasting doors:
> And the King of glory will come in.
> Who is the King of glory?
> Jehovah strong and mighty,
> Jehovah mighty in battle.
> Lift up your heads, O ye gates;
> Yea, lift them up, ye everlasting doors:

---

[1] 2 Samuel 1 [18].

[2] "The book of Jashar" would be translated literally "the book of the Upright," as in the margin of the R. V. A familiar example of the diminutive form of the name is found in the song of Deuteronomy 15, "Jeshurun waxed fat and kicked."

> And the King of glory will come in.
> Who is this King of glory?
> Jehovah of hosts,
> He is the King of glory.

The first six verses of this Psalm offer a conception of God attained through the insight of Israel's prophets five hundred years after David's time.

Only less marked is the contrast between the ancient poetic bit in Psalm 60 $^{6-10a}$ and the remainder of the poem. The ancient portion is an oracle assigning the east and west Jordan territory to Israel and promising victory over the Philistines, with Edom and Moab reduced to the position of slaves.

> Yahweh spake in His sanctuary:
> "I will exult, I will divide Shechem;
> And the Valley of Succoth will I mete out.
> Gilead is Mine, and Mine is Manasseh;
> Ephraim also is the defence of My head;
> Judah is My commander's staff.
> Moab is My washpot;
> Unto Edom will I cast My sandal;
> Over Philistia will I shout in victory."
> O that one would conduct me to the entrenched city?
> O that one would lead me unto Edom?
> Wilt not Thou (Yahweh)? [1]

The later portions which envelop this utterance of confident youth breathe the sense of Jehovah's rejection, so characteristic of the Babylonian exile and the generations following.

A comparison of modern hymns as they appear in successive collections will show that they are modified from time to time, in a surprising number of cases. The hymns of ancient Israel evidently suffered successive editings and combinations before they assumed their final form in the late, post-exilic book of Psalms. If we are to find genuine songs of the days of the United Kingdom in the book, it can only be through a process of rigid criticism that separates the late elements from the early. We may well believe that the book of Psalms in its ultimate form contains much that

---

[1] Translation of Professor Briggs, *Psalms*, in *Int. Crit. Com.*, II, p. 58.

arose during the monarchy, and that some of this came from the time of David and Solomon. In only a few instances, however, is it possible to distinguish these early portions with even approximate certainty.[1]

---

[1] Professor Briggs finds, in addition to the portions of 24 and 60 noted above, as genuine products of the Davidic age: 7 [1-4a], [5], [12-16], 18 [2-19], [28-44], [46-48], [50], and possibly 13 [1-5]. 23 he would place possibly in the reign of Solomon. *Psalms, Int. Crit. Com.*

CHAPTER IV

BEGINNINGS OF CONNECTED PROSE WRITING

(*Before 900 B.C.*)

THE years of struggle between Canaanite, Philistine, and Hebrew for possession of the vine-covered hills and fertile valleys of Palestine produced noble songs and prose tales, handed down by word of mouth, but not connected prose writing. So, too, the years of struggle of Celt and Saxon for possession of Britain called forth gleeman's song rather than historian's narrative. This came later. Comparison between the early English and Hebrew literature may be carried far, for the history of early prose writing in our own literature offers closest analogy to that of Israel.[1]

It was not till near the middle of the sixth century A.D., in Christian England, that Gildas the Wise wrote his Epistle concerning the wickedness and corruption of the British State and Church. This he introduced by an historical sketch, "clearly derived," it is maintained, "from oral tradition."[2] This historical introduction was used more than a century later in the compilation of the *Historia Britonum*, "a curious congeries of writings" compiled somewhere about the year 679 A.D., with additions in later times. About the year 800, one Nennius is supposed to have made a recension of the whole; although, in accordance with another view, the original compilation is ascribed to Nennius. In either case, whether the original *Historia* dates from the last quarter of the seventh century or from 800, the earliest connected narrative known to us dealt with comparatively recent history, resting on

---

[1] Carpenter and Harford-Battersby (*The Hexateuch*, I, p. 4 f.) and Dr. John P. Peters (various writings) have noted some of the similarities in the literary history. The subject was first suggested to the present writer by Peters, *Early Hebrew Story*. The working out of the analogies in the present volume has been along almost wholly independent lines.

[2] See *Cambridge History of English Literature*, Vol. I, p. 73.

oral traditions, and this was used as one document in the earliest direct attempt to write the history of the Britons, which was itself a compilation rather than original composition of digested material. Again Gildas, and, probably, the *Historia Britonum*, were among the sources used by Bede, in the first half of the eighth century, in his ecclesiastical history of England, a work which carries the history from the landing of Cæsar down to the time of the writer. Bede's history and other materials were used in the *Saxon Chronicle*, begun in Alfred's time (ninth century) and continued by various hands on into the twelfth century. In this latter century, Florence of Worcester attempted to write a universal history, beginning with the creation. He styled it *Chronicon ex Chronicis*, a name which suggests its real nature as a compilation. The basis of the earlier portions was the Universal Chronicle of the Irish monk Marianus Scotus, who, for the early portion of his history, was a compiler from Bede and the Old English Chronicle. Other monks continued the work of Florence after his death. Thus, during the six centuries, from the day when Gildas the Wise wrote, rather incidentally, connected history from oral tradition, to Florence of Worcester and his *Chronicon ex Chronicis*, historical writing in England advanced largely through the process of compilation. Again, we may note that historical writing dealt at first with comparatively recent events and that gradually the historians extended their view backward. Bede reached back to the conquest of Britain by Cæsar, and, several centuries later, Marianus and Florence strove to write the story from the creation on.

In Israel it is certainly not earlier than the era of David and Solomon that we can find connected prose writings. They come only when the nation has been united and comparative peace secured. As in the case of Gildas's Epistle, the earliest concern not the distant past, but more recent events; they are current stories handed down orally with much lifelike detail. The story of David's court and family life, which makes up the greater part of 2 Samuel, is very commonly spoken of as the earliest connected prose writing of Israel; the narratives of Saul and David, however, beginning at 1 Samuel 9, may be as early or even earlier.

The work of Gildas, we have seen, was embodied in a later

composition, the *Historia Britonum*, and this reëdited by Nennius; Gildas and the *Historia*, with other sources, were used by Bede, and so on, through the *Saxon Chronicle* and the compilation of Florence. So the early Saul and David narratives were combined with other narratives of Samuel, Saul, and David, and ultimately, some four hundred years after their times, were edited in the present books of Samuel. In the study of each literature, the long and patient work of many critics, building upon and correcting each other, has so far unravelled the various documents compiled that we can now select with considerable certainty the portions belonging to the earlier and later strands. Apparently the students of each literature have commonly worked in ignorance of the details of the work being done in the other, so that the closely analogous results are the more notable.

The analysis, now made with confidence, gives a group of early Saul stories which probably constituted at first a separate cycle of narratives, written down by a different hand from that which gathered the David-Saul stories. In order to appreciate the Saul stories in their individual character, as they first existed in a separate document, it is necessary to read them through by themselves.[1]

Now there was a man of Benjamin, whose name was Kish, the son of Abiel, the son of Zeror, the son of Becorath, the son of Aphiah, the son of a Benjamite, a mighty man of valor. And he had a son, whose name was Saul, a young man and a goodly: and there was not among the children of Israel a goodlier person than he: from his shoulders and upward he was higher than any of the people. And the asses of Kish, Saul's

[1] They now constitute the following sections of 1 Samuel: 9 $^{1-10}$, ^{16}, 11 $^{1-11}$, ^{15}, 13 $^{2-7}$, $^{16-18}$, ^{23}, 14 $^{1-46}$. Some of the grounds for the separation of this material and the David-Saul stories from the later strand of Samuel lie on the surface. There are in 1 Samuel two different conceptions of the position held by Samuel, the one viewing him as a prophet, the other as a "judge." With these go different views of Samuel's attitude toward the founding of the monarchy; the narrative that pictures him as a "judge" views the kingdom from the standpoint of its later defects. There are, too, several duplicate narratives: two introductions of David to Saul, two origins of the saying concerning Saul among the prophets, two accounts of the sparing of Saul's life, with striking similarities, etc. The analysis of 1 Samuel into its earlier and later strands relieves difficulties that puzzle even the young Sunday school scholar. The character of the later document will be considered in Chapter XIV.

father, were lost. And Kish said to Saul his son, Take now one of the servants with thee, and arise, go seek the asses. And he passed through the hill-country of Ephraim, and passed through the land of Shalishah, but they found them not : then they passed through the land of Shaalim, and there they were not : and he passed through the land of the Benjamites, but they found them not.

When they were come to the land of Zuph, Saul said to his servant that was with him, Come, and let us return, lest my father leave off caring for the asses, and be anxious for us. And he said unto him, Behold now, there is in this city a man of God, and he is a man that is held in honor ; all that he saith cometh surely to pass : now let us go thither ; peradventure he can tell us concerning our journey whereon we go. Then said Saul to his servant, But, behold, if we go, what shall we bring the man ? for the bread is spent in our vessels, and there is not a present to bring to the man of God : what have we ? And the servant answered Saul again, and said, Behold, I have in my hand the fourth part of a shekel of silver : that will I give to the man of God, to tell us our way. (Beforetime in Israel, when a man went to inquire of God, thus he said, Come, and let us go to the seer ; for he that is now called a Prophet was beforetime called a Seer.) Then said Saul to his servant, Well said ; come, let us go. So they went unto the city where the man of God was.

As they went up the ascent to the city, they found young maidens going out to draw water, and said unto them, Is the seer here ? And they answered them, and said, He is ; behold, *he is* before thee : make haste now, for he is come to-day into the city ; for the people have a sacrifice to-day in the high place. As soon as ye are come into the city, ye shall straightway find him, before he goeth up to the high place to eat ; for the people will not eat until he come, because he doth bless the sacrifice ; *and* afterwards they eat that are bidden. Now therefore get you up ; for at this time ye shall find him. And they went up to the city ; *and* as they came within the city, behold, Samuel came out toward them, to go up to the high place.

Now Jehovah had revealed unto Samuel a day before Saul came, saying, To-morrow about this time I will send thee a man out of the land of Benjamin, and thou shalt anoint him to be prince over my people Israel ; and he shall save my people out of the hand of the Philistines : for I have looked upon my people, because their cry is come unto me. And when Samuel saw Saul, Jehovah said unto him, Behold, the man of whom I spake to thee ! this same shall have authority over my people. Then Saul drew near to Samuel in the gate, and said, Tell me, I pray thee, where the seer's house is. And Samuel answered Saul, and said, I am the seer ;

E

go up before me unto the high place, for ye shall eat with me to-day: and in the morning I will let thee go, and will tell thee all that is in thy heart. And as for thine asses that were lost three days ago, set not thy mind on them; for they are found. And for whom is all that is desirable in Israel? Is it not for thee, and for all thy father's house? And Saul answered and said, Am not I a Benjamite, of the smallest of the tribes of Israel? and my family the least of all the families of the tribe of Benjamin? wherefore then speakest thou to me after this manner?

And Samuel took Saul and his servant, and brought them into the guest-chamber, and made them sit in the chiefest place among them that were bidden, who were about thirty persons. And Samuel said unto the cook, Bring the portion which I gave thee, of which I said unto thee, Set it by thee. And the cook took up the thigh, and that which was upon it, and set it before Saul. And *Samuel* said, Behold, that which hath been reserved! set it before thee and eat; because unto the appointed time hath it been kept for thee, for I said, I have invited the people. So Saul did eat with Samuel that day.

And when they were come down from the high place into the city, he communed with Saul upon the housetop. And they arose early: and it came to pass about the spring of the day, that Samuel called to Saul on the housetop, saying, Up, that I may send thee away. And Saul arose, and they went out both of them, he and Samuel, abroad. As they were going down at the end of the city, Samuel said to Saul, Bid the servant pass on before us (and he passed on), but stand thou still first, that I may cause thee to hear the word of God.

Then Samuel took the vial of oil, and poured it upon his head, and kissed him, and said, Is it not that Jehovah hath anointed thee to be prince over his inheritance? When thou art departed from me to-day, then thou shalt find two men by Rachel's sepulchre, in the border of Benjamin at Zelzah; and they will say unto thee, The asses which thou wentest to seek are found; and, lo, thy father hath left off caring for the asses, and is anxious for you, saying, What shall I do for my son? Then shalt thou go on forward from thence, and thou shalt come to the oak of Tabor; and there shall meet thee there three men going up to God to Bethel, one carrying three kids, and another carrying three loaves of bread, and another carrying a bottle of wine: and they will salute thee, and give thee two loaves of bread, which thou shalt receive of their hand. After that thou shalt come to the hill of God, where is the garrison of the Philistines: and it shall come to pass, when thou art come thither to the city, that thou shalt meet a band of prophets coming down from the high place with a psaltery, and a timbrel, and a pipe, and a harp, before them; and they will be prophesying: and the Spirit of Jehovah will come mightily upon thee, and thou shalt prophesy with them, and shalt be turned into another man. And let it be, when these signs are come unto thee, that thou do as occasion shall serve thee; for God is with thee. And thou shalt go down before me to Gilgal; and, behold, I will come down unto thee, to offer burnt-offerings, and to sacrifice sacrifices of peace-offerings: seven days shalt thou tarry, till I come unto thee, and show thee what thou shalt do.

And it was so, that, when he had turned his back to go from Samuel, God gave him another heart: and all those signs came to pass that day. And when they came thither to the hill, behold, a band of prophets met him; and the Spirit of God came mightily upon him, and he prophesied among them. And it came to pass, when all that knew him beforetime saw that, behold, he prophesied with the prophets, then the people said one to another, What is this that is come unto the son of Kish? Is Saul also among the prophets? And one of the same place answered and said, And who is their father? Therefore it became a proverb, Is Saul also among the prophets? And when he had made an end of prophesying, he came to the high place.

And Saul's uncle said unto him and to his servant, Whither went ye? And he said, To seek the asses; and when we saw that they were not found, we came to Samuel. And Saul's uncle said, Tell me, I pray thee, what Samuel said unto you. And Saul said unto his uncle, He told us plainly that the asses were found. But concerning the matter of the kingdom, whereof Samuel spake, he told him not.

Then Nahash the Ammonite came up, and encamped against Jabesh-gilead: and all the men of Jabesh said unto Nahash, Make a covenant with us, and we will serve thee. And Nahash the Ammonite said unto them, On this condition will I make it with you, that all your right eyes be put out; and I will lay it for a reproach upon all Israel. And the elders of Jabesh said unto him, Give us seven days' respite, that we may send messengers unto all the borders of Israel; and then, if there be none to save us, we will come out to thee. Then came the messengers to Gibeah of Saul, and spake these words in the ears of the people: and all the people lifted up their voice, and wept. And, behold, Saul came following the oxen out of the field; and Saul said, What aileth the people that they weep? And they told him the words of the men of Jabesh.

And the Spirit of God came mightily upon Saul when he heard those words, and his anger was kindled greatly. And he took a yoke of oxen, and cut them in pieces, and sent them throughout all the borders of Israel by the hand of messengers, saying, Whosoever cometh not forth after Saul and after Samuel, so shall it be done unto his oxen.   And the dread of Jehovah fell on the people, and they came out as one man.   And he numbered them in Bezek.   And they said unto the messengers that came, Thus shall ye say unto the men of Jabesh-gilead, To-morrow, by the time the sun is hot, ye shall have deliverance.   And the messengers came and told the men of Jabesh; and they were glad. Therefore the men of Jabesh said, To-morrow we will come out unto you, and ye shall do with us all that seemeth good unto you.   And it was so on the morrow, that Saul put the people in three companies; and they came into the midst of the camp in the morning watch, and smote the Ammonites until the heat of the day : and it came to pass, that they that remained were scattered, so that not two of them were left together.   And all the people went to Gilgal; and there they made Saul king before Jehovah in Gilgal; and there they offered sacrifices of peace-offerings before Jehovah; and there Saul and all the men of Israel rejoiced greatly.

Saul chose him three thousand men of Israel, whereof two thousand were with Saul in Michmash and in the mount of Bethel, and a thousand were with Jonathan in Gibeah of Benjamin : and the rest of the people he sent every man to his tent.   And Jonathan smote the garrison of the Philistines that was in Geba ; and the Philistines heard of it.   And Saul blew the trumpet throughout all the land, saying, Let the Hebrews hear. And all Israel heard say that Saul had smitten the garrison of the Philistines, and also that Israel was had in abomination with the Philistines. And the people were gathered together after Saul to Gilgal.

And the Philistines assembled themselves together to fight with Israel, thirty thousand chariots, and six thousand horsemen, and people as the sand which is on the sea-shore in multitude : and they came up, and encamped in Michmash, eastward of Beth-aven.   When the men of Israel saw that they were in a strait (for the people were distressed), then the people did hide themselves in caves, and in thickets, and in rocks, and in coverts, and in pits.   Now some of the Hebrews had gone over the Jordan to the land of Gad and Gilead; but as for Saul, he was yet in Gilgal, and all the people followed him trembling.

And Saul, and Jonathan his son, and the people that were present with them, abode in Geba of Benjamin : but the Philistines encamped in Michmash.   And the spoilers came out of the camp of the Philistines in three companies : one company turned unto the way that leadeth to Ophrah, unto the land of Shual; and another company turned the way to Beth-horon; and another company turned the way of the border that looketh down upon the valley of Zeboim toward the wilderness.   And the garrison of the Philistines went out unto the pass of Michmash.

Now it fell upon a day, that Jonathan the son of Saul said unto the young man that bare his armor, Come, and let us go over to the Philistines' garrison, that is on yonder side. But he told not his father. And Saul abode in the uttermost part of Gibeah under the pomegranate-tree which is in Migron: and the people that were with him were about six hundred men; and Ahijah, the son of Ahitub, Ichabod's brother, the son of Phinehas, the son of Eli, the priest of Jehovah in Shiloh, wearing an ephod. And the people knew not that Jonathan was gone. And between the passes by which Jonathan sought to go over unto the Philistines' garrison, there was a rocky crag on the one side, and a rocky crag on the other side: and the name of the one was Bozez, and the name of the other Seneh. The one crag rose up on the north in front of Michmash, and the other on the south in front of Geba.

And Jonathan said to the young man that bare his armor, Come, and let us go over unto the garrison of these uncircumcised: it may be that Jehovah will work for us; for there is no restraint to Jehovah to save by many or by few. And his armorbearer said unto him, Do all that is in thy heart: turn thee, behold, I am with thee according to thy heart. Then said Jonathan, Behold, we will pass over unto the men, and we will disclose ourselves unto them. If they say thus unto us, Tarry until we come to you; then we will stand still in our place, and will not go up unto them. But if they say thus, Come up unto us; then we will go up; for Jehovah hath delivered them into our hand: and this shall be the sign unto us. And both of them disclosed themselves unto the garrison of the Philistines: and the Philistines said, Behold, the Hebrews come forth out of the holes where they had hid themselves. And the men of the garrison answered Jonathan and his armorbearer, and said, Come up to us, and we will show you a thing. And Jonathan said unto his armorbearer, Come up after me; for Jehovah hath delivered them into the hand of Israel. And Jonathan climbed up upon his hands and upon his feet, and his armorbearer after him: and they fell before Jonathan; and his armorbearer slew them after him. And that first slaughter, which Jonathan and his armorbearer made, was about twenty men, within as it were half a furrow's length in an acre of land. And there was a trembling in the camp, in the field, and among all the people; the garrison, and the spoilers, they also trembled; and the earth quaked: so there was an exceeding great trembling.

And the watchmen of Saul in Gibeah of Benjamin looked; and, behold, the multitude melted away, and they went hither and thither. Then said Saul unto the people that were with him, Number now, and see who is gone from us. And when they had numbered, behold, Jonathan and his armorbearer were not there.   And Saul said unto Ahijah, Bring hither the ark of God.   For the ark of God was there at that time with the children of Israel.   And it came to pass, while Saul talked unto the priest, that the tumult that was in the camp of the Philistines went on and increased : and Saul said unto the priest, Withdraw thy hand.   And Saul and all the people that were with him were gathered together, and came to the battle : and, behold, every man's sword was against his fellow, and there was a very great discomfiture.   Now the Hebrews that were with the Philistines as beforetime, and that went up with them into the camp, from the country round about, even they also turned to be with the Israelites that were with Saul and Jonathan.   Likewise all the men of Israel that had hid themselves in the hill-country of Ephraim, when they heard that the Philistines fled, even they also followed hard after them in the battle.   So Jehovah saved Israel that day : and the battle passed over by Beth-aven.

And the men of Israel were distressed that day ; for Saul had adjured the people, saying, Cursed be the man that eateth any food until it be evening, and I be avenged on mine enemies.   So none of the people tasted food.   And all the people came into the forest ; and there was honey upon the ground.   And when the people were come unto the forest, behold, the honey dropped : but no man put his hand to his mouth ; for the people feared the oath.   But Jonathan heard not when his father charged the people with the oath : wherefore he put forth the end of the rod that was in his hand, and dipped it in the honeycomb, and put his hand to his mouth ; and his eyes were enlightened.   Then answered one of the people, and said, Thy father straitly charged the people with an oath, saying, Cursed be the man that eateth food this day.   And the people were faint. Then said Jonathan, My father hath troubled the land : see, I pray you, how mine eyes have been enlightened, because I tasted a little of this honey.   How much more, if haply the people had eaten freely to-day of the spoil of their enemies which they found ? for now hath there been no great slaughter among the Philistines.

And they smote of the Philistines that day from Michmash to Aijalon. And the people were very faint ; and the people flew upon the spoil, and took sheep, and oxen, and calves, and slew them on the ground ; and the people did eat them with the blood.   Then they told Saul, saying, Behold, the people sin against Jehovah, in that they eat with the blood.   And he said, Ye have dealt treacherously : roll a great stone unto me this day. And Saul said, Disperse yourselves among the people, and say unto them, Bring me hither every man his ox, and every man his sheep, and slay them here, and eat ; and sin not against Jehovah in eating with the blood.

And all the people brought every man his ox with him that night, and slew them there. And Saul built an altar unto Jehovah: the same was the first altar that he built unto Jehovah.

And Saul said, Let us go down after the Philistines by night, and take spoil among them until the morning light, and let us not leave a man of them. And they said, Do whatsoever seemeth good unto thee. Then said the priest, Let us draw near hither unto God. And Saul asked counsel of God, Shall I go down after the Philistines? wilt thou deliver them into the hand of Israel? But he answered him not that day. And Saul said, Draw nigh hither, all ye chiefs of the people; and know and see wherein this sin hath been this day. For, as Jehovah liveth, who saveth Israel, though it be in Jonathan my son, he shall surely die. But there was not a man among all the people that answered him. Then said he unto all Israel, Be ye on one side, and I and Jonathan my son will be on the other side. And the people said unto Saul, Do what seemeth good unto thee. Therefore Saul said unto Jehovah, the God of Israel, Show the right. And Jonathan and Saul were taken by lot; but the people escaped. And Saul said, Cast lots between me and Jonathan my son. And Jonathan was taken.

Then Saul said to Jonathan, Tell me what thou hast done. And Jonathan told him, and said, I did certainly taste a little honey with the end of the rod that was in my hand; and, lo, I must die. And Saul said, God do so and more also; for thou shalt surely die, Jonathan. And the people said unto Saul, Shall Jonathan die, who hath wrought this great salvation in Israel? Far from it: as Jehovah liveth, there shall not one hair of his head fall to the ground; for he hath wrought with God this day. So the people rescued Jonathan, that he died not. Then Saul went up from following the Philistines; and the Philistines went to their own place.

In many respects this might be styled one story, rather than a group of stories; one character is central almost throughout and one theme runs through the whole. There is, too, an excellent point of beginning and a climax which leaves the mind at rest: "Then Saul went up from following the Philistines; and the Philistines went to their own place." Yet we note that from the raid on Michmash forward, Saul ceases to be truly the hero. While the theme, the choice of Saul to deliver from the Philistines, continues to be the same, the central interest is now in Jonathan, his heroic exploits and his escape from the tragic end which a blind fate, or his father's folly, had almost made inevitable. It is better to count this a separate story, though an important member of the group.

The paragraphs connecting this story with that which ends at Saul's formal recognition in Gilgal may be thought of as due to the collector of the cycle, for the new story really begins, "Now it fell upon a day that Jonathan the son of Saul." The narratives of Saul's selection by Samuel and of the public exploit which led to his acknowledgment by the people may also have been separate stories; each has its own main event, and each opens in a way to catch and fix the attention. The second begins, "Then Nahash the Ammonite came up and encamped against Jabesh-gilead."

One can hardly read this cycle of Saul stories for the first time without being impressed by their "swiftness" and "unerring sense of effective detail." [1] There is constant action, and the actions selected are "so significant that each stage makes us eager for the next until the attention is released and the imagination satisfied by the climax." [2] The first Saul story occupies 3 pages, as printed above. In this brief compass, we have the introduction of Saul and his family, the hunt for the asses, the discussion of Saul with his servant, the meeting with the maidens, Samuel's preparation for the meeting with Saul, the meeting, the feast, the evening talk upon the housetop, the anointing, the foretelling of experiences, Saul among the prophets, the uncle's questioning, Saul's partial answer. Yet it is no barren summary of events, nor is there unpleasant sense of hurry; everything is told that need be, and the movement seems even leisurely. The stories of this cycle meet the rhetorician's formal tests of well-told tales: I. A central person and event, or unity and climax; II. The right beginning to fix the attention and fix it in a way that leads on to what is to follow; III. Movement, which involves both action and selection. [3]

To select the earliest strand of narrative in 1 Samuel 15–30 is more difficult than in the case of chapters 9–14. A rough analysis

---

[1] J. H. Gardiner, *The Bible as English Literature*. The characterization is applied by Gardiner to Israel's early prose as a whole.

[2] Charles Sears Baldwin, *How to Write*. The phrases quoted are used in a general discussion of the qualities of good prose as exemplified in the Bible.

[3] Baldwin, *How to Write*.

will give 16 $^{14-23}$, 18 $^{6-13,}$ $^{20-29a}$, 19 $^{11-17}$, 21 $^{1-9}$, 22 ^{1,} ^{2,} $^{6-23}$, 23 $^{1-14}$, 25, 27–28^2, 29–30 as the earliest group of narratives concerning David and Saul in their tangled relations. Possibly some material should be added to that selected, and, quite certainly, some clauses should be excised, as due to an editor who united this early cycle with a later; but these sections give a generally self-consistent group of stories. Saul is not the hero here; David is everywhere the central figure. We shall not go far astray, if we assign the former stories, in their origin, to Saul's own tribe of Benjamin, and these to Judah; though it may well be that the two cycles in which Saul was prominent were already combined as a single document before they came to form a part of one of the two great histories which were ultimately interwoven to form our books of Samuel.

The whole group has the unity of a central theme, but what the climax shall be depends upon the point at which we separate it from the next group. If we look at it as primarily the story of David's struggle with Saul, the natural conclusion and climax is found in the first chapter of 2 Samuel.[1]

The writer of this cycle, if he included David's Lament over Saul and Jonathan, professedly had a written source for one bit, namely, the *Book of Jashar* (2 Samuel 1^{18}), although, as in the history of Saul's establishment in the kingdom, the document, as a whole, is close to the oral tradition. The insertion of poems, such as David's laments, in early prose narratives finds analogy in the *Saxon Chronicle*, where we read, for example, the lyric celebrating the victory of Æthelstan at Brunanburh, inserted under the year 937.

Equally with the Saul cycle, this group of narratives would fully meet the formal tests of well-told stories. The opening (16 ^{14} $^{ff.}$) is, "Now the Spirit of Jehovah departed from Saul, and an evil spirit from Jehovah troubled him, and Saul's servants said unto him, Behold now, an evil spirit from God troubleth thee. Let our lord now command thy servants, that are before thee, to seek out a man who is a skilful player on the harp: and it shall come to pass, when the evil spirit from God is upon thee, that he

---

[1] The division between 1 and 2 Samuel is late and not particularly happy.

shall play with his hand, and thou shalt be well." It was this sad change in Saul, recorded so simply, that brought David into the king's household and led on to the whole series of entanglements. In beginning, in unity, and in progress, the stories offer little opportunity for aught but intellectual and æsthetic satisfaction. Yet some stand out with especial distinction, as the sack of Ziklag and David's consequent pursuit of the Amalekites, and the story of David, Nabal, and Abigail. In the one, we have rapid action with a quick succession of sharply drawn pictures — the little city where fire and rapine have done their work; the maddened followers ready to stone David; the inquiry of Jehovah by the priest with the ephod; the heart-breaking pursuit that proved too swift for fully one-third of the men; the finding of the famished Egyptian; the camp of the Amalekites in revelry; the smiting and recovery; the establishment at the brook Besor of the ordinance concerning the division of the spoil; the distribution of gifts to the elders of Judah and neighboring clans. In the other, there is chiefly dialogue in which, despite the conventional phrases of oriental courtesy, character is distinctly revealed. Few scenes show more clearly the true David, but he is not the chief figure of this story. The interest centres rather in "Abigail, wife of 'the fool,' Nabal, such a fearless, self-possessed, gracious woman as is not often met." The gentle power of the woman that so quickly calmed and wrought sweet reasonableness in the soul of David, the outlaw chief, hot for vengeance, must have been deeply felt throughout the generations. It has remained for a woman, writing in the twentieth century A.D., to put into words a most sympathetic interpretation of this woman of the eleventh century B.C. Elaborating the fine characterization quoted above, this writer goes on: "Not in all the Old Testament, hardly in all eastern literature, is there another speech of woman so dignified, appropriate, and winning as the words Abigail addressed to David to restrain him from avenging himself with his own hand. There is all the loyalty of the wife who, though mated with a clown, is yet true to him. 'Upon me, my Lord, upon me be the iniquity, for my husband is not accountable, being Nabal — a fool.' There is all the fearlessness of the woman who, though in danger, is mistress of the situation, able to remind the freebooting chieftain how unworthy of him it would be to avenge himself with his own hand. There is all the discretion and tact of a woman entirely mistress of herself and perspicacious as to the character of him to whom her plea was addressed, in her promise that when at last better days should have dawned — David's soul 'bound in the bundle of life with Jehovah, and the souls of his enemies slung out by God as from the hollow of a sling' — then 'this shall be no grief unto thee, nor offence of heart unto my lord, either that thou hast shed blood causeless or that my lord hath avenged himself.'" [1]

In the David-Saul stories, the interest of each is well led up to the climax, and is led on, too, through the successive narratives, till the hero reaches the most critical point when escape from fighting against his own people seems impossible. David is the trusted vassal of one of the Philistine kings, having been forced to flee from all Saul's domain. The Philistines are mustering all their forces for a united effort to establish once more the dominance that Saul has broken, and David and his men come perforce to the great muster in the train of their liege lord Achish. What is David to do in the crisis? The story gives an unexpected release from the entanglement that a moment before seemed hopeless. David carries out his assumed rôle with consummate bravado, and then turns back with his six hundred followers.

No better example could be found of the simple objectiveness of early stories in contrast to the conscious psychological analysis characteristic of modern writers. One may note this objectivity in any early literature, whether it be in Greece, or our own England, or the land of Israel. Is it not equally characteristic of Beowulf, the Iliad, or Æneid, and the David-Saul stories? "Brave deeds nobly done, but with few reflections concerning them" might characterize any one of these immortal tales almost as well as another.[2] A modern student of Biblical literature has drawn an effective contrast between Browning's picture of David's inner struggles as he goes to play before Saul in one of his terrible moods, and the simple, objective narrative of our early document. He remarks that "the thought of the East was essentially simple. It

---

[1] Louise Seymour Houghton, *Hebrew Life and Thought*, pp. 157–158.

[2] The characterization is that given of Beowulf in *The Cambridge History of English Literature*, Vol. I, p. 47.

knew only the objective and solid facts of which man has direct
sensation, and the simple and primitive emotions which are his
reactions to them. It has no perception of the subtler shades and
shadows of feeling in which modern writers delight, nor of the
complicated webs of thought which grow from men's efforts to
reason out the universe." [1]

Returning to David's strange plight at Aphek, we may speculate
whimsically as to how Browning, or Mrs. Ward, or even George
Eliot would have revelled in depicting the conflicting emotions
of the hero of the tale. The old story gives us a dramatic scene
— Achish and the princes of the Philistines in heated discussion,
and then Achish and David; but psychological analysis? Far
be it from the unspoiled story-teller of early East or early West!

The story of the sack of Ziklag follows. While intense enough
in itself, it seems, in relation to the whole, an interlude, occupying
the time while the army of Israel is in its death struggle miles
away. In its closing scene, however, when David sends gifts of
the booty to the elders of Judah and the neighboring clans, it
throws much light on the course that led David so soon to the
throne of the southern portion of the Hebrew confederation.
The vivid narrative of David's receiving the news of Saul's death
follows, and his noble dirge may have formed the conclusion — it
would have been a strong and fitting one — of the original David-
Saul cycle of stories.

As was noticed in Chapter III, the military leader selected by
Samuel proved the right man to crystallize diffused enthusiasm
into sudden action, but he did not add the qualities on which stable
results could rest. He and his house went down to ruin, to be
followed by a dashing leader who had also much of the tact and
patience of the true statesman. This one was, it is true, a child of
his age, ethically immature and superstitious in religion, but
intensely loyal to the God of Israel as he understood such loyalty.
He was a leader who so attached his personal followers that, even
when his cause was in desperate case, his sigh for a draught of

---

[1] J. H. Gardiner, *The English Bible as Literature*, p. 86. As indicated
in the text, this admirable description seems to fit early occidental literature equally well.

water from the old home spring was answered at the jeopardy of life. To the power of inspiring blind devotion, characteristic of the born leader of men, he added the wisdom of a Washington, recognizing that "we must use men as they are, not as we would have them" — witness the efficient service that was his through all his long reign from that bloody brute, but consummate fighter, Joab.

After years of struggle, David's skill in allaying jealousies, and the military ability at his command, gave him the rule over a fairly united people. In desperate struggle, the hegemony of the Philistines was thrown off; by a quick assault the natural stronghold of Jerusalem was captured from the Canaanites, who had held it all through the loose rule of Saul. This neutral, defensible place, lying between the mutually jealous northern and southern tribes, was chosen as the political capital and was started toward its age-long religious preëminence by the bringing of the ancient ark. The neighboring peoples to the south, east, and north were subdued or entered into alliance, and the brief era of Israel's national glory and peace was begun.

Within the king's motley family, the wives, incident to marriage alliances with various tribes and clans, and their sons, furnished the conditions necessary for bitter rivalry, intrigue, and tragedy. The man whose native talents had raised him from obscurity and outlawry to the rule of the kingdom, which he had himself welded, saw no reason why he should not take to himself any woman that he would. Under the influence of one of those unique personalities whose work made Israel ultimately the world's teacher, he repented deeply, it is true, but his eldest son followed the course of his sin rather than his penitence. The fire kindled burst out repeatedly and could not be quenched.

The dramatic incidents of David's court life, which resulted in the murder of Amnon, the rebellion and death of Absalom, the birth of Solomon, the judicial murder of Adonijah, and the final establishment of Solomon on the throne, furnished the material for a remarkable narrative. This now forms essentially chapters 9–20 of 2 Samuel and 1 and 2 of 1 Kings. It is universally acknowledged as bearing all the marks of a substantially contemporaneous record. It is singularly free from unconscious allusions to subsequent conditions and other anachronisms that almost inevitably betray the later hand, as well as from those legendary accretions by which oral transmission is so sure to show itself. Yet it is no mere chronicle kept from month to month or year to year; it is the finished work of one who looks back from a time at least as late as Solomon's reign and sees the events of David's court life in perspective and in their ultimate issue. Perhaps the story was written during the reign of Solomon, though hardly with the king's knowledge and sanction; if after Solomon's death, it seems a little strange that the writer betrays no knowledge of the division of the kingdom.

In picturesque details and charming side touches, the narrative shows all the marks of the unspoiled story-teller, accustomed to the quick, responsive appreciation of simple, childlike listeners. It is the story-teller who relieves the strain between the account of Joab's cold-blooded slaughter of Absalom and David's pathetic grief, by the story of the foot-race between the Cushite runner sent by Joab and the eager Ahimaaz who, though handicapped at the start, outruns the Cushite. We seem to see almost a hint of tender sentiment in Joab as he tries to dissuade Ahimaaz from running with the unwelcome tidings.[1] It is the story-teller who takes us suddenly to David sitting between the two gates and the watchman on the roof of the gate. He delays just long enough with the coming of one runner into sight and then the other, and the questioning conversation of David and the watchman, before he lets the blow fall on the head of the father, more concerned for the fate of his handsome, wayward son than for his kingdom. It is the *raconteur*, too, who says, "But when David saw that his servants were whispering together, David perceived that the child was dead,"[2] or again, "The woman took and spread the covering over the well's mouth, and strewed bruised grain thereon; and nothing was known."[3]

In sharp contrast with the stories considered in the present chapter, the prose narratives of events antedating the rise of the monarchy bear the marks of a considerable period of oral transmission, and this accords with other facts which suggest that we are not far from the beginning of connected prose writing in ancient

[1] 2 Samuel 18 19-23.   [2] 2 Samuel 12 19.   [3] Samuel 17 19.

Israel. On the other hand, the comparative complexity of the
story of David's court and family life shows a conscious literary
art that may imply predecessors for our narrative, which have left
no other trace of their existence.

The working out of the plot in the interplay of its parts is worth
noting in detail. At the outset, Jonathan's surviving son,
Meribaal, appears in a vivid scene, which has a certain significance
in itself as revealing the character and temper of David early in
his reign, but seems to have no especial connection with the story
as a whole, until troubles are clouding thick about the old monarch
fleeing from a people in rebellion. Finally, in the epilogue of the
long Absalom incident, Meribaal appears again in a sharply drawn
picture, which still leaves us wondering whether his servant Ziba
was a blackguard or Meribaal was a snivelling ingrate. Perhaps
the writer did not know; evidently David did not, and so settled
their affairs with a compromise, giving each the benefit of the
doubt. This side story throws light upon David's character and
purposes at the three significant points where it appears; it serves
to darken the hour of his misfortune and to help complete the
picture of his general magnanimous, though rather rough-handed
justice, at the time of restoration to the throne.

The central story begins with the political action of sending
ambassadors to Hanun, the new king of Ammon. Does the writer
have a certain appreciation of the coarse humor in the insult given
David by the treatment of his representatives? He tells the
incident with frank detail, at any rate. The Hanun incident
leads on to the Ammonite war, and this to the story of Uriah and
Bathsheba, from which comes the narrative of the birth of Solomon,
whose secure settlement upon the throne will be the conclusion
of this entire narrative. This can be achieved only after the
removal of the older sons, Amnon and Absalom, and all that
involves a complicated chain of events. Amnon, the elder, wrongs
Absalom's sister. After two years of waiting, Absalom takes
bloody vengeance. David's dealing with this matter eventuates,
years later, in Absalom's rebellion and death. David's restoration is followed almost immediately by the account of the closing
scenes of his life. The introduction of the beautiful Shunammite
prepares for the ultimate removal by death of Solomon's elder

brother, Adonijah, whose ill-starred attempt to secure the throne
is frustrated by Nathan and Bathsheba.

Many characters have each their part to play, and many striking
scenes exhibit the long and complex series of events necessary to
unfold the story.   Joab the general, Nathan the prophet, the wise
woman of Tekoa, Hushai the shrewd counsellor and wily rhetorician,
and many more appear in clear-cut and significant scenes or furnish
material for subordinate plots that in themselves are full of deep
human interest.   How tragic, for example, is the brief story of the
wise, gentle, beautiful Tamar !   How living is the scene where the
wise woman of Tekoa tells her skilfully concocted story to David,
and the shrewd old king, after hearing her through, asks, "Is the
hand of Joab with thee in all this?"   The modern novel hardly
offers a greater number of clearly differentiated characters or a
greater variety of conflicting purposes and significant incidents
than we find interwoven and worked out to an issue in this early
narrative of ancient Israel.

The various scenes depend for their sustained interest more
upon the interplay of well-drawn characters than upon shifting
scenery.   The value of variety in setting is not overlooked, but
the writer spends little more time on the careful painting of the
background than was given in the Shakespearean theatre; he
permits his readers some imagination.   He uses very sparingly, in
his own person, those picturesque touches from animal life and
nature's processes, so instinctive with the rural bred; but when he
makes the orator Hushai speak, within five verses, there are comparisons with a bear robbed of her whelps, the heart of a lion, the
sand for multitude, and the dew falling on the ground.

We have been considering the selection and arrangement of
material as bearing upon the central theme of Solomon's secure
establishment upon the throne with all possible claimants removed;
but the narrative is not merely of interest as a dramatic account
of important historical events.   The moral and religious aspect of
the events is felt throughout; and it is noticeable, as we see in the
case of other early narratives, that the writer has no hard and fast
theory of providential government to illustrate from the history,
and no mechanical, ecclesiastical ideals to uphold.   Both of these
tendencies, which so largely color the Old Testament history in its

final form, appear only in later ages. In this early story, the simple comment upon David's conduct in the matter of Bathsheba and Uriah is "The thing that David had done displeased Jehovah." Then Nathan is introduced, rousing, with homely parable, the king's native sense of justice, and adding to this an appeal to his strong religious sense, "Wherefore hast thou despised the word of Jehovah to do that which is evil in his sight?" "By this deed thou hast given great occasion to the enemies of Jehovah to blaspheme." The terrible tragedy of lust unbridled, leading on inevitably to wretched woe, unfolds without any obtrusive pointing of the moral in such a way that the facts speak their own high lesson.

How far the writer may have entered into philosophizing upon the cause and effect of it all we cannot be sure. We do feel, however, that the events are recorded by one to whom religion has begun to be ethical. Occasionally his childlike faith in the direct control of God is definitely expressed, as in the statement "Jehovah had ordained to defeat the good counsel of Ahithophel, to the intent that Jehovah might bring evil upon Absalom." Even such expressions as this are rare in this grandly simple and impressive narrative of men and events.

CHAPTER V

(Before 800 B.C.)

EVEN while David lived, jealousies between the northern and southern tribes threatened dissolution of the union. A policy of centralization with the establishment of fortresses at strategic points made secession impossible during the reign of Solomon. Yet, before Solomon's death, an able young officer whom he had put in charge of the task-work of the great tribe of Ephraim "lifted up his hand against the king" and then fled to Egypt, where he was harbored by Shishak. This Pharaoh represented a new dynasty with ambitions for foreign conquest, and his reception of Jeroboam was ominous. Within Israel itself, prophets of the type that had loyally served and dared to rebuke David turned away from Solomon in despair; one of them enkindled, we are told, the thought of future rule in the heart of Jeroboam.[1]

Looking back over the centuries it is easy to see that the division of the kingdom was inevitable, unless Solomon should leave a son of consummate tact or iron hand. When the separation came, by far the greater portion of the land, the people, and the natural wealth of all sorts fell to Jeroboam. A large portion also of the patriotic and religious memories and traditions were the especial heritage of the northern kingdom. Even the sanctuaries at Dan and Bethel had been places of worship for Israel far longer than the Temple mount. The separation of Northern Israel from Judah probably had behind it the forces of religious conservatism, as well as the political conservatism that protested against a despotism new to the tribes of Israel. Shishak of Egypt soon plundered the accumulated wealth of Jerusalem; yet Judah has her advantages, which in the ultimate issue will prove the more

[1] 1 Kings 11 29-39.

vital. Her land is relatively compact, sheltered, and defensible, and her reigning house firmly established on the throne. In the generations to come, Northern Israel will have to bear the first attacks of Syria and Assyria from without, and within will pass through revolution after revolution. In Judah the Temple will become more and more a unifying and inspiring force; while already, at the time of the division, there is in the south a literary culture which will give the people a means of preserving and developing ideals only tardily won in the north.

There was much material for literature in the north, but we cannot ascribe any prose writing of Northern Israel to the first century of her independent existence. In the first half century, times were often troublous. Jeroboam ruled seventeen years, but his son, after only two years' reign, was assassinated by the commander of the army, who made himself king. This monarch, Baasha, made alliance with Damascus against Judah, Solomon's great-grandson, then reigning in Judah, bought off the ally, who proceeded to attack Israel. Baasha's son ruled only two years when he was killed. The able general of the army, Omri, soon overcame the assassin and established a dynasty that lasted nearly fifty years and won considerable power for Northern Israel. The rule of this new line coincided substantially with the second half of the first century. This period was one of much foreign warfare, sometimes successful, but often very disastrous to Israel. On the whole, the conditions were unfavorable for literary development, though there may have been some writings now lost. References in Kings indicate that at least state annals were kept.

In Judah, in spite of some warfare, prose literature grew from generation to generation. Royal annals which had been begun under the United Kingdom were carried forward, while true prose literature developed through the gathering of oral traditions and written fragments from the past into a great narrative work that sought to trace history back to the beginning of man's life on earth.

In the previous chapter, the analogy between the growth of the early historical narratives of England and Israel was not completed. In addition to successive compilations, revisions, and continuations forward, paralleled in Israel's writing, the progress of historical composition in England showed successive extensions backward — to Cæsar's conquest, to the creation. In the great Judean history of the ninth century B.C., writers of Judah attempted for their nation that which Florence of Worcester undertook in the England of the twelfth century A.D. For the early millenniums the English narrative was the Hebrew, borrowed by Christian England. Here the analogy of spontaneous growth is interrupted, since the English history is only an imitation and reproduction of the Hebrew. There seems to be no adequate parallel, in any early literature, to the great effort made in Judah, in the century after Solomon's death, to tell the story of the past. With all our admiration for the intellect of the Greeks, we must admit that it never set itself this noble task on any such comprehensive plan as that of the early Judean writers.[1]

Probably the Judean writers at first reached back from the rise of the monarchy only to the era of the conquest and settlement and gathered into a written document the heroic tales of the deliverers whom we call Judges. Their narrative was free from that rigid interpretation of the events given in our present book of Judges.[2] Like the early Saul and David stories, these stories were told in free, spontaneous form, with little of reflective interpretation. One example will indicate the general literary character of all.

Because of Midian the children of Israel made them the dens which are in the mountains, and the caves, and the strongholds. And so it was, when Israel had sown, that the Midianites came up, and the Amalekites, and the children of the east; they came up against them; and they encamped against them, and destroyed the increase of the earth, till thou come unto Gaza, and left no sustenance in Israel, neither sheep, nor ox, nor ass. For they came up with their cattle and their tents; they came in as locusts for multitude; both they and their camels were without number: and they came into the land to destroy it. And Israel was brought very low because of Midian:

And the angel of Jehovah came, and sat under the oak which was in Ophrah, that pertained unto Joash the Abiezrite: and his son Gideon

---

[1] As Eduard Meyer states, true historical literature had a wholly independent origin only among the Israelites and Greeks (*Geschichte des Altertums*, II (1910), § 131).

[2] See Chapter XVIII.

was beating out wheat in the winepress, to hide it from the Midianites.
And the angel of Jehovah appeared unto him, and said unto him, Jehovah
is with thee, thou mighty man of valor. And Gideon said unto him,
Oh, my lord, if Jehovah is with us, why then is all this befallen us? and
where are all his wondrous works which our fathers told us of, saying,
Did not Jehovah bring us up from Egypt? but now Jehovah hath cast us
off, and delivered us into the hand of Midian. And Jehovah looked upon
him, and said, Go in this thy might, and save Israel from the hand of
Midian: have not I sent thee? And he said unto him, Oh, Lord, wherewith shall I save Israel? behold, my family is the poorest in Manasseh,
and I am the least in my father's house. And Jehovah said unto him,
Surely I will be with thee, and thou shalt smite the Midianites as one man.
And he said unto him, If now I have found favor in thy sight, then show
me a sign that it is thou that talkest with me. Depart not hence, I pray
thee, until I come unto thee, and bring forth my present, and lay it before
thee. And he said, I will tarry until thou come again.

And Gideon went in, and made ready a kid, and unleavened cakes of
an ephah of meal: the flesh he put in a basket, and he put the broth in a
pot, and brought it out unto him under the oak, and presented it. And
the angel of God said unto him, Take the flesh and the unleavened cakes,
and lay them upon this rock, and pour out the broth. And he did so.
Then the angel of Jehovah put forth the end of the staff that was in his
hand, and touched the flesh and the unleavened cakes; and there went
up fire out of the rock, and consumed the flesh and the unleavened cakes;
and the angel of Jehovah departed out of his sight. And Gideon saw
that he was the angel of Jehovah; and Gideon said, Alas, O Lord Jehovah!
forasmuch as I have seen the angel of Jehovah face to face. And Jehovah
said unto him, Peace be unto thee; fear not: thou shalt not die. Then
Gideon built an altar there unto Jehovah, and called it Jehovah-shalom:
unto this day it is yet in Ophrah of the Abiezrites.

But the Spirit of Jehovah came upon Gideon; and he blew a trumpet;
and Abiezer was gathered together after him.

And Gideon came to the Jordan, and passed over, he, and the three
hundred men that were with him, faint, yet pursuing. And he said unto
the men of Succoth, Give, I pray you, loaves of bread unto the people
that follow me; for they are faint, and I am pursuing after Zebah and
Zalmunna, the kings of Midian. And the princes of Succoth said, Are
the hands of Zebah and Zalmunna now in thy hand, that we should give
bread unto thine army? And Gideon said, Therefore when Jehovah
hath delivered Zebah and Zalmunna into my hand, then I will tear your
flesh with the thorns of the wilderness and with briers. And he went up

thence to Penuel, and spake unto them in like manner; and the men of Penuel answered him as the men of Succoth had answered. And he spake also unto the men of Penuel, saying, When I come again in peace, I will break down this tower.

Now Zebah and Zalmunna were in Karkor, and their hosts with them, about fifteen thousand men, all that were left of all the host of the children of the east; for there fell a hundred and twenty thousand men that drew sword. And Gideon went up by the way of them that dwelt in tents on the east of Nobah and Jogbehah, and smote the host; for the host was secure. And Zebah and Zalmunna fled; and he pursued after them; and he took the two kings of Midian, Zebah and Zalmunna, and discomfited all the host.

And Gideon the son of Joash returned from the battle from the ascent of Heres. And he caught a young man of the men of Succoth, and inquired of him: and he described for him the princes of Succoth, and the elders thereof, seventy and seven men. And he came unto the men of Succoth, and said, Behold Zebah and Zalmunna, concerning whom ye did taunt me, saying, Are the hands of Zebah and Zalmunna now in thy hand, that we should give bread unto thy men that are weary? And he took the elders of the city, and thorns of the wilderness and briers, and with them he taught the men of Succoth. And he brake down the tower of Penuel, and slew the men of the city.

Then said he unto Zebah and Zalmunna, What manner of men were they whom ye slew at Tabor? And they answered, As thou art, so were they; each one resembled the children of a king. And he said, They were my brethren, the sons of my mother: as Jehovah liveth, if ye had saved them alive, I would not slay you. And he said unto Jether his firstborn, Up, and slay them. But the youth drew not his sword; for he feared, because he was yet a youth. Then Zebah and Zalmunna said, Rise thou, and fall upon us; for as the man is, so is his strength. And Gideon arose, and slew Zebah and Zalmunna and took the crescents that were on their camels' necks.[1]

Whether the inference is correct that the Judean historians gathered first the hero stories of the age of settlement in Canaan and later prefixed the traditions of the Exodus, of the early tribal wanderings, and of the beginnings of humanity, it is clear that, within about a century after the division of the kingdom, Judah had an incomparable collection of stories of the past, brought together in a masterly way by those who gave the whole a certain

[1] Judges 6 2b-6a, 11-24, 34, 8 4-21.

literary unity. This history was later interwoven with one of similar character composed in Northern Israel, and, after subsequent revision, centuries later, sections from the composite work thus produced were fitted into a new and independent historical outline to form our books of Genesis, Exodus, Numbers, and Joshua. The narratives of Judges and Samuel escaped the last stage of this process, but received, at an earlier date, abundant additions and interpretations. The tracing of this long literary history will furnish matter for subsequent chapters. We are concerned now only with the earliest strand, compiled in Judah during the first century and a quarter of the divided kingdom. This must be fragmentary, as we can now recover it, and yet the portions preserved are sufficient to discover the general plan and scope of the Early Judean History of Antiquity.

It begins with the story of the Garden in Genesis 2 : — [1]

In the day that Jehovah God made earth and heaven, no plant of the field was yet in the earth, and no herb of the field had yet sprung up; for Jehovah God had not caused it to rain upon the earth: and there was not a man to till the ground; but there went up a mist from the earth, and watered the whole face of the ground. And Jehovah God formed man of the dust of the ground, and breathed into his nostrils the breath of life; and man became a living soul. And Jehovah God planted a garden eastward, in Eden; and there he put the man whom he had formed. And out of the ground made Jehovah God to grow every tree that is pleasant to the sight, and good for food; the tree of life also in the midst of the garden, and the tree of the knowledge of good and evil. And a river went out of Eden to water the garden; and from thence it was parted, and became four heads. The name of the first is Pishon: that is it which compasseth the whole land of Havilah, where there is gold; and the gold of that land is

[1] Genesis 2 is sharply distinguished from chapter 1 in vocabulary, style, and point of view. Chapter 2 is picturesque and naïve, conceiving God as working with materials, in human fashion, and associating with his creatures; chapter 1 is orderly, repetitious, with a lofty and spiritualized conception of God. It is not difficult, by these and other criteria, to distinguish the continuations of each of these narratives in later chapters. The first key to the analysis was found in the use of the divine names. In chapter 1 it is uniformly God, in 2, Yahweh God. In chapter 15 there begins a third document using the name God, but otherwise more closely related to the document of chapter 2, from which it cannot always be discriminated with certainty. See p. 99.

good : there is bdellium and the onyx stone.   And the name of the second
river is Gihon : the same is it that compasseth the whole land of Cush.
And the name of the third river is Hiddekel : that is it which goeth in
front of Assyria.   And the fourth river is the Euphrates.   And Jehovah
God took the man, and put him into the garden of Eden to dress it and to
keep it.   And Jehovah God commanded the man, saying, Of every tree
of the garden thou mayest freely eat : but of the tree of the knowledge of
good and evil, thou shalt not eat of it : for in the day that thou eatest
thereof thou shalt surely die.

And Jehovah God said, It is not good that the man should be alone ;
I will make him a help meet for him.   And out of the ground Jehovah
God formed every beast of the field, and every bird of the heavens ; and
brought them unto the man to see what he would call them : and whatsoever the man called every living creature, that was the name thereof.
And the man gave names to all cattle, and to the birds of the heavens,
and to every beast of the field ; but for man there was not found a help
meet for him.   And Jehovah God caused a deep sleep to fall upon the
man, and he slept ; and he took one of his ribs, and closed up the flesh
instead thereof : and the rib, which Jehovah God had taken from the man,
made he a woman, and brought her unto the man.   And the man said,
This is now bone of my bones, and flesh of my flesh : she shall be called
Woman, because she was taken out of Man.   Therefore shall a man
leave his father and his mother, and shall cleave unto his wife : and they
shall be one flesh.   And they were both naked, the man and his wife, and
were not ashamed.

This narrative is continued by the temptation and fall, the first
murder, and the beginnings of civilization through Cain's descendants.   Lamech's song is included here.[1]   The account of the flood
follows : —[2]

And it came to pass, when men began to multiply on the face of the
ground, and daughters were born unto them, that the sons of God saw
the daughters of men that they were fair ; and they took them wives of
all that they chose.   And Jehovah said, My spirit shall not strive with
man for ever, for that he also is flesh : yet shall his days be a hundred and
twenty years.   The Nephilim were in the earth in those days, and also
after that, when the sons of God came in unto the daughters of men, and
they bare children to them : the same were the mighty men that were of
old, the men of renown.

[1] Genesis 4 23-24.   See p. 13.
[2] 6 1-8, 7 1-5, 7-10, 12, 16b-17, 22-23, 8 2b-3a, 6-12, 13b, 20-22.

And Jehovah saw that the wickedness of man was great in the earth, and that every imagination of the thoughts of his heart was only evil continually. And it repented Jehovah that he had made man on the earth, and it grieved him at his heart. And Jehovah said, I will destroy man whom I have created from the face of the ground; both man, and beast, and creeping things, and birds of the heavens; for it repenteth me that I have made them. But Noah found favor in the eyes of Jehovah.

And Jehovah said unto Noah, Come thou and all thy house into the ark; for thee have I seen righteous before me in this generation. Of every clean beast thou shalt take to thee seven and seven, the male and his female; and of the beasts that are not clean two, the male and his female: of the birds also of the heavens, seven and seven, male and female, to keep seed alive upon the face of all the earth. For yet seven days, and I will cause it to rain upon the earth forty days and forty nights; and every living thing that I have made will I destroy from off the face of the ground. And Noah did according unto all that Jehovah commanded him. And Noah went in, and his sons, and his wife, and his sons' wives with him, into the ark, because of the waters of the flood. Of clean beasts, and of beasts that are not clean, and of birds, and of everything that creepeth upon the ground, there went in two and two unto Noah into the ark, male and female, as God commanded Noah. And it came to pass after the seven days, that the waters of the flood were upon the earth. And the rain was upon the earth forty days and forty nights. And Jehovah shut him in. And the flood was forty days upon the earth; and the waters increased, and bare up the ark, and it was lifted up above the earth. All in whose nostrils was the breath of the spirit of life, of all that was on the dry land, died. And every living thing was destroyed that was upon the face of the ground, both man, and cattle, and creeping things, and birds of the heavens; and they were destroyed from the earth: and Noah only was left, and they that were with him in the ark. And the rain from heaven was restrained; and the waters returned from off the earth continually:

And it came to pass at the end of forty days, that Noah opened the window of the ark which he had made: and he sent forth a raven, and it went forth to and fro, until the waters were dried up from off the earth. And he sent forth a dove from him, to see if the waters were abated from off the face of the ground; but the dove found no rest for the sole of her foot, and she returned unto him to the ark; for the waters were on the face of the whole earth: and he put forth his hand, and took her, and brought her in unto him into the ark. And he stayed yet other seven days; and again he sent forth the dove out of the ark; and the dove came in to him at eventide; and, lo, in her mouth an olive leaf plucked off: so Noah knew that the waters were abated from off the earth. And he stayed yet other seven days, and sent forth the dove; and she returned not again unto him any more. And Noah removed the covering of the ark, and looked, and, behold, the face of the ground was dried.

And Noah builded an altar unto Jehovah, and took of every clean beast, and of every clean bird, and offered burnt-offerings on the altar. And Jehovah smelled the sweet savor; and Jehovah said in his heart, I will not again curse the ground any more for man's sake, for that the imagination of man's heart is evil from his youth; neither will I again smite any more everything living, as I have done. While the earth remaineth, seedtime and harvest, and cold and heat, and summer and winter, and day and night shall not cease.

Presumably the story of Noah's drunkenness and the oracular curse on Cain that now follow the flood narrative [1] originally stood before it.[2] Descendants of Cush and Shem are next given and, in this connection, the traditional founding of Nineveh.[3] The naïve story of the tower of Babel with the scattering of the nations [4] ends this group of traditions concerning the beginnings of world history.

Abram and his family are briefly introduced in the narrative [5] which passes immediately to his departure to Shechem and Bethel [6] and then to Egypt.[7]

And there was a famine in the land: and Abram went down into Egypt to sojourn there; for the famine was sore in the land. And it came to pass, when he was come near to enter into Egypt, that he said unto Sarai his wife, Behold now, I know that thou art a fair woman to look upon: and it will come to pass, when the Egyptians shall see thee, that they will say, This is his wife: and they will kill me, but they will save thee alive. Say, I pray thee, thou art my sister; that it may be well with me for thy sake, and that my soul may live because of thee. And it came to pass, that, when Abram was come into Egypt, the Egyptians beheld the woman that she was very fair. And the princes of Pharaoh saw her, and praised her to Pharaoh: and the woman was taken into Pharaoh's house. And he dealt well with Abram for her sake: and he had sheep, and oxen, and he-asses, and men-servants, and maid-servants, and she-asses, and camels. And Jehovah plagued Pharaoh and his house with great plagues because of Sarai, Abram's wife. And Pharaoh called

[1] 9 18-27.   [2] See Kent, *Beginnings of Hebrew History*, p. 60.
[3] 10 8-19, 21, 25-30.   [4] 11 1-9.   [5] 11 28-30.   [6] 12 1-4a, 6-9.   [7] 12 10-20.

Abram and said, What is this that thou hast done unto me? Why didst thou not tell me that she was thy wife? why saidst thou, She is my sister, so that I took her to be my wife? now therefore behold thy wife, take her, and go thy way. And Pharaoh gave men charge concerning him: and they brought him on the way, and his wife, and all that he had.

The return to Bethel and the separation of Abram and Lot are recounted,[1] and the promise of the land is then given to Abram.[2]

And Jehovah said unto Abram, after that Lot was separated from him, Lift up now thine eyes, and look from the place where thou art, north-ward and southward and eastward and westward: for all the land which thou seest, to thee will I give it, and to thy seed for ever. And I will make thy seed as the dust of the earth: so that if a man can number the dust of the earth, then may thy seed also be numbered. Arise, walk through the land in the length of it and in the breadth of it; for unto thee will I give it. And Abram moved his tent, and came and dwelt by the oaks of Mamre, which are in Hebron, and built there an altar unto Jehovah.

The flight of Hagar offers incidental opportunity to explain the name Beer-lahai-roi.[3] The entertainment of the heavenly visitors and the destruction of Sodom and Gomorrah give a series of vivid pictures.[4]

The stories of this document are all picturesque, full of human interest, appealing alike to child and cultured man of letters. Professor Gardiner speaks of their "intense interest in human life," and, classing them along with the narratives of the same general age in Samuel and Kings, declares that "for swiftness, for the unerring sense of effective detail, these stories are our standard in English." "One thinks first of all," he adds, "of their simplicity, clearness, and vividness."[5] We need only recall the picture with which the whole story opens; or the narrative of temptation, sin, and shame; the account of the first murder; the vivid scene at Babel; the entertainment of the heavenly visitors at Abraham's tent, to feel the justice of this high estimate from a man of letters. One need only read the stories to the more infallible critics, story-loving children, to test their unchanging vitality.

[1] 13 1-5, 6b-11a, 12b-13.   [2] 13 14-18.   [3] 16 1b-2, 4-14.   [4] 18, 19 1-28.
[5] J. H. Gardiner, *The Bible as English Literature*, p. 37.

Human beings of alert mind are interested to know how things come to be as they are — 'tis the common impulse of early myth, of proud philosophy, and of arrogant science. Few if any early documents are more alive to this universal craving of keen intellects than the early Judean history. It can hardly let a name or custom find mention without some explanation of its origin. The rise of the different arts and occupations, the sources of the universal joys and sorrows of life are all of vital moment in this earliest attempt at a universal history of humanity. Sociologist and poet alike may find their spiritual progenitors in the narrators of these ancient tales, to whom " nothing human" was " foreign." The stories seek to tell why the marriage relation exists, why "men must work and women must weep," why the nations suffer the inconvenience of talking different languages, and so on, *ad indefinitum*. They love, too, the folksong that comes down from the hearts and lives of the people.

The same qualities are seen throughout the history of the patriarchal wanderings, the Egyptian sojourn, the wilderness era, the struggle for the land. A few selections made almost at random illustrate : —

THE DELIVERANCE AT THE SEA

And it was told the king of Egypt that the people were fled : and the heart of Pharaoh and of his servants was changed towards the people, and they said, What is this we have done, that we have let Israel go from serving us ? And he made ready his chariot, and took his people with him : and all the chariots of Egypt.

And when Pharaoh drew nigh, the children of Israel lifted up their eyes, and, behold, the Egyptians were marching after them ; and they were sore afraid :

And they said unto Moses, Because there were no graves in Egypt, hast thou taken us away to die in the wilderness ? wherefore hast thou dealt with us, to bring us forth out of Egypt ? Is not this the word that we spake unto thee in Egypt, saying, Let us alone, that we may serve the Egyptians ? For it were better for us to serve the Egyptians, than that we should die in the wilderness. And Moses said unto the people, Fear ye not, stand still, and see the salvation of Jehovah, which he will work for you to-day : for the Egyptians whom ye have seen to-day, ye shall see them again no more for ever. Jehovah will fight for you, and ye shall hold your peace.

And the pillar of cloud removed from before them, and stood behind them; yet gave it light by night: and the one came not near the other all the night. And Jehovah caused the sea to go back by a strong east wind all the night, and made the sea dry land. And it came to pass in the morning watch, that Jehovah looked forth upon the host of the Egyptians through the pillar of fire and of cloud. And he bound their chariot wheels, and they drove them heavily; so that the Egyptians said, Let us flee from the face of Israel; for Jehovah fighteth for them against the Egyptians. And the sea returned to its strength when the morning appeared; and the Egyptians fled against it; and Jehovah overthrew the Egyptians in the midst of the sea. There remained not so much as one of them.

Thus Jehovah saved Israel that day out of the hand of the Egyptians; and Israel saw the Egyptians dead upon the seashore.[1]

SENDING THE QUAILS

And the mixed multitude that was among them lusted exceedingly: and the children of Israel also wept again, and said, Who shall give us flesh to eat? We remember the fish, which we did eat in Egypt for nought; the cucumbers, and the melons, and the leeks, and the onions, and the garlic: but now our soul is dried away; there is nothing at all save this manna to look upon. And the manna was like coriander seed, and the appearance thereof as the appearance of bdellium. The people went about, and gathered it, and ground it in mills, or beat it in mortars, and boiled it in pots, and made cakes of it: and the taste of it was as the taste of fresh oil. And when the dew fell upon the camp in the night, the manna fell upon it.

And Moses heard the people weeping throughout their families, every man at the door of his tent: and the anger of Jehovah was kindled greatly; and Moses was displeased. And Moses said unto Jehovah, Wherefore hast thou dealt ill with thy servant? and wherefore have I not found favor in thy sight, that thou layest the burden of all this people upon me? Have I conceived all this people? have I brought them forth, that thou shouldst say unto me, Carry them in thy bosom, as a nursing-father carrieth the suckling child, unto the land which thou swarest unto their fathers? Whence should I have flesh to give unto all this people? for they weep unto me, saying, Give us flesh, that we may eat. I am not able to bear all this people alone, because it is too heavy for me. And if thou deal thus with me, kill me, I pray thee, out of hand, if I have found favor in thy sight; and let me not see my wretchedness.

* * * * * * * *

[1] Exodus 14 5-6, 7b, 10a, 11-14, 19b, 20b, 21b, 24a, 25, 27b, 28b, 30.

And Moses went out, and told the people the words of Jehovah:

And there went forth a wind from Jehovah, and brought quails from the sea, and let them fall by the camp, about a day's journey on this side, and a day's journey on the other side, round about the camp, and about two cubits above the face of the earth.   And the people rose up all that day, and all the night, and all the next day, and gathered the quails: he that gathered least gathered ten homers: and they spread them all abroad for themselves round about the camp.   While the flesh was yet between their teeth, ere it was chewed, the anger of Jehovah was kindled against the people, and Jehovah smote the people with a very great plague. And the name of that place was called Kibroth-hattaavah, because there they buried the people that lusted.   From Kibroth-hattaavah the people journeyed unto Hazeroth; and they abode at Hazeroth.[1]

JOSHUA'S SONG

Then spake Joshua to Jehovah in the day when Jehovah delivered up the Amorites before the children of Israel; and he said in the sight of Israel,

> Sun, stand thou still upon Gibeon;
> And thou, Moon, in the valley of Aijalon.
> And the sun stood still, and the moon stayed,
> Until the nation had avenged themselves of their enemies.

Is not this written in the book of Jashar?   And the sun stayed in the midst of heaven, and hasted not to go down about a whole day.   And there was no day like that before it or after it, that Jehovah hearkened unto the voice of a man: for Jehovah fought for Israel.[2]

The theology and ethics of this history are primitive.   Abram lies about his wife and never dreams of chivalrous protection, but he is not condemned for it.   God is thought of as little more than a powerful man whose majesty is threatened by the height of Babel's tower, who has to come down to see what men are doing, who walks and talks with men; with him prophets like Abraham and Moses may argue and persuade.   The culmination of wickedness is explained as due to the intermarriage of the sons of God with the daughters of men.   Despite the primitive thought of these narratives, there is a great moral and religious theme running through them.   We have fully entered the era when religion is becoming ethical.   The great truth that man's sin brings separation from God and countless woes is set forth with dramatic power

[1] Numbers 11 4-15, 31-35.   [2] Joshua 10 12-14.

as the story advances from stage to stage. The other side of the picture is also winsomely presented, with the primitive virtues of generosity, hospitality, and childlike piety embodied in attractive personalities. This is called the early Judean *prophetic* history because it contains the beginnings of the moral and spiritual teachings which were the great gift and glory of Israel's prophets. We have left behind the age when the God of Israel was little more than the God of battles.

Allusion was made, in the opening chapter, to the fact that the stories of Eden and Babel indicate on their face their origin in the Tigris-Euphrates valley. The garden is planted "eastward," and, of the rivers, two are clearly the Tigris and Euphrates.[1] The tower of Babel is placed in the Babylonian plain, Shinar, where the building material was regularly brick, the bitumen ("slime") springs were abundant, and great, towerlike structures were erected from the earliest times. The flood story is not so obviously set in the Tigris-Euphrates valley, but the close parallels to it in the earlier Babylonian flood stories indicate no less certainly that it, too, comes from this centre of early Semitic culture. The fullest version that has reached us is contained in the eleventh tablet of the Gilgamesh Epic, found in the library of King Ashurbanipal of Nineveh (seventh century B.C.). Fragments of the story have been found that were written long before the migration of Israel's progenitors to Canaan. It is conceivable that the tradition was brought from Mesopotamia in the Abramic migration, but more probable that it was adopted by the Hebrews after their entrance into Canaan.[2]

The Hebrew form of the story is introduced by a strange bit of ancient mythology concerning the sons of God and daughters of men, and is characterized by the childlike conceptions of the ninth century B.C.; yet it is distinguished by a lofty conception of the action of one God who brings on the flood as a just judgment, in most startling contrast to the cowering and bickering gods that appear in the seventh-century form of the Babylonian story. The Babylonian narrative is one form of the original tradition that

[1] The Pishon and Gihon are probably two of the artificial rivers of Babylonia.

[2] See Chapter I, p. 7.

probably grew out of some early devastating flood in the Tigris-Euphrates valley.   The early Judean form of the story shows how completely the prophetic conception of Jehovah, even in its earlier stages, transfused and transformed all that the sons of Israel received of Semitic tradition.   In Babylon and Assyria the story was handed down unchanged in its fundamental conceptions.   In Israel, such details as the process of calking the ark or sending out birds to see whether the waters had abated might remain almost unchanged while the story was transformed in its entire significance.   The Babylonian story should be read in comparison with the Judean.

THE BABYLONIAN DELUGE NARRATIVE [1]

Gilgamesh has come after great struggles to the abode of Utnapishtim, hero of the flood.

Gilgamesh speaks to him, to Utnapishtim, the far-removed:
"I gaze at thee, Utnapishtim.
Thy appearance is not different.   As I am, so art thou.
And thou art not different.   As I am, so art thou.
Thou art completely ready for the fray.
. . . thou hast placed upon thee.
Tell me how thou didst enter into the assembly of the gods and secure life."

Utnapishtim spoke to Gilgamesh:
"I will reveal to thee, Gilgamesh, a secret story,
And the decision of the gods I will tell thee.
The city Shurippak,[2] a city which thou knowest,
(The one that) lies on the Euphrates,
That city was old and the gods thereof
Induced the great gods to bring a cyclone over it.
It was planned (?) by their father Anu
(By) their counsellor, the warrior Enlil,
(By) their herald Ninib,
(By) their leader En-nugi
Nin-igi-azag,[3] Ea, was with them,
He repeated their decision to the reed-hut.
Reed-hut, reed-hut, wall, wall,
Reed-hut, hear!   Wall, give ear."

[1] Revised translation by Professor Morris Jastrow, Jr., Ph.D.
[2] Now identified as the site of the mound Fara.
[3] Or Nin-igi-ku title of Ea as "lord of the shining eye."

O man of Shurippak, son of Ubaru-Tutu,
Break up the house, build a ship,
Abandon your property, seek life.
Throw aside your possessions, and preserve life,
Bring into the ship seed of all living things.
The ship that thou shalt build,
Its dimensions shall be measured,
Its breadth and length made to correspond.

     *   *   *   *   *   *

I understood and spoke to Ea my lord.
(The command) of my lord which thou hast commanded as
I have understood (it) I will carry out
But what shall I answer the city, the people, and the elders?
Ea opened his mouth and spoke
(As answer) thus speak to them :
(Know that) Enlil has taken hatred towards me,
So that I can no longer dwell (in your city)
(On) Bel's territory I dare no longer set my face.
Therefore, I go to the 'deep' to dwell with Ea my lord.

Over you I will cause blessing to rain down
(Catch of) bird, catch of fish,
And . . . rich crops.
Shamash had fixed the time
" (When) the rulers of darkness at evening will cause a destructive rain-
    storm to come down.
Enter the ship, close thy door." [1]
That time drew nigh.
The rulers of darkness at evening brought on a destructive rainstorm.
I looked at the aspect of the day.
The sight of the day was terrible,
I entered the ship and closed my door.
To the pilot of the ship, the boatsman Puzur-schadu-rabu [2]
I entrusted the large structure [3] and its contents.
As morning dawned
There arose on the firmament of heaven, black clouds,
Ramman thundered therein ;
Nebo and Lugal march in advance,
The ship's pole Urra [4] tears out.
Ninib marches, commanding the attack,

[1] Variant " thy ship."   [2] Variant Puzur-kur-gal.
[3] Lit. "palace."   [4] " God of pestilence."

G

The Anunnaki lift the torches
Illuminating the land with their sheen,
Ramman's roar reaches to heaven,
All light is changed to darkness.

*   *   *   *   *   *

One day the hurricane raged . . .
Storming furiously . . .
Like a combat over . . .
Brother sees not brother;
The people of heaven [1] do not know one another.
The gods are terrified at the cyclone,
They flee and mount to the heaven of Anu; [2]
The gods crouch like dogs in an enclosure.
Ishtar cries aloud like one in birth throes,
The mistress of the gods howls aloud:
"That day be turned to clay [3]
When I in the assembly of the gods commanded evil,
For the destruction of my people ordered a combat.
Did I bring forth my people
That like fish they should fill the sea?"
The gods of the Anunnaki weep with her,
The gods sit down, depressed and weeping.
Their lips are closed . . .
Six days and nights . . .
The storm, cyclone (and) hurricane continued sweeping over the land.
When the seventh day approached, the hurricane and cyclone ceased the
        combat
After having fought like . . .
The sea grew quiet, the evil storm abated, the cyclone was restrained.
I looked at the day and the roar had quieted down.
And all mankind had turned to clay
Like an enclosure . . . had become.

I opened a window and light fell on my face,
I bowed down and sat down (and) wept,
Tears flowed on my face,
I looked in all directions to the horizon of the sea
At a distance, of 12 (miles) [4] an island appeared
At Mount Nizir the ship stood still,
Mount Nizir took hold of the ship so that it could not move.

---

[1] *I.e.* the gods.   [2] *I.e.* the highest part of heaven.
[3] *I.e.* be cursed with destruction.   [4] Or after a space of twelve double hours.

One day, two days Mount Nizir, three days and four days Mount Nizir, etc.[1]

Five days, six days, Mount Nizir, etc.[1]

When the seventh day arrived,

I sent forth a dove, letting it free.

The dove went hither and thither.

Not finding a resting-place it came back.

I sent forth a swallow, letting it free.

The swallow went hither and thither.

Not finding a resting-place, it came back.

I sent forth a raven, letting it free.

It ate, croaked, but did not turn back.

Then I let (all?) out to the four regions (and) brought an offering.

I brought a sacrifice on the mountain top.

Seven and seven *adagur* jars I arranged.

Beneath them I strewed reeds, cedarwood and myrtle.

The gods smelled the odor,

The gods smelled the sweet odor.

The gods like flies gathered around the sacrificer.

As soon as the mistress of the gods [2] had arrived

She raised on high the large precious stones which Anu had made, according to his plan.

"Ye gods here, as surely as I will not forget the lapis lazuli at my neck

So I will remember these days — never to forget them.

Let the gods come to the sacrifice,

But Enlil should not come to the sacrifice

Because without reflection he brought on the cyclone,

And decreed my people to destruction."

As soon as Enlil arrived,

He saw the ship, and Enlil was enraged,

Filled with anger at the Igigi.

"Who now has escaped with his life?

No man was to survive the destruction!"

Ninib opened his mouth and spake,

Said to the warrior Enlil,

"Who except Ea can plan any affair?

Ea indeed knows every order."

Ea opened his mouth and spoke, saying to the warrior Enlil:

"Thou art the leader (and) warrior of the gods,

---

[1] Sign of reduplication, *i.e.* "Mount Nizir took hold of the ship so that it could not move."   [2] Ishtar.

But why didst thou, without reflection, bring on the cyclone?
On him who has sinned impose his sin,
On the evil-doer impose his evil,
But be merciful so as not to root out completely,
Be considerate not (to destroy altogether).
Instead of bringing on a cyclone,
O that lions had come and diminished man!
Instead of bringing on a cyclone,
O that jackals had come and diminished man!
Instead of bringing on a cyclone,
O that famine had come and overwhelmed the land!
Instead of bringing on a cyclone,
O that Urra[1] had come and destroyed the land!
I did not reveal the oracle of the great gods,
I sent Atra-Khasis [2] a dream and he heard the oracle.
Now take counsel for him."
Enlil mounted the ship,
Took hold of my hand and led me up,
Led up and caused my wife to kneel at my side,
Touched our forehead, stepped between us (and) blessed us.
Hitherto Utnapishtim was a man;
Now Utnapishtim and his wife shall be gods like us.
Utnapishtim shall dwell in the distance, at the confluence of the streams.
Then they took me and settled me at the confluence of the streams.

While the Babylonian tablets have not as yet yielded any such extensive and close parallel to the other stories of the Judean history, they do at times throw interesting light upon the Hebrew narratives. A notable example is found in the recognition in the Code of Hammurabi of Babylon (c. 2000 B.C.) of the legal fiction that a wife may obtain a son through giving her slave maid to her husband. The custom which figures so prominently in the stories of Abram and Jacob was evidently an ancient Semitic usage.

The story of Noah, the first vineyard keeper,[3] though standing among the narratives supposed to precede the first entrance of Israel's ancestors into Canaan, seems to have been of Canaanite origin, where the vine played so prominent a part in the life of the people. Of the later stories preserved in Genesis many group themselves about ancient sacred spots such as the oak at Mamre

---

[1] God of pestilence.   [2] Meaning "the very wise one."   [3] Genesis 9 20-28.

and the natural sanctuary at Bethel. When the Hebrews settled among the Canaanites, they doubtless adopted many traditions connected with the ancient sanctuaries of the land, and with these may have mingled recollections of their early tribal wanderings, and of their own early experiences in the land.[1]

In the story of Joseph, there is preserved, it seems quite possible, a modified form of one of the most famous of Egyptian tales, The Story of Two Brothers, Anpu and Bata.[2] Even if the Egyptian tale is the original of this narrative of Joseph and his master's wife, it is but an episode in the Hebrew Joseph narratives, and serves to illustrate how completely foreign material might be assimilated.

As the Hebrew narrative advances through the story of the Exodus to the days of the Judges the genuinely historical elements grow more and more prominent, while it becomes evident that this early document is far superior in historical value to the late framework of the Pentateuch. In the narrative of the deliverance at the sea, for example, the Judean history gives an account that does not presuppose the suspension of the laws of physics while the waters stand in a wall on either hand. That conception belongs rather to the late strand of the book of Exodus.[3] In the settlement of Canaan, it has already been noted that these earlier sources represent the conquest as a gradual occupation and settlement among the former inhabitants.[4] The later writers conceived it rather as a triumphal march which has the double disadvantage of being intrinsically improbable and quite out of accord with subsequent conditions as revealed in the earliest, sometimes contemporary, documents. Thus, from the point of view of the historian, the Early Judean History contains usually the earliest and best accounts that have been preserved of ages already traditional when Hebrew writers began to search the distant past.

This great example of early prose writing is more than historical chronicle. The wonderful literary genius of Judah, in the ninth

---

[1] See Gunkel, *Legends of Genesis*, pp. 91–93; Kent, *Beginnings of Hebrew History*, Introduction I.

[2] The story is given in *Egyptian Tales, Second Series*, by M. Flinders Petrie, pp. 36–86.

[3] Exodus 14 [22, 29].   [4] Page 6.

century B.C., gathered together the priceless lore of the past, preserved in song and prose tale, in written document and oral tradition, and shaped it all under the majestic thought that Jehovah had created man instinct with his own breath, and that man's sin and separation from his creator had brought separation from his fellow-man and countless woe; but that there had ever been faithful and obedient individuals whom Jehovah could bless and direct into paths of righteousness and peace. The narrative is alive to every human interest, to the origin of all arts, customs, names even, to the details of individual lives in their loves and hates, their failures and successes, with the whole mass of material so mastered and moulded that these incidental interests do not divert the main stream from its even flow. In rational order, the story is told from the beginnings of all history, through the separation and wanderings of Israel's reputed ancestors, down to a time almost contemporary with the writers. Although this great work has been preserved interwoven with later documents, in excerpts that do not give the whole, yet its comparative continuity of narrative and its progressive unity of conceptions make it one of the most remarkable literary products of antiquity.

CHAPTER VI

EARLY PROSE NARRATIVES OF NORTHERN ISRAEL

(About 850 to 800 B.C.)

IT was noted in the previous chapter that the first fifty years
of Northern Israel's separate history were marked by at least
two assassinations and consequent changes of dynasty. Then
the able general Omri established himself on the throne, and was
succeeded by his son Ahab, whose two sons reigned after him in
succession. These three generations of rulers bring the history
down to the latter part of the ninth century B.C. Omri seems to
have made alliance with Damascus, whose growing power King
Baasha had felt; but Ahab waged bitter war with the Syrian
kingdom.

In 1 Kings 20 and 22, we have vivid accounts of two periods in
this struggle which probably come from a history composed soon
after the events. A brief selection from each may serve to give
the flavor of this early narrative.

And Benhadad sent unto him, and said, The gods do so unto me, and
more also, if the dust of Samaria shall suffice for handfuls for all the people
that follow me. And the king of Israel answered and said, Tell him, Let
not him that girdeth on his armor boast himself as he that putteth it off.
And it came to pass, when Benhadad heard this message, as he was drinking, he and the kings, in the pavilions, that he said unto his servants,
Set yourselves in array. And they set themselves in array against the
city.

And they went out at noon. But Benhadad was drinking himself
drunk in the pavilions, he and the kings, the thirty and two kings that
helped him. And the young men of the princes of the provinces went
out first; and Benhadad sent out, and they told him, saying, There are
men come out from Samaria. And he said, Whether they are come out
for peace, take them alive; or whether they are come out for war, take
them alive. So these went out of the city, the young men of the princes

of the provinces, and the army which followed them. And they slew every one his man; and the Syrians fled, and Israel pursued them: and Benhadad the king of Syria escaped on a horse with horsemen. And the king of Israel went out, and smote the horses and chariots, and slew the Syrians with a great slaughter.[1]

So the king of Israel and Jehoshaphat the king of Judah went up to Ramoth-gilead. And the king of Israel said unto Jehoshaphat, I will disguise myself, and go into the battle; but put thou on thy robes. And the king of Israel disguised himself, and went into the battle. Now the king of Syria had commanded the thirty and two captains of his chariots, saying, Fight neither with small nor great, save only with the king of Israel. And it came to pass, when the captains of the chariots saw Jehoshaphat, that they said, Surely it is the king of Israel; and they turned aside to fight against him: and Jehoshaphat cried out. And it came to pass, when the captains of the chariots saw that it was not the king of Israel, that they turned back from pursuing him. And a certain man drew his bow at a venture, and smote the king of Israel between the joints of the armor: wherefore he said unto the driver of his chariot, Turn thy hand, and carry me out of the host; for I am sore wounded. And the battle increased that day: and the king was stayed up in his chariot against the Syrians, and died at even; and the blood ran out of the wound into the bottom of the chariot. And there went a cry throughout the host about the going down of the sun, saying, Every man to his city, and every man to his country.[2]

The document from which these chapters were taken by the compiler of Kings probably contained the vivid stories of the expedition against Edom in which Elisha participated (2 Kings 3), of the relief of Samaria (2 Kings 6 24–7 17), and of the revolution of Jehu (2 Kings 9–10). Various indications of later additions are found in these sections, especially in the last, but the main kernel may be ascribed to a Northern Israelitish history written not long after the close of the first century of the divided kingdom. We may count these narratives the earliest relics of connected prose writing in the northern kingdom.

The northern narratives lack the full charm of the Saul and David stories, which held a similar position of priority in the literary history of the South, but are still fine specimens of the story-telling gifts of Israel's early writers. How extensive the

---

[1] 1 Kings 20 10-12, 16-21.   [2] 1 Kings 22 29-36.

work may have been from which these excerpts were taken we cannot tell, but there is no reason to suppose that it extended back into what were then ancient times. As in Judah, and Britain too, the probability is that the earliest historical writing dealt with recent events.

A brief piece of narrative writing, contemporary with that which we have just been considering, is found on the famous Moabite Stone, erected by King Mesha to commemorate his successes in winning back territory which Omri had taken from Moab.[1] The alphabet and the language are practically identical with those found in the earliest Hebrew inscriptions, while the ideas and modes of expression are quite similar to those of Israel's earliest narratives. A translation follows: —

MESHA'S INSCRIPTION

I am Mesha, son of Chemosh . . . king of Moab the Dibonite. My father was king over Moab thirty years, and I became king after my father. And I made this high place for Chemosh in Karhoh (?) in (gratitude for) deliverance, because he saved me from all assailants (?) and because he made me see my desire upon all those who hated me.

Omri was king of Israel and he afflicted Moab many days, because Chemosh was angry with his land. And his son succeeded him; and he also said, 'I will afflict Moab.' In my days he said . . . but I saw my desire upon him and upon his house, and Israel perished for ever. Omri, however, took possession of the land of Medeba; and he occupied it during his own days and half of his sons' days, forty years; but Chemosh restored it in my days.

And I fortified Baal-meon; and I made in it the reservoir; and I fortified Kirjathaim. And the men of Gad had occupied the land of Ataroth from of old; and the king of Israel built Ataroth for himself. And I fought against the city and took it. And I slew all the people; the city (became) a gazing-stock to Chemosh and to Moab. And from there I brought the altar-hearth of Dodoh (?); and I dragged it before Chemosh in Kerioth; and I caused the men of Sharon (?) to dwell there, and also the men of . . .

Then Chemosh said to me, 'Go and take Nebo against Israel.' So I went by night and fought against it from the break of dawn until noon, and I took it and slew them all — seven thousand men and women and

[1] The Moabite Stone was discovered at the ruins of ancient Dibon, east of the Jordan, in 1868, by a German missionary, F. A. Klein. It is now in the Louvre.

. . . female slaves — for I had devoted it to Ashtar-chemosh. And the king of Israel had fortified Jahaz, and occupied it while he fought against me. But Chemosh drove him out before me. I took two hundred men of Moab — all its poverty-stricken citizens — and I brought them into Jahaz and took possession of it, to add it to Dibon.

I fortified Karhoh (?), the wall of the forests and the wall of the acropolis. And I built its gates; and I built the royal palace; and I constructed the sluices of the reservoir (?) for the water in the midst of the city. And there was no cistern in the midst of the city, in Karhoh (?); so I said to the people, 'Each of you make a cistern in his own house.' And I cut the trenches (?) for Karhoh (?) with the help of the prisoners of Israel.

I built Aroer, and I made the highway by the Arnon. I rebuilt Beth-bamoth, for it had been overthrown. I rebuilt Bezer, for it was in ruins, (with the help of) fifty men of Dibon, for all Dibon was obedient. And I reigned over a hundred (chiefs) (?) in the cities which I added to the land. And I built Medeba and Beth-diblathaim and Beth-baal-meon. And there I placed (those who bred the small) (?) sheep of the land.

And at Horonaim dwelt the . . . And Chemosh said to me, Go down, fight against Horonaim; so I went down (and fought against the city many days, and) Chemosh (restored it) in my days . . .'.[1]

During the reign of Ahab there appeared one of the great creative personalities of history, the desert prophet Elijah. He announced the complete overthrow of Ahab's house, and, at the instigation of his successor, Elisha, the impetuous general Jehu accomplished the destruction. Elijah was the forerunner and leader of a social and religious movement without which the history and literature of Israel would not be worth prolonged consideration. Elijah did his work alone, though not without sympathizers and followers. Among these, the stories of his wonderful deeds and words were fondly treasured and rehearsed and, before many years had passed, were committed to writing. The stories which appear as chapters 17–19 and 21 of 1 Kings clearly show that they are excerpts from a more complete narra-tive. The sudden introduction of Elijah (17 [1]) is hardly explicable except on the supposition that the beginning of the original narrative has not been preserved. Chapter 18, too, suggests that some account had previously been given of the persecution of Jehovah's prophets by Jezebel.

[1] Kent, *Israel's Historical and Bibliographical Narratives*, p. 495.

In this son of the Gilead hills the narrators had a hero to kindle the imagination. His sudden appearances and vanishings created mystery; his physical prowess was such that he could run twelve miles ahead of Ahab's chariot; his speech came forth a burning fire. Note his power of quick, crushing retort, "When Ahab saw Elijah, Ahab said unto him, 'Is it thou, thou troubler of Israel?' And he answered, 'I have not troubled Israel; but thou, and thy father's house;'"[1] "'Hast thou found me, O mine enemy?' And he answered, 'I have found thee, because thou hast sold thyself to do that which is evil in the sight of Jehovah.'"[2] Note again his scathing sarcasm to the priests of Baal, "Cry aloud; for he is a god: either he is musing, or he is gone aside, or he is on a journey, or peradventure he sleepeth and must be awaked."[3] This scene has been vividly reproduced in Tennyson's Palace of Art: —

> One was the Tishbite whom the raven fed,
>   As when he stood on Carmel steeps,
> With one arm stretched out bare, and mocking said,
>   "Come cry aloud — he sleeps."
>
> Tall, eager, lean, and strong, his cloak wind borne
>   Behind, his forehead heavenly bright
> From the clear marble pouring glorious scorn,
>   Lit as with inner light.

The stories also give us a picture of the hour of reaction after the great contest and its apparent fruitlessness. The juniper tree has become a proverbial symbol for an experience common to all high natures that dare undertake great things.

And Ahab told Jezebel all that Elijah had done, and withal how he had slain all the prophets with the sword. Then Jezebel sent a messenge, unto Elijah, saying, So let the gods do to me, and more also, if I make not thy life as the life of one of them by to-morrow about this time. And when he saw that, he arose, and went for his life, and came to Beersheba, which belongeth to Judah, and left his servant there. But he himself went a day's journey into the wilderness, and came and sat down under a juniper-tree: and he requested for himself that he might die, and said, It is enough; now, O Jehovah, take away my life; for I am not better than my fathers. And he lay down and slept under a juniper-tree; and, behold, an angel touched him, and said unto him, Arise and eat. And he

---

[1] 1 Kings 18 17-18.   [2] 1 Kings 21 20.   [3] 1 Kings 18 27.

looked, and, behold, there was at his head a cake baken on the coals, and a cruse of water. And he did eat and drink, and laid him down again. And the angel of Jehovah came again the second time, and touched him, and said, Arise and eat, because the journey is too great for thee. And he arose, and did eat and drink, and went in the strength of that food forty days and forty nights unto Horeb the mount of God.[1]

From the juniper tree, God's message sent the prophet to Horeb, where Israel had first entered into covenant with the God who revealed himself to Moses in the cloud-hidden peak. The wind, the trembling earth, and flashing lightning were still there to affright; but Jehovah, of old the God of cloud and thunder, now spoke to his sorely tried servant, in "a voice of gentle stillness," a message of comfort and of courage that sent him hence to a work more significant than any yet accomplished.

In the Elijah narratives, there is the same unerring selection of material and rapidity of movement that characterize the early Judean prose. The dialogue never overflows its banks and runs sluggish, as it so often does in modern stories; it is just sufficient to give the situation and general temper of each of the characters. Obadiah, the royal chamberlain, reveals himself perfectly in his one meeting with Elijah.

And as Obadiah was in the way, behold, Elijah met him: and he knew him, and fell on his face, and said, Is it thou, my lord Elijah? And he answered him, It is I: go, tell thy lord, Behold, Elijah is here. And he said, Wherein have I sinned, that thou wouldest deliver thy servant into the hand of Ahab, to slay me? As Jehovah thy God liveth, there is no nation or kingdom, whither my lord hath not sent to seek thee: and when they said, He is not here, he took an oath of the kingdom and nation, that they found thee not. And now thou sayest, Go, tell thy lord, Behold, Elijah is here. And it will come to pass, as soon as I am gone from thee, that the Spirit of Jehovah will carry thee whither I know not; and so when I come and tell Ahab, and he cannot find thee, he will slay me: but I thy servant fear Jehovah from my youth. Was it not told my lord what I did when Jezebel slew the prophets of Jehovah, how I hid a hundred men of Jehovah's prophets by fifty in a cave, and fed them with bread and water? And now thou sayest, Go, tell thy lord, Behold, Elijah is here; and he will slay me. And Elijah said, As Jehovah of hosts

[1] 1 Kings 19 1-8.

liveth, before whom I stand, I will surely show myself unto him to-day. So Obadiah went to meet Ahab, and told him.[1]

He's a good man and true, but very cautious for his own safety. What English novel is without this type of servant — small editions of Ahab's chamberlain!

Ahab's character is most consistent throughout all the scenes. He covers his fear when Elijah meets him with a show of bravado, but he does just what Elijah tells him to do. "Is it thou, thou troubler of Israel?" "I have not troubled Israel; but thou, and thy father's house. . . . Now therefore send, and gather to me all Israel unto Mount Carmel. . . ." "So Ahab sent . . . and gathered." At Naboth's vineyard, the king meets Elijah with "Hast thou found me, O mine enemy?" Then Elijah speaks, and no further word is heard from Ahab. These glimpses through well-managed dialogue, are quite consistent with the picture we have of Ahab sulking because he cannot get the playground he wants, and scorned by his wife who, whatever else she may have been, was to the last a woman of strength and courage.

In the Elijah stories, Northern Israel had a book of narratives hardly inferior, from a purely literary point of view, to the Saul and David stories written in Southern Israel a hundred and fifty years earlier.[2] Elisha appeared in the historical narrative that we counted the earliest connected prose of Northern Israel, but the greater part of the narratives concerning him probably belong later than the Elijah stories and seem, on the whole, inferior both in historical and literary value.

However far Northern Israel may have been behind Judah in date of the beginnings of connected prose writing, in the teachings of Elijah there is a great advance on anything previously formulated in Israel or Judah. Elijah stood for two epoch-making principles. One was the total exclusion of the recognition of any god but Jehovah in Israel. This was of deep and far-reaching political significance. International alliances demanded international marriages in the days of Ahab, or Solomon, as in modern Europe. The Tell-el-Amarna tablets contain numerous references

[1] 1 Kings 18 [7-16a].

[2] Ahab was killed about 850 B.C., and we may infer that these Elijah stories were in written form some fifty years later.

to such marriages between the widely separated rulers of the Nile and Euphrates valleys, six hundred years before Ahab's time. The letter of Amenophis III, for example, to Kadashman-Bel shows that the Babylonian ruler had raised question in a previous letter as to whether the Egyptian queen, his sister, is being properly treated, and Kadashman-Bel, writing to Amenophis, says "As for the damsel, my daughter, for the marriage of whom thou hast written me, she is mature and marriageable; send and let her be taken." When Solomon introduced this ancient practice in Israel on a large scale, it was but one of the various steps he took in the direction of making Israel a nation among the nations. His marriage with an Egyptian princess was matter of great pride in his own day and even later. Such intermarriage meant, as a matter of course, the introduction at the capital of various foreign religions; had the Egyptian princess been refused the right to worship her own gods in her own way, the marriage alliance would quickly have proved cause of international quarrel rather than international comity. The "high places" which Solomon built for his queens stood for full three hundred years, until King Josiah, under the impulse of the new law of Deuteronomy, destroyed them.

Men writing later than Elijah saw in Solomon's foreign marriages great evil, but there is no indication that they were especially condemned in Solomon's day. Elijah was the first prophet to maintain definitely that Jehovah alone should be worshipped in the land of Israel. The issue was raised in his day by the fact that Omri had, in developing a strong national policy, espoused his son Ahab to the daughter of the Phœnician king, Ethbaal, and she proved an earnest propagator of her father's religion.

An international policy like that of Omri and Ahab meant, not only the introduction of foreign gods, but the reintroduction of despotic rule, such as Israel had shaken off at the death of Solomon. It did not occur to Ahab of Israel, however greedy he might be of the vineyard adjoining his estate in Jezreel, that he could take Naboth's ancestral land by force or guile. He made his offers of money or exchange of land, and when the private citizen refused, there was nothing left for the king but acquiescence. Private property rights, even against the king, were sacred in Israel. To Jezebel, trained in the Phœnician court, one seemed no king who could not obtain anything he chose from his subject. "Dost thou now govern the kingdom of Israel?" she cried, "Arise, and eat bread, and let thy heart be merry; I will give thee the vineyard of Naboth the Jezreelite." She avoids a possible popular outbreak by using Israel's ancient machinery of justice, the village court of elders. With suborned witnesses and a mock trial, she secures the judicial murder of Naboth, and the desired land reverts to the king.

To the daughter of the Phœnician king, it is simple enough; but in Israel there is a force which the Phœnician does not understand, a force that will grind to powder the royal house daring to violate the right of the private citizen. It was not in connection with the introduction of Baal worship that Elijah appeared to announce the complete destruction of the house of Omri and Ahab, but in Naboth's vineyard when Ahab had "killed and taken possession."

The two great principles, for which Elijah stood and which make him one of the most significant figures in the history of civilization, were really one, and that one was absolute loyalty to a God who cares for the rights of the common citizen. Religion and politics were wedded in ancient Israel; they are not divorceable where religion is the worship of a God who cares.

CHAPTER VII

THE GREAT EPHRAIMITE HISTORY

(*About 800 to 750 B.C.*)

ELIJAH announced the downfall of Ahab's house, and Elisha took active measures to realize the prediction, sending his servant to anoint the impetuous general of the army as king, in the place of Ahab's reigning son. The rebellion, instantly roused, directed itself to the bloody extermination of all ho had adopted the worship of the Phœnician Baal and, especially, of Ahab's family; the uprising was successful and established a dynasty that ruled for a full century. The struggle was, however, terribly costly in life and left the nation, for a time, sadly weakened. The picture on the obelisk of Shalmaneser of Assyria with its inscription, "Tribute of Jehu son of Omri: silver, gold, a golden bowl, golden goblets, a golden ladle, golden pitchers, bars of lead, a staff for the hand of the king, spear shafts, I received from him," bears testimony to the heavy price that the new king had to pay to Assyria, the advancing power of the east. Twelve years before, Israel had first come into contact with Assyria, when Ahab, in alliance with his Syrian neighbors, had met the Assyrian army in the battle of Karkar, north of Palestine.

In subsequent years, Assyria was to play a decisive part in Israel's history, but the force of Shalmaneser's next campaign fell upon Syria rather than Israel, and left Jehu's son able to cope on more than equal terms with Damascus. Then there was a period of fifty years of respite from further serious advance westward on the part of Assyria, and the house of Jehu enjoyed such prosperity as troubled Israel had not known since the death of Solomon. Jehu's son was able to defeat the weakened Syrians, and his son regained Israel's old, east-Jordan territory. The king of the next generation, Jeroboam II, ruled for more than forty years (781–740) over an extensive territory, troubled by no powerful invader.

96

It was evidently during this era of peace and prosperity that men of northern Israel gathered the writings and traditions of their people's past and compiled a great historical work similar to that which had been composed in Judah during the previous century. Generations later, material from this document was inwoven with the Judean history to make a more complete national history. The two documents were so closely interwoven and were so similar in their form and thought that it is often impossible to separate them with any certainty. A careful examination, however, of the narrative books of the Hexateuch[1] makes it clear that two histories, each of which had assumed a fairly complete form by the middle of the eighth century B.C., were inwoven; some duplications of material and certain recurring differences in language and point of view are satisfactorily explained only on this hypothesis. It is possible, too, in the case of a large part of the material, to separate the strands with much of certainty.

It is not as clear that these two documents continue through the book of Judges, though the indications seem to warrant the conclusion that they do. This view was adopted in Chapter V, in the consideration of the Judean history, and it is probable also that the Ephraimite history contained, from the outset, stories of the days of the Judges.[2] That the book is composite is unquestionable, and that its materials are, in some instances, the product of the North and, in others, of the South, is perfectly clear. Sometimes an individual story gives evidence of compilation from two narratives, in other cases an entire story is an original literary unit preserved in Israel or Judah. The Gideon history has furnished an interesting problem for analysis. A story of one, Jerubbaal, who pursued and successfully attacked the Midianites with a small band of followers is assimilated with the story of Gideon who accomplished the same feat. In Chapter V, the Judean Gideon story was given; the Jerubbaal story, a part of which is printed below, is probably to be assigned to the Ephraimite document.

---

[1] The term Hexateuch has come into use to emphasize the fact that Joshua is in its origin one with the Pentateuch; it was compiled from the same great histories, which originally extended through the early conquest.

[2] See Moore, *Judges, Int. Crit. Com.*, pp. xxv–xxxiii.

Then Jerubbaal, who is Gideon, and all the people that were with him, rose up early, and encamped beside the spring of Harod: and the camp of Midian was on the north side of them, by the hill of Moreh, in the valley.

And Jehovah said unto Gideon, The people that are with thee are too many for me to give the Midianites into their hand, lest Israel vaunt themselves against me, saying, Mine own hand hath saved me. Now therefore proclaim in the ears of the people, saying, Whosoever is fearful and trembling, let him return and depart from mount Gilead. And there returned of the people twenty and two thousand; and there remained ten thousand.

And Jehovah said unto Gideon, The people are yet too many; bring them down unto the water, and I will try them for thee there: and it shall be, that of whom I say unto thee, This shall go with thee, the same shall go with thee; and of whomsoever I say unto thee, This shall not go with thee, the same shall not go. So he brought down the people unto the water: and Jehovah said unto Gideon, Every one that lappeth of the water with his tongue, as a dog lappeth, him shalt thou set by himself; likewise every one that boweth down upon his knees to drink. And the number of them that lapped, putting their hand to their mouth, was three hundred men: but all the rest of the people bowed down upon their knees to drink water. And Jehovah said unto Gideon, By the three hundred men that lapped will I save you, and deliver the Midianites into thy hand; and let all the people go every man unto his place. So the people took victuals in their hand, and their trumpets; and he sent all the men of Israel every man unto his tent, but retained the three hundred men: and the camp of Midian was beneath them in the valley.

And it came to pass the same night, that Jehovah said unto him, Arise, get thee down into the camp; for I have delivered it into thy hand. But if thou fear to go down, go thou with Purah thy servant down to the camp: and thou shalt hear what they say; and afterward shall thy hands be strengthened to go down into the camp. Then went he down with Purah his servant unto the outermost part of the armed men that were in the camp. And the Midianites and the Amalekites and all the children of the east lay along in the valley like locusts for multitude; and their camels were without number, as the sand which is upon the sea-shore for multitude. And when Gideon was come, behold, there was a man telling a dream unto his fellow; and he said, Behold, I dreamed a dream; and, lo, a cake of barley bread tumbled into the camp of Midian, and came unto the tent, and smote it so that it fell, and turned it upside down, so that the tent lay flat. And his fellow answered and said, This is nothing else save the sword of Gideon the son of Joash, a man of Israel: into his hand God hath delivered Midian, and all the host.

And it was so, when Gideon heard the telling of the dream, and the interpretation thereof, that he worshipped; and he returned into the camp of Israel, and said, Arise; for Jehovah hath delivered into your hand the host of Midian. And he divided the three hundred men into three companies, and he put into the hands of all of them trumpets, and empty pitchers, with torches within the pitchers. And he said unto them, Look on me, and do likewise: and, behold, when I come to the outermost part of the camp, it shall be that, as I do, so shall ye do. When I blow the trumpet, I and all that are with me, then blow ye the trumpets also on every side of all the camp, and say, For Jehovah and for Gideon.

So Gideon, and the hundred men that were with him, came unto the outermost part of the camp in the beginning of the middle watch, when they had but newly set the watch: and they blew the trumpets, and brake in pieces the pitchers that were in their hands. And the three companies blew the trumpets, and brake the pitchers, and held the torches in their left hands, and the trumpets in their right hands wherewith to blow; and they cried, The sword of Jehovah and of Gideon. And they stood every man in his place round about the camp; and all the host ran; and they shouted, and put them to flight. And they blew the three hundred trumpets, and Jehovah set every man's sword against his fellow, and against all the host; and the host fled as far as Beth-shittah toward Zererah, as far as the border of Abelmeholah, by Tabbath. And the men of Israel were gathered together out of Naphtali, and out of Asher, and out of all Manasseh, and pursued after Midian.

In reading Genesis, the first trace of the northern history that one meets is in chapter 15. The attempt is often made to distinguish between the material taken from it and that from the Judean history in this chapter, but the results are by no means certain. The section gives the account of the promise to Abram that his seed shall be as the stars of heaven in number and shall possess the land of the Amorite. It is generally assumed that the northern history did not attempt to carry the story much further back and began with the reputed ancestor of Israel; if this be so, the historians of Israel undertook a less ambitious task than those of Judah, who began with the creation of man and sought to trace the origin of civilization.

[1] Judges 7 [1-23].

The Ephraimite history is not met again until the twentieth chapter of Genesis, the story of Abraham in Gerar.

And Abraham journeyed from thence toward the land of the South, and dwelt between Kadesh and Shur: and he sojourned in Gerar. And Abraham said of Sarah his wife, She is my sister: and Abimelech king of Gerar sent, and took Sarah. But God came to Abimelech in a dream of the night, and said to him, Behold, thou art but a dead man, because of the woman whom thou hast taken; for she is a man's wife. Now Abimelech had not come near her: and he said, Lord, wilt thou slay even a righteous nation? Said he not himself unto me, She is my sister? and she, even she herself said, He is my brother: in the integrity of my heart and the innocency of my hands have I done this. And God said unto him in the dream, Yea, I know that in the integrity of thy heart thou hast done this, and I also withheld thee from sinning against me: therefore suffered I thee not to touch her. Now therefore restore the man's wife; for he is a prophet, and he shall pray for thee, and thou shalt live: and if thou restore her not, know thou that thou shalt surely die, thou, and all that are thine.

And Abimelech rose early in the morning, and called all his servants, and told all these things in their ears: and the men were sore afraid. Then Abimelech called Abraham, and said unto him, What hast thou done unto us? and wherein have I sinned against thee, that thou hast brought on me and on my kingdom a great sin? thou hast done deeds unto me that ought not to be done. And Abimelech said unto Abraham, What sawest thou, that thou hast done this thing? And Abraham said, Because I thought, Surely the fear of God is not in this place; and they will slay me for my wife's sake. And moreover she is indeed my sister, the daughter of my father, but not the daughter of my mother; and she became my wife: and it came to pass, when God caused me to wander from my father's house, that I said unto her, This is thy kindness which thou shalt show unto me: at every place whither we shall come, say of me, He is my brother. And Abimelech took sheep and oxen, and men-servants and women-servants, and gave them unto Abraham, and restored him Sarah his wife. And Abimelech said, Behold, my land is before thee: dwell where it pleaseth thee. And unto Sarah he said, Behold, I have given thy brother a thousand pieces of silver: behold, it is for thee a covering of the eyes to all that are with thee; and in respect of all thou art righted. And Abraham prayed unto God: and God healed Abimelech, and his wife, and his maid-servants; and they bare children. For Jehovah had fast closed up all the wombs of the house of Abimelech, because of Sarah, Abraham's wife.

This narrative is commonly regarded as a variant of the very similar story of the Judean history, Genesis 12. It shows, perhaps, a slight ethical advance upon that account which indicated no consciousness that Abraham's conduct was discreditable. This writer makes it clear that Abraham's lie was only a half lie — from our point of view, no less reprehensible, but possibly indicating in the narrator a slight advance upon the naïveté of the earlier writing. Another difference may be noted in God's method of communicating; here it is through a dream instead of by direct speech. This doubtless represents an advance upon the childlike ideas of the earlier historians and seems to be characteristic of the Ephraimite history.

In passing, it is of interest to note the writer's idea of a prophet, "He is a prophet, and he shall pray for thee, and thou shalt live." Obviously "prophet" is not used here in its ordinary English sense of predictor, but rather as indicating one who is in close and intimate relation with God. Such relations are not, however, incompatible with dishonest and unchivalrous conduct; the ethical ideals of the age are still very crude. Is it possible that there is a bit of sarcasm in the words of Abimelech to Sarah, "Behold I have given thy *brother* a thousand pieces of silver"? The word italicized is surely ironical from our point of view.

A considerable part of chapter 21 is ascribed to this document.[1] This section affords another instance of the writer's avoidance of anthropomorphic pictures; an angel calls down from heaven, but God does not come down and speak in any bodily form. The narrative seeks to account for the name Beersheba, a place important later on in the story, but, in general, the Ephraimite narratives show less tendency to explain the origin of everything than the Judean exhibited.

The story of the offering of Isaac follows: —

And it came to pass after these things, that God did prove Abraham, and said unto him, Abraham; and he said, Here am I. And he said Take now thy son, thine only son, whom thou lovest, even Isaac, and get thee into the land of Moriah; and offer him there for a burnt-offering upon one of the mountains which I will tell thee of. And Abraham rose early in the morning, and saddled his ass, and took two of his young men

[1] vv. 1 f., 6, 8–24, 27, 31.

with him, and Isaac his son; and he clave the wood for the burnt-offering, and rose up, and went unto the place of which God had told him.   On the third day Abraham lifted up his eyes, and saw the place afar off.   And Abraham said unto his young men, Abide ye here with the ass, and I and the lad will go yonder; and we will worship, and come again to you. And Abraham took the wood of the burnt-offering, and laid it upon Isaac his son; and he took in his hand the fire and the knife; and they went both of them together.   And Isaac spake unto Abraham his father, and said, My father: and he said, Here am I, my son.   And he said, Behold, the fire and the wood: but where is the lamb for a burnt-offering?   And Abraham said, God will provide himself the lamb for a burnt-offering, my son: so they went both of them together.

And they came to the place which God had told him of; and Abraham built the altar there, and laid the wood in order, and bound Isaac his son, and laid him on the altar, upon the wood.   And Abraham stretched forth his hand, and took the knife to slay his son.   And the angel of Jehovah called unto him out of heaven, and said, Abraham, Abraham: and he said, Here am I.   And he said, Lay not thy hand upon the lad, neither do thou anything unto him; for now I know that thou fearest God, seeing thou hast not withheld thy son, thine only son, from me.   And Abraham lifted up his eyes, and looked, and, behold, behind him a ram caught in the thicket by his horns: and Abraham went and took the ram, and offered him up for a burnt-offering in the stead of his son.   And Abraham called the name of that place Jehovah-jireh: as it is said to this day, In the mount of Jehovah it shall be provided.   And the angel of Jehovah called unto Abraham a second time out of heaven, and said, By myself have I sworn, saith Jehovah, because thou hast done this thing, and hast not withheld thy son, thine only son, that in blessing I will bless thee, and in multiplying I will multiply thy seed as the stars of the heavens, and as the sand which is upon the sea-shore; and thy seed shall possess the gate of his enemies; and in thy seed shall all the nations of the earth be blessed; because thou hast obeyed my voice.   So Abraham returned unto his young men, and they rose up and went together to Beersheba; and Abraham dwelt at Beersheba.[1]

This is one of the best-told stories in the entire collection, as its perennial attractiveness would indicate, though it seems to lack something of the perfection of form that the best Judean stories possess; the movement seems just a little labored in comparison with those.   But, it would be difficult to excel

[1] Genesis 22 1-19.

in any selections from the Judean history the Ephraimite form of the Joseph stories.

And they laded their asses with their grain, and departed thence. And they came unto Jacob their father unto the land of Canaan, and told him all that had befallen them, saying, The man, the lord of the land, spake roughly with us, and took us for spies of the country. And we said unto him, We are true men; we are no spies: we are twelve brethren, sons of our father; one is not, and the youngest is this day with our father in the land of Canaan. And the man, the lord of the land, said unto us, Hereby shall I know that ye are true men: leave one of your brethren with me, and take grain for the famine of your houses, and go your way; and bring your youngest brother unto me: then shall I know that ye are no spies, but that ye are true men: so will I deliver you your brother, and ye shall traffic in the land.

And it came to pass as they emptied their sacks, that, behold, every man's bundle of money was in his sack: and when they and their father saw their bundles of money, they were afraid. And their heart failed them, and they turned trembling one to another, saying, What is this that God hath done unto us? And Jacob their father said unto them, Me have ye bereaved of my children: Joseph is not, and Simeon is not, and ye will take Benjamin away: all these things are against me. And Reuben spake unto his father, saying, Slay my two sons, if I bring him not to thee: deliver him into my hand, and I will bring him to thee again.[1]

The story of the finding of Moses is another of the most charming in this document.

And there went a man of the house of Levi, and took to wife a daughter of Levi. And the woman conceived, and bare a son: and when she saw him that he was a goodly child, she hid him three months. And when she could not longer hide him, she took for him an ark of bulrushes, and daubed it with slime and with pitch; and she put the child therein, and laid it in the flags by the river's brink. And his sister stood afar off, to know what would be done to him. And the daughter of Pharaoh came down to bathe at the river; and her maidens walked along by the riverside; and she saw the ark among the flags, and sent her handmaid to fetch it. And she opened it, and saw the child: and, behold, the babe wept. And she had compassion on him, and said, This is one of the Hebrews' children. Then said his sister to Pharaoh's daughter, Shall I go and call thee a nurse of the Hebrew women, that she may nurse the

[1] Genesis 42 26, 29-35, 28b, 36-37.

child for thee? And Pharaoh's daughter said to her, Go. And the maiden went and called the child's mother. And Pharaoh's daughter said unto her, Take this child away, and nurse it for me, and I will give thee thy wages. And the woman took the child, and nursed it. And the child grew, and she brought him unto Pharaoh's daughter, and he became her son. And she called his name Moses, and said, Because I drew him out of the water.[1]

The northern history was perhaps even more fond of embodying old poems than the southern. To it we owe the preservation of the Miriam and Deborah songs and the significant reference to the *Book of the Wars of Yaweh*.[2] That the northern history had also its own version of the Balaam oracles was noticed in Chapter III.

Viewing the two histories in the large, the northern seems less imbued with the thought of the divine control of the course of events and the consequence of conduct than the Judean. The interest centres more in the " dominant personalities " and in " the methods by which they kept in touch with God."[3] The stories are so well told that it is difficult to see where they fall short of the Judean narratives of Saul and David or of the ninth century history of the earlier times; but, usually, they lack the spontaneous charm and strength of these. It would seem that cold reflection has touched them just enough to spoil the perfect bloom.

If, on the other hand, one were to compare all the prose thus far considered with that of the later ages of Israel's literature, it would all become fused into one class, sharply distinguished from the later types. The Saul and David stories of the tenth century, the great Judean history of the ninth, the earliest narratives of Northern Israel in the latter half of the ninth, the Elijah stories, written near the close of that century, and the great Ephraimite history of antiquity, all belong to the creative age of prophetic narration. During these two centuries of prose writing, the stories, whether they concerned the nearer or more remote past, were still close to the mouth of the *raconteur* who tells a story for the sake of the story. Great conceptions may be embodied in the narratives, but they are not " sicklied o'er " with abstract reflection. The story as such still prevails.

[1] Exodus 2 1-10.   [2] Numbers 21 14.
[3] Sanders and Fowler, *Outlines Biblical History and Literature*, p. 46.

CHAPTER VIII

Amos and Hosea

(*About 750 to 735 B.C.*)

No one of the many books of prose or poetry considered in the preceding chapters has come down to us in its original form. The Wars of Yahweh, the Book of Jashar, the Judean History, the Ephraimite History, and all the rest are known only as they are referred to in later books or as they may be unravelled from other strands with which they were later inwoven in the processes of compilation. This should not seem strange if we recall the fact that many of the most famous books of antiquity belonging to other literatures are known only as preserved in later writings and in the most fragmentary form.

It was in the later years of Jeroboam II, about 750 B.C., that a tiny book was written which has survived the vicissitudes of the centuries and exists to-day with relatively slight changes from its original form. It is the book of Amos. Printed in modern form it would make a pamphlet of a few pages; a single instalment of almost any serious magazine article is longer. Ancient books were usually brief in comparison with modern,[1] but this one was a very small affair among the little books of antiquity. In later Jewish times, it was customary to write it along with eleven others, some longer and some shorter, on one roll which came to be known as *The Book of the Twelve*.

Commonly styled "minor" because of its brevity, somewhat obscure to readers separated from its time by centuries, until recent years, the book of Amos has been much neglected; yet it

[1] One has but to recall the bulk of almost any volume of the famous classical writings, even when printed with introduction, copious notes, and glossary, to realize this fact.

should be a book of profound interest, not merely because it is the first preserved from ancient Israel, but because it is one of the most significant mile-posts in the upward progress of humanity.

In literary form, the book is quite different from any previous writing of which we have knowledge. Amos was the first of the so-called "writing prophets,"[1] a group of writers of whom it has recently been said by a man of letters: "One who has read the Hebrew prophets, the Greek dramatists, and Shakespeare has a view of the essentials of life in its greatness that requires little supplementing; his reading thereafter is for definition and detail, for the temporal modeling of life in different periods and races and nations, for the illumination of it in exceptional men and women and in high types of character or romantic circumstances; it is, in general, rather verification of old truth than anything new that he finds."[2] In our study of the Hebrew prophets we shall strive to appreciate their development in relation to the general history of Israel, the distinctive qualities of their means of self-expression, and their interpretation of the meaning of life.

The book of Amos is made up chiefly of the prophet's addresses,

---

[1] That is, the prophets who themselves wrote down their messages, or whose words were recorded as separate books by their immediate followers. These books are commonly known among Christian readers simply as "the prophets"; but the Jews class Joshua, Judges, Samuel, and Kings also as "prophets," and, in recent years, it has become widely prevalent among Biblical scholars to style the Judean and Ephraimite documents of the Pentateuch as prophetic writings — a usage already followed in earlier chapters of this volume. Evidently in any full appreciation of the development and significance of Hebrew prophecy, much Old Testament material in addition to the books commonly styled prophets must be taken into account; the writing prophets had forerunners, whether considered from the point of view of their thought and work or of their literary form. The earlier book that most nearly resembled Amos and Isaiah, so far as we know the earlier books, was the Elijah document. While this may be acknowledged, it would be difficult to point out in any literature a more distinct step to a new literary form and to new thought than that marked by the book of Amos.

To avoid cumbrous terminology in this and succeeding chapters "prophetic literature" or "prophecy" will be used to designate the writing prophets alone, except where it may seem necessary for some special purpose to adopt the more inclusive use of the terms.

[2] Woodberry, *The Appreciation of Literature*, p. 192.

preserved in brief form and not always clearly distinguished from one another. If we arrange the material in accordance with its natural divisions, it will appear as made up of : (1) An opening address, chapters 1 and 2 ; (2) a series of three supplementary addresses, chapter 3, chapter 4, chapters 5 and 6 ; (3) a section made up chiefly of visions described in public address, chapters 7–9. In the last main division, there appear an interjected historical statement (7 $^{10-17}$) and an address similar to those of the second section (8 $^{4-14}$). For an understanding of the thought of the book, a knowledge of the historical events lying behind the addresses as first delivered is essential. Amos was a man keenly alive to the conditions and events of his own day and entirely familiar with the history of previous generations.

The opening address of the book is bristling with allusions to the late wars with Syria, in which the east-Jordan Hebrews had suffered terribly, to the conduct of Philistia and Phœnicia, who had taken advantage of Israel's misfortunes in war to sell her captives as slaves, to the ruthless action of Edom and Moab, and to the social injustices and debauchery of Israel herself. A mere reading by one who is not familiar with the historical situation is about as confusing as for a citizen of South Africa to read the report of a political speech or reform sermon delivered in America. Should such a reader study the American address thoughtfully, he might begin to see what the general conditions were which called it forth, and should he follow this with reading upon the national, state, and municipal developments of America in the nineteenth and early twentieth centuries, he would come to understand vastly more of what the address meant. Similarly, the thought of Israel's prophets is being restored to the world through the study of their writings with attention to their literary form and to the events and conditions that called them forth. The prophets were first of all men of their time.[1]

The example used of modern political orations or reform sermons may serve to illustrate the prophetic writings with respect to their character as addresses dealing with current history and conditions which the speaker would see reformed ; beyond this the illustra-

---

[1] James Robertson, *The Old Testament and Its Contents*, p. 85.

tion can hardly serve; such orations and sermons are not ordinarily to be classed as literature and certainly not in the form that they are reported. When, however, one has a Demosthenes or an Amos discussing the conditions on which alone national independence may be preserved, then the address, when written down, is a part of the world's literature.

The general subject and period are indicated in what we may style the title page of the book (1 ¹): —

THE WORDS OF AMOS
WHO WAS AMONG THE HERDSMEN OF TEKOA
WHICH HE SAW
CONCERNING ISRAEL

IN THE DAYS OF
UZZIAH KING OF JUDAH
AND IN THE DAYS OF
JEROBOAM THE SON OF JOASH KING OF ISRAEL
TWO YEARS BEFORE THE EARTHQUAKE

The long reigns of Jeroboam the son of Joash (Jeroboam II) and of Uzziah were almost synchronous, extending from the early part of the eighth century to 740 and 737 B.C., respectively. The brief account of Jeroboam's reign in 2 Kings 14 $^{23-29}$ speaks of his success in restoring the ancien borders of Israel to the far north of Palestine and to the east. Amos alludes again and again to the prosperity and national confidence of the people. He speaks of the winter house and the summer house, of the houses of ivory and of hewn stone. He pictures the people lying upon beds of ivory, stretching themselves upon their couches, singing idle songs to the sound of the viol, drinking wine in bowls and anointing themselves with the chief oils. In the mountain of Samaria, they are secure and say, "Have we not taken to us horns by our own strength?" Such allusions doubtless reflect the conditions of the latter half of Jeroboam's reign when successful warfare has been waged and its demoralizing fruits have begun to be manifest.

The place and immediate circumstances of the prophet's preaching are indicated in the historical section of chapter 7.

Then Amaziah the priest of Bethel sent to Jeroboam king of Israel, saying, Amos hath conspired against thee in the midst of the house of Israel: the land is not able to bear all his words. For thus Amos saith, Jeroboam shall die by the sword, and Israel shall surely be led away captive out of his land. Also Amaziah said unto Amos, O thou seer, go, flee thou away into the land of Judah, and there eat bread, and prophesy there: but prophesy not again any more at Bethel; for it is the king's sanctuary, and it is a royal house.[1]

Though Amos was a herdsman of Tekoa, a little mountain hamlet twelve miles south of Jerusalem, he comes to the royal sanctuary of Northern Israel where Jeroboam's priest is in charge and where, no doubt, the people have assembled in large numbers to observe the ritual practices of their religion. Here they hold their solemn assemblies and offer to Jehovah their burnt offerings, meal offerings, and peace offerings of their fat beasts; here is heard the noise of their songs and melody of their viols.[2]

To the priest whose bread is gained by performing his professional duties at the sanctuary, it seems that the seer from Judah is seeking his living at the king's sanctuary, where he has no right, save as he comes to divine things favorable to the king's rule. Amos understands the implication in the command to go to his own country "and there eat bread," and indignantly denies that he belongs to the professional prophets.

Then answered Amos, and said to Amaziah, I was no prophet, neither was I a prophet's son; but I was a herdsman, and a dresser of sycomore-trees: and Jehovah took me from following the flock, and Jehovah said unto me, Go, prophesy unto my people Israel. Now therefore hear thou the word of Jehovah: Thou sayest, Prophesy not against Israel, and drop not thy sword against the house of Isaac; therefore thus saith Jehovah: Thy wife shall be a harlot in the city, and thy sons and thy daughters shall fall by the sword, and thy land shall be divided by line; and thou thyself shalt die in a land that is unclean, and Israel shall surely be led away captive out of his land.[3]

It is not expressly stated that all of Amos's addresses were delivered at the Bethel sanctuary, but, from the entirely secondary character of all allusions to Judah, the prophet's own nation, it is clear that Amos's message was designed for Israel, and it is prob-

[1] vv. 10–13.   [2] 5 21–23.   [3] 7 14–17.

able that all the addresses of the book were delivered to the gay
holiday throngs which came to the feasts at the great sanctuary
of ancient renown, and there practised the demoralizing rites from
which Jehovah's religion was with much difficulty kept pure.[1]

We may picture the opening address of the book as delivered at
the sanctuary of Israel.   The keen-eyed son of the wilderness had
grown up in a high and desolate region, whence the crags broke
downward in indescribable confusion, some four thousand feet
to the silent shores of the Dead Sea.   Scott has given a vivid
picture of the desolation upon which, from boyhood, Amos had
looked out to the eastward, in the description of the ride to Engedi
with which the *Talisman* opens, and Professor George Adam Smith,
who has written upon Biblical history and geography with all the
vividness and much of the insight of a novelist, is at his best in his
description of this region.   "When you climb . . . the hill of
Tekoa, and, looking east, see those fifteen miles of chaos, sinking
to a stretch of the Dead Sea, you begin to understand the influence
of the desert on Jewish imagination and literature.   It gave the
ancient natives of Judea, as it gives the mere visitor of to-day, the
sense of living next door to doom; the sense of how narrow is
the border between life and death; the awe of the power of God
who can make contiguous regions so opposite in character.   He
turneth rivers into a wilderness, and water-springs into a thirsty
ground.   The desert is always in face of the prophets, and its
howling of beasts and its dry sand blow mournfully across their
pages the foreboding of judgment. . . . Amos lived to the south
of Jerusalem, at Tekoa.   No one can read his book without
feeling that he haunted heights and lived in the face of very wide
horizons.   But from Tekoa you see the exact scenery of his visions.
The slopes on which Amos herded his cattle show the mass of
desert hills with their tops below the spectator, and therefore
displaying every meteoric effect in a way they could not have done
had he been obliged to look up to them.   The cold wind that
blows off them after sunset; through a gap the Dead Sea, with
its heavy mists; beyond the gulf the range of Moab, cold and
gray, till the sun leaps from behind his barrier, and in a moment
the world of hill-tops below Tekoa is flooded with light — that

was the landscape of Amos."[1]   Here the herdsman of the stunted breed of sheep that live on the scant herbage of the region eked out his frugal livelihood by the culture of the sycomore figs, food only of the poor.

To one thus bred, the sudden wealth and luxury of an era of national expansion might in itself seem wickedness, but the herdsman was not a man simply of the mountain pastures.   The movements of nations, past and present, were subjects of his daily meditations; he alludes to the fact that Israel had come from Egypt and had dispossessed the Amorite of his land, that the Philistines were another immigrant people in Canaan, as were the Syrians also in their land.   For more than a generation, the people beyond Damascus had ceased their westward advance, yet Amos saw in them the sure instrument of coming destruction.   In the hour of national prosperity and peace, he alone looked beyond Damascus to the distant danger.   To the far southwest he knows of Ethiopia, and he is familiar too with the strange phenomenon of the Nile's annual rise and fall.   Nor is the herdsman unskilled in the writing of his native tongue; he is able, when the time comes, to write the substance of his impassioned orations in rugged, generally pure Hebrew, and to express his thought in the parallelism and accentual rhythm of Hebrew poetry.[2]   Whether they were originally delivered in metrical form is perhaps an insoluble question; that they may have been is not at all improbable.   Certainly, in one instance, Amos announced himself as about to sing a dirge (a Qina), and the lines that immediately follow furnish a very exact specimen of elegiac metre: Hear ye this word which I take up for a lamentation over you, O house of Israel :—

[1] G. A. Smith, *Historical Geography*, pp. 314–315. Cf. also *The Book of the Twelve* (*Expositor's Bible*), Vol. I, pp. 74–76; C. F. Kent, *Biblical Geography and History*, pp. 177 f.

[2] One of the most interesting examples of the power of a tradition that has a great name behind it is found in the persistent life of St. Jerome's dictum that Amos was "rude in speech but not in knowledge." For more than fourteen centuries this was repeated by commentators, until, in the scientific spirit of the nineteenth century, it occurred to a student of Hebrew to examine the facts. When these were found to be contrary to the estimate of Jerome, it was noticed that the context of his statement suggested that the ancient scholar was drawing an inference from Amos's occupation rather than an induction from his Hebrew.

> Fallen, no more shalt thou rise, virgin of Israel.
> Forsaken she lieth prone, no one uplifting.[1]

Throughout a large part of the opening address the structure shows as close an approach to uniform stanzas as Hebrew poetry often exhibits. The whole is a doom-song of great rhythmical power. In impassioned oratory, balanced clauses with some one recurring phrase are frequent, but this address seems to show a parallelism and symmetry of structure quite beyond anything which would occur in a prose oration; it suggests rather the structure of Mark Antony's speech in Shakespeare's verse than any actual oration in classical or modern history. Yet this is no imaginary address; however artistic the form, the purpose is intensely practical.

A quatrain of trimeters forms the prelude. Lines 1 and 2 and 3 and 4 show perfect synonymous parallelism, while the second distich stands in synthetic relation to the first.

> Yahweh from Zion shall roar,
>   From Jerusalem utter his voice;
> The shepherd's pastures shall mourn
>   The crest of Carmel wither.

Each of the seven or eight[2] stanzas following is introduced by "Thus sayeth Yahweh."[3]

> Thus sayeth Yahweh:
>   For three transgressions of Damascus,
>   Yea four, I will not revoke it;
>   For their threshing with iron, Gilead.
>   I will send a fire on Hazael's house,

[1] 5 1-2.

[2] The stanza concerning Judah is probably a late insertion, imitating the form of Amos's lines, but introducing thought that is out of harmony with the rest of the address and belongs rather to a later age.

[3] The first two lines following this phrase are trimeters, while the third line is puzzling. In the first and third stanzas it seems to be a four-beat line, but in the second and fourth, it is a five-beat or three, two-beat. In the fifth and seventh, it is a full distich of three-beat lines, but in the sixth it is apparently one long line. The translation seeks to follow as far as possible the form of the Hebrew lines as they stand, save where, as in the transposition of the line "And break Damascus's gate-bar," there is some probable emendation of the text.

To devour Benhadad's palaces.
I will cut off inhabitant from Aven-valley
    And holder of sceptre from Eden-house,
And break Damascus's gate-bar;
    So Syrians shall go captive to Kir,[1]
                        Sayeth **Yahweh.**

Thus sayeth Yahweh:
    For three transgressions of Gaza,
        Yea four, I will not revoke it;
    For their exiling a full captivity,
        To deliver to Edom.
    I will send a fire on Gaza's wall,
        To devour her palaces,
    Will cut off inhabitant from Ashdod
        And holder of sceptre from Ashkelon,
    And turn my hand upon Ekron;
        So Philistine remnant shall perish,
                        Sayeth **Yahweh.**

Thus sayeth Yahweh:
    For three transgressions of Tyre,
        Yea four, I will not revoke it;
    For their delivering a full captivity to Edom.
        Brothers' bond they forgot.
    I will send a fire on Tyre's wall,
        To devour her palaces.

Thus sayeth Yahweh:
    For three transgressions of Edom,
        Yea four, I will not revoke it;
    For pursuing with sword his brother,
        And breaking kinship.
    He kept forever his anger,
        Yea his wrath he guarded alway.
    I will send a fire on Teman,
        To devour Bozrah's palaces.

Thus sayeth Yahweh:
    For three transgressions of Bene-**Ammon,**
        Yea four, I will not revoke it;
    For ripping up women of Gilead,

---

[1] Back to their original home. Cf. 9 [7].

I

So to enlarge their boundary.
I will kindle a fire on Rabbah's wall,
    To devour her palaces,
With shouting in battle's day,
    With tempest in day of storm-wind.
Their king shall go into exile
    He and his princes together,

                                    Sayeth Yahweh.

Thus sayeth Yahweh:
    For three transgressions of Moab,
        Yea four, I will not revoke it;
    For his burning the bones of Edom's king to lime,
    I will send a fire on Moab;
        It shall devour Kerioth's palaces,
    And in battle-din Moab shall perish,
        With shouting, and with trumpet sound.
    I will cut off judges from her midst,
        And all her princes will kill,

                                    Sayeth Yahweh.

Thus sayeth Yahweh:
    For three transgressions of Israel,
        Yea four, I will not revoke it;
    For their selling for silver the righteous,
        And needy for a couple of sandals.
    Who crush the head of the poor,
        And turn aside the way of the meek,
    A man and his father go to the sacred harlot,
        So they profane my holy name.
    Upon garments pledged they lie,
        Beside every altar.
    And wine of the fined they drink,
        In the house of their God.
    Yet I, I cut off before them Amorite,
        Whose height was like the cedar's height,
        And strong was he as oak;
    His fruit from above, his root from below.
    Yet I, I brought you up from Egypt-land,
    And led you forty years through wilderness,
        To inherit the land of Amorite,
    And raised up your sons for prophets,

Your young men for Nazirites,
Is it not even so, Bene-Israel?

Oracle of Yahweh.

And ye gave the Nazirites wine,
    And the prophets commanded,
    Saying, " Prophesy not."
Behold I will make a quaking beneath you,
    As quakes your rolling cart,
    When o'erloaded with sheaves.
Flight shall fail the swift;
    The strong shall not confirm his force;
The mighty shall not save his life;
    The bowman shall not stand.
The swift of foot shall not save,
    Nor rider on steed, save his life;
And the stout of heart among the mighty,
    Naked away shall flee, that day.[1]

Oracle of Yahweh.

As the menace of Amos's opening lines fell on the ears of the gay throng, there may have been a startled moment, followed soon by approval of the prophet's oracle. Doom upon Damascus, Philistia, Tyre, Edom, Ammon, for the cruel sufferings that they had inflicted upon the fathers of the listeners, in the wars that had been waged a generation or two before, was an announcement to which every son of Israel would give ready ear and assent. With rare skill, the speaker is taking his hearers the first step toward the recognition of a principle never before fully apprehended and enunciated in human speech. He has gained their ready assent to the truth that Jehovah is sure to inflict just punishment on those who are selfishly cruel toward Israel. The next doom, that upon Moab, advances another step, in its assertion that the God of Israel will also inflict punishment for the vindictive cruelty of Moab toward the king of Edom. Back of this lies the great conception of Jehovah as just arbiter among the nations.

The hearers do not comprehend all this, but the swing of the prophet's song and their hatred of the ancient rival nation carry

[1] The beat of the last line suggests, perhaps, the sound of the flight. Arom yanus bayyom hahu. Cf. the onomatopoetic line describing the retreat in the Deborah Song, p. 23.

them on, no doubt, to ready acquiescence in the doom of Moab. This yielded, the prophet has secured recognition of a great principle, indefinitely above and beyond anything met in earlier writings. This is nothing less than the audacious reach of faith to a God of nations whose dealings with the peoples are determined by their conduct toward one another.

This point reached, he quickly applies his principle to Israel, where injustice is rampant in the economic, political, and religious life of the nation. The righteous are sold for silver and the very money used for the purchase of the wine needed in the sacrificial feasts is gained from unjust fines. While the sensual character of the Bethel worship is prominent in the prophet's thought, the selfish cruelty of the ways by which the means for this worship are obtained is even more emphasized, and the whole is counted ingratitude toward the God who has blessed Israel. Amos's opening address is much more notable as an example of skilful oratory than as a poetic utterance.

The succeeding addresses expand and defend the crushing indictment and sentence of the first. Upon the mountains of Samaria are oppressions; they store violence and robbery in their palaces; the women of wealth oppress the poor, calling upon their lords to supply their drinking feasts; the one who speaks upright reproof is abhorred; the wealthy litigant bribes, and the poor man cannot get justice before the elders who hold court at the city gate. In the similar section of chapter 8, the merchants are represented as formally observing the Sabbath with cessation of their business, while eagerly longing to be back at their trading with false measures and weights, and selling the refuse of the wheat. With such counts the prophet expands his earlier indictment of selfish, cruel conduct in Israel at this era of sudden wealth.

Nothing of all this seems to the people inconsistent with religious faith and practice. Jehovah, they feel, has greatly blessed them and they are looking for more marked manifestations of his favor.[1] They maintain all their religious rites with abundant offerings; their solemn assemblies are held and their songs rise to their God.[2] It is evident that the mass of the people of Israel have not apprehended the thought that the religion of Jehovah

[1] 5 18-20.   [2] 5 21-23.

has any concern with business. We have seen the conception that Jehovah's demands are ethical, beginning to take shape at an earlier date; but the story of Naboth's vineyard was unknown to the people or its lesson uncomprehended. The mass of Israel was, where the followers of nearly all the world's religions have still remained, in the stage of development which regards religion as a matter merely of ceremonial usage and time-honored institutions.

Turning our thought from the indictment to the sentence with which the first address closes, we note that this too is made more definite in the succeeding addresses. No instrument of punishment was mentioned at first, but the second address threatens that an adversary shall plunder the land to repletion. The fourth address promises an adversary who shall afflict the land from end to end and plainly indicates Assyria in its threat of captivity beyond Damascus.

The description of visions which occupies the major part of chapters 7–9 adds very little, if any, new thought to the addresses considered. The section does, however, serve to illustrate the varied modes adopted by the prophet in his effort to make his message reach and rouse the hearers. For the Oriental, ever fond of figurative speech, rejoicing in "dark sayings," these visions had a charm and power which it may not be possible for us to realize.

In seeking to apprehend Amos's thought, we are led to formulate it into general statements, but we must remember that the Hebrew mind did not group in that way. Amos presented his thought in concrete, vivid pictures, not in abstract statements. We have already noted, in our examination of Israel's early narratives, that a picture or story conveying a lesson was not ridden by any statement of its moral. In the stirring oratory of the social reformer we see the same poetic freedom.

In addition to the definite pictures which Amos draws of existing conditions and his symbolic visions, his words are full of illustrations from nature, characteristic reflections of his rural life. We may enumerate of these, in barren summary: the lion's defiant roar over his prey; the bird caught in the snare; the heedless cattle that trample underfoot; the drought coming when the latter rains should assure the harvest; blasting and mildew; the palmer worm devouring gardens, vineyards, fig and olive trees; the mountains and wind in their majesty and power; the Pleiades and Orion overhead. Only one who had lived close to nature and simple, rural life could think in the pictures so strikingly characteristic of Amos.

We have no literary categories under which to classify the prophetic writings. Professor Moulton's term "prophetic rhapsody" is as happy as any, if we must give a name derived from the Greek, whence we get our literary forms and terms. He says, "So far as form is concerned prophecy is not distinctive, but comprehensive; all types of literature are attracted towards it, and the various literary forms are fused together into a new form in the prophetic rhapsody."[1] He is evidently using the term "rhapsody," not in its original Greek meaning, but in its modern sense as applied to poetry and music, indicating "something especially exalted and free from limitations of form."[2] The different parts of a prophetic book may often be subjected to literary classification, but the change from one literary form to another is bewilderingly swift, and for some forms our technical terminology fails. Even Professor Moulton, who tends to assimilate distinctive Semitic forms with European, styles the third section of Amos simply "vision prophecy." For this the European has no technical term.

Such facts as the foregoing make it very difficult to discuss the prophetic writings as a part of literature. Only one who has read them attentively and sympathetically and whose mind is not too rigidly fixed in occidental channels can apprehend the beauty and power of this wonderful instrument for the expression of "the essentials of life in its greatness." The other great, flexible, comprehensive literary form, with which prophecy has been so appreciatively grouped by Professor Woodberry, is likewise a complex, composite form. The Greek drama grew in the first instance out of a combination of the collected songs of the rhapsodists[3] and the Bacchic chorus, and, later, it gradually

[1] R. G. Moulton, *The Literary Study of the Bible*, p. 112.
[2] *Idem*, p. 369.
[3] Rhapsody — from rhapto = stitch together; odé = song.

developed its elastic dialogue element. We understand, more or less clearly, this composite form, when the term "drama" is used, and so we must come to understand a less organized, but not less distinct, composite literary form, when the term "prophecy" is used.

Even when it has developed to its greatest perfection, the form of prophetic literature has the marks of its ancestry. Ecstasy was characteristic of the early prophets of Israel; we have seen it in the Balaam oracles and in the experience of Saul among the prophets. Music, with which the bands of travelling prophets accompanied their prophesying no doubt had its part to play in inducing ecstasy. Intense emotion continued to characterize the prophets of Israel long after they had left far behind the primitive practices, for the speaker felt that he was uttering words whose source was outside his own mind and will. In the writing prophets, it is not always easy to tell whether the preacher is speaking in his own person or as the voice of God, or again, as the mouthpiece of his people. Narrative, direct address, soliloquy, and dialogue are puzzlingly intermingled. Yet, however rhapsodical the prophecy, all the great prophets of the eighth and seventh centuries had, like Amos, a keen sense of present fact. This combination of the grasp of concrete realities with great emotion Professor Gardiner emphasizes as the mark of the climax in the development of any school of literature.[1]

In Hosea the union of emotion and reality is perhaps even more notable than in Amos. This book opens with a narrative of Hosea's family experience that from the start is seen to be a parable of Jehovah's experience with Israel. The two elements, the personal history of Hosea and the application to Israel, are kept reasonably distinct throughout the first paragraph.

When Jehovah spake at the first by Hosea, Jehovah said unto Hosea, Go, take unto thee a wife of whoredom and children of whoredom; for the land doth commit great whoredom, departing from Jehovah. So he went and took Gomer the daughter of Diblaim; and she conceived, and bare him a son. And Jehovah said unto him, Call his name Jezreel; for yet a little while, and I will avenge the blood of Jezreel upon the

[1] Gardiner, *The Bible as English Literature*, p. 216.

house of Jehu, and will cause the kingdom of the house of Israel to cease. And it shall come to pass at that day, that I will break the bow of Israel in the valley of Jezreel.   And she conceived again, and bare a daughter. And Jehovah said unto him, Call her name Lo-ruhamah; for I will no more have mercy upon the house of Israel, that I should in any wise pardon them. But I will have mercy upon the house of Judah, and will save them by Jehovah their God, and will not save them by bow, nor by sword, nor by battle, by horses, nor by horsemen.   Now when she had weaned Lo-ru-hamah, she conceived, and bare a son.   And Jehovah said, Call his name Lo-ammi; for ye are not my people, and I will not be your God.[1]

The second paragraph, with its sudden recollection of ancient promise and glorious vision of hope, cuts free from Hosea's personal affairs and deals wholly with the contrasted future.

Yet the number of the children of Israel shall be as the sand of the sea, which cannot be measured nor numbered; and it shall come to pass that, in the place where it was said unto them, Ye are not my people, it shall be said unto them, Ye are the sons of the living God.   And the children of Judah and the children of Israel shall be gathered together, and they shall appoint themselves one head, and shall go up from the land; for great shall be the day of Jezreel.   Say ye unto your brethren, Ammi; and to your sisters, Ruhamah.[2]

In the second chapter, the domestic and the national tragedy are so fused in the crucible of the prophet's heart, that it is quite impossible to distinguish one from the other.

Contend with your mother, contend; for she is not my wife, neither am I her husband; and let her put away her whoredoms from her face, and her adulteries from between her breasts; lest I strip her naked, and set her as in the day that she was born, and make her as a wilderness, and set her like a dry land, and slay her with thirst.   Yea, upon her children will I have no mercy; for they are children of whoredom; for their mother hath played the harlot; she that conceived them hath done shamefully; for she said, I will go after my lovers, that give me my bread and my water, my wool and my flax, mine oil and my drink.   There-fore, behold, I will hedge up thy way with thorns, and I will build a wall against her, that she shall not find her paths.   And she shall follow after her lovers, but she shall not overtake them; and she shall seek them, but shall not find them: then shall she say, I will go and return to my first husband; for then was it better with me than now.

---

[1] Hosea 1 2-9.   [2] 1 10-2 1.

For she did not know that I gave her the grain, and the new wine, and the oil, and multiplied unto her silver and gold, which they used for Baal. Therefore will I take back my grain in the time thereof, and my new wine in the season thereof, and will pluck away my wool and my flax which should have covered her nakedness.   And now will I uncover her lewdness in the sight of her lovers, and none shall deliver her out of my hand.   I will also cause all her mirth to cease, her feasts, her new moons, and her sabbaths, and all her solemn assemblies.   And I will lay waste her vines and her fig-trees, whereof she hath said, These are my hire that my lovers have given me; and I will make them a forest, and the beasts of the field shall eat them.   And I will visit upon her the days of the Baalim, unto which she burned incense, when she decked herself with her ear-rings and her jewels, and went after her lovers, and forgat me, saith Jehovah.[1]

The third chapter is spoken in calmer vein, and, again, the national conditions are clearly distinguished from the personal experiences of Hosea which illustrate them.

And Jehovah said unto me, Go again, love a woman beloved of her friend, and an adulteress, even as Jehovah loveth the children of Israel, though they turn unto other gods, and love cakes of raisins.   So I bought her to me for fifteen pieces of silver, and a homer of barley, and a half-homer of barley; and I said unto her, Thou shalt abide for me many days; thou shalt not play the harlot, and thou shalt not be any man's wife; so will I also be toward thee.   For the children of Israel shall abide many days without king, and without prince, and without sacrifice, and without pillar, and without ephod or teraphim: afterward shall the children of Israel return, and seek Jehovah their God, and David their king, and shall come with fear unto Jehovah and to his goodness in the latter days.

Back of Hosea's message of judgment and hope lie two groups of facts : (1) Hosea's wife has been faithless to him, a wanton pursuing her lovers; his sense of wrong is bitter, but he loves her with an unquenchable love.   In imagination, he sees himself luring her back to such promises as she gave him in her youth; in reality, he must buy her back, for, deserted of her lovers, she has become a slave, and her husband's love she does not yet comprehend.   She must experience purification through many days of enforced abiding by him as no man's wife, while he voluntarily remains without wife. (2) Israel has been faithless to Jehovah and has sought other gods. Though he has provided the nation with food and money, it has not known that these came from him, and has lavished them on Baal, the Canaanite god of fertility, and has thought thus to gain prosperity. The prophet sees that only after Israel has remained long without government or means of worship will she come to seek Jehovah. These may be disentangled as the two groups of stern, terrible realities that are fused in Hosea's vivid imagination by the intense fire of his emotion. In these opening chapters we have the gist of Hosea's book.

Interpreting Hosea's words with precise literalness, it would seem that he received a divine command deliberately to marry a woman already a wanton, and so known to him. Prophets often performed some strange act in order to impress a lesson needed by the nation, but the idea that the God of Israel, the God who demanded social purity such as was undreamed of in other religions, could have commanded such conduct has so greatly shocked moral sense that the story has often been interpreted as a mere parable. Such it may be, but an historical study of Hebrew prophecy seems to establish two facts which suggest another interpretation. First, in describing early convictions leading them to their life work, the prophets read their early thoughts in the light of subsequent experience and speak of what in reality has come to them in slow realization through the experience of the years, as having been revealed to them, told them, or commanded them, by God himself. This is in perfect accord with the laws of mental life as we know them in others than prophets. Second, the prophets acquired their greatest truths in connection with their own experience of life, interpreted in the light of their fundamental convictions.

Viewing Hosea's opening chapters from the point of view of these general facts, Biblical students have come to believe that this man, who loved his wife with a certain chivalry hardly ever suggested in ancient literature, married one whom he supposed to be pure. He gave to his first child the name of Jezreel to emphasize his conviction that Jehu's bloody rebellion demanded Jehovah's judgment. As time went on and other children were born, he came to know that his wife was indifferent to his love, and sought other lovers, blind to his cherishing care for her; the names of the later children, certainly of the third child, contained suggestion not only of Israel's doom, but of the wife's faithlessness as well. Through his own bitter anguish, he grew to understand something of the sorrow in Jehovah's heart for a people blind to his provident care, and turned to other gods. Where there was such complete failure to comprehend love, he saw that, though one might dream of bringing back the old days of pure love's covenant by pleading, in reality, it was impossible. But he learned more than this through his own great love, a love that asked for itself only opportunity to reclaim from sin to purity; he came to understand the unalterable love of Jehovah for Israel. When, at length, he wrote down the story of his life with the message that had grown out of it, he looked back over the years and felt that through these deep waters God had called him to pass, so he might know and teach. Then, with the vivid speech of a Hebrew prophet who never cared to state all the intermediate steps, he put the whole in a word — God had commanded him to take a wife of whoredom and children of whoredom.

Chapters 4–14 belong to a later era than 1–3. In the double dating of Hosea's book (1¹), the years given by the kings of Judah (Uzziah, Jotham, Ahaz, and Hezekiah) and those given by the king of Israel (Jeroboam) are not wholly synchronous; the reigns of the Judean kings carry us quite beyond Jeroboam's death in 740. The dating by Judean kings was probably added by a later hand, after Hosea was dead and Israel was obliterated as a nation, for Hosea was a prophet of Israel and not of Judah. This later editor possibly knew that Hosea's ministry extended beyond the days of Jeroboam, although none of his extant prophecies seem as late as the time of Hezekiah.

Anarchy and confusion followed the long reign of Jeroboam, and this is often reflected in chapters 4–14; Jeroboam's son had reigned only six months when the assassin's hand struck him down, and the murderer was in turn killed after a month's reign. The new ruler who then came to the throne was forced to pay tribute to Assyria, but he seems to have died a natural death and was succeeded by his son; this son was killed by the head of the army, who established himself as king. In his days, Assyria took the east-Jordan and Galilean districts from Israel and left one Hoshea as vassal king over the sadly diminished territory of Northern Israel. All these changes occurred within about six years. Twelve years more, and rebellion against Assyria brought the destruction of Samaria, the deportation of many thousands of its inhabitants, and the end of the history of the northern kingdom.

The words of Hosea (7 7), "All their kings are fallen," referring evidently to Israel, or again, "As for Samaria, her king is cut off as foam upon the water" (10 7), would be appropriate at almost any time after Jeroboam's death, but hardly when he had been reigning prosperously for a generation and when his fathers had enjoyed prosperous reigns for years previously. Nor would the picture of Israel as swallowed up among the nations, as gone up to Assyria for help (8 8, 9) be appropriate before the time of Menahem's tribute.[1] Indeed, in Hosea, rapid change of kings, a weak and vacillating policy, with almost complete anarchy dominant at home, are constantly reflected. Following the events of the year 735 came the devastating and cutting off from Israel of Gilead, yet Hosea speaks of this district as though it still belonged to Israel, and makes no reference to any judgment fallen upon it. The words of chapters 4–14 are probably, therefore, to be assigned to the years 740 to 735 B.C., in which occurred the assassinations of kings Zechariah, Shallum, and Pekahiah, and the tribute of Menahem to Assyria.

It is sometimes maintained that Hosea could not have put his own prophecies in their present form, because of their lack of orderly arrangement. The book certainly does suggest fragmentary literary remains gathered after the prophet's death, somewhat as the Koran was collected, but if Hosea himself put the material together, there is no reason for wonder that it has no more orderly form. The Semitic, the Oriental mind, in general, does not work according to Occidental ideas of law and order; and Hosea's mind, in particular, never would have thought of giving a mass of material even such order as is seen in the grouping of the various elements of Amos. Amos's mind worked much more after the fashion of ours than did those of most of the great

[1] 2 Kings 15 19-20.

prophets of Israel. Hosea's thought and speech are never progressive, but are full of swift alternations of despair and hope,
of denunciation and pity.

Hosea's intense, imaginative identifying of himself, now with
God and now with the people, gives dramatic power to his words,
but he does not work out dramatic dialogue in any such orderly
way as some of the later prophets. In the early verses of chapter 4
it is difficult to determine whether the prophet is speaking in his
own person or that of God. From verse 6 on, it seems to be
Jehovah who speaks; this continues through chapter 5, though
in each chapter, God is often named in the third person. Chapter
6 opens with the voice of the people; at verse 4, Jehovah speaks,
addressing the people in the second person, which is quickly
changed to the third. This continues through 7 4, when suddenly
the prophet speaks in his own person; but a little later it seems
to be Jehovah speaking, and so on.

Come, and let us return unto Jehovah; for he hath torn, and he will
heal us; he hath smitten, and he will bind us up. After two days will
he revive us: on the third day he will raise us up, and we shall live before
him. And let us know, let us follow on to know Jehovah: his going
forth is sure as the morning; and he will come unto us as the rain, as the
latter rain that watereth the earth.

O Ephraim, what shall I do unto thee? O Judah, what shall I do unto
thee? for your goodness is as a morning cloud, and as the dew that goeth
early away. Therefore have I hewed them by the prophets; I have
slain them by the words of my mouth: and thy judgments are as the light
that goeth forth. For I desire goodness, and not sacrifice; and the
knowledge of God more than burnt-offerings. But they like Adam
have transgressed the covenant; there have they dealt treacherously
against me. Gilead is a city of them that work iniquity; it is stained
with blood. And as troops of robbers wait for a man, so the company of
priests murder in the way toward Shechem; yea, they have committed
lewdness. In the house of Israel I have seen a horrible thing: there
whoredom is found in Ephraim, Israel is defiled. Also, O Judah, there is
a harvest appointed for thee, when I bring back the captivity of my people.

When I would heal Israel, then is the inquity of Ephraim uncovered,
and the wickedness of Samaria; for they commit falsehood, and the thief
entereth in, and the troop of robbers ravageth without. And they
consider not in their hearts that I remember all their wickedness: now

have their own doings beset them about; they are before my face. They make the king glad with their wickedness, and the princes with their lies. They are all adulterers; they are as an oven heated by the baker; he ceaseth to stir the fire from the kneading of the dough, until it be leavened.

On the day of our king the princes made themselves sick with the heat of wine; he stretched out his hand with scoffers. For they have made ready their heart like an oven, while they lie in wait: their baker sleepeth all the night; in the morning it burneth as a flaming fire. They are all hot as an oven, and devour their judges; all their kings are fallen: there is none among them that calleth unto me.[1]

Elsewhere the dramatic form of speech is changed, and the words of Ephraim are narrated by Jehovah (12 8), but a moment later, the prophet in his own person speaks of God. One must needs be alert to follow these dramatic changes; once in the spirit of it the utterance has great power. The form, not unfamiliar in the impassioned oratory of other peoples and ages, is peculiarly prominent in Israel's prophets.

We can hardly imagine Hosea working out an address or poem like that of Amos 1 and 2, with its regular structure and its advancing stages of thought, or even that of chapter 3; nor would he give a series of formal visions like those of Amos 7 ff. — "Thus the Lord Jehovah showeth me and behold." Indeed, it would be difficult to find better illustrations of the saying "the style is the man" than Amos and Hosea afford. Amos used effective illustrations which seem spontaneous, but Hosea "thinks in pictures." This characteristic has already been indicated in the discussion of the first three chapters of the prophecy. Forceful examples from the later chapters are those of 7 8-12, 10 1, 12 1, 7 : —

Ephraim, he mixeth himself among the peoples; Ephraim is a cake not turned. Strangers have devoured his strength, etc.

Israel is a luxuriant vine, that putteth forth his fruit: according to the abundance of his fruit he hath multiplied his altars; according to the goodness of their land they have made goodly pillars.

Ephraim feedeth on wind, and followeth after the east wind: he continually multiplieth lies and desolation; and they make a covenant with Assyria, and oil is carried into Egypt.

[1] 6 1–7 7.

He is a trafficker, the balances of deceit are in his hand: he loveth to oppress.

Unusually beautiful examples are found in the early part of chapter 6, printed above, and in the description of Israel and the Father : —

When Israel was a child, then I loved him, and called my son out of Egypt.   The more the prophets called them, the more they went from them : they sacrificed unto the Baalim, and burned incense to graven images.   Yet I taught Ephraim to walk; I took them on my arms; but they knew not that I healed them.   I drew them with cords of a man, with bands of love; and I was to them as they that lift up the yoke on their jaws; and I laid food before them.

How shall I give thee up, Ephraim? how shall I cast thee off, Israel? how shall I make thee as Admah? how shall I set thee as Zeboiim? my heart is turned within me, my compassions are kindled together.   I will not execute the fierceness of mine anger, I will not return to destroy Ephraim: for I am God, and not man; the Holy One in the midst of thee; and I will not come in wrath.   They shall walk after Jehovah, who will roar like a lion; for he will roar, and the children shall come trembling from the west.   They shall come trembling as a bird out of Egypt, and as a dove out of the land of Assyria; and I will make them to dwell in their houses, saith Jehovah.[1]

The character of the pictures or illustrations is also significant. Amos's are more often from the wilder aspects of nature and Hosea's from the calm and beautiful; while the spirit and ideas of Hosea are quite as much in contrast to Amos as the mode of thought or form of expression.

The dominant idea of Amos is justice, that of Hosea love and mercy.   Like most bald statements, this one may convey an absolutely false impression.   Justice demands judgment, so does love; or rather, justice demands judgment; love sees that it is inherent, and so inevitable.   Amos could not know and give Hosea's message because he had not Hosea's nature and Hosea's experience.   Only one who had loved and been wronged and loved still could be the first to know unquenchable love in God.   Only one who had loved thus and had loved one who was incapable of comprehending and returning the love in kind could be the first to realize

[1] 11 1-4, 8-11.

that judgment and expiation must precede the possibility of reunion and blessing. Paying the price to her owner and taking her back to his home and tender care could not give Hosea again his wife.

History affords a partial parallel to the marriage story of Hosea in that of Andrea del Sarto whose wife's beautiful face was so graven on his heart that every woman's face he put upon the canvas had her features. Browning pictures the artist pleading with her one evening when he restrained her with him for a little time till she fled away to gayer company : —

> Had you, with these the same, but brought a mind
> Some women do so.   Had the mouth there urged
> God and the glory ! never care for gain.
> If you would sit thus by me every night
> I should work better, do you comprehend ?
> I mean that I should earn more, give you more.

The wife of Andrea del Sarto could not understand, he knew, "better work," save as it meant "more money," as Hosea's wife could not comprehend the constraining love which would speak to her heart.

So, Hosea saw that Israel was destroyed for lack of knowledge; the spirit of whoredoms is in the midst of them and they have not *known* the Lord.[1] In their ignorance they think to please him with sacrifices and burnt offerings, but those were not what he wanted; he longed rather for the spirit of kindness in their hearts and knowledge of himself.[2] Israel was like a silly dove without understanding.[3]

In chapter 11, we have seen the figure changed from that of husband and faithless wife to that of father and indifferent child : I taught Ephraim also to walk; I took them on my arms; but they knew not that I healed them. Brutish insensibility makes the true relation between Israel and God impossible. Hosea sees, even more deeply than Amos, the inevitable consequences of Israel's sin, because he sees that those consequences are not inflicted, but are inherent in the nature of personality.

Never before Amos, so far as we can know to-day, had any one clearly grasped and presented the theory of history that he held

[1] 4 6, 5 4.   [2] 6 6.   [3] 7 11.

— the conviction that above all life's inequalities and cruel injustices between individuals and nations stood a God who could and would work out perfect justice. Whether one can share Amos's faith or not, anyone with a spark of soul can but glory in the splendid audacity and upward reach of the man, who with eyes fully open to the injustices of life, dared first to affirm such a faith in unequivocal terms.

Never before Hosea, so far as we can know to-day, had any one clearly grasped and presented the theory of life that he held — the conviction that above all man's brutish insensibility, and cruel lust and hate, stood a God who, though he must punish to reform, yet loved with unquenchable love those who were utterly indifferent to him. Even those who may not be able to share Hosea's faith, can revere as almost more than human the man who from the ashes of his own love-dream rose to that sublime faith. This twofold message of justice and mercy was given with all the power of orator and poet to a blind nation rushing to its speedy end.

K

CHAPTER IX

(Before 722 B.C.)

THE Deborah-song would, in itself, prove that poetry had reached a high stage of development in Northern Israel before the rise of the monarchy. When the Ephraimite history was composed, probably during the earlier part of the reign of Jeroboam II, the writer embodied many songs sung in Israel and made reference to whole books of poems already existing. We cannot question that many poems had been composed in Northern Israel during the age of settlement and conquest and of the united and divided Kingdoms. The greater part of the stories of the Judges arose in these regions, and it may well be that back of these lay old songs, in other cases than that of the great deliverance by the waters of Megiddo.

The history of the divided kingdom, as given in the books of Kings, preserves very little of song; but the so-called "Blessing of Moses," embodied in the book of Deuteronomy, was probably written in Northern Israel during the prosperous reign of Jeroboam II, and was thus nearly contemporary with the oracle of Amos. It is similar to the earlier "Blessing of Jacob," and like that has comparatively little of literary charm.

The ancient sacred spots of Northern Israel were centres where many traditions were preserved which found their ultimate place in the Ephraimite narrative; the suggestion has *a priori* probability that many songs to Jehovah were treasured at the same places. Amos, who speaks of Bethel and Gilgal as sanctuaries, condemns the noise of songs and viols along with the sacrifices at the solemn assemblies in honor of Jehovah. At the king's sanctuary of Bethel, where organized worship was carried on throughout the entire history of Northern Israel, we may feel very confident that there was a special collection of religious songs.

Whether we can identify any extant songs as belonging to this collection is a matter of more uncertainty; yet we find in Israel's great song book certain hymns which seem to emanate from the Joseph tribes, at least in their original form.   In the first stanza, for example, of Psalm 80, we are in the hill country of Samaria where Benjamin was at the southern border, Manasseh on the northern slopes, and the great tribe of Ephraim in the central district.

> Give ear, O Shepherd of Israel,
> Thou that leadest Joseph like a flock;
> Thou that sittest above the cherubim, shine forth.
> Before Ephraim and Benjamin and Manasseh, stir up thy might,
> And come to save us.
> Turn us again, O God;
> And cause thy face to shine, and we shall be saved.

The time is one of distress for these regions.   As Mesha, king of Moab, pictured his god, Kemosh, angry with him,[1] so the poet of Israel finds Jehovah, God of hosts, angry with his people.

> O Jehovah God of hosts,
> How long wilt thou be angry against the prayer of thy people?
> Thou hast fed them with the bread of tears,
> And given them tears to drink in large measure.
> Thou makest us a strife unto our neighbors;
> And our enemies laugh among themselves.
> Turn us again, O God of hosts;
> And cause thy face to shine, and we shall be saved.[2]

In Psalm 81 also, Joseph seems to be the portion of Israel that is in the thought of the poet.   The new moon as a feast day recalls Amos's picture of practices in this region, and the thought seems almost to echo Hosea as the song progresses.

> Sing aloud unto God our strength:
> Make a joyful noise unto the God of Jacob.
> Raise a song, and bring hither the timbrel,
> The pleasant harp with the psaltery.
> Blow the trumpet at the new moon,
> At the full moon, on our feast-day.

[1] See p. 89.   [2] 80 1-4.

For it is a statute for Israel
An ordinance of the God of Jacob.
He appointed it in Joseph for a testimony,
When he went out over the land of Egypt,
Where I heard a language that I knew not.
I removed his shoulder from the burden :
His hands were freed from the basket.
Thou calledst in trouble, and I delivered thee ;
I answered thee in the secret place of thunder ;
I proved thee at the waters of Meribah.
Hear, O my people, and I will testify unto thee :
O Israel, if thou wouldest hearken unto me !
There shall no strange god be in thee ;
Neither shalt thou worship any foreign god.
I am Jehovah thy God,
Who brought thee up out of the land of Egypt :
Open thy mouth wide, and I will fill it.
But my people hearkened not to my voice ;
And Israel would none of me.
So I let them go after the stubbornness of their heart,
That they might walk in their own counsels.
Oh that my people would hearken unto me,
That Israel would walk in my ways !
I would soon subdue their enemies,
And turn my hand against their adversaries.
The haters of Jehovah should submit themselves unto him :
But their time should endure for ever.
He would feed them also with the finest of the wheat ;
And with honey out of the rock would I satisfy thee.

In Psalm 77, with its echoes of Deborah's picture of Jehovah's
advance, as the God of the thunder storm, Joseph is again
prominent.

Thou art the God that doest wonders :
Thou hast made known thy strength among the peoples.
Thou hast with thine arm redeemed thy people,
The sons of Jacob and Joseph.
The waters saw thee, O God ;
The waters saw thee, they were afraid :
The depths also trembled.
The clouds poured out water ;

The skies sent out a sound:
Thine arrows also went abroad.
The voice of thy thunder was in the whirlwind;
The lightnings lightened the world:
The earth trembled and shook.
Thy way was in the sea,
And thy paths in the great waters,
And thy footsteps were not known.
Thou leddest thy people like a flock,
By the hand of Moses and Aaron.

That all of these psalms were originally composed in Northern Israel, in the particular region occupied by the Joseph tribes, seems highly probable. In our book of Psalms, they are all assigned to an Asaph collection. From this earlier book evidently Psalms 50 and 73 to 83 were taken. In several other songs of this group there are indications of Israelite rather than Judean origin. We may note that in 50 [7] and 73 [1] the address is to Israel, and that in 75 [9] and 76 [6] God is the God of Jacob. This is his title in the psalms of only the Asaph and Korah groups, and is in harmony with a theory of Northern Israelitish origin.

The suggestion that the original Asaph collection may have been the hymnal of the Bethel sanctuary, which stood in Ephraim's territory, is a most attractive one.[1] Whether it be a true surmise or not, we may feel much confidence that many of the poems in the collection were composed in Ephraim and so antedate in their original form the downfall of Samaria in 722 B.C. To date the songs more precisely is in most cases quite impracticable, though we may note, for example, in Psalm 76 [4-8] a majestic description of Israel's God as the God of War, which suggests the early days when the wars of Jehovah were still the great theme of his people's song.

[1] The writer desires to acknowledge his indebtedness to the lectures of Dr. John P. Peters, delivered at Brown University in January, 1910, for the noting of the data and their interpretation in the above discussion of the Asaph Psalter, as also in the following discussion of the Korahite. The writer's own examination of the evidence, made since hearing the lecture discussion, has led him to feel more assurance that the Asaph collection may well be the Bethel hymnal than Dr. Peters ventured to express. Students of the Psalms must eagerly await Dr. Peters's forthcoming commentary.

Glorious art thou and excellent,
From the mountains of prey.
The stouthearted are made a spoil,
They have slept their sleep;
And none of the men of might have found their hands.
At thy rebuke, O God of Jacob,
Both chariot and horse are cast into a dead sleep.
Thou, even thou, art to be feared;
And who may stand in thy sight when once thou art angry?
Thou didst cause sentence to be heard from heaven:
The earth feared, and was still.

Again, the opening of 82, with its thought of God judging among the gods, seems primitive. In the later verses, however, there comes an outcry for judgment such as Amos promised, and this portion seems certainly later than the preaching of that great prophet. It is conceivable that one who had heard Amos composed this prayer in the days of injustice which continued for a short generation before the final judgment fell on Israel.

Of the Korahite collection, Psalms 42–49 and 84–89, several bear marks of far northern origin, not in Samaria but Galilee. In the last Psalm of the collection, Tabor and Hermon are pictured as rejoicing in Jehovah's name. This line could hardly have been written after Gilead and Galilee had been devastated by Tiglath-pileser in 734, and had been taken away from Israel. We are brought to the northern districts during the prosperous days of the kingdom. Much of the poem may have been added later, but some of the verses accord well with a relatively early origin.

O Jehovah God of hosts,
Who is a mighty one, like unto thee, O Jehovah?
And thy faithfulness is round about thee.
Thou rulest the pride of the sea;
When the waves thereof arise, thou stillest them.
Thou hast broken Rahab in pieces, as one that is slain;
Thou hast scattered thine enemies with the arm of thy strength.
The heavens are thine, the earth also is thine:
The world and the fulness thereof, thou hast founded them.

The north and the south, thou hast created them:
Tabor and Hermon rejoice in thy name.
Thou hast a mighty arm;
Strong is thy hand, and high is thy right hand.[1]

Psalm 42 has commonly been interpreted as the sad cry of one of the exiles carried to Babylon in 597 or 586 B.C. Its bitter sorrow over the apparent helplessness of God to care for his people is in thought and expression identical with that which found utterance at the time of the great exile. On the other hand, the picture of deep calling unto deep at the noise of thy waterfalls has seemed strange in a poem, the occasion of which is the last glimpse of Palestine from a shoulder of Hermon. It may be that the nucleus of the poem was a song in honor of God manifest in the wonderful living spring at Dan that constitutes one of the Jordan's sources.[2] This spring, no doubt, was the ancient natural sanctuary at which migrating Dan established the Levite as priest with image and ephod [3] and which Jeroboam I selected as the northern sanctuary for his kingdom.

O my God, my soul is cast down within me:
Therefore do I remember thee from the land of the Jordan,
And the Hermons, from the hill Mizar.
Deep calleth unto deep at the noise of thy waterfalls:
All thy waves and thy billows are gone over me.
Yet Jehovah will command his lovingkindness in the daytime;
And in the night his song shall be with me,
Even a prayer unto the God of my life.
I will say unto God my rock, Why hast thou forgotten me?
Why go I mourning because of the oppression of the enemy?[4]

The opening verses of 46 suggest the same sacred spot.

God is our refuge and strength,
A very present help in trouble.
Therefore will we not fear, though the earth do change,
And though the mountains be shaken into the heart of the seas;
Though the waters thereof roar and be troubled,
Though the mountains tremble with the swelling thereof.

[1] Psalm 89 [8-13].
[2] For the sacred character of springs see Chapter II, p. 14.
[3] Judges 17 and 18.   [4] Psalm 42 [6-9].

It is an attractive suggestion that the Korahite collection goes back to the old temple at Dan and that the Korahite rebellion was really the Dan schism.[1]

The royal marriage hymn, Psalm 45, is a notable member of this collection, and one very commonly recognized as belonging to the period of the monarchy.   In the earlier part of the poem, the praise is of the royal bridegroom, while the latter part is filled with praise and admiration for the bride and hope for the princely line.

> My heart overfloweth with a goodly matter;
> I speak the things which I have made touching the king:
> My tongue is the pen of a ready writer.
> Thou art fairer than the children of men; ·
> Grace is poured into thy lips:
> Therefore God hath blessed thee for ever.
> Gird thy sword upon thy thigh, O mighty one,
> Thy glory and thy majesty.
> And in thy majesty ride on prosperously,
> Because of truth and meekness and righteousness:
> And thy right hand shall teach thee terrible things.
> Thine arrows are sharp;
> The peoples fall under thee;
> They are in the heart of the king's enemies.
> Thy throne, O God, is for ever and ever:
> A sceptre of equity is the sceptre of thy kingdom.
> Thou hast loved righteousness, and hated wickedness:
> Therefore God, thy God, hath anointed thee
> With the oil of gladness above thy fellows.
> All thy garments smell of myrrh, and aloes, and cassia;
> Out of ivory palaces stringed instruments have made thee glad.
> Kings' daughters are among thy honorable women:
> At thy right hand doth stand the queen in gold of Ophir.
> Hearken, O daughter, and consider, and incline thine ear;
> Forget also thine own people, and thy father's house:
> So will the king desire thy beauty;
> For he is thy Lord; and reverence thou him.
> And the daughter of Tyre shall be there with a gift.
> The rich among the people shall entreat thy favor.
> The king's daughter within the palace is all glorious:

[1] This, too, is the suggestion of Dr. Peters, made in the lectures referred to above.

Her clothing is inwrought with gold.
She shall be led unto the king in broidered work:
The virgins her companions that follow her
Shall be brought unto thee.
With gladness and rejoicing shall they be led:
They shall enter into the king's palace.
Instead of thy fathers shall be thy children,
Whom thou shalt make princes in all the earth.
I will make thy name to be remembered in all generations:
Therefore shall the peoples give thee thanks for ever and ever.

There is no more complex and difficult problem in the study of
Israel's ancient literature than the history of the Psalter. The
editorial headings of the individual psalms suggest that back of
its present division into five books lie still earlier collections which
were gathered together from time to time. The duplication of
certain psalms and many other indications point in the same
direction as indicating a slow and complex process of compilation.
In the text itself, as well as the headings, editorial work is manifest,
and there is perhaps no early psalm which has not suffered considerable emendation. It is only when the later stages of the
development of this great treasury of Israel's song are reached that
one can speak upon its history with any approach to definiteness.
It is, however, probable that somewhere in the book there are
many relics of the psalmody of Northern Israel, and the Korahite
and Asaphite psalters may have been collections made in the
kingdom ended in 722 B.C.

With the book of Hosea, the literature of Northern Israel comes
to its climax and completion. Though the development of prose
writing was later in Israel than in Judah, it reached great beauty
and power in the Elijah stories and in Hosea. In 721 thousands
of the inhabitants of Ephraim were carried exile to remote regions
and settled in separate districts where they could never again
unite for effective rebellion against the rule of Assyria. Pagan
peoples from other conquered districts were moved into Israel's
territory, and a mixed population was formed from these and the
remnants of Israel. This composite population in time learned
to worship Jehovah, who had now come to be regarded as the god
of the land, and ultimately became the Samaritan people.

All that has been preserved of the literature of Northern Israel was taken over and handed down by Judah. Many passages in Hosea referring to Judah come awkwardly in their context and were probably added to give the writing application to the nation which preserved it. We may well imagine that faithful followers of Jehovah fled from the self-doomed nation of Israel during its later years of anarchy and apostasy and found a refuge in Judah, and that they brought with them their literary treasures. Thus, we may suppose, the lost histories of the northern kingdom and the Elijah and Elisha stories, from which the compiler of our books of Kings got his material for the events of the north, the great Ephraimite prophetic history of the earlier times, the book of Hosea, and, it may be, collections of psalms were preserved from the destruction which must have overtaken the large body of the literature of Northern Israel in the extinction of the nation. The literary history of Northern Israel terminated just when it had entered upon its great era of prose writing.

There is no cause for wonder that no more literature has been preserved from Israel. It is, rather, difficult to see how so much could have survived the extinction of the nation, except as we believe that the influence of a nation which had produced Deborah, Samuel, Elijah, and Hosea, and which could tell in such noble verse and prose the story of its leaders, could not perish.

CHAPTER X

ISAIAH

(*737 to 701 B.C.*)

IT was about the time of Hosea's latest prophecies that Isaiah began his work in Jerusalem, where the life of Jehovah's people was henceforth to centre; the year that king Uzziah died, that is, the year that Menahem assassinated Shallum in Samaria, Isaiah became aware of his mission.

Uzziah, in his later years, had been a leper, and his son Jotham had served as regent. This son survived his father two years only. Before his death, there was an alarming coalition formed against him. Damascus, which had been prostrate since its terrible defeat by Assyria in 797, had begun to revive; its natural resources made this inevitable when it was not swept by devastating war. The king, Rezin, made confederacy with Pekah of Israel against Judah, and Jotham, dying, left his twenty year old son to face this crisis. It is almost certain that the cause of the union against Judah was refusal to unite in rebellion against Assyria. Two years earlier, just before the death of Uzziah, when Menahem was king of Israel, a coalition of nineteen states, including the region from the Euphrates to Judah, had been formed to check the advance of an aggressive king on the throne of Assyria, who sought to realize the dreams of earlier kings by extending his power to the Mediterranean. This confederation had proved fruitless in checking the advance of the mighty Tiglath-pileser who appears to have marched down the coast plain of Palestine and to have reached the farthermost limits of the confederate district, while both Menahem and Uzziah paid tribute. That, too, was the year that king Uzziah died.

139

The coalition of two years later, in which Damascus and Israel were united against Judah, brought Tiglath-pileser once more into the westland. After capturing Damascus, he took away from Israel and practically depopulated her territory east of the Jordan and north of the plain of Esdraelon. It was now that Pekah was killed and Hoshea placed upon the throne of the little kingdom that was to be ruled from the city of Samaria.[1] These events gave the *terminus ad quem* for the latest preaching of Hosea. According to the narrative in Kings, Ahaz sought help from Assyria as a humble vassal, and so Tiglath-pileser came at just this time.[2] Ahaz went to meet the Assyrian overlord at Damascus, and Judah thus renewed her vassalage to the eastern power. She maintained this allegiance some thirty years longer, and so escaped when foolish rebellion caused the downfall of Northern Israel.

The first period of Isaiah's ministry may be counted as extending over the twelve years from the last year of Uzziah to the final revolt and beginning of the long siege of Samaria. Many of the prophecies delivered by Isaiah during these years require a knowledge of the general facts of the history for an appreciation of their significance.

The account of Isaiah's call, chapter 6, is an example of vision prophecy that may recall Amos 7–9 in its form.

In the year that king Uzziah died I saw the Lord sitting upon a throne, high and lifted up; and his train filled the temple. Above him stood the seraphim: each one had six wings; with twain he covered his face, and with twain he covered his feet, and with twain he did fly. And one cried unto another, and said, Holy, holy, holy, is Jehovah of hosts: the whole earth is full of his glory. And the foundations of the thresholds shook at the voice of him that cried, and the house was filled with smoke. Then said I, Woe is me! for I am undone; because I am a man of unclean lips, and I dwell in the midst of a people of unclean lips: for mine eyes have seen the King, Jehovah of hosts.

Then flew one of the seraphim unto me, having a live coal in his hand, which he had taken with the tongs from off the altar: and he touched my mouth with it, and said, Lo, this hath touched thy lips; and thine iniquity is taken away, and thy sin forgiven. And I heard the voice of the

[1] 2 Kings 15 29ff.   [2] 2 Kings 16 7–9.

Lord, saying, Whom shall I send, and who will go for us? Then I said, Here am I; send me. And he said, Go, and tell this people, Hear ye indeed, but understand not; and see ye indeed, but perceive not. Make the heart of this people fat, and make their ears heavy, and shut their eyes; lest they see with their eyes, and hear with their ears, and understand with their heart, and turn again, and be healed. Then said I, Lord, how long? And he answered, Until cities be waste without inhabitant, and houses without man, and the land become utterly waste, and Jehovah have removed men far away, and the forsaken places be many in the midst of the land. And if there be yet a tenth in it, it also shall in turn be eaten up: as a terebinth, and as an oak, whose stock remaineth, when they are felled; so the holy seed is the stock thereof.

Vision experience, explain it as we may in terms of scientific psychology, has been notably characteristic of great religious leaders throughout history. The Hebrew prophets, Paul, Mohammed, Savonarola, Luther, come instantly to mind, and Christ himself may have recounted to his followers in the form of objective visions the struggle through which he passed just before entering upon his public career.

It is impossible to determine just how far this form of recorded experience may have been a truly ecstatic condition with Isaiah and other great prophets of ancient Israel, and how far it may have developed into a consciously poetic method of describing the growth of convictions. In the picture as we have it in Chapter 6, it seems that the experiences of later years must be included. On the other hand there is no reason for doubting that the great convictions which set Isaiah to his long, life task culminated in some sort of a trance, probably in the temple, the year that king Uzziah died, the year the nation paid tribute to Assyria. Before the inner experience of that day was committed to writing in its present form, consciously or unconsciously later thoughts must have become mingled with the initial convictions. All these fine-spun distinctions, inevitable to those influenced by modern psychological science, were no doubt absolutely foreign to the thought of the great prophet, and, even to-day, the best test of the visions of religious enthusiasts and teachers is not psychological analysis, but the objective moral and spiritual worth of the visions.

The notable fact is not that the Hebrew prophets had symbolic visions, but that their visions kept so close to the actual needs of their days and could be described in a form containing moral and spiritual truth still eminently sober, sane, and valid.   Isaiah saw, it is true, the Lord sitting upon an exalted throne, with his train filling the temple, the heavenly beings, the house filled with smoke, and all the rest of that nature; but he saw, at the same time, the sin of his own life, the sin and insensibility of his nation, and the inevitable consequences.   These were hard, sober facts that give the vision validity to our scientific minds.

Again, we may trace through the vision the steps of Isaiah's inner experience: First, a conviction of an exalted God; next, a sense of his own unholiness and that of his people; then, assurance that God can purify his unholy members; finally the hearing of the Divine call, "Whom shall I send and who will go for us?" and the ready answer.   The experience is in substance that of men in all ages of history; normal even down to the twentieth century, known to many a man who never saw any such vision as that recorded here.   The form of Isaiah's vision may be foreign to us, but woe worth the day when the essential experience which it embodies becomes wholly unknown.[1]

[1] It certainly is an experience familiar to any one who comes at all into contact with the inner life of young men and women to-day.   One who has had unusual opportunities for such contact writes: "In his 'Spiritual Significance of Modern Socialism,' John Spargo asks what he evidently regards as an unanswerable question: 'Where to-day are the dreamers of dreams setting the hearts of men aflame with holy enthusiasms, setting the feet of young men and maidens marching toward the vision? Where is there faith in mankind, faith in the future of the race, in the capacity of mankind to rise higher and higher, to complete the chain of evolution from brute to brother?'

"Where?   In all our American colleges, North and South, East and West.   There is no lack of dreamers; of hearts aflame with holy enthusiasm; of young men and maidens eager to march toward the vision; of faith in the capacity of mankind to complete the chain of evolution from brute to brother.   What these young men and maidens need is not chiefly greater enthusiasm, inspiring them to march, but wise counsel teaching them in what direction to march; not more vision, but more practical knowledge, and more wise self-reliance, that they may make the vision real.   In these ten years of college experience I have had a few come to me with the question, How to escape from some pit into which, through ignorance or sudden gust of passion, they have fallen; but I

Chapters 2–5 seem to form a distinct group of prophecies assignable to the earliest years of Isaiah's ministry, coming therefore shortly after the inaugural vision of chapter 6. They begin with their own heading: The word that Isaiah the son of Amoz saw concerning Judah and Jerusalem.[1] The thought of Jehovah's exaltation, dominant in the opening vision, here finds its sequel in Isaiah's characteristic pronouncement of judgment on all that is proud, haughty, and lifted up. This recurs several times.

That Isaiah had caught the spirit and probably the very words of Amos may be seen in such a passage as

Jehovah standeth up to contend and standeth to judge the peoples. Jehovah will enter into judgment with the elders of his people, and the princes thereof: It is ye that have eaten up the vineyard; the spoil of the poor is in your houses: what mean ye that ye crush my people, and grind the face of the poor? saith the Lord, Jehovah of hosts.

The wanton luxury of wealthy women which Amos so vividly portrayed as the destructive trampling of heedless kine, is pictured with more of realistic detail by Isaiah.

Moreover Jehovah said, Because the daughters of Zion are haughty, and walk with outstretched necks and wanton eyes, walking and mincing as they go, and making a tinkling with their feet; therefore the Lord will smite with a scab the crown of the head of the daughters of Zion, and Jehovah will lay bare their secret parts. In that day the Lord will take away the beauty of their anklets, and the cauls, and the crescents; the pendants, and the bracelets, and the mufflers; the headtires, and the ankle chains, and the sashes, and the perfume-boxes, and the amulets; the rings, and the nose-jewels; the festival robes, and the mantles, and the shawls, and the satchels; the hand-mirrors, and the fine linen, and the turbans, and the veils. And it shall come to pass, that instead of sweet spices there shall be rottenness; and instead of a girdle, a rope; and instead of well set hair, baldness; and instead of a robe, a girding of sackcloth; branding instead of beauty. Thy men shall fall by the sword, and thy mighty in the war. And her gates shall lament and mourn;

have had hundreds come to me with the question, How can I best serve my fellow-men; how best promote universal brotherhood? And this counsel has been sought alike by men intending to go into the ministry, into law, into business, into teaching, into journalism."—Lyman Abbott, in *The Outlook*, August, 1909.

[1] 2 [1].

and she shall be desolate and sit upon the ground.   And seven women shall take hold of one man in that day, saying, We will eat our own bread, and wear our own apparel: only let us be called by thy name; take thou away our reproach.[1]

Here the contrast between the unimaginative picture of the city man and that of the herdsman of Tekoa is notable. Both in the dignity of a certain reserve and in poetic power the advantage, in this instance, seems to be wholly with the herdsman; the passage is not a fair example of Isaiah's poetic power, though a wonderful instance of concrete description.

Like Amos, Isaiah could on occasion assume the rôle of minstrel and, with winsome spirit, begin in the lively measure of a love-song. It would be difficult to excel the charming translation of Canon Cheyne, who has caught this spirit of the song in chapter 5 [1-7].

> A song will I sing of my friend,
>   A love-song touching his vineyard.
>
> A vineyard belongs to my friend,
>   On a hill that is fruitful and sunny;
> He digged it, and cleared it of stones,
>   And planted there vines that are choice;
> A tower he built in the midst,
>   And hewed also therein a wine-vat;
> And he looked to find grapes that are good,
>   Alas! it bore grapes that are wild.
>
> Ye, in Jerusalem dwelling,
>   And ye, who are freemen of Judah,
> Judge ye, I pray, between me
>   And my cherished vineyard.
> What could have been done for my vineyard
>   That I had not done?
> When I looked to find grapes that are good,
>   Why bore it grapes that are wild?
>
> And now let me give you to know
>   What I purpose to do to my vineyard:
> I will take away its hedge,
>   That it be eaten up,

[1] 3 [16]–4 [1].

> I will break through its walls,
>> That it be trodden down;
> Yea, I will make it a waste,
>> Neither pruned nor weeded;
>
> It shall shoot up thorns and briers,
> And the clouds will I enjoin that they rain not upon it.
> For the vineyard of Yhvh Sabaoth is the House of Israel,
> And the men of Judah his cherished plantation;
> And he looked for justice, but behold! bloodshed,
> For righteousness, but behold! an outcry.[1]

The closing lines give a striking play upon words in the contrasted "justice" and "bloodshed," "righteousness" and "outcry"; the words are mishpat and mispah, tsedhaqa and tseaqa.[2]

The lines that follow in chapter 5 begin with the weird lament of the mourners so often heard in Jerusalem's streets — "Hoy!" Thus they lamented for the man of God slain by the lion in the early years of the kingdom, "Hoy! my brother." Thus Jeremiah forbad them to mourn for Josiah's unworthy son, saying "Hoy! my brother" or "Hoy! my sister," or "Hoy! lord," or "Hoy! his glory!"[3] Isaiah's lament is not, however, for the dead, but for the living and the prosperous; it is over the wealthy land that he utters the mourner's cry.

In the prosperous reigns of Jeroboam II and Uzziah, sudden national expansion had given opportunity for great increase of wealth to a certain ruthless type of man who always comes to the front under the social conditions prevailing at such a time. Amos had painted him and his vulgar wife, in strong, unfading colors, at their coarse enjoyments, and in their brutal indifference to the sufferings of the poor. Isaiah gives the economic condition, in one respect more clearly than Amos. The small, independent landowner, the very bone and sinew of the nation, is being crushed out, for these strong brutes by use of their increasing resources are laying field to field till there is no room and they are made to dwell alone in the midst of the land.[4]

In the days of Ahab, more than a century before, the influence

---

[1] Cheyne, *Isaiah*, Polychrome Bible.
[2] The second contrast might be suggested by *righteousness* and *riotousness*.   [3] Jeremiah 22 18.   [4] 5 8.

of the Phœnician princess, whom the king married, had led him to override the rights of a private citizen in his ancestral vineyard, and the great prophet of the ninth century had pronounced awful curse upon the royal line. Now, not the king merely, but many who had gained the necessary economic power, were displacing the freeholder. The economic inequalities which manifested themselves particularly in this tendency were doubtless one chief element of the circumstances that gave rise to Israel's great prophetic movement.

Isaiah sang the doom : —

> Woe to the joiners of house to house.
>   Field they add to field,
> Till there's an end of room ;
>   And ye are made to dwell alone.
>
> Therefore hath Jehovah of Hosts to me sworn :[1]
> In truth, many houses shall desolate be ;
> Houses great and fair, uninhabited.[2]

The remainder of chapter 5, as well as the verses translated above, shows that wonderful blending of emotion and hard fact which was discussed in connection with Hosea. Verses 11, 12, 22, 23 offer excellent examples.

Woe unto them that rise up early in the morning, that they may follow strong drink; that tarry late into the night, till wine inflame them ! And the harp and the lute, the tabret and the pipe, and wine, are in their feasts; but they regard not the work of Jehovah, neither have they considered the operation of his hands.

Woe unto them that are mighty to drink wine, and men of strength to mingle strong drink; that justify the wicked for a bribe, and take away the righteousness of the righteous from him !

The last line may mean nothing more than the justice of the just man's case, but it suggests the possibility that the ancient poet saw something of the truth embodied in the familiar lines of the modern seer : —

> He who steals my purse steals trash ;
> But he who filches my good name, etc.

---

[1] Adopting an emendation of text. See Kittel, *Bib. Heb. in loc.*
[2] Isaiah 5 [8-10].

Whether the ancient prophet saw the greater injustice done by the bribed court than the mere taking of property, he certainly does, at times, go far deeper than matters of external conduct in analyzing the national situation.   He follows, for example, in the line of profound insight that Hosea had first suggested and that found its culmination only in the teaching of him who spake as never man spake; echoing Hosea, Isaiah cries, My people are gone into captivity for lack of knowledge;[1] and he adds something which is a great advance in the analysis of this phase of the nation's need, Woe unto them that call evil good and good evil, that put darkness for light and light for darkness.[2]   More than seven hundred years later, Jesus would declare guilty of eternal sin only those who called the good evil, who counted deeds of mercy the work of Beelzebub; moral perversity that could not comprehend the light of love when it shone was the one condition in man of which Jesus despaired.[3]   Like the greater one to follow, Isaiah would not stop with surface indications, whether these were cruel monopoly, bribery, or drunken debauchery.

In addition to this penetrating insight into actual social and spiritual conditions and their underlying causes, we may note the imaginative power of this great age in literature when fact and emotion are still united.

Therefore Sheol hath enlarged its desire, and opened its mouth without measure; and their glory, and their multitude, and their pomp, and he that rejoiceth among them, descend into it.   And the mean man is bowed down, and the great man is humbled, and the eyes of the lofty are humbled, but Jehovah of hosts is exalted in justice, and God the Holy One is sanctified in righteousness.   Then shall the lambs feed as in their pasture, and the waste places of the fat ones shall wanderers eat.

Woe unto them that draw iniquity with cords of falsehood, and sin as it were with a cart rope; that say, Let him make speed, let him hasten his work, that we may see it; and let the counsel of the Holy One of Israel draw nigh and come, that we may know it![4]

And he will lift up an ensign to the nations from far, and will hiss for them from the end of the earth; and, behold, they shall come with speed swiftly.   None shall be weary nor stumble among them; none shall slumber nor sleep; neither shall the girdle of their loins be loosed, nor the latchet of their shoes be broken: whose arrows are sharp, and all their

[1] 5 [13].   [2] 5 [20].   [3] Mark 3 [22-30], Matthew 12 [24-31].   [4] 5 [14-19].

bows bent; their horses' hoofs shall be accounted as flint, and their wheels as a whirlwind: their roaring shall be like a lioness, they shall roar like young lions; yea, they shall roar, and lay hold of the prey, and carry it away safe, and there shall be none to deliver. And they shall roar against them in that day like the roaring of the sea: and if one look unto the land, behold, darkness and distress; and the light is darkened in the clouds.[1]

If no other words of Isaiah had been preserved than those of the early group of prophecies now forming chapters 2–5 of his book, the author's reputation as orator, poet, and seer would be amply established. The last lines printed above afford a fine example of the splendid sweep of the prophet's pictures of the future, when he lets his imagination soar above all present evils and beyond their consequences, buoyed by his sure faith in the God who will ultimately bring all nations to Himself. The rush of picture upon picture, figure changing to figure, is most characteristic of Isaiah who, despite his rapid changes, rarely mixes a figure or becomes turbid. The last four lines illustrate the poet's wonderful sense of sound and love of sudden contrast. When he speaks of roaring like the roaring of the sea, the vowels are largely broad and full. In the sudden change of attention from the sea to the storm-tossed mariner looking keenly for the light on the shore, the vowels become short and thin, followed often by sharp dentals or linguals. As we pronounce the Hebrew words, our vocal organs are forced into almost strained constriction, so characteristic of tense feeling. If the Lange-James theory of emotion be true, then the ancient poet, playing upon his reader as upon an instrument, superinduces in him, through the emotional reaction from the physical action required to pronounce the words, the anxiety of the sailor pictured. Isaiah adds to Amos's and Hosea's wealth of figures from inland nature a profound appreciation of the sea's majesty and power, familiarity with the mariner's dangers, and a sense of ocean's organ tones.

One of the most notable examples of Isaiah's wealth of figurative language is found in "the great arraignment" which forms the opening chapter of the book. It is possible to enumerate in the chapter some fifteen or sixteen distinct figures or illustrations

[1] 5 26-30. "Thereof" omitted on ground of slight emendation of text. See Kittel, *Bib. Heb. in loc.*

from home and farm life, from industry, nature, and history; all are so perfect that even for slow Occidental wit, the rapid succession serves to make the thought effective. This chapter is an admirable example, too, of the prophetic type of address. Though the whole, in the form we have it, could be delivered in less than five minutes, it contains apostrophe to the heavens and the earth, mandatory address to rulers of Sodom and people of Gomorrah, tender appeal by Jehovah of hosts, the mighty one of Israel, followed by glorious promises. The great thoughts wrought out by the two unique and distinct personalities, Amos and Hosea, are here poured forth in rapid succession, yet in a form that is quite Isaiah's own, so that one familiar with the work of the two earlier prophets would never think of ascribing this address to either of them. The thought of Jehovah as the holy one of Israel and the conception of a remnant to be left are distinctively Isaiah's.

While this address deals specifically with existing conditions, it does not allude to any great political events which would connect it clearly with some one period of Isaiah's ministry. The devastation of the land may have been that of the Syro-Ephraimitish war, two years after the prophet's inaugural vision, or it may have been due to one of the Assyrian invasions a few years later.

Were we arranging the volume of Isaiah's sermons we should put first the title page, verse 1 of chapter 1 : —

THE VISION

OF

ISAIAH THE SON OF AMOZ

WHICH HE SAW

CONCERNING JUDAH AND JERUSALEM

IN THE DAYS OF

UZZIAH, JOTHAM, AHAZ, AND HEZEKIAH

KINGS OF JUDAH

and then the inaugural vision of chapter 6. The address of chapter 1, however, whether it was delivered early or late in the ministry, forms an admirable starting-point for the appreciation of Isaiah's message in its relation to the preceding prophets and in certain of its distinctive elements.

Viewing chapters 1–6 as a whole, we find in them a noble sequel for Judea to the twofold message which had just been given to Israel. In literary form, they furnish notable examples of the symbolic vision, song, and effective rhetoric which are so mingled in the greatest prophetic literature.

If one reads on into chapter 7, he comes suddenly upon simple narrative in which Isaiah is spoken of in the third person. It is a section about the prophet similar in form to the stories of Elijah or the brief narrative in the seventh chapter of the book of Amos. The story tells of the coalition between Rezin and Pekah against Ahaz of Judah, and of Isaiah's efforts to prevent Ahaz from calling in the aid of Assyria. The scene of the fateful interview is at the end of the conduit of the upper pool, whither the king had gone, probably to look after the water-supply of the city in view of the threatened siege. With Isaiah is his son, Shear-Jashub, whose name is a standing, twofold prophecy; "a remnant shall return" contains both menace and promise — menace of coming exile, promise that the nation shall not utterly perish.

Isaiah's description of the kings of Israel and Damascus as two stumps of smoking firebrands is inimitable. Two years before, Judah had been united with eighteen other states in an imposing alliance against Assyria, that fell to pieces at the advance of the Assyrian king. Pekah's predecessor had humbly paid tribute, to save his neck and state, and the Assyrian had entered Damascus. Now the stumps of these firebrands, just smoking, hoped to kindle an effective conflagration. Ahaz was wise in refusing to ally himself with them; Isaiah was wiser in bidding him not to seek Assyrian aid, the price of which would be complete vassalage. Jerusalem with its great natural advantages was capable always of enduring prolonged siege, and the stumps would soon consume themselves.

The king is determined to carry out his own plan, and so Isaiah offers him a sign from Jehovah, such as he shall himself choose. With feigned reverence, Ahaz declines to put God to the test, and the prophet, in Jehovah's name, determines the sign to be given. As soon as a young woman [1] can bear a child and that

---

[1] The Hebrew word translated "virgin" means simply a young woman of marriageable age, whether maid or newly married.

child can grow to the earliest choice of good and evil, nay sooner, the land whose two kings thou abhorrest shall be forsaken. The time element is surely a main feature of the prediction, but Isaiah's words are not merely a general poetic statement of time; he refers to some particular child to be born to whom the symbolic name God-with-us, Immanuel, is to be given.

This promise of deliverance from the present threatening danger is followed by impassioned, figurative predictions of coming judgment from the more distant regions of Egypt and Assyria. If they were originally spoken as a part of the Immanuel prophecy, the connection of thought would seem to be warning against the proposed Assyrian alliance.

The following chapter (8) returns to the promise of the coming downfall of Samaria and Damascus, timed by the period of conception and early infancy. In the presence of faithful witnesses, the prophet writes on a great tablet ominous words. He then begets a son, named at birth with the words that his father wrote, Maher-shalal-hash-baz — Spoil-speedeth-prey-hasteth. Before this child shall be able to utter his first "abi" and "immi," [1] Assyria shall carry away the relics of Damascus and the spoil of Samaria. A moment later, in an exalted outcry, the prophet speaks of "Thy land, O Immanuel." The prophecies of the two children, with name of doom and name of hope, are strangely inwoven and strangely similar. Possibly it is one child only, whose birth and infancy mark the period of delay of doom for the present enemies and of God's manifestation of his presence with Judah.

The section which began (7 [1ff.]) with simple narrative in the third person closes (8 [9] – 9 [7]) with rhapsodical promises for the future, when Jehovah shall be an inviolate place of refuge for those who fear him, but a stumbling-stone and snare for the others of his people, when there shall be a ruler on David's throne called Wonderful, Counsellor, Mighty God, Everlasting Father, Prince of Peace. The child of the closing vision whose rule is thus described can hardly be, it would seem, the one to be born in Ahaz's day as a sign to make that king yield practical trust to Jehovah. The prediction of a child named God-with-us has carried the prophet on eagle wings.

[1] "My father," "my mother."

The oracle of doom on Damascus and Ephraim that forms verses 1–11 of chapter 17 must be assigned to the same era as the prophecies just considered.   It is an example of the more direct form of prophetic address, in which Isaiah's characteristic thought that Jehovah's judgment shall not absolutely destroy his people is applied to Israel as well as Judah.

And it shall come to pass in that day, that the glory of Jacob shall be made thin, and the fatness of his flesh shall wax lean.   And it shall be as when the harvestman gathereth the standing grain, and his arm reapeth the ears; yea, it shall be as when one gleaneth ears in the valley of Rephaim.   Yet there shall be left therein gleanings, as the shaking of an olive-tree, two or three berries in the top of the uppermost bough, four or five in the outmost branches of a fruitful tree, saith Jehovah, the God of Israel.[1]

Ahaz was unmoved by all Isaiah's threats, promises, and pleadings.   In his stubborn weakness he sent messengers.

So Ahaz sent messengers to Tiglath-pileser king of Assyria, saying, I am thy servant and thy son: come up, and save me out of the hand of the king of Syria, and out of the hand of the king of Israel, who rise up against me.   And Ahaz took the silver and gold that was found in the house of Jehovah, and in the treasures of the king's house, and sent it for a present to the king of Assyria.   And the king of Assyria hearkened unto him; and the king of Assyria went up against Damascus, and took it, and carried the people of it captive to Kir, and slew Rezin.

And king Ahaz went to Damascus to meet Tiglath-pileser king of Assyria, and saw the altar that was at Damascus; and king Ahaz sent to Urijah the priest the fashion of the altar, and the pattern of it, according to all the workmanship thereof.   And Urijah the priest built an altar: according to all that king Ahaz had sent from Damascus, so did Urijah the priest make it against the coming of king Ahaz from Damascus.   And when the king was come from Damascus, the king saw the altar: and the king drew near unto the altar, and offered thereon.   And he burnt his burnt-offering and his meal-offering, and poured his drink-offering, and sprinkled the blood of his peace-offerings, upon the altar.

*   *   *   *   *   *   *   *

And king Ahaz cut off the panels of the bases, and removed the laver from off them, and took down the sea from off the brazen oxen that were under it, and put it upon a pavement of stone.   And the covered way for the sabbath that they had built in the house, and the king's entry

[1] 17 4-6.

without, turned he unto the house of Jehovah, because of the king of Assyria.[1]

Such were some of the immediate internal effects upon Judah of Ahaz's conduct.   Upon Israel, the effects were more obviously disastrous.   The summary statement of 2 Kings 15 [29] is impressive : —

In the days of Pekah king of Israel came Tiglath-pileser king of Assyria, and took Ijon, and Abel-beth-maacah, and Janoah, and Kedesh, and Hazor, and Gilead, and Galilee, all the land of Naphtali ; and he carried them captive to Assyria.

The latter part of Isaiah 9 may belong to this time ; it pictures vividly the fact that not even the reduction of Israel's territory to the mere hill country of Ephraim can destroy the ill-founded confidence of the people and lead them to turn to Jehovah, recognizing that it is really he who has smitten.

The Lord sent a word into Jacob, and it hath lighted upon Israel. And all the people shall know, even Ephraim and the inhabitant of Samaria, that say in pride and in stoutness of heart, The bricks are fallen, but we will build with hewn stone ; the sycomores are cut down, but we will put cedars in their place.   Therefore Jehovah will set up on high against him the adversaries of Rezin, and will stir up his enemies, the Syrians before, and the Philistines behind ; and they shall devour Israel with open mouth.   For all this his anger is not turned away, but his hand is stretched out still.

Yet the people have not turned unto him that smote them, neither have they sought Jehovah of hosts.[2]

Later, we shall see Isaiah definitely declaring to Judah that Assyria is the rod of Jehovah's anger.

The opening verses of chapter 28 picture again the blind folly of the men of Ephraim.   Whether the prophet means to represent them as actually besotted with liquor and so unable to understand the terrible dangers threatening or whether drunkenness is but a figure to express their maudlin exaltation, the picture is a terrible one when

even these reel with wine, and stagger with strong drink ; the priest and the prophet reel with strong drink, they are swallowed up of wine, they stagger with strong drink ; they err in vision, they stumble in judgment. For all tables are full of vomit and filthiness, so that there is no place clean.

[1] 2 Kings 16 [7-13, 17-18].   [2] 9 [8-13].

In their stupid assurance, the people object to being taught like
weaned children, "precept upon precept, line upon line, here a
little, there a little." In towering indignation, the prophet promises
them Jehovah's precept upon precept, line upon line, from strange
lips, and with another tongue. As he goes on, Judah and its rulers
seem to be central in his thought. Either an earlier prophecy
uttered against Samaria before its final downfall is inwoven with
later warning and promises to Judah or the whole was written
before 721, and the prophet, starting with lament over the blind
folly of Samaria, passes on to similar errors in the rulers of his own
people.

From the picture of drunken self-confidence, the prophecy goes
on with the figure of a flood or scourge passing through Judah.
As the Hebrew text stands, and the English versions translate,
Isaiah is made guilty of a strangely mixed figure, an "overflowing
scourge"! Did Isaiah, who would change the figure every few
lines, without confusing himself or his reader, perpetrate, in a
figure carried through a passage of three hundred words, the
"overflowing whip"? The two words, shôt shôteph (a scourge
overflowing), are so nearly alike that a slight change in either
will make it of essentially the same root meaning as the other.
We may with some of the early versions read an overflowing, or
rushing, *flood*, or we may follow the emendation of others and read
a scourge *moving eagerly* or *quickly*.[1] Neither emendation is more
difficult than those the student is forced constantly to make in the
text that has come down to us in the earliest Hebrew manuscripts,
already copied and recopied for more than fifteen hundred years
after Isaiah wrote. As a matter of purely literary judgment, it
is not necessary to believe that Israel's ancient master of figurative
speech was guilty of this solecism.

In verse 20, we pass without warning from the rushing flood to
one of the homeliest and most intensely expressive figures in Isaiah's

---

[1] See Kittel, *Bib. Heb.* Dillmann notes that *shot shoteph* gives a
paronomasia. Whether he thinks that this accounts for the mixed figure
is not clear. *Isaiah, Handbuch z. A. T.*, p. 255. Kent suggests that it is
the scornful reference of the people to the figure of an overwhelming
flood which Isaiah frequently uses. *Sermons, Epistles and Apocalypses
of Israel's Prophets*, p. 128.

writings. It may be just a current proverb that Isaiah throws in — For the bed is shorter than that a man can stretch himself on it; and the covering narrower than that he can wrap himself in it. If Isaiah originated this, he created a word that might well have become proverbial. Can one recall any proverb which more effectively pictures a vexingly intolerable situation? The chapter closes with a parable much in the spirit and tone of some of the quaint poems on manners found in the book of Proverbs, very different from the usual speech of the prophets.

Give ye ear, and hear my voice; hearken, and hear my speech. Doth he that ploweth to sow plow continually? doth he continually open and harrow his ground? When he hath levelled the face thereof, doth he not cast abroad the fitches, and scatter the cummin, and put in the wheat in rows, and the barley in the appointed place, and the spelt in the border thereof? For his God doth instruct him aright, and doth teach him. For the fitches are not threshed with a sharp threshing instrument, neither is a cart wheel turned about upon the cummin; but the fitches are beaten out with a staff, and the cummin with a rod. Bread grain is ground; for he will not be always threshing it: and though the wheel of his cart and his horses scatter it, he doth not grind it. This also cometh forth from Jehovah of hosts, who is wonderful in counsel, and excellent in wisdom.[1]

Chapter 20 brings us down to a time more than twenty-five years after the opening of Isaiah's ministry, to the year of an Assyrian expedition against Philistia, when Judea as Assyrian vassal seems to have escaped any serious consequences from the proximity of the Assyrian army, but when Isaiah evidently knew that his people were in danger of compromising intrigue with the Ethiopian dynasty, now on the throne of Egypt. The brief narrative tells how Isaiah went about the streets stripped of his outer garment and barefoot like a captive, as a sign of Egypt's coming conquest by Assyria. This suggests another of the prophet's varied methods of enforcing his lessons, symbolic action. With all his rhetorical and poetic gifts, Isaiah found it necessary to adopt this striking device in order to enforce his lesson upon the people.

This prophecy introduces us to an international situation that later largely shaped Isaiah's activity. More than a quarter of a century before, Hosea had pictured Israel as a silly dove looking

[1] 28 23-29.

now to Egypt and now to Assyria for help; ten years more and Judah's foolish cooing to Egypt will bring an Assyrian army to her gates. The coming of the Assyrians in the campaign of 701 against Palestine and Egypt is indeed the next great event, or series of events, about which Isaiah's prophecies group themselves. Isaiah had been unable to convince the nation that trust in Egypt against Assyria was hopeless. Some doubtless followed the prophet, trusting his clear vision of the national destinies of Assyria and Egypt, but there was a strong party in Jerusalem which favored throwing off Assyrian vassalage in reliance on Egypt.

At this era, Palestine was feeling the force of her peculiar position as the buffer between two ancient seats of power, the Tigris-Euphrates valley and the Nile valley. Assyria had been for years at the borders of Egypt, and her ambition was not yet sated. Egypt's policy was to foment rebellion among the tributary states of Syria which lay between her and the centre of Assyrian power. As the prophets saw matters, both Northern Israel and Judah needed a consistent national policy. Isaiah, early in his ministry, had tried to keep Ahaz from seeking closer dependence upon Assyria; that vassalage once assumed, he saw the madness of breaking it in reliance upon Egyptian help. Perhaps it was in no small measure due to the fact that the Assyrian was having trouble on his southern borders with his Babylonian vassal that the Egyptian party was at length able to have its way in Judah. The deposed king of Babylon even sent an embassy to Judea; he was doubtless seeking to stir up revolt in the west so that his own chance of successful rebellion might be improved. At any rate, Judah became utterly compromised against her overlord, and the terrible Assyrian army that had destroyed her sister, twenty years before, was threatening her in 701.

A large number of Isaiah's prophecies connect themselves with this crisis. Those contained in chapters 29–32 may be regarded as a group all dating from the year before the invasion. Possibly this group begins at 28 [7] (the chapter division is late) and only the first six verses belong to the time before the fall of Samaria, where we considered the entire chapter. The thought of 28 [7ff] is very similar to that of 29.

The latter chapter opens with a lament over Jerusalem which

Jehovah is to besiege and bring to great distress, and then to deliver.   The hearers are blind to what is coming; all vision is to them as a sealed book or written characters to a man who cannot read.   Here we see that which appears in the description of the inaugural vision — the prophet forced to talk to those who have a fat heart, heavy ears, and shut eyes.   They hear, but understand not; they see, but perceive not; with the mouth they honor Jehovah, but their heart is far removed from him.   The next chapter shows wherein their alienation is especially evident; they are rebellious children in that they go down to Egypt for help.   Chapter 31 also pronounces woe upon those who go down to Egypt, who trust in horses and chariots, but look not unto the Holy One of Israel.   Through threat and promise in swift alternation, Isaiah seeks to convince the blinded people that Jehovah, not Egypt, can help them.

To the prophet's mind, the policy adopted means wasting of the land and siege of the city by the Assyrians; yet he constantly holds out hope of ultimate victory over Assyria.   The heroic stature of Isaiah's personality is herein revealed.   Though the party which seemed to him utterly wicked and foolish is having its own way and leading his people into the greatest peril that it has yet faced, he still believes that Jehovah will deliver.

In a passage of uncertain date, it may have been uttered in connection with the crisis of 701, we have an even more striking example of the prophet's catholic outlook.   Assyria, the dreaded overlord, and Egypt, the would-be ally, luring Judah to her ruin, are to be in peaceful intercourse, with Israel a blessing in the midst.   To some it seems impossible that Isaiah, with his attitude toward Assyria and Egypt and in the international situation of his day could have pictured such a consummation.

In that day shall there be an altar to Jehovah in the midst of the land of Egypt, and a pillar at the border thereof to Jehovah.   And it shall be for a sign and for a witness unto Jehovah of hosts in the land of Egypt; for they shall cry unto Jehovah because of oppressors, and he will send them a saviour, and a defender, and he will deliver them.   And Jehovah shall be known to Egypt, and the Egyptians shall know Jehovah in that day; yea, they shall worship with sacrifice and oblation, and shall vow a vow unto Jehovah, and shall perform it.   And Jehovah will smite Egypt, smiting and healing; and they shall return unto Johovah, and he will be entreated of them, and will heal them.

In that day shall there be a highway out of Egypt to Assyria, and the Assyrian shall come into Egypt, and the Egyptian into Assyria; and the Egyptians shall worship with the Assyrians.

In that day shall Israel be the third with Egypt and with Assyria, a blessing in the midst of the earth; for that Jehovah of hosts hath blessed them, saying, Blessed be Egypt my people, and Assyria the work of my hands, and Israel mine inheritance.[1]

In the terrible crisis of 701, the addresses of Isaiah show all the resources of his poetry and rhetoric. The weird lament, Hoy, is sounded again and again, for the city of David, for those who seek deep to hide their counsel from Jehovah, for the rebellious children, and for those who seek help from Egypt. The poet's imagination adds figure to figure, picture to picture, to catch the dull eyes of those who see but perceive not. The orator's irony holds up to the scorn of generations to come those who say to their seers, "See not," and to the prophets, " Prophesy not unto us right things; speak unto us smooth things; prophesy deceits." Then, in the majesty of the spokesman of Israel's Holy One, he announces a shattering like the breaking of a potter's vessel. From fierce mood, he passes quickly to gentle pleading; and therefore will the Lord wait, that he may be gracious upon you, and therefore will he be exalted that he may have mercy upon you. . . . He will be very gracious unto thee at the voice of thy cry; when he shall hear it, he will answer thee.

Sometimes the figures follow in such quick succession, as in 30 [28], that we may, perhaps, call them a little mixed, though there is nothing like an overflowing whip. Elsewhere they are exceedingly effective. Such are the pictures of the besiegers disappointed like a hungry man who dreams that he eats,[2] the lion over his prey growling defiance to the shepherds,[3] the shadow of a great rock in a weary land.[4]

The section 10 [5]–11 [9] probably comes a little later, when the Assyrian army is already advancing and even the Egyptian party must see the impending danger. An important thing to note in this section is Isaiah's clear theory of God's government in the

---

[1] Isaiah 19 [19-25].   [2] 29 [8].   [3] 31 [4].   [4] 32 [2].

movements of the nations.   The theory, as seen in the particular situation, is this — Here is mighty Assyria (one of the most brutal, conquering nations known in history) which has laid waste all the great cities from the borders of Mesopotamia to Samaria, coming on toward Judah to carry out its own cruel purposes.[1] In reality this self-confident nation is just a rod in Jehovah's hand to punish Judah.   When God has used the Assyrian's ambition for this purpose, he will punish him who has thought himself to be acting in his own strength and wisdom while he was gratifying his own cruel rapacity.

A very striking passage is that beginning at 10 [28].   The Assyrian army is advancing along the summit of the central range of Palestine.   From the territory which had belonged to Northern Israel, over the natural boundary at Michmash, where the steep-sided cross-valley cuts the road, they come on toward Jerusalem. The inhabitants of the little towns north of the city flee in terror and the striding giant stands just north of the city, shaking his threatening arm at the hill of Jerusalem.

He is come to Aiath, he is passed through Migron; at Michmash he layeth up his baggage; they are gone over the pass; they have taken up their lodging at Geba; Ramah trembleth; Gibeah of Saul is fled. Cry aloud with thy voice, O daughter of Gallim! hearken, O Laishah! O thou poor Anathoth! Madmenah is a fugitive; the inhabitants of Gebim flee for safety.   This very day shall he halt at Nob: he shaketh his hand at the mount of the daughter of Zion, the hill of Jerusalem.

Behold, the Lord, Jehovah of hosts, will lop the boughs with terror: and the high of stature shall be hewn down, and the lofty shall be brought low.   And he will cut down the thickets of the forest with iron, and Lebanon shall fall by a mighty one.

When Sennacherib really came, his advance was the usual one down along the coast plain.   With Judea in alliance with Egypt, it was necessary to cut off all possibility of aid from that quarter before undertaking the siege of the mountain stronghold, and besides, Egypt was the really important enemy; little Judea could well be left for later consideration.   In Isaiah's wonderfully vivid description of the Assyrian advance concrete, imaginative picturing is carried to its extreme.   The vivid description is really given for

[1] 10 [7-11].

the sake of what follows, the promise of Jehovah's sure deliverance. When the danger actually came, it was hardly less immediate and the deliverance was no less dramatic than in the imaginative picture painted in advance.

From the present danger and promised deliverance, the prophecy passes into one of the wonderful Messianic passages of this book:—

And there shall come forth a shoot out of the stock of Jesse, and a branch out of his roots shall bear fruit.   And the Spirit of Jehovah shall rest upon him, the spirit of wisdom and understanding, the spirit of counsel and might, the spirit of knowledge and of the fear of Jehovah.   And his delight shall be in the fear of Jehovah; and he shall not judge after the sight of his eyes, neither decide after the hearing of his ears; but with righteousness shall he judge the poor, and decide with equity for the meek of the earth; and he shall smite the earth with the rod of his mouth; and with the breath of his lips shall he slay the wicked.   And righteous-ness shall be the girdle of his waist, and faithfulness the girdle of his loins.

And the wolf shall dwell with the lamb, and the leopard shall lie down with the kid; and the calf and the young lion and the fatling together; and a little child shall lead them.   And the cow and the bear shall feed; their young ones shall lie down together; and the lion shall eat straw like the ox.   And the sucking child shall play on the hole of the asp, and the weaned child shall put his hand on the adder's den.   They shall not hurt nor destroy in all my holy mountain; for the earth shall be full of the knowledge of Jehovah, as the waters cover the sea.[1]

With the earlier part of the general section just considered we may connect the effective bit in 14 [24-27].

Jehovah of hosts hath sworn, saying, Surely, as I have thought, so shall it come to pass; and as I have purposed, so shall it stand: that I will break the Assyrian in my land, and upon my mountains tread him under foot: then shall his yoke depart from off them, and his burden depart from off their shoulder.   This is the purpose that is purposed upon the whole earth; and this is the hand that is stretched out upon all the nations.   For Jehovah of hosts hath purposed, and who shall annul it? and his hand is stretched out, and who shall turn it back?

This is one of several similar, short oracles, of which Isaiah seems to have uttered very many.   One of the finest of these may per-haps come from this period.

[1] 11 [1-9].

Ah, the uproar of many peoples, that roar like the roaring of the seas; and the rushing of nations, that rush like the rushing of mighty waters! The nations shall rush like the rushing of many waters: but he shall rebuke them, and they shall flee far off, and shall be chased as the chaff of the mountains before the wind, and like the whirling dust before the storm. At eventide, behold, terror; and before the morning they are not. This is the portion of them that despoil us, and the lot of them that rob us.

The translation does remarkably well in preserving something of the sound effect of the original. As one reads of the rushing of nations, that rush like the rushing of mighty waters (ûsheôn leummim kisheôn mayim kabbirim yishsha'ûn), one recalls Homer's favorite poluphloisboio thalasses, loud-roaring sea, in which we hear so marvellously the boom of the breaker followed by the swishing rush of the water on the beach.[1] Homer was fond of onomatopoetic lines, and Isaiah, too, knew how to suit the sound to the thought. The very repetition of the same sound and even the same word, which would be so offensive were it undertaken by any one other than one of the world's masters of words, gives us the full impression of the terrible, swift advance of great armies.

With Jehovah's rebuke the figure changes to express the change in that figured. The armies are no longer rushing masses, like mighty waters, but multitudes of driven individuals, like chaff before the wind of the mountain threshing floor, like dust before the storm-wind. No longer have we the uproar of many peoples (hamon ammim rabbim), but the chaff before the wind and the whirl of dust before the storm-wind (mots liphne-ruach and galgal liphne supha). Then the whole fate of the scattered army is summed up: —

> At eventime, and behold terror!
> Not yet morning; they are not.[2]

Isaiah's power of emotional suggestion is exemplified also in his prophecy concerning the Ethiopian embassy: —

---

[1] *E.g.* Iliad A 34.

βῆ δάκέων παρὰ θῖνα πολυφλοίσβοιο θαλάσσης,

She went in silence along the shore of the loud roaring sea.

[2] Seeking to give the terse effect of the Hebrew by a slavishly literal translation.

M

> Hoy, land of whirring wings,
> Which is beyond the rivers of Cush;
> That sendeth envoys by the sea,
> In vessels of reed upon waters.

The creepy effect of the opening mourners' cry is heightened by the description of the far distant land where the air is resonant with the superabundant insect life of the tropics. It suggests lonesome, dank, impenetrable regions.

Literary qualities somewhat similar to those of the prophecies just considered are seen also in the "burden of the valley of vision,"[1] the exact occasion of which is uncertain. The picturing of the tumult in the city, of the prophet's anguish; of the breaches in the wall with the houses torn down to repair the holes, of the mad revelry of the people — "Let us eat and drink," they say, "for to-morrow we shall die"— is all in Isaiah's style, as is also the sudden contrast at the close — Surely this iniquity shall not be purged from you till ye die, saith the Lord Jehovah of hosts.

As a matter of sober history, Sennacherib suddenly withdrew from Palestine and Jerusalem was spared, though not through aid of Egypt. Whatever the immediate cause, Isaiah's faith was vindicated and the prestige of Jerusalem as Jehovah's unconquerable dwelling place was greatly enhanced. Isaiah's fame too was established, and many later prophecies were added to the rather fragmentary literary remains of his long and eventful ministry. Such, for example, are the dooms pronounced upon Babylon, the oppressing city, given in chapters 13 and 14. They would have been meaningless to the contemporaries of Isaiah the son of Amoz.

All of Isaiah's genuine prophecies are to be found in chapters 1–35 of the book bearing the prophet's name. To this collection of prophecies, most of which were written or spoken by Isaiah, was added a narrative section in which Isaiah figures prominently, chapters 36–39. These narratives are found almost in duplicate in 2 Kings 18 [13]–20 [19]. This was probably material preserved among the disciples of Isaiah, much as the narratives concerning Elijah were treasured by his followers.[2] The noble prophecies added to the book of Isaiah which once terminated with 36–39 will be considered in connection with the later ages from which they emanate.[3]

[1] 22 [1-14].   [2] See Chapter VI.   [3] Chapter XIX.

CHAPTER XI

(*About 722 to 680? B.C.*)

WHILE Isaiah was active in the affairs of state in Jerusalem, the prophet Micah was writing or speaking in the borderland district of Judea, near the Philistine frontier. He is, indeed, often called a younger contemporary of Isaiah.

In many respects Micah suggests the man Amos who also lived in the rural portion of Judea. His home, Maresha, was at the edge of the foothills, just above the Philistine plain, not much more than twenty miles to the westward of Amos's home at Tekoa. From Jerusalem it lay about twenty-seven miles distant, toward the southwest.[1]

Although Isaiah had attacked those who were dispossessing the small landowners, his vision was not so filled with the economic problems of the times as that of these prophets who dwelt among the poor peasants and better understood their lot. The terribly expressive figure that Micah used to describe the cruel oppression of the people is not surpassed by any of Amos's pictures.

> And I said, Hear, I pray you, ye heads of Jacob, and rulers of the house of Israel: is it not for you to know justice? ye who hate the good, and love the evil; who pluck off their skin from off them, and their flesh from off their bones; who also eat the flesh of my people, and flay their skin from off them, and break their bones, and chop them in pieces, as for the pot, and as flesh within the caldron.[2]

Amos was stirred to the depths of his nature by the moral obliquity of a people who could say that Jehovah was with them, while they trampled upon the poor,[3] and Micah was no less deeply moved by the sight of those who used high and responsible position for mercenary ends, and yet leaned upon the Lord, saying, "Is not

---

[1] For description of the region, see Kent, *Biblical Geography and History*, p. 186 f.   [2] 3 1-3.   [3] Amos 5 11-14.

Jehovah in the midst of us, no evil shall come upon us.[1] Such moral perversity, with its natural accompaniment of hatred and opposition to all who saw and taught moral truth, greatly roused both these teachers of elemental righteousness.[2]

Micah's song of woe to the land-monopolists is highly suggestive of Isaiah's.[3]

> Woe to those who devise wrong on their couch,[4]
> With morning light they perform it,
> Since 'tis in their power.
> They covet fields and grasp,
> Yea houses, and take them away.
> They wrong master and house,
> Yea,[5] a man and his heritage.[6]

Yet, both in spirit and thought, we find Micah more closely kindred with Amos than with Isaiah. Such a passage as this might easily have been written by Amos, who indignantly repudiated the insinuation of the Bethel priest that he was prophesying as a means of livelihood. Both the insinuation and hot denial may be more fully appreciated after noting Micah's picture of the professional prophets "that make my people to err; that bite with their teeth, and cry, Peace; and whoso putteth not into their mouths they even prepare war against him."[7]

In clear moral insight into the conditions of their times, in bold and stern denunciation of evil, and also in power of concrete picturing and the use of homely, effective illustrations, these two champions of the common people were kindred spirits. Though Micah may have been familiar with the teaching of his greater predecessor, he was no mere imitator; his thought and his style were his own.

In one passage he gives one of the most remarkable series of plays upon names that was ever devised. It is one of the instances in which we see that the Hebrew punned not as a witty exercise, but for the purpose of making his thought pierce dull ears. Canon Farrar has thus attempted to represent it in English: —

[1] Micah 3 [11].   [2] Amos 5 [10], Micah 2 [6].   [3] See p. 146.
[4] Kittel, *Bib. Heb.* Note *in loc.*   [5] Kittel, *Bib. Heb. in loc.*
[6] Micah 2 [1-2].   [7] Micah 3 [5].

'In Gath (Tell-town) tell it not;
In Akko (Weep-town) weep not!
In Beth-le-Aphrah (Dust-town) roll thyself in dust.
Pass by, thou inhabitress of Shaphir (Fair-town) in nakedness and
    shame!
The citizen of Zaanan (March-town) marched not forth.
The mourning of Bethezel (Neighbour-town) taketh from you its stand-
    ing-place.
The inhabitress of Maroth (Bitter-town) is in travail about good,
Because evil hath come down from Jehovah to the gate of Jerusalem.
Bind the chariot to the swift horse, thou inhabitress of Lachish (Horse-
    town);
She was the beginning of sin for the daughter of Zion,
For the transgressions of Israel were found in thee.
Therefore wilt thou (Oh Zion) give dismissal (farewell presents) to Mor-
    esheth-Gath (The Possession of Gath).
The houses of Achzib (False-spring) become Achzab (a disappointing
    brook) to Israel's kings.
Yet will I bring the heir (namely, Sargon, king of Assyria) to thee, thou
    citizen of Mareshah (Heir-town).
Unto Adullam (the wild beasts' cave) shall the glory of Israel come!
Make thyself bald (O Zion) for the children of thy delight.
Enlarge thy baldness as the vulture,
For they are gone into captivity from thee. [1]

It was not Micah's lot to give the world its first formulated
statement of some great, epoch-making truth, as Amos and Hosea
did, nor to awe with the splendor of his rhetoric and poetry as
Isaiah. He was the least of the four eighth-century prophets,
but he was not an unworthy member of that glorious company,
even though he gave us only chapters 1 to 3 of the book bearing
his name.

In regard to the remainder of the book, it must be acknowledged
that chapters 4 and 5 are, in form and thought, much more like
the Jewish writings of a later age than those of the eighth or even
the seventh century prophets. They were probably composed
at a much later date. It is generally admitted further, that that
chapters 6 and 7 could not have been written until after 685 B.C.,
when Manasseh succeeded Hezekiah. They reflect a time when

---

[1] Farrar, *Minor Prophets*, pp. 130–131.

the statutes of Omri are kept and all the works of the house of Ahab;[1] when the prince asketh for a reward;[2] when one cannot trust in neighbor, friend, or wife.[3] All the sources unite in representing Hezekiah as obedient to the divine instruction given by the prophets Isaiah and Micah, so that the words of chapters 6 and 7 seem more suitable to the times of moral and religious reaction introduced by Manasseh than to any of the later years of Hezekiah's reign. It may well be, however, that these chapters, at least as far as 7 [6], were written by Micah before Manasseh succeeded in drowning the voice of true prophecy with the stream of martyr's blood that he caused to flow.[4]

If Micah did write chapter 6, he is to be credited with a piece of dramatic dialogue unsurpassed in prophetic literature. The writer of this wonderful bit grasped the vital part of the message of Amos, Hosea, and Isaiah, and formulated it into a well-nigh perfect statement of human duty: What doth Jehovah require of thee, but to do justly, and to love kindness, and to walk humbly with thy God?[5] Whoever wrote those words is to be credited with one of the most perfect, diamond-like utterances ever made. Hardly a word could be added and none could be taken from it. Mercy without justice is corrupting; justice without mercy is horrible; both without humility are detestable. Can one match this winged word in any literature? We think only and inevitably of the supreme insight which combined the commands from Deuteronomy and Leviticus and gave the whole law in two words that were one: Thou shalt love the Lord thy God with all thy heart, and soul, and strength, and mind, and thy neighbor as thyself.

The opening section of the dramatic dialogue of Micah 6 which culminates at verse 8 is: —

Hear ye now what Jehovah saith: Arise, contend thou before the mountains, and let the hills hear thy voice. Hear, O ye mountains, Jehovah's controversy, and ye enduring foundations of the earth; for Jehovah hath a controversy with his people, and he will contend with Israel. O my people, what have I done unto thee? and wherein have I

---

[1] Micah 6 [16].   [2] Micah 7 [3].   [3] Micah 7 [5].

[4] Kent (Sermons, Epistles, and Apocalypses of Israel's Prophets, p. 145 f.) thinks that chapter 6 may be as early as 701.   [5] 6 [8].

wearied thee? testify against me. For I brought thee up out of the land of Egypt, and redeemed thee out of the house of bondage; and I sent before thee Moses, Aaron, and Miriam. O my people, remember now what Balak king of Moab devised, and what Balaam the son of Beor answered him; remember from Shittim unto Gilgal, that ye may know the righteous acts of Jehovah.

Wherewith shall I come before Jehovah, and bow myself before the high God? shall I come before him with burnt-offerings, with calves a year old? will Jehovah be pleased with thousands of rams, or with ten thousands of rivers of oil? shall I give my first-born for my transgression, the fruit of my body for the sin of my soul? He hath showed thee, O man, what is good; and what doth Jehovah require of thee, but to do justly and to love kindness, and to walk humbly with thy God?

The first verses suggest a great assize with the everlasting hills judges. Canaan's mountains and hills were ever instinct with life to the ancient Hebrew prophet and poet. The fancy of the Greek peopled every grove and cave with nymph and satyr, and every majestic object in nature with its god or gods. Such fancies filled the world with fascinating mystery and poetry; we enter into the delight as we may do playfully into the imaginations of a child, but after all, it's a child's life and not ours, and we soon put it off for maturer things.

The personifying of the great objects of nature to which the Hebrew prophet and poet invite is something larger and more mature. His loftier religious thought kept the fancy of Israel's poet within bounds. This distinguished him from other Semites as well as from men of different race. His cousin, the bedouin Arab of the desert, even down to the present day when he is supposed to worship only Allah, has ever peopled all things with spirits innumerable. His other cousins, the wonderfully civilized people of Babylonia, let their fancy run riot in picturing Tiamat, black chaos, mother of horrible brood, or the demon of the northwest wind with his hard-cut, sharp features and wicked grin, or their whole pantheon of gods of sun and moon, of air and water, of this place and that place. The fervid imagination of Hebrew prophet and poet, though it did not always confine itself to our standards of unity ran no such riot.

As the Hebrew prophets were gradually learning to think of

one God, spirit unpicturable, over all, through all, and in all, such childlike fancies as those of Greek and Babylonian were early outgrown; yet nature did not become to them a prose waste of blind law. The mountains, winds, water, and stars above were not gods, not peopled with gods or demigods; they were living realities, now rejoicing or trembling at the presence of the Almighty, now doing his will in beneficent purpose toward his children; now listening as majestic court while God himself deigns to plead his cause against his recreant people.

Is it fanciful to count the Hebrew poets, in their treatment of nature, far nearer to the poets of the nineteenth century and the philosophers of the twentieth than were those of other ancient peoples? To Wordsworth and Tennyson nature is not peopled with spirits but is itself living, and the life in it all is the life of God. Our philosophy to-day tends to find one principle of life in all things visible and thinkable. If it finds God at all, it finds him not distinct from nature, but immanent in all. So it comes about that even in this machine-made, science-swept-and-garnished age of ours we can without too much effort enter into the fancy of the poet as he writes: Arise, contend thou before the mountains, and let the hills hear thy voice.

The poet does not describe the outward appearance of God who comes to plead with his people, but he ventures to represent him speaking in his own person and in accents deep and tender: "O my people, what have I done unto thee? and wherein have I wearied thee?" and he goes on to recall his guardian care in the past. The people in sudden penitence ask: "Wherewith shall I come before Jehovah?" The prophet answers in his own person: "He hath showed thee, O man, what is good."

Next we hear the voice of Jehovah crying unto the city: "Are there yet treasures of wickedness in the house of the wicked, and a scant ephah that is abominable? Shall I be pure with wicked balances and with a bag of deceitful weights?" We are reminded strongly of Amos, who had especially condemned the small ephah measure and the balances of deceit with which the merchants of his day dealt. The prophet goes on to threaten: "Thou shalt sow, but shalt not reap; thou shalt tread the olives, but shalt not anoint with oil; and the vintage, but shalt not drink the wine."

We are still further reminded of the earlier prophet of doom who had told the wealthy oppressors of the poor that though they had built houses of hewn stone they should not dwell in them, and though they had planted pleasant vineyards they should not drink the wine thereof.[1]

The song of lament that follows is most effective in its opening:—

> Woe, woe is me, for I have become
> Like the gatherings of harvest, like the gleanings of the vintage:
> Not a cluster to eat,
> Not a fig that any one desires.[2]

Whether actually written by the youngest of the eighth-century prophets or by a later hand, the section Micah 6 1–7 6 is the appropriate conclusion of eighth-century prophecy which we must count one of the most significant movements in the history of human thought. It was a movement which comes closer to the most vital thinking of the present day than almost any other that we can name in ancient literature.

As in the slow evolution of physical life there comes, at times, a sudden leap when accumulated forces manifest themselves, so in the slow progress of thought there come sudden outflowerings when the pent up forces of the spirit find splendid expression. The comparatively crude, but profoundly significant moral interpretations of history seen in the Judean and Ephraimite narratives of the ninth and early eighth centuries, and, more especially, in the work of the great Elijah of the ninth century indicate the gathering forces. Among the conditions that tended to bring to outflowering the growing moral insight of Hebrew prophets, we must count the foreign influences of Ahab's court; the national expansion when Syrian and Assyrian pressure were temporarily withdrawn, with the opportunity that this expansion gave for sudden luxury and monopolistic developments, and for their accompanying bribery and graft in the state and its church; and, finally, the new advance of Assyria, with the fall of Syria and then of Northern Israel.

---

[1] Amos 5 11.

[2] Translation of Kent in *Sermons, Epistles, and Apocalypses of Israel's Prophets*.

Israel stood in peculiar relation to her God. Other Semitic peoples worshipped a god originally belonging either to the particular tribe or the district in which they lived. Jehovah had entered into voluntary relations with these tribes and had, through long struggle with Dagan, Chemosh, and the Baalim of the Canaanites, vindicated his power in the land. But, before Amos's time, he had not been definitely conceived as one who ruled in the affairs of other lands and nations, save as the champion of his chosen people. We see in the tenth-century narrative that, if David is driven across the border of Judea, he is thought of as cut off from the possibility of worshipping Jehovah.[1] The thought is similar to that of the Syrian officer who cannot worship Jehovah unless he has a little Palestinian earth in Syria.[2] In the ninth-century narrative, Jacob is represented as crying out, "Jehovah is in this place and I knew it not."[3] In the narrative of Judges Jephthah speaks to Ammon[4] of the land which Chemosh their god had given them, as Jehovah had given a land to Israel.[5] Elijah felt that to get closest contact with his God he must go to Horeb. It was a slow, hard lesson to learn that the God of Sinai was able to rule the land of Canaan. The advance from this to the thought of him as God of nations, caring even for Moab's treatment of Edom, using self-confident Assyria as the rod of his anger, purposing to bring Egypt and Assyria to worship him, was one of the most stupendous that the history of human thought records. Two centuries after Amos's time, the exiles in Babylonia still had no grasp of this conception; in the early years of exile, many of Ezekiel's visions were directed to convincing his contemporaries that Jehovah had come to Babylon with them, while the marvellous literary gifts of the prophet of the closing years of exile were again and again put to their utmost stretch in emphasizing the power of Jehovah as above that of the Babylonian gods.

Yet, in the middle of the eighth century B.C., the herdsman of Tekoa grasped the thought of a God of nations and presented it in majestic form. Israel was about to feel the full force of her position between the rival centres of world power, when Amos

---

[1] Samuel 26 [19].   [2] 2 Kings 5 [17].   [3] Genesis 28 [16].
[4] Properly Moab, whose god Chemosh is.   Milcom is the god of Ammon. See Moore, *Judges, in loc. Enc. Bib.* § Chemosh.   [5] Judges 11 [24].

made his great affirmation of one God ruling in the movements of nations. The extending of Jehovah's rule from Sinai to Canaan, and from his earlier worshippers to tribes that had not known him, had prepared the way for the sudden leap in Amos's great affirmation.

The fact that Jehovah was not originally the God of Israel, but had voluntarily elected this people, had entered into covenant with them, and they with h m, gave a peculiar possibility of demands in his name. Though Chemosh might be angry with his people and permit them to suffer loss for a time,[1] he could not cast them off altogether; the relation between them was inherent. This was true generally of the Semitic peoples; their gods were bound to the particular tribes. On the other hand, Jehovah and Israel had entered into voluntary contract. When Israel broke this, he might cast her off absolutely.[2] When therefore Amos affirmed a just God ruling over the nations, dealing with them according to their righteousness, he could denounce complete destruction upon them on the very ground of their relation to that God — You only have I known of all the families of the earth; therefore I will visit upon you all your iniquities.[3] The only hope lay in a complete change on Israel's part from injustice to justice in all her social, economic, and religious life.

Through personal experience, interpreted in the light of closest sympathy with national needs, Hosea came to see that hope lay only in Jehovah's unchangeable choice of love; but he saw, too, the deeper lesson that love is powerless unless it can win a voluntary response. It can, through tender care and stern restraint, seek to purify and bring to a new appreciation, but until answering love comprehends love, even God can do nought but restrain and wait.

The great forward movements of history for the past twenty-six centuries have been movements toward the ideals of Amos and Hosea. This is clearly manifest in the history of Jewish and Christian religion. Amos made religion ethical. The work of

---

[1] See Moabite Stone, p. 89.

[2] For further discussion of the peculiar relation of Israel and Yahweh, see Budde, *Religion of Israel to the Exile*, especially pp. 35–38; Marti, *Religion of the Old Testament*, pp. 56–66.   [3] Amos 3 [2].

John the Baptist and of Jesus Christ was to make religion ethical. The great struggle going on in the church of to-day concerns the fundamentally ethical character of religion. In the spirit of Amos, and of Christ himself, Christianity is coming to recognize that its mission includes the establishment of justice between man and man, between nation and nation.[1] Amos, and Isaiah after him, saw that all worship from a people practising injustice in economic and political affairs is hateful to God. Christ Jesus taught the same truth with his deeper interpretation of humanity as composed of neighbors and brothers. Paul, interpreting the spirit of Christ for his generation, broke the bonds of ritualism that would have kept Christianity a sect of Judaism. Luther worked as a disciple of Paul, and, in the nineteenth century, the same forward movement has given us Reformed Judaism. To-day, in the Jewish church as in the Christian, there is a sharp division between those who make religious organization and its ritual requirements fundamental and those who count these only means, good so far as they help toward the end which Amos,

---

[1] Since writing the present chapter, it has been the writer's privilege to read, in proof, the first part of the forthcoming book by Louis Wallis, on The *Sociological Study of the Bible*. As the title suggests, this writer approaches the study of the Bible from the sociologist's view point. After quoting from Walker, *Religious Life in New England*, a description of the transformation from the conception of "Christianity as an agency for individual rescue and salvation" to the thought of its function "as the savior of society," he adds: "The change of emphasis thus described is due, primarily, not to intellectual or spiritual or theoretical causes, but to the increasing pressure of the social problem. And since the religion of the Bible has the social character just noted, the social awakening of the church brings it into a new attitude with reference to the Bible. The conditions of religious life and thought are now in process of rapid change; and there is growing interest in Bible-study from the ethical and social standpoints. In this field a great surprise awaits the rank and file of the church. For if the modern scientific school of Bible scholarship had been expressly raised up for the purpose of guiding and controlling the new social thought of the church, it could scarcely have had a better preparation for the task now looming before it. The new view of the Bible, which prevails at all the great centres of learning, is in harmony with the present social awakening in the religious world; whereas the older, traditional view of the Bible agrees equally with the former, one-sided emphasis upon individualism." — Part I, Introduction.

Isaiah, and Christ placed unequivocally above organization and ritual.

If this is clear within the religious bodies, it is hardly less plain outside, in the whole story of the progress of economic and political life. In our own day, as in centuries gone, many who own no allegiance to Christian or Jewish church give heart and life to the realization of the ideal of Amos — let justice roll down as waters and righteousness as a perennial stream. In the story of the upward progress of humanity it was Amos who first made this principle on which human society depends, the recognized demand for the relation of social class to social class and of nation to nation.

Hosea saw that the fundamental difficulty with Israel was incapacity to apprehend the love of God. He saw, in a measure at least, that Israel's salvation must be through fellowship with the God of love, and that the brutish insensibility of Israel made God's higher blessing of her just as impossible as true marriage fellowship between himself and his lewd wife, as impossible as true parental and filial fellowship between a fostering father and a wandering son. Christ Jesus came to make fellowship between child and Father possible. The Gospel of John, which especially emphasizes this side of Jesus's mission and which declares that such understanding fellowship is eternal life,[1] is the perfect sequel of the book of Hosea.

The Reformers of the sixteenth century did not see the truth given by Hosea and developed in John's picture of Christ, or permitted it to be obscured by other emphasis. The most advanced Christian thinking of to-day is just beginning to give full weight to this deep interpretation of life in its greatness, that was first given by Hosea, was made palpable in Jesus Christ, fully stated only in the Gospel of John, and is now at last becoming central in Christian thought and endeavor. The modern study of the Gospel story and the modern study of the nature of mental life are uniting to bring Hosea's thought to prominence in the thinking of many.[2]

In these and other phases of the thinking of the eighth-century prophets, it is not difficult to support the claim that the best social

---

[1] John 17 [2].

[2] For illustration see, for example, *The Atoning Life*, by Henry S. Nash.

and religious thinking of to-day is moving in the channels first clearly indicated by Israel's prophets of the eighth century B.C. We have already noted that their interpretation of nature never fully came to its own till the poets of the nineteenth century wrote; we add to this that their interpretation of life never came to its own among any large number of men, till the great economic and religious crises of the present age called hundreds and thousands of devoted men and women to give their lives to making real in individual and society the ideals of Israel's prophets.

CHAPTER XII

Deuteronomy

(*Before 621*)

LAW-BOOKS do not usually form a part of literature, but there was a law-book written in Israel which cannot be omitted from any historical survey of the nation's literature. Its influence upon the form and spirit of later writing was revolutionary, and, in itself, it is an attractive literary work, infused with sublime ideas nobly expressed. When the historical origin of the book is realized, its quality ceases to be wholly inexplicable.

We have seen how the eighth-century prophets started currents of thought that made their half-century one of the most notable in the progress of the world's thinking. These currents were such as touch the springs of human emotion in many ways; but, early in the next century, all public expression of this thought was suddenly checked by a great reactionary movement. The nation could not be carried forward from its lower ideas with such a rush as the prophetic outburst of the eighth century demanded. When King Hezekiah died in 686, there came to the throne his twelve-year-old son Manasseh, who evidently fell under the control of the anti-prophetic party which succeeded in rousing this great reactionary movement. Tradition has it that Isaiah was sawn asunder during this reign. We have already seen some indication that Micah lived till this time and cried out against the corruption of all classes of society. If so, he probably suffered a martyr's death; Manasseh's reign is chiefly notable for its bloody persecution of the prophets of Jehovah and its reinstatement of the practices which they had denounced.[1]

[1] 2 Kings 21 [1-18], Jeremiah 2 [30], 15 [4].

The reaction is not difficult of explanation. The prophets had not simply enunciated revolutionary theological ideas; they had applied their ideas of God's justice and mercy to the entire civic, economic, social, and religious life of their day. In emphasizing these principles they had opposed powerful and unscrupulous business and political interests and had minimized or denounced time-honored forms of religious worship. When Hezekiah carried out his reforms under the influence of Isaiah and Micah, it was as though, to-day, those who believe that the religion of a just and merciful God means the suppression of special privilege should get control of all government long enough to put out the "grafters" and largely to break up oppressive monopolies of all sorts, and as though they should say to those orthodox Christians who have no sympathy with the great social and ethical awakening of the time, "All your prayers and hymns are loathesome to God; away with them. What he demands is not these things, but rather to do justly, love mercy, and walk humbly with him." With Manasseh's accession, it was as though, following this, all who believe that religion is primarily a matter of institutions and ceremonies and that revolutionary ideas in religion are necessarily wrong, with the "grafters" and monopolists, should come back to complete control.

Some elements of the situation we can hardly imagine in our day. Those who had stood for a religion that expressed itself in putting down bribery and monopoly were put to death, if they so much as taught their doctrines. The reform has utterly failed; government, as well as business, social, and religious life all seem in worse state than before it was undertaken. Some true and earnest souls have seen a great light and have faith in the ultimate outcome; if they do anything to carry their doctrines into immediate effect, their blood flows in the streets of Jerusalem. Many bear witness through death; others labor secretly, formulating into detailed and practical working shape for the everyday life of their countrymen the ideals which the prophets have set forth and have tried to apply whole.

These chastened reformers have ready at hand a brief code of laws dealing with religious, social, and economic practices based upon just principles, so far as it goes. This code has been itself a slow growth ; it includes elements of great antiquity, it is already embodied in the national history, and is revered by the nation. They make this code the basis of their work.[1] In one important respect they must make a change, for which the division of the kingdom and the downfall of Northern Israel, with its ancient sanctuaries, has done much to prepare the way. The old code presupposed the worship of Jehovah in many places, but experience has showed that, at the scattered local sanctuaries, his worship is wont to be mingled or confused with that of the local deities, and that debasing practices are thus associated with the worship of Jehovah. Amos had seen the situation with perfect clearness and had attacked it rough handed, after his fashion. The reformers of this century see that they must revise the old laws at this point. They accordingly leave out the part at the opening that seems to permit altars to Jehovah in any and every place,[2] and formulate definite requirements that all sacrificial worship shall be performed at the temple of Solomon.

The law of the central sanctuary is the most prominent feature of their revised code ; but they go deeper than this, for they have Hosea, as well as Amos and Isaiah, and they have given their hearts to the God of love and righteousness. The old code does not emphasize absolute devotion to God or provide for the detailed enforcement of justice and consideration between man and man. So they add new motives for the carrying out of the old laws, and they modify, expand, and add to those laws until they produce a code that is at once old and new. To this they prefix a wonderful exhortation, embodying the noblest religious and social thought ever expressed by human speech.

They cast the whole, law code as well as exhortation, in the literary form of addresses delivered by Moses. In this their age would see nothing strange. We have seen that the idea of individual authorship and proprietorship by the author of a book is relatively modern. In addition to this, their work is, after all, only a revision and expansion of earlier laws that were regarded as of Mosaic origin. Even in modern times a work may be greatly revised and expanded by later hands and yet continue to be issued

---

[1] The code is now found in Exodus 20 20 – 23 33, commonly called the "Book of the Covenant."   [2] Exodus 20 22-25.

N

under the name of the original author.[1] Again we know that among the Jewish writers a few centuries later it was a regular literary method to represent one's own thoughts as uttered by some ancient man of renown. Our book indeed was not the first example of the practice, although it may not have been carried out on so elaborate a scale before Manasseh's reign.

The weary years of Manasseh's reign grew into decades; a half century passed and still this practically pagan king lived and ruled. No opportunity appeared for giving any publicity to the new law code. When, at the end of fifty-five years of rule, the old king died full of years and cruel wickedness, his son, bearing the name of an Egyptian god, proved a ruler worthy of this ill omen. The new law-book was preserved somewhere about the temple, but its authors may have been dead and it was completely forgotten.

Happily the reign of Manasseh's son Amon is brief, and he is succeeded by his son, still a boy. The father removed, in some way this son seems to grow up under good influences. As the years go by the voice of faithful prophets is heard once more. Zephaniah and Jeremiah dare to reprove and rebuke the evils which have persisted from the reigns of Manasseh and Amon.

After a time the king, Josiah, having attained full manhood, undertakes the repair of the temple which has fallen into sad estate. During these repairs the law-book, written in Manasseh's reign, is brought to light. When it is read to the king, he is deeply moved. He cannot fail to see how utterly different its provisions are from the practices of the land. He is moved to undertake a great reform of the nation, based upon this law. Such, in general, is the history of the writing and first publication of the Book of Deuteronomy as it is read to-day by the student of Israel's literary and religious history.[2]

Now, for the first time, there was a thoroughgoing attempt to centralize the nation's worship in Jerusalem. Whatever Hezekiah

[1] When the present writer entered college, he had a new *Webster's Unabridged Dictionary*. It was fully twice as large as the *Webster's Unabridged* that his father had in his college days; yet Noah Webster had died before that earlier edition was published.

[2] The law book as composed before 621 B.C. did not include more than chapters 5–26, 28 of the present book of Deuteronomy.

may have done in this direction,[1] his zeal did not extend to the destruction of the high places that Solomon had built before Jerusalem for the foreign deities.[2] Prior to Josiah's reform in 621 B.C., Israel's greatest religious leaders show no knowledge of the central requirement of Deuteronomy that all sacrificial worship shall be limited to the Jerusalem temple.

The great hortatory address of chapters 5–11 begins with the writer's statement that "Moses called unto all Israel and said unto them"; but from this point on the address is given in the first person. It begins : —

Hear, O Israel, the statutes and the ordinances which I speak in your ears this day, that ye may learn them, and observe to do them. Jehovah our God made a covenant with us in Horeb. Jehovah made not this covenant with our fathers, but with us, even us, who are all of us here alive this day. Jehovah spake with you face to face in the mount out of the midst of the fire (I stood between Jehovah and you at that time, to show you the word of Jehovah : for ye were afraid because of the fire, and went not up nto the mount), saying,

With verse 6 begin ten commandments, slightly modified from the familiar form in which they appear in Exodus 20.[3] The most notable difference is found in the motive assigned for observing the Sabbath day, in the third commandment. Deuteronomy reads : —

Observe the sabbath day, to keep it holy, as Jehovah thy God commanded thee. Six days shalt thou labor, and do all thy work; but the seventh day is a sabbath unto Jehovah thy God : in it thou shalt not do any work, thou, nor thy son, nor thy daughter, nor thy man-servant, nor thy maid-servant, nor thine ox, nor thine ass, nor any of thy cattle, nor thy stranger that is within thy gates; that thy man-servant and thy maid-servant may rest as well as thou. And thou shalt remember that thou wast a servant in the land of Egypt, and Jehovah thy God brought thee out thence by a mighty hand and by an outstretched arm : therefore Jehovah thy God commanded thee to keep the sabbath day.

The motive here given is in perfect accord with the rest of the book, in which thoughtful consideration for the rights and comfort of others is constantly manifest, and the memory of the Egyptian

[1] 2 Kings 18 [3-4]. [2] 2 Kings 23 [13]. [3] In the Ephraimite Prophetic History.

bondage is repeatedly urged as a ground for kindly treatment of the unfortunate.

Throughout the long hortatory introduction to the law proper, there is a notable emphasis on God's love for Israel, reëchoing Hosea's great truth.   We may note, for example, in chapter 7:—

but because Jehovah loveth you, and because he would keep the oath which he sware unto your fathers, hath Jehovah brought you out with a mighty hand, and redeemed you out of the house of bondage, from the hand of Pharaoh king of Egypt.   Know therefore that Jehovah thy God, he is God, the faithful God, who keepeth covenant and lovingkindness with them that love him and keep his commandments to a thousand generations, and repayeth them that hate him to their face, to destroy them: he will not be slack to him that hateth him, he will repay him to his face, and he will love thee, and bless thee, and multiply thee.[1]

Amos and Isaiah seem to speak again in the recognition of God's majesty; such, for example, as that of chapter 10.

Behold, unto Jehovah thy God belongeth heaven and the heaven of heavens, the earth, with all that is therein.   For Jehovah your God, he is God of gods, and Lord of lords, the great God, the mighty, and the terrible, who regardeth not persons, nor taketh reward.   He doth execute justice for the fatherless and widow, and loveth the sojourner, in giving him food and raiment.[2]

God's love is made the ground of demand that in turn the people love him:—

Thy fathers went down into Egypt with threescore and ten persons; and now Jehovah thy God hath made thee as the stars of heaven for multitude.

Therefore thou shalt love Jehovah thy God, and keep his charge, and his statutes, and his ordinances, and his commandments, alway.[3]

God's espousal of the cause of the defenceless is ground for mercy toward these on the part of his people.

He doth execute justice for the fatherless and widow, and loveth the sojourner, in giving him food and raiment.   Love ye therefore the sojourner; for ye were sojourners in the land of Egypt.[4]

Such generous motives are repeatedly urged in this great discourse, but perhaps almost more prominent is the motive of

[1] vv. 8–10, 13 a.   [2] vv. 14, 17–18.   [3] 10 22–11 1.   [4] 10 18–19.

national self-interest. The principle of the Divine government is presented as one of reward and punishment according to faithfulness. We should note that the interest to which appeal is made is not personal but national. The thought of Israel's prophetic writers has not yet reached the stage of clearly marked individualism. Hosea had not pictured God as loving the individual, but the nation — that was his wife, his son; and Deuteronomy makes its appeal to national self-interest rather than individual motives.

All the commandment which I command thee this day shall ye observe to do, that ye may live, and multiply, and go in and possess the land which Jehovah sware unto your fathers. And it shall be, if thou shalt forget Jehovah thy God, and walk after other gods, and serve them, and worship them, I testify against you this day that ye shall surely perish. As the nations that Jehovah maketh to perish before you, so shall ye perish; because ye would not hearken unto the voice of Jehovah your God.[1]

The subsequent experience of the nation was of a character to burn deep into the consciousness of the people the doctrine of Deuteronomy, that the national prosperity and especially the possession of the land were contingent upon faithfulness to Jehovah. The result was that for a time this idea became as dominant in the literature of Israel as the doctrine of evolution is in the thought of to-day.

Under the influence of Deuteronomy it was natural that faithfulness to Jehovah should be interpreted in terms of the law of the central sanctuary; so the subsequent age that had lost the superb moral fervor and insight of the great age of prophecy tested conduct once more in terms of ritual rather than justice, kindness, and humility. Such a change is inevitable when the noblest ethical and spiritual thought becomes dogma.

In the book of Deuteronomy itself, in the law code as well as in the great exhortation of chapters 5–11, the profound moral and spiritual life of the great eighth-century prophets still throbs through the whole. Such laws as these may serve to illustrate : —

Thou shalt not see thy brother's ox or his sheep go astray, and hide thyself from them : thou shalt surely bring them again unto thy brother.

[1] 8 1 19-20, cf. 7 12-16 11 8-9, 13-17 22-25.

And if thy brother be not nigh unto thee, or if thou know him not, then thou shalt bring it home to thy house, and it shall be with thee until thy brother seek after it, and thou shalt restore it to him.   And so shalt thou do with his ass; and so shalt thou do with his garment; and so shalt thou do with every lost thing of thy brother's, which he hath lost, and thou hast found: thou mayest not hide thyself.   Thou shalt not see thy brother's ass or his ox fallen down by the way, and hide thyself from them: thou shalt surely help him to lift them up again.

When thou buildest a new house, then thou shalt make a battlement for thy roof, that thou bring not blood upon thy house, if any man fall from thence.[1]

Thou shalt not oppress a hired servant that is poor and needy, whether he be of thy brethren, or of thy sojourners that are in thy land within thy gates: in his day thou shalt give him his hire, neither shall the sun go down upon it (for he is poor, and setteth his heart upon it); lest he cry against thee unto Jehovah, and it be sin unto thee.

Thou shalt not wrest the justice due to the sojourner, or to the father-less, nor take the widow's raiment to pledge; but thou shalt remember that thou wast a bondman in Egypt, and Jehovah thy God redeemed thee thence: therefore I command thee to do this thing.

When thou reapest thy harvest in thy field, and hast forgot a sheaf in the field, thou shalt not go again to fetch it: it shall be for the sojourner, for the fatherless, and for the widow; that Jehovah thy God may bless thee in all the work of thy hands.   When thou beatest thine olive-tree, thou shalt not go over the boughs again: it shall be for the sojourner, for the fatherless, and for the widow.   When thou gatherest the grapes of thy vineyard, thou shalt not glean it after thee: it shall be for the sojourner, for the fatherless, and for the widow.   And thou shalt remember that thou wast a bondman in the land of Egypt; therefore I command thee to do this thing. [2]

Amos found a people who really thought that Jehovah was bound to bless them just because they were his people and were offering sacrifices to him.   In his emphasis upon the moral quality of religion in contrast to the people's thought and practice, he flouted all forms of worship.   In this extreme attitude, he was largely followed by Hosea, Isaiah, and Micah; the newly apprehended truths must be burned into the hearts of the people.   This is ever the work of the prophet; his contemporaries style him a fanatic, but if he is to do the work of a prophet, he cannot stop to

[1] 22 1-4, 8.   [2] 24 14-15, 17-18, 19-22.

weigh and appraise his truth in its relation to other truths. If he be a true prophet, his truth is *the* truth that his hearers must learn, and the time for its modification and limitation by other truths, and for its proper placement in the hierarchy of permanent principles will come later.

In the seventh-century work of Deuteronomy, we have not only an attempt to interpret into workable form for everyday life the moral and spiritual principles of the eighth-century prophets; we have also a comprehensive attempt to synthesize these with the worship elements of life. Here it is no longer "kindness and not sacrifice" but kindness and sacrifice, or, more significant than that, kindness *in* sacrifice.

Seven weeks shalt thou number unto thee : from the time thou beginnest to put the sickle to the standing grain shalt thou begin to number seven weeks. And thou shalt keep the feast of weeks unto Jehovah thy God with a tribute of a freewill-offering of thy hand, which thou shalt give, according as Jehovah thy God blesseth thee : and thou shalt rejoice before Jehovah thy God, thou, and thy son, and thy daughter, and thy man-servant, and thy maid-servant, and the Levite that is within thy gates, and the sojourner, and the fatherless, and the widow, that are in the midst of thee, in the place which Jehovah thy God shall choose, to cause his name to dwell there. And thou shalt remember that thou wast a bondman in Egypt: and thou shalt observe and do these statutes.

Thou shalt keep the feast of tabernacles seven days, after that thou hast gathered in from thy threshing-floor and from thy winepress: and thou shalt rejoice in thy feast, thou, and thy son, and thy daughter, and thy man-servant, and thy maid-servant, and the Levite, and the sojourner, and the fatherless, and the widow, that are within thy gates.[1]

And, now, behold, I have brought the first of the fruit of the ground, which thou, O Jehovah, hast given me. And thou shalt set it down before Jehovah thy God, and worship before Jehovah thy God: and thou shalt rejoice in all the good which Jehovah thy God hath given unto thee, and unto thy house, thou, and the Levite, and the sojourner that is in the midst of thee.

When thou hast made an end of tithing all the tithe of thine increase in the third year, which is the year of tithing, then thou shalt give it unto the Levite, to the sojourner, to the fatherless, and to the widow, that they may eat within thy gates, and be filled.[2]

[1] 16 9–14.   [2] 26 10–12.

Heretofore, it would seem that the prophetic element in Israel's religion had developed almost independently of the priestly element; the inevitable conflict of the two was hardly foreshadowed until prophecy reached its sudden maturity. Then came the marvellous synthesis of the next century which seems, for the moment, to make possible the dwelling together of the two in perfect harmony; but Deuteronomy is after all, at its heart and centre, a law code, and law is by its nature the ally of priest rather than of prophet. When, in the latter part of the seventh century, Deuteronomy becomes the inspiration and guide of Josiah's reform, reawakened prophecy suddenly becomes ominously silent[1] and the history of the reform records almost exclusively purification and centralization of worship.[2] The spiritual and moral requirements of Deuteronomy are amenable to royal decree in only a very limited extent. Thus, when the book first becomes effective, as well as in its influence upon Israel's later literature, the priestly elements of Deuteronomy, rather than the prophetic, are emphasized. Deuteronomy grows out of the brief age of prophecy, but foreshadows the long "night of legalism."

In its language and style, Deuteronomy is fully as influential in the literary history of Israel as it is in thought. Very rarely will any one familiar with the flavor of Israel's earlier prose and with Deuteronomy be in any doubt as to whether a piece of Hebrew narrative antedates or follows the publication of Deuteronomy in 621 B.C. In the only important instance where historical students of Israel's literature have not yet come to substantial agreement, the document in question is of essentially the same age as Deuteronomy, so that the only uncertainty is whether it was directly influenced by Deuteronomy or, slightly antedating it, was the outgrowth of the same era.[3]

The imaginary addresses of Deuteronomy are singularly different in style from the actual addresses of Amos and Isaiah or any other of Israel's great public speakers. Deuteronomy has its own glories of style, but they are not those of Israel's oratory. Compare, for example, the burning utterances of Amos, in his

---

[1] See p. 200.   [2] 2 Kings 23 [1-25].
[3] The late Samuel document.   See pp. 207–211.

fourth address, with the words ascribed to Moses contemplating the immediate passage of the Jordan.

Hear ye this word which I take up for a lamentation over you, O house of Israel. The virgin of Israel is fallen; she shall no more rise: she is cast down upon her land; there is none to raise her up. For thus saith the Lord Jehovah: The city that went forth a thousand shall have a hundred left, and that which went forth a hundred shall have ten left, to the house of Israel.

For thus saith Jehovah unto the house of Israel, Seek ye me, and ye shall live; but seek not Bethel, nor enter into Gilgal, and pass not to Beersheba: for Gilgal shall surely go into captivity, and Bethel shall come to nought. Seek Jehovah, and ye shall live; lest he break out like fire in the house of Joseph, and it devour, and there be none to quench it in Bethel. Ye who turn justice to wormwood, and cast down righteousness to the earth, seek him that maketh the Pleiades and Orion, and turneth the shadow of death into the morning, and maketh the day dark with night; that calleth for the waters of the sea, and poureth them out upon the face of the earth (Jehovah is his name); that bringeth sudden destruction upon the strong, so that destruction cometh upon the fortress.[1]

All the commandment which I command thee this day shall ye observe to do, that ye may live, and multiply, and go in and possess the land which Jehovah sware unto your fathers. And thou shalt remember all the way which Jehovah thy God hath led thee these forty years in the wilderness, that he might humble thee, to prove thee, to know what was in thy heart, whether thou wouldest keep his commandments, or not. And he humbled thee, and suffered thee to hunger, and fed thee with manna, which thou knewest not, neither did thy fathers know; that he might make thee know that man doth not live by bread only, but by everything that proceedeth out of the mouth of Jehovah doth man live. Thy raiment waxed not old upon thee, neither did thy foot swell, these forty years. And thou shalt consider in thy heart, that, as a man chasteneth his son, so Jehovah thy God chasteneth thee. And thou shalt keep the commandments of Jehovah thy God, to walk in his ways, and to fear him. For Jehovah thy God bringeth thee into a good land, a land of brooks of water, of fountains and springs, flowing forth in valleys and hills; a land of wheat and barley, and vines and fig-trees and pomegranates; a land of olive-trees and honey; a land wherein thou shalt eat bread without scarceness, thou shalt not lack anything in it; a land whose stones are iron, and out of whose hills thou mayest dig copper. And thou shalt eat and be full,

[1] Amos 5 1-9.

and thou shalt bless Jehovah thy God for the good land which he hath given thee.[1]

In contrast, Deuteronomy is leisurely and quiet; a solemn earnestness and a certain formal dignity make its quality. This is perhaps even more noticeable in one of the noblest passages of the book, compared by way of contrast, with the great arraignment of Isaiah 1.

Hear, O Israel: Jehovah our God is one Jehovah: and thou shalt love Jehovah thy God with all thy heart, and with all thy soul, and with all thy might. And these words, which I command thee this day, shall be upon thy heart; and thou shalt teach them diligently unto thy children, and shalt talk of them when thou sittest in thy house, and when thou walkest by the way, and when thou liest down, and when thou risest up. And thou shalt bind them for a sign upon thy hand, and they shall be for frontlets between thine eyes. And thou shalt write them upon the door-posts of thy house, and upon thy gates.

And it shall be, when Jehovah thy God shall bring thee into the land which he sware unto thy fathers, to Abraham, to Isaac, and to Jacob, to give thee great and goodly cities, which thou buildedst not, and houses full of all good things which thou filledst not, and cisterns hewn out, which thou hewedst not, vineyards and olive-trees which thou plantedst not, and thou shalt eat and be full; then beware lest thou forget Jehovah, who brought thee forth out of the land of Egypt, out of the house of bondage. Thou shalt fear Jehovah thy God: and him shalt thou serve, and shalt swear by his name. Ye shall not go after other gods, of the gods of the peoples that are round about you; for Jehovah thy God in the midst of thee is a jealous God; lest the anger of Jehovah thy God be kindled against thee, and he destroy thee from off the face of the earth.

Ye shall not tempt Jehovah your God, as ye tempted him in Massah. Ye shall diligently keep the commandments of Jehovah your God, and his testimonies, and his statutes, which he hath commanded thee. And thou shalt do that which is right and good in the sight of Jehovah; that it may be well with thee, and that thou mayest go in and possess the good land which Jehovah sware unto thy fathers, to thrust out all thine enemies from before thee, as Jehovah hath spoken.[2]

The vision of Isaiah the son of Amoz, which he saw concerning Judah and Jerusalem, in the days of Uzziah, Jotham, Ahaz, and Hezekiah, kings of Judah.

[1] Deuteronomy 8 1-10.   [2] 6 4-19.

Hear, O heavens, and give ear, O earth; for Jehovah hath spoken: I have nourished and brought up children, and they have rebelled against me. The ox knoweth his owner, and the ass his master's crib; but Israel doth not know, my people doth not consider. Ah sinful nation, a people laden with iniquity, a seed of evil-doers, children that deal corruptly! they have forsaken Jehovah, they have despised the Holy One of Israel, they are estranged and gone backward. Why will ye be still stricken, that ye revolt more and more? the whole head is sick, and the whole heart faint. From the sole of the foot even unto the head there is no soundness in it; but wounds and bruises, and fresh stripes: they have not been closed, neither bound up, neither mollified with oil. Your country is desolate; your cities are burned with fire; your land, strangers devour it in your presence, and it is desolate, as overthrown by strangers. And the daughter of Zion is left as a booth in a vineyard, as a lodge in a garden of cucumbers, as a besieged city. Except Jehovah of hosts had left unto us a very small remnant, we should have been as Sodom, we should have been like unto Gomorrah.[1]

It will be recalled that this chapter of Isaiah was counted a perfect example of the prophetic type of speech with its rapid succession of apostrophe, mandatory address, tender appeal, and glorious promise, and its wealth of figurative language. It has, too, its own dignity and rolling phrases, but its wave crests are lashed into white foam, very different from the dead-swell of Deuteronomy's deep sea.

The passage of Deuteronomy that most closely resembles the genuine oratory of Israel is that which gives the threatened consequences of disobedience, chapter 28 [15ff]. It begins: —

But it shall come to pass, if thou wilt not hearken unto the voice of Jehovah thy God, to observe to do all his commandments and his statutes which I command thee this day, that all these curses shall come upon thee, and overtake thee. Cursed shalt thou be in the city, and cursed shalt thou be in the field. Cursed shall be thy basket and thy kneading-trough. Cursed shall be the fruit of thy body, and the fruit of thy ground, the increase of thy cattle, and the young of thy flock. Cursed shalt thou be when thou comest in, and cursed shalt thou be when thou goest out.

Jehovah will send upon thee cursing, discomfiture, and rebuke, in all that thou puttest thy hand unto to do, until thou be destroyed, and until thou perish quickly; because of the evil of thy doings, whereby thou

[1] Isaiah 1 [1-9].

hast forsaken me. Jehovah will make the pestilence cleave unto thee, until he have consumed thee from off the land, whither thou goest to possess it. Jehovah will smite thee with consumption, and with fever, and with inflammation, and with fiery heat, and with the sword, and with blasting, and with mildew; and they shall pursue thee until thou perish.

And thy heaven that is over thy head shall be brass, and the earth that is under thee shall be iron. Jehovah will make the rain of thy land powder and dust: from heaven shall it come down upon thee, until thou be destroyed.[1]

Even the strictly legal portion of the code exhibits the characteristic style of the purely hortatory sections. The law of the king may serve as an example.

When thou art come unto the land which Jehovah thy God giveth thee, and shalt possess it, and shalt dwell therein, and shalt say, I will set a king over me, like all the nations that are round about me; thou shalt surely set him king over thee whom Jehovah thy God shall choose: one from among thy brethren shalt thou set king over thee; thou mayest not put a foreigner over thee, who is not thy brother. Only he shall not multiply horses to himself, nor cause the people to return to Egypt, to the end that he may multiply horses; forasmuch as Jehovah hath said unto you, Ye shall henceforth return no more that way. Neither shall he multiply wives to himself, that his heart turn not away: neither shall he greatly multiply to himself silver and gold.

And it shall be, when he sitteth upon the throne of his kingdom, that he shall write him a copy of this law in a book, out of that which is before the priests the Levites: and it shall be with him, and he shall read therein all the days of his life; that he may learn to fear Jehovah his God, to keep all the words of this law and these statutes, to do them; that his heart be not lifted up above his brethren, and that he turn not aside from the commandment, to the right hand, or to the left: to the end that he may prolong his days in his kingdom, he and his children, in the midst of Israel.

In contrast with the simple, direct, story-telling style of Israel's earlier prose writers, Deuteronomy at times suggests the finished style of the Greek writers who were trained in the rules of expression. Prose has become almost a conscious art; henceforth we may not expect to find the charming, naïve narratives that were

[1] 28 15-23.

written from the days of Solomon to those of Jeroboam II.   With the coming of great generalizations into thought, spontaneous emotion must be checked by the cold grasp of reflection, and poetic interest in the vicissitudes of individual heroes must give place to the recording and interpreting of national movements.

CHAPTER XIII

REAWAKENING OF PROPHECY IN JOSIAH'S REIGN

Zephaniah, Jeremiah, and Nahum

(626 to 608 B.C.)

PROPHECY was so effectually silenced under Manasseh that it is not until his grandson Josiah has been upon the throne a dozen years that the prophetic voice is again audible.[1] At this time there occurred a great invasion of southwestern Asia by the barbaric Scythian hordes from the north, vividly described by Herodotus.[2] These dread foes swept down over the Tigris-Euphrates valley and, while they had no enginery to capture a strong city like Nineveh, they wrought its ultimate ruin hardly less surely by their devastation of all the neighboring country. It does not appear that the invaders came up into the Judean hills, but they occupied the coast plains of Palestine, where their presence must have made an impression of horror upon the inhabitants of the hills.

The little book of Zephaniah is generally regarded as showing in its imagery the influence of the Scythian invasion. It threatens destruction to Judah and Nineveh, such as would be wrought by a dreadful foe.

I will utterly consume all things from off the face of the ground, saith Jehovah. I will consume man and beast; I will consume the birds of the heavens, and the fishes of the sea, and the stumblingblocks with the wicked; and I will cut off man from off the face of the ground, saith Jehovah . . . for the day of Jehovah is at hand: for Jehovah hath prepared a sacrifice, he hath consecrated his guests. . . . And their wealth shall become a spoil, and their houses a desolation: . . . a day of the trumpet and alarm, against the fortified cities, and against the high battlements . . . and their blood shall be poured out as dust, and their

---

[1] See p. 178.   [2] I, 103–106.

flesh as dung. . . . And he will stretch out his hand against the north, and destroy Assyria, and will make Nineveh a desolation, and dry like the wilderness. And herds shall lie down in the midst of her, all the beasts of the nations: both the pelican and the porcupine shall lodge in the capitals thereof; their voice shall sing in the windows; desolation shall be in the thresholds: for he hath laid bare the cedar-work. This is the joyous city that dwelt carelessly, that said in her heart, I am, and there is none besides me: how is she become a desolation, a place for beasts to lie down in! every one that passeth by her shall hiss, and wag his hand.[1]

Since the book was evidently, on other grounds, written not long before the Deuteronomic reform, it was probably the Scythian invasion that suggested the form in which doom was threatened, if this invasion was not indeed an influential element in the circumstances calling forth the prophecy.

The religious and moral conditions pictured by the prophet seem the aftermath of the great heathen reaction of the seventh century.

And I will stretch out my hand upon Judah, and upon all the inhabitants of Jerusalem; and I will cut off the remnant of Baal from this place, and the name of the Chemarim with the priests; and them that worship the host of heaven upon the housetops; and them that worship, that swear to Jehovah and swear by Malcam; and them that are turned back from following Jehovah; and those that have not sought Jehovah, nor inquired after him.

Woe to her that is rebellious and polluted! to the oppressing city! She obeyed not the voice; she received not correction; she trusted not in Jehovah; she drew not near to her God. Her princes in the midst of her are roaring lions; her judges are evening wolves; they leave nothing till the morrow. Her prophets are light and treacherous persons; her priests have profaned the sanctuary, they have done violence to the law. Jehovah in the midst of her is righteous; he will not do iniquity; every morning doth he bring his justice to light, he faileth not; but the unjust knoweth no shame.[2]

Zephaniah's theme is the day of the Lord, a day of darkness and gloom, a day of the trumpet and alarm. It will be recalled that Amos was the first to picture the day of the Lord as darkness and

---

[1] Zephaniah 1 2-3, 7b, 13a, 16, 17b. 2 13-15.   [2] Zephaniah 1 4-6, 3 1-5.

not light. Zephaniah was familiar with the prophetic writings of the previous century, and applied their teachings to the conditions of his own generation.

Not far from the time when Zephaniah gave his brief message, a far greater than he became conscious of the prophet's task as his divinely appointed destiny. The later record of the inner experience forms the first chapter of our book of Jeremiah. It lacks the majestic quality of Isaiah's inaugural vision, in which profound yet typical inner experience was so impressively pictured. Jeremiah's account is given in the simplest form. It begins: —

Now the word of Jehovah came unto me, saying, Before I formed thee in the belly I knew thee, and before thou camest forth out of the womb I sanctified thee; I have appointed thee a prophet unto the nations. Then said I, Ah, Lord Jehovah! behold, I know not how to speak; for I am a child. But Jehovah said unto me, Say not, I am a child; for to whomsoever I shall send thee thou shalt go, and whatsoever I shall command thee thou shalt speak.[1]

The description becomes more impressive as it goes on.

Be not afraid because of them; for I am with thee to deliver thee, saith Jehovah. Then Jehovah put forth his hand, and touched my mouth; and Jehovah said unto me, Behold, I have put my words in thy mouth: see, I have this day set thee over the nations and over the kingdoms, to pluck up and to break down and to destroy and to overthrow, to build and to plant.[2]

This is followed by the account of two symbolic visions, the first of which is far from impressive to us.

Moreover the word of Jehovah came unto me, saying, Jeremiah, what seest thou? And I said, I see a rod of an almond-tree. Then said Jehovah unto me, Thou hast well seen: for I watch over my word to perform it.[3]

The only significance of the almond-tree rod seems to be that pointed out by the revisers in their notes, which indicate the play upon the word "watching" in "almond tree" — shokedh, shakedh. Again we are reminded that such plays were not the trivial matters with the Hebrews that they are with us.[4]

[1] Jeremiah 1 4-7.   [2] Jeremiah 1 8-10.   [3] Jeremiah 1 11-12.

[4] The Puritans practised plays upon names in the most serious connections. "When the Rev. Samuel Stone, the successor of Thomas Hooker

The next vision, that of the boiling caldron with its face from the north, has more of inherent significance.

And the word of Jehovah came unto me the second time, saying, What seest thou? And I said, I see a boiling caldron; and the face thereof is from the north. Then Jehovah said unto me, Out of the north evil shall break forth upon all the inhabitants of the land. For, lo, I will call all the families of the kingdoms of the north, saith Jehovah; and they shall come, and they shall set every one his throne at the entrance of the gates of Jersualem, and against all the walls thereof round about, and against all the cities of Judah. And I will utter my judgments against them touching all their wickedness, in that they have forsaken me, and have burned incense unto other gods, and worshipped the works of their own hands.[1]

As in the case of the opening paragraph, this rises to greater power toward the close, where Jehovah is represented encouraging Jeremiah to the greatness of his mission.

Thou therefore gird up thy loins, and arise, and speak unto them all that I command thee: be not dismayed at them, lest I dismay thee before them. For, behold, I have made thee this day a fortified city, and an iron pillar, and brazen walls, against the whole land, against the kings of Judah, against the princes thereof, against the priests thereof, and against the people of the land. And they shall fight against thee; but they shall not prevail against thee: for I am with thee, saith Jehovah, to deliver thee.[2]

On the whole, Jeremiah's opening vision gives small promise of originality of thought or power of expression, and suggests little of strong or attractive personality. Amos, Micah, and Isaiah are men of strength who must do great work despite their defects; Hosea is from the first a man of fire, capable of the most intense love, but one who must learn patience through the strength of his

at Hartford, died in 1663, his colleagues vied with one another in their fervid appreciations of his virtues. He was compared to the stone which Jacob set up and called Eben-ezer, and also the stone with which David slew Goliath; he was termed

'Whetstone, that edgefy'd th' obtusest mind;
Loadstone, that drew the iron heart unkind.'"
    — W. E. Simonds, *History of American Literature*, p. 33.

[1] Jeremiah 1 [13–16].   [2] Jeremiah 1 [17–19].

O

burning love. Jeremiah appears crushed at the thought of responsibility; to be one driven to his work by a relentless sense that it is his work. He will never love the struggle nor greet his fate with a shout; yet under his shrinking exterior, there is resistless conviction that he has been predestined before birth to do a great work. Jeremiah will never do his work in spite of his defects; he is not a man like his great predecessors in whom "the defects of his virtues" are obvious. Rather he is a supreme example of the possibilities of one who possesses the virtues of his defects; it was the very tenacity of his weakness that made Jeremiah an original force in the upward progress of humanity.

In the heading of the book, the first date is given as the thirteenth year of Josiah's reign, that is, 626 B.C. We can follow Jeremiah's activities for full forty years after that time, until after the downfall of Jerusalem in 586 B.C. It is not impossible that the Scythian invasion may have been the immediate occasion for the opening of his ministry as well as that of Zephaniah. The picture of the boiling caldron may well have been suggested by this.

Very probably we are to find the earliest of Jeremiah's recorded sermons in chapter 2. One is here strongly reminded of Hosea; the address opens with his thought of Israel as Jehovah's bride in the wilderness.[1]

And the word of Jehovah came to me, saying, Go, and cry in the ears of Jerusalem, saying, Thus saith Jehovah, I remember for thee the kindness of thy youth, the love of thine espousals; how thou wentest after me in the wilderness, in a land that was not sown. Israel was holiness unto Jehovah, the first-fruits of his increase: all that devour him shall be held guilty; evil shall come upon them, saith Jehovah.[2]

Brutish insensibility to the divine care and guidance has been the attitude of the people.

Hear ye the word of Jehovah, O house of Jacob, and all the families of the house of Israel; Thus saith Jehovah, What unrighteousness have your fathers found in me, that they are gone far from me, and have walked after vanity, and are become vain? Neither said they, Where is Jehovah that brought us up out of the land of Egypt, that led us through the wilderness, through a land of deserts and of pits, through a land of drought and of the shadow of death, through a land that none passed through, and

---

[1] Compare Hosea 2 14-23.   [2] Jeremiah 2 1-3.

where no man dwelt? And I brought you into a plentiful land, to eat the fruit thereof and the goodness thereof; but when ye entered, ye defiled my land, and made my heritage an abomination.[1]

The priests, rulers, and prophets have been faithless.

The priests said not, Where is Jehovah? and they that handle the law knew me not: the rulers also transgressed against me, and the prophets prophesied by Baal, and walked after things that do not profit.[2]

The husband's pleading is tender though searching, with its appeal to the common conduct of the nations which do not change their gods, though they be no gods at all.

Wherefore I will yet contend with you, saith Jehovah, and with your children's children will I contend. For pass over to the isles of Kittim, and see; and send unto Kedar, and consider diligently; and see if there hath been such a thing. Hath a nation changed its gods, which yet are no gods? but my people have changed their glory for that which doth not profit.[3]

Suddenly the figurative representation of God as the husband who cares bountifully for his bride is changed to that of a fountain of living waters contrasted to broken cisterns that cannot hold even their stale, stored-up waters. Again, Israel is a beast of burden, whose yoke has been broken, a choice vine planted that has degenerated into an alien vine, a young camel galloping aimlessly,[4] a wild ass of the wilderness, a detected thief. Isaiah himself could scarcely heap figure upon figure in more rapid succession; yet, as is usually the case with Isaiah, the total effect is not confusing. If the reader is alert, he finds each changing figure flashing its ray of light upon Israel's character and conduct.

Be astonished, O ye heavens, at this, and be horribly afraid, be ye very desolate, saith Jehovah. For my people have committed two evils: they have forsaken me, the fountain of living waters, and hewed them out cisterns, broken cisterns, that can hold no water. Is Israel a servant? is he a home-born slave? why is he become a prey? The young lions have roared upon him, and yelled; and they have made his land waste: his cities are burned up, without inhabitant.

---

[1] Jeremiah 2 4-7.   [2] Jeremiah 2 8.   [3] Jeremiah 2 9-11.
[4] Literally, twisting herself, entangling her ways.

The children also of Memphis and Tahpanhes have broken the crown of thy head. Hast thou not procured this unto thyself, in that thou hast forsaken Jehovah thy God, when he led thee by the way? And now what hast thou to do in the way to Egypt, to drink the waters of the Shihor? or what hast thou to do in the way to Assyria, to drink the waters of the River? Thine own wickedness shall correct thee, and thy backslidings shall reprove thee : know therefore and see that it is an evil thing and a bitter, that thou hast forsaken Jehovah thy God, and that my fear is not in thee, saith the Lord, Jehovah of hosts.

For of old time I have broken thy yoke, and burst thy bonds; and thou saidst, I will not serve; for upon every high hill and under every green tree thou didst bow thyself, playing the harlot. Yet I had planted thee a noble vine, wholly a right seed : how then art thou turned into the degenerate branches of a foreign vine unto me? For though thou wash thee with lye, and take thee much soap, yet thine iniquity is marked before me, saith the Lord Jehovah. How canst thou say, I am not defiled, I have not gone after the Baalim? see thy way in the valley, know what thou hast done; thou art a swift dromedary traversing her ways; a wild ass used to the wilderness, that snuffeth up the wind in her desire; in her occasion who can turn her away? all they that seek her will not weary themselves; in her month they shall find her. Withhold thy foot from being unshod, and thy throat from thirst. But thou saidst, It is in vain; no, for I have loved strangers, and after them will I go.

As the thief is ashamed when he is found, so is the house of Israel ashamed; they, their kings, their princes, and their priests, and their prophets; who say to a stock, Thou art my father; and to a stone, Thou hast brought me forth : for they have turned their back unto me, and not their face; but in the time of their trouble they will say, Arise, and save us. But where are thy gods that thou hast made thee? let them arise, if they can save thee in the time of thy trouble : for according to the number of thy cities are thy gods, O Judah.[1]

The literary promise of the opening chapter was not great, but the address of chapter 2 tells us that another poet-prophet has arisen in Israel. The thought of God's tender care and of Israel's wanton insensibility to his love, so effectively expanded in Isaiah's great arraignment (chapter 1), is again presented in an original and effective form.

The four chapters following are most naturally assigned to the earlier years of Jeremiah's preaching, before 621, when the prophet

[1] Jeremiah 2 12-28.

must still have been a comparatively young man. In these early addresses one discovers that the young man, like Zephaniah, had been a diligent student of the earlier prophets, but finds, as yet, no great, new contributions to the prophetic interpretation of life.

Clearly, Jeremiah's spirit is most closely akin to that of Hosea. He does not merely adopt and repeatedly use Hosea's characteristic figure; he has genuinely entered into Hosea's interpretation of life. He, too, sees that it is insensibility to the goodness of God that is the root troub e with Israel — nothing purely external. They do not know God; this is the fundamental lack. He cries out in God's name: For my people is foolish, they have not known me; they are sottish children, and they have none understanding; they are wise to do evil, but to do good they have no knowledge.

Hosea first learned the lesson through the death he died when he found that the one to whom he had given his unbounded love was incapable of understanding or caring. Jeremiah's tender, sensitive heart made him able, even in the years of his immaturity, before he had come to his own life, to understand the significance of Hosea's truth. He, too, saw God desiring soul union and communion with his people as a true husband or father, and saw his people absolutely unresponsive to this yearning love.

As we read Jeremiah's early sermons and feel the voice and heart of Hosea on every page, we may note also the message of Amos and Isaiah, spoken once again with hardly less of strength and poetic power than in its original form. Injustice to the weak in the law court; riches gained through oppression and dishonesty;[1] the divine judgment threatened through a nation from afar;[2] yet a remnant to be spared;[3] sacrifices hateful to God;[4] glossing over of evil, crying peace, peace when there is no peace[5] — in all these and many other notes that we catch in Jeremiah's earlier discourses, we may recognize the influence of the masters over whose recorded messages he must have pored and pondered, listening to the voices of the past, in the barren years of his youth, when no prophet spoke publicly. Yet throughout these early

[1] 5 26-29.　　[2] 5 15, 6 22.　　[3] 5 18.　　[4] 6 20.　　[5] 6 13-14.

sermons, Jeremiah's voice is no mere echo, even though his own distinctive message has not yet shaped itself.

An individual note which we catch in these chapters, and which we shall come to recognize as a distinctive mark of Jeremiah's personality, is the inner compulsion to give his message of plucking up and breaking down.

For thus hath Jehovah of hosts said :
Hew down trees and cast up a mound against Jerusalem.
This is the faithless city ; there is only oppression in her midst.
As a fountain keepeth fresh its waters, so she keepeth fresh her wickedness ;
Acts of violence and oppression are heard in her ;
Before me continually are wounds and blows.
Receive instruction, O Jerusalem, lest I be alienated from thee ;
Lest I make thee a desolation, an uninhabited land.
Thus saith Jehovah of hosts :
Glean thoroughly, as a vine, the remnant of Israel,
Put forth again your hand as a grape gatherer toward the young vines.

To whom shall I speak and testify that they may hear ?
Behold, their ear is uncircumcised and they cannot hearken ;
Behold, the word of Jehovah has become to them a reproach, they have no pleasure in it.
Therefore I am full of the wrath of Jehovah ; I am weary of restraining myself.
I must pour it out upon the children in the street and upon the assembly of young men,
For both the husband and the wife shall be taken, the aged and him that is advanced in years.
And their houses shall be turned over to others, their fields to robbers ;
For from the least even to the greatest of them, each greedily robs,
And from the prophet even to the priest each deals deceitfully.[1]

This is akin to the relentless conviction noted in connection with the inaugural vision.

We imagine Amos almost exulting in his message of doom, his sense of justice is so dominant ; Isaiah's doom and hope sweep on in majestic current, splendid, but cold at times, or else again, a

[1] Jeremiah 6 6-13. Translation of C. F. Kent, in *Sermons, Epistles, and Apocalypses of Israel's Prophets*, p. 184.

consuming fire; never restrained by tender sympathy; Jeremiah would not utter words that separate him from the understanding and companionship of everyday men, but a burning fire within compels him to be a prophet against his will.

Understanding, as Jeremiah does, that the transformation of society is inwardly conditioned, its purification seems hopeless even to the young man.

They are all grievous revolters, going about with slanders ;
They are brass and iron ; they all of them deal corruptly.
The bellows blow fiercely ; the lead is consumed of the fire :
In vain do they go on refining ; for the wicked are not plucked away.
Refuse silver shall men call them, because Jehovah hath rejected them.[1]

The preaching of Jeremiah and Zephaniah must have helped prepare the way for the reform of Josiah, undertaken five years after the beginning of Jeremiah's ministry. What part, if any, these prophets may have taken in the actual reform movement is a question that we cannot solve. In the history of Josiah's reign, as given in Kings, no mention is made of either prophet, and no internal evidence leads to the dating of any of their extant messages in the period of the Deuteronomic reform, except the passage of Jeremiah 11 [1-8].

The word that came to Jeremiah from Jehovah, saying, Hear ye the words of this covenant, and speak unto the men of Judah, and to the inhabitants of Jerusalem; and say thou unto them, Thus saith Jehovah the God of Israel : Cursed be the man that heareth not the words of this covenant, which I commanded your fathers in the day that I brought them forth out of the land of Egypt, out of the iron furnace, saying, Obey my voice, and do them, according to all which I command you : so shall ye be my people, and I will be your God; that I may establish the oath which I sware unto your fathers, to give them a land flowing with milk and honey, as at this day. Then answered I, and said, Amen, O Jehovah.

And Jehovah said unto me, Proclaim all these words in the cities of Judah, and in the streets of Jerusalem, saying, Hear ye the words of this covenant, and do them. For I earnestly protested unto your fathers in the day that I brought them up out of the land of Egypt, even unto this day, rising early and protesting, saying, Obey my voice. Yet they obeyed

---

[1] Jeremiah 6 [23-30].

not, nor inclined their ear, but walked every one in the stubbornness of
their evil heart: therefore I brought upon them all the words of this
covenant, which I commanded them to do, but they did them not.

This seems like an account of Jeremiah's preaching Deuteronomy
in Jerusalem and the cities of Judah. The reference to the
covenant commanded the fathers in the day that they were brought
up out of the land of Egypt and to the curse upon him that hears
not the words of this covenant seems to refer to Deuteronomy.

If the passage be rightly interpreted and authentic, Jeremiah
entered into the reform of Josiah and became a preacher of Deuteronomy.   To some, the thought that the prophet Jeremiah,
with his insight into the inner conditions of true reform, took
such part in this religious reform by royal authority is absurd.
On the other hand it seems that Jeremiah might be glad to see
the temptations connected with the local high places diminished
by their destruction, and there is assuredly much in the book of
Deuteronomy in its appeal to the love of God and remembrance of
his past mercies that is in closest accord with the early preaching
of Jeremiah.[1]   In the large amount of discourse and biographical
material from Jeremiah there is almost no other clear reference
to the Deuteronomic reform.   Either the prophet's activity was
rather small in this connection, or, when he caused his memoirs
to be written, after Josiah's death, he did not care to retain much
that concerned this period of his life.   It is certain that in the
later years of his ministry he fully understood the temporary
character of a reform based on exhortation to obey the law.

We know almost nothing of Jeremiah's activity during the years
from 621 till Josiah's death in 609.   They were years of peace
and prosperity such as Judah had not known for more than a
century, and they were years in which the nation, at least outwardly, was observing a law which combined much that was best
in the priestly and prophetic elements of its religion.

At the close of this period, the movements of the great nations
once more began to affect the little Judean state.   The Medes
from the northeast of Assyria, and the Chaldeans on the south,

[1] Even though the narrative of 11 1-8 may not have been written at
Jeremiah's dictation, it may still contain an authentic tradition.

were renewing their attacks on Nineveh, whose territory had been so ravaged by the Scythians a few years before. This in itself could bring only satisfaction to the Hebrews; the foe that had so mercilessly oppressed is now about to receive the wages of cruel ambition.

The brief prophecy of Nahum shows how one prophet, who believed in the righteous vengeance of Jehovah, welcomed the prospect of Nineveh's fall. "I will break his yoke from off thee and will burst thy bonds in sunder,"[1] he cries. With a riot of lurid color, he paints the siege and downfall of Nineveh, as though already accomplished, that den of the lions and feeding place of the young lions, where the lion and the lioness walked, the lion's whelp, and none made them afraid.[2] Within the city,

> In the streets, the chariots are mad;
> They rush to and fro in the squares.
> Their appearance is as torches;
> As lightnings they dart.
> The besiegers are without the city;
> They haste to its wall,
> The mantlet is prepared.
> The river gates are opened,
> The palace crumbles.[3]

The prophet hears, with inner ear, the actual din of the siege and reports with words that echo it to-day.

> Sound of whip and sound of rattling wheel,
> And galloping horse, and bounding chariot.
> Horseman mounting,
> And flame of sword, and flash of spear.
> Many slain; a mass of corpses;
> And no end to the carcasses.
> They stumble on the carcasses.[4]

Ironically Nahum calls upon the Assyrians to prepare for the siege : —

Draw thee water for the siege; strengthen thy fortresses; go into the clay, and tread the mortar; make strong the brickkiln.[5]

Then he triumphantly promises them : —

[1] Nahum 1 [13].   [2] 2 [11].   [3] 2 [4, 5].   [4] 3 [2-3a].   [5] 3 [14].

There shall the fire devour thee; the sword shall cut thee off; it shall devour thee like the canker-worm: make thyself many as the canker-worm; make thyself many as the locust.[3]

Nahum was unexcelled as a word painter. It is possible to make this sweeping statement, though he has left us only a tract of five pages.

The first chapter has no definite references to Nineveh; it is a general song of praise to the avenging Jehovah. It shows some signs of having been designed originally as an alphabetic poem, the successive lines beginning with the letters of the alphabet in order. Though the text seems to be in much confusion, it is clear that it was an effective psalm. It probably began,

> A requiting God is Jehovah;
> He avengeth and is lord of wrath.
> In wind and storm is his way,
> And clouds are the dust of his feet.
> He rebuketh the sea, and dries it,
> And all rivers he makes run dry.[2]

Whether this psalm was written by Nahum as a prelude to his more specific prophecy or was prefixed by some other hand as an appropriate introduction to his brief discourse, we cannot say. In any case, Nahum adds nothing to the body of prophetic truth and reaches only the lower levels of the common thought. With the sin and real needs of his people he does not deal. The approaching downfall of the cruel enemy, that had obliterated the northern nation and held the southern long in vassalage, as the act of a requiting God fills his vision.

In Egypt, the Pharaoh was anticipating the partition of the Assyrian domain, and so he marched across Palestine, on his way to the Euphrates to annex as much as he might be able. Josiah, who had assumed the rule over the old northern territory since the Assyrian domination had been relaxed, disputed the passage of the Egyptians and encountered them near where the great battle had been fought in Deborah's day. The Pharaoh was victorious, and Judah's noble king met his death.

---

[1] 3 [15].   [2] Translation based on the revised text of Kittel, *Bib. Heb.*

CHAPTER XIV

NARRATIVE WRITING FROM THE TIME OF AMOS TO THE PUBLICATION OF DEUTERONOMY

(750 to 621 B.C.)

LITERARY analysis has undertaken to show that many parts of the great Judean History of Antiquity, discussed in Chapter V as the product of the ninth century B.C., could not have been written quite as early as that time.   There is nothing inherently improbable in the view that this great narrative was revised and enlarged from time to time; indeed, our knowledge of the history of Old Testament literature and of other ancient literatures makes it highly probable that such was the case.   Ancient historical narratives grew, not only by being brought down to date and extended backward, but by the insertion of kindred material as it came to light.

The purpose of the present volume does not make it desirable to follow the delicate and often uncertain analysis of the Judean history into the earlier and later strands.   If called upon to name a date for the actual completion of the Judean history, it will be in the middle of the seventh century rather than in the ninth, yet the later work is merely supplementary, and it is better to think of the Judean history as the literary product of the ninth century, when it took shape and character.

Much the same may be said concerning the Ephraimite History of Antiquity.   It had taken definite form before the middle of the eighth century and yet it too was largely supplemented during the next one hundred years.   How this could have gone on after the downfall of Northern Israel it is difficult to see, except as we recall the probability that during the twenty years of anarchy preceding 721 B.C., many faithful worshippers of Jehovah took refuge in Judah.[1]   Literary analysis certainly seems to find satisfactory evi-

[1] See Chapter IX, p. 138.

dence that the great Ephraimite history continued to grow for three-quarters of a century after the fall of Samaria and the partial repopulation of its territory with heathen peoples. This growth was probably the work of those who took refuge in Judah before or after the fall of Samaria.

The revision of the two great histories was checked only by the compilation of the two into one. This seems to have occurred about the third quarter of the seventh century B.C., in the latter part of the reign of Manasseh or early part of that of Josiah, not long before the publication of Deuteronomy. Apparently the writer of Deuteronomy 5–11 had before him both this composite work and the separate Ephraimite history.[1] The compilation generally made the Judean history the framework and inwove the Ephraimite material with this. Only the Judean history was available for the pre-Abramic period. With the promise of the land of Canaan to Abram the first material from the Ephraimite history appears. Here the method of the compiler was close interweaving of the two accounts. From the Judean history followed the story of the birth of Ishmael and flight of Hagar, the visit of the angels, promise of Isaac, the destruction of Sodom and Gomorrah, and the incestuous origin of Moab and Ammon. Then, from the Ephraimite history was taken the story of Abraham's sojourn in Gerar with the taking of Sarah by king Abimelech — the story so like that of the Egyptian sojourn recorded in the Judean history (Genesis 12 $^{10-20}$). After this follows the Ephraimite account of the driving out of Hagar and Ishmael, evidently a variant account of that already taken from the Judean history. From the Ephraimite document comes also the principal narrative of the Beer-sheba covenant with Abimelech, although some elements from the Judean history appear here interwoven. The testing of Abraham in the matter of offering Isaac was next inserted from the Ephraimite story, and thus the compilation went forward, sometimes with the two accounts of some events closely interwoven; sometimes with an incident or series of incidents taken out of one history, with no interwoven material from the other; sometimes with a narrative which is evidently a doublet of one taken from the other history, but with a different setting and

[1] See Cornill, *Introduction Old Testament*, p. 140.

different details, making it seem another incident. At times the hand of the editor who combined the two may be seen in connecting phrases, harmonistic changes, or even noticeable expansions. An example of the last is found in 22 [14b-18].

As it is said to this day, In the mount of Jehovah it shall be provided. And the angel of Jehovah called unto Abraham a second time out of heaven, and said, By myself have I sworn, saith Jehovah, because thou hast done this thing, and hast not withheld thy son, thine only son, that in blessing I will bless thee, and in multiplying I will multiply thy seed as the stars of the heavens, and as the sand which is upon the sea-shore; and thy seed shall possess the gate of his enemies; and in thy seed shall all the nations of the earth be blessed; because thou hast obeyed my voice.

As the work goes forward, some parts show more independent work on the part of the editor than one finds in Genesis. Occasionally "the narrative is, with considerable skill, to some extent, 'composed' on the basis of the sources"; [1] but the portion of the history summarized above gives a fair idea of the method of compiling followed in the composition of the great history of antiquity from the union of the northern and southern documents.

This composite narrative contained by far the larger part of our Genesis, Exodus, Numbers, Joshua, and Judges, but it was still to pass through further editing and compiling with another great document before it assumed the form in which it has come down to us. No one of the first six books of our Bible was as yet in anything like its present form when the central part of Deuteronomy was published in 621 B.C. If this edition of the great prophetico-legal writing contained, as we have supposed, chapters 5–26 and 28, though it lacked 1–4, 27, and 29–34, it was more nearly our present book than was any other book of the Hexateuch.

When discussing the beginnings of connected prose writing, the early Saul stories, early David-Saul stories, and stories of David's court and family life were separated from the remaining material of 1 and 2 Samuel. There remain, after this analysis, large portions of 1 Samuel and small parts of 2 Samuel, which offer puzzling problems for the literary critic. To some the material seems strongly influenced by Deuteronomy, and so to have taken

---

[1] Cornill, *Introduction Old Testament*, p. 139.

form after 621.   On the other hand there appear marked affinities
to the Ephraimite history of the earlier centuries, and the view
seems consistent that a large part of this material is to be associated closely with the late portions of this history.   It would then
be so nearly contemporary with Deuteronomy that it might
naturally show many affinities without being directly influenced
by Deuteronomy.   We may therefore discuss the latest document
used by the compiler of 1 and 2 Samuel as a product of the seventh
century, written prior to the publication of Deuteronomy.

In the early Saul stories, Samuel appeared as a local seer who
recognized in Saul the possible leader of a united movement
against Philistine domination.   As a prophet, he anointed Saul
and brought him into touch with the religio-patriotic enthusiasts,
the sons of the prophets, who first appear in Israel's history at
this crisis.   Thus, in the cycle of stories which probably took
permanent form in Saul's tribe of Benjamin, Samuel appears as the
enlightened patriot, to whose sagacity and private initiative the
monarchy is due.   Still, he is known to only a small part of Israel,
and the popular acclaim is for Saul and David.   The picture is
simple, natural, and in harmony with the conditions of Israel as
revealed in other early sources.

Later tradition in Ephraim could not rest content with such a
noble but relatively obscure rôle for this great representative of
the tribe.   So there grew up a Samuel tradition which made him
a prophet, more like Elijah and Isaiah in assumption of continued
supervision over the throne, and, growing beyond this, even represented him as a great military leader or judge who commanded
a united Israel against the Philistines before Saul was ever heard
of, and who won such successes that the early struggle of Saul
is quite inexplicable, if not wholly unnecessary.

Then came the word of Jehovah unto Samuel, saying, It repenteth
me that I have set up Saul to be king; for he is turned back from following
me, and hath not performed my commandments.   And Samuel was wroth;
and he cried unto Jehovah all night.   And Samuel rose early to meet
Saul in the morning; and it was told Samuel, saying, Saul came to Carmel, and, behold, he set him up a monument, and turned, and passed on,
and went down to Gilgal.   And Samuel came to Saul; and Saul said
unto him, Blessed be thou of Jehovah: I have performed the command-

ment of Jehovah. And Samuel said, What meaneth then this bleating of the sheep in mine ears, and the lowing of the oxen which I hear? And Saul said, They have brought them from the Amalekites: for the people spared the best of the sheep and of the oxen, to sacrifice unto Jehovah thy God; and the rest we have utterly destroyed. Then Samuel said unto Saul, Stay, and I will tell thee what Jehovah hath said to me this night. And he said unto him, Say on.

And Samuel said, Though thou wast little in thine own sight, wast thou not made the head of the tribes of Israel? And Jehovah anointed thee king over Israel; and Jehovah sent thee on a journey, and said, Go, and utterly destroy the sinners the Amalekites, and fight against them until they be consumed. Wherefore then didst thou not obey the voice of Jehovah, but didst fly upon the spoil, and didst that which was evil in the sight of Jehovah? And Saul said unto Samuel, Yea, I have obeyed the voice of Jehovah, and have gone the way which Jehovah sent me, and have brought Agag the king of Amalek, and have utterly destroyed the Amalekites. But the people took of the spoil, sheep and oxen, the chief of the devoted things, to sacrifice unto Jehovah thy God in Gilgal. And Samuel said, Hath Jehovah as great delight in burnt-offerings and sacrifices, as in obeying the voice of Jehovah? Behold, to obey is better than sacrifice, and to harken than the fat of rams. For rebellion is as the sin of witchcraft, and stubbornness is as idolatry and teraphim. Because thou hast rejected the word of Jehovah, he hath also rejected thee from being king.

And Saul said unto Samuel, I have sinned; for I have transgressed the commandment of Jehovah, and thy words, because I feared the people, and obeyed their voice.

And Samuel said, Gather all Israel to Mizpah, and I will pray for you unto Jehovah. And they gathered together to Mizpah, and drew water, and poured it out before Jehovah, and fasted on that day, and said there, We have sinned against Jehovah. And Samuel judged the children of Israel in Mizpah. And when the Philistines heard that the children of Israel were gathered together to Mizpah, the lords of the Philistines went up against Israel. And when the children of Israel heard it, they were afraid of the Philistines. And the children of Israel said to Samuel, Cease not to cry unto Jehovah our God for us, that he will save us out of the hand of the Philistines. And Samuel took a sucking lamb, and offered it for a whole burnt-offering unto Jehovah: and Samuel cried unto Jehovah for Israel; and Jehovah answered him. And as Samuel was offering up the burnt-offering, the Philistines drew near to

[1] 1 Samuel 15 [10-24].

battle against Israel; but Jehovah thundered with a great thunder on that day upon the Philistines, and discomfited them; and they were smitten down before Israel. And the men of Israel went out of Mizpah, and pursued the Philistines, and smote them, until they came under Bethcar.

Then Samuel took a stone, and set it between Mizpah and Shen, and called the name of it Ebenezer, saying, Hitherto hath Jehovah helped us. So the Philistines were subdued, and they came no more within the border of Israel: and the hand of Jehovah was against the Philistines all the days of Samuel. And the cities which the Philistines had taken from Israel were restored to Israel, from Ekron even unto Gath; and the border thereof did Israel deliver out of the hand of the Philistines. And there was peace between Israel and the Amorites.

And Samuel judged Israel all the days of his life. And he went from year to year in circuit to Bethel, and Gilgal, and Mizpah; and he judged Israel in all those places. And his return was to Ramah, for there was his house; and there he judged Israel; and he built there an altar unto Jehovah.[1]

Samuel looms large in this later tradition of his own tribe, but his work is far less truly noble and significant than in the early Saul story. No longer is he the real founder of the monarchy, a true prophet and patriot whose enlightened vision sees the need of his generation, who is able, in his own obscure place, to direct the rising tide of popular dissatisfaction into channels that make possible independence of Philistia and a united kingdom, and that advance the people far toward the possibility of ultimate monotheistic religion.

In the later tradition, he is a highly successful ruler, deeply opposed to the establishment of a formal monarchy, himself *de facto* king. After a special revelation from God, he gives assent to the selection of a king, but warns the people of dreadful evils to follow their folly. This was a view of the monarchy natural for those whose vision was filled by its evils developed under Solomon, Ahab, and the succession of assassin kings who ruled Israel after the death of Jeroboam II. With a longer perspective, we cannot question that the monarchy was a great blessing to Israel, in contrast with the loose tribal organization and rude conditions that preceded. The genuine Samuel of the early

[1] 1 Samuel 7 5-17.

tradition so recognized it, and, as a true prophet, worked with the best available human instruments and made it possible.

Not only is the Samuel of the later history less noble and his work less significant, the narratives themselves lack much of the charm of those of the earlier day. This later Samuel document is, from the literary point of view, a transition one between the great age of stories and the era when prose writers are to be dominated by hard-and-fast theories of how things must have happened in accordance with certain theological dogmas. The new tendency has not reached its development in the later Samuel stories, which have much of the naturalness and beauty of the earlier age, yet a cold, withering hand is laid upon literature when stories are no longer told for their simple human interest, but to illustrate and teach certain theories.

In the earlier stories, a childlike faith in God's guidance of human affairs and a sound moral sense gave moral and religious significance to the narratives without, as we have so often noted, any obtrusion of the lesson. In these later Samuel stories, a developed and formal theory of God's control of human affairs is already in evidence. Deep earnestness and conviction lend their dignity to the literature, but one who looks at the narrative purely from the literary point of view feels the change. It is especially noticeable in the barren and unnatural story of Samuel's victory over the Philistines and the long account of the rejection of Saul, both of which were printed above. The elaborate discourse attributed to Samuel is another example. It begins: —

And Samuel said unto all Israel, Behold, I have hearkened unto your voice in all that ye said unto me, and have made a king over you. And now, behold, the king walketh before you; and I am old and grayheaded; and, behold, my sons are with you and I have walked before you from my youth unto this day. Here I am: witness against me before Jehovah, and, before his anointed: whose ox have I taken? or whose ass have I taken? or whom have I defrauded? whom I have oppressed? or of whose hand have I taken a ransom to blind mine eyes therewith? and I will restore it you. And they said, Thou hast not defraudest us, nor oppressed us, neither hast thou taken aught of any man's hand. And he said unto them, Jehovah is witness against you, and his anointed is witness

P

this day, that ye have not found aught in my hand. And they said, He is witness.

And Samuel said unto the people, It is Jehovah that appointed Moses and Aaron, and that brought your fathers up out of the land of Egypt. Now therefore stand still, that I may plead with you before Jehovah concerning all the righteous acts of Jehovah, which he did to you and to your fathers. When Jacob was come into Egypt, and your fathers cried unto Jehovah, then Jehovah sent Moses and Aaron, who brought forth your fathers out of Egypt, and made them to dwell in this place. But they forgat Jehovah their God; and he sold them into the hand of Sisera, captain of the host of Hazor, and into the hand of the Philistines, and into the hand of the king of Moab; and they fought against them. And they cried unto Jehovah, and said, We have sinned, because we have forsaken Jehovah, and have served the Baalim and the Ashtaroth: but now deliver us out of the hand of our enemies, and we will serve thee. And Jehovah sent Jerubbaal, and Bedan, and Jephthah, and Samuel, and delivered you out of the hand of your enemies on every side; and ye dwelt in safety.[1]

In contrast to the qualities represented in the more extreme examples cited, the story of the child Samuel is highly attractive, yet the swift movement of an earlier age has disappeared, the dialogue is less natural than in earlier times, and the real working out of events is obscured by an artificial conception.

And the child Samuel ministered unto Jehovah before Eli. And the word of Jehovah was precious in those days; there was no frequent vision. And it came to pass at that time, when Eli was laid down in his place (now his eyes had begun to wax dim, so that he could not see), and the lamp of God was not yet gone out, and Samuel was laid down to sleep, in the temple of Jehovah, where the ark of God was; that Jehovah called Samuel: and he said, Here am I. And he ran unto Eli, and said, Here am I; for thou calledst me. And he said, I called not; lie down again. And he went and lay down. And Jehovah called yet again, Samuel. And Samuel arose and went to Eli, and said, Here am I; for thou calledst me. And he answered, I called not, my son; lie down again. Now Samuel did not yet know Jehovah, neither was the word of Jehovah yet revealed unto him. And Jehovah called Samuel again the third time. And he arose and went to Eli, and said, Here am I; for thou calledst me. And Eli perceived that Jehovah had called the child.

[1] 1 Samuel 12 1-11.

Therefore Eli said unto Samuel, Go, lie down: and it shall be, if he call thee, that thou shalt say, Speak, Jehovah; for thy servant heareth. So Samuel went and lay down in his place.

And Jehovah came, and stood, and called as at other times, Samuel, Samuel. Then Samuel said, Speak; for thy servant heareth. And Jehovah said to Samuel, Behold, I will do a thing in Israel, at which both the ears of every one that heareth it shall tingle. In that day I will perform against Eli all that I have spoken concerning his house, from the beginning even unto the end. For I have told him that I will judge his house for ever, for the iniquity which he knew, because his sons did bring a curse upon themselves, and he restrained them not. And therefore I have sworn unto the house of Eli, that the iniquity of Eli's house shall not be expiated with sacrifice nor offering for ever.

And Samuel lay until the morning, and opened the doors of the house of Jehovah. And Samuel feared to show Eli the vision. Then Eli called Samuel, and said, Samuel, my son. And he said, Here am I. And he said, What is the thing that Jehovah hath spoken unto thee? I pray thee, hide it not from me: God do so to thee, and more also, if thou hide anything from me of all the things that he spake unto thee. And Samuel told him every whit, and hid nothing from him. And he said, It is Jehovah: let him do what seemeth him good.[1]

It is impossible to determine how soon the later Samuel history was compiled with the earlier groups of stories. Possibly they were inwoven almost immediately. If this is the case, the death of David, now recorded in 1 Kings, was included in the composite work and the miscellaneous material of 2 Samuel 21–24, which interrupts the dramatic story of David's court and family life, was inserted in its present place by the later editors who compiled the books of Kings and gave the finishing touches to Samuel. In the composition the material was so arranged that the later picture, representing Samuel as the recognized leader of all Israel, was given priority, and quite obscured the earlier and nobler picture of the true founder of the Hebrew kingdom.

The earlier and later groups of stories are combined with only very slight harmonistic touches until the summary of David's reign, 2 Samuel 8. From this point forward the early narrative of David's court and family life stands almost without alteration or interruption.

[1] 1 Samuel 3 1–18.

CHAPTER XV

Jeremiah, Habakkuk

(608 to 586 B.C.)

AFTER the death of Josiah the kingdom fell temporarily under the sway of Egypt, and Pharaoh-Necho decided which of the Judean princes should rule as vassal king. The ruler selected, Jehoiakim, was distinctly hostile to the spirit and policy of his father; his reign was marked by the backrush of all the heathen practices which had been driven out. Egypt remained suzerain only four or five years, and then the Babylonian Nebuchadrezzar, who had defeated the Egyptians in a decisive battle, became ruler of Palestine. For a time Jehoiakim paid tribute, but after a few years, trusting to Egypt for help, he undertook to throw off the Babylonian rule. Jehoiakim himself died in time to escape the consequences of his folly, and his son ruled only three months when the Babylonian army was before Jerusalem. The new king, surrendering at discretion, was carried a prisoner to Babylon. With him were taken 10,000 men, besides women and children, the flower of the little state — nobles, soldiers, and skilled artisans. Thus the partial exile began in 597 B.C. In Jerusalem an uncle of the captive king, a son of Josiah, was placed upon the throne by the Babylonians. Matters went from bad to worse in the government of the little devastated state, where the new rulers attributed their exemption from deportation to the special favor of God, and, after a few years, refused the Babylonian tribute. Jerusalem stood a long siege, but in 586 B.C. the city was captured, plundered, and razed to the ground; the brief, impressive statement in Kings is : —

And he burnt the house of Jehovah, and the king's house; and all the houses of Jerusalem, even every great man's house burnt he with

212

fire. And all the army of the Chaldeans, that were with the captain of the guard, brake down the walls of Jerusalem round about.[1]

A few thousand more were now deported to Babylonia, so that in all, men, women, and children, there must have been some 50,000 Judeans in that distant region. There were now three chief centres of Jewish population, for many had fled to Egypt in the troublous times, and many, largely the peasantry, were left in Judea.

We have fuller information concerning the experiences of Jeremiah, during the next twenty-three years after the death of Josiah, than in the case of any other of the Old Testament prophets. His teachings during this period have been preserved mingled with a large amount of biographical and historical information. It is possible, therefore, to gather from the book of Jeremiah a vivid picture of the inner and outer life of the prophet and the intimate life of Jerusalem during the years 608 to 586. The impression of these things quite overshadows the sermons themselves which generally lack the literary power found in the addresses of the eighth-century prophets. Jeremiah's significance lies in the insight which he reached in the later years of his ministry, and this insight we are able to appreciate as we follow him through the inner and outer struggles incident to the time of his nation's downfall.

We may see him in the temple court, warning the worshippers who have come thither from the cities of Judah, or at the temple gate denouncing the confidence of those who trust in the sanctuary while they are guilty of moral and religious wrongs; we may see him going to the palace to address king and nobles, or follow him to the potter's house, where he will learn a lesson as he watches the workman change his plan for the particular vessel to be made, or again we may go out with him to the valley of the son of Hinnom by the east gate, whither he goes to shiver in pieces an earthen vessel, before a gaping crowd. His striking sermon of judgment, preached on this occasion, gave excuse for the ruler of the temple to put Jeremiah in the public stocks, in the gate of Benjamin, which was by the house of the Lord.

In the case of most prophets who delivered their message orally, as Jeremiah did his, we are left to infer how it came to be written

[1] 2 Kings 25 9-10.

down. The confused state, for example, of Isaiah's oracles strongly suggests that these were gathered by his disciples, after his death; the orderly arrangement of Amos's memoirs, on the other hand, makes it probable that he himself put the substance of his preaching into permanent form, after returning from his Bethel misson. — All this is inference. In the case of Jeremiah we have a definite account of his dictating to Baruch in the fourth year of Jehoiakim, what he had preached during the twenty-two years of his ministry. When King Jehoiakim contemptuously cut up and burned this precious book, Jeremiah had it rewritten and expanded by the addition of many like words.[1]

This second and enlarged edition of Jeremiah's oracles must have contained the inaugural vision and early addresses, already discussed, and also the original discourses and narratives that connect themselves with the first four years of Jehoiakim's reign. The theme of this little roll was "Words *against* Israel, Judah, and all the nations";[2] Jehoiakim's reactionary reign certainly furnished ample occasion for oracles of this character. As we examine our present book of Jeremiah, a still later and greatly enlarged edition, it is impossible to determine always which discourses were delivered early enough in Jehoiakim's reign to be included in the original roll written in the fourth year; probably a comparatively small amount of material outside of chapters 1–17 belonged to this collection.

Jeremiah's silence during the later years of Josiah's reign[3] is broken with his lament for King Jehoahaz or Shallum whom the people had chosen to succeed Josiah. Pharaoh-Necho carried the newly appointed king in bonds to Egypt, and Jeremiah would stay the mourning for the dead king with thought for this second national loss.

> Weep ye not for the dead; nor mourn for him.
> Weep sore for him who has gone, for he shall not return,
> To see the land of his nativity.[4]

Soon after Jehoiakim's reign is begun, Josiah's reform, with its destruction of the high places and enforcement of the law, is as though it had not been.

[1] Jeremiah 36 1–32.   [2] Jeremiah 36 2, 32.
[3] See Chapter XIII, p. 200.   [4] 22 10.

And Jehovah said unto me, A conspiracy is found among the men of Judah, and among the inhabitants of Jerusalem.   They are turned back to the iniquities of their forefathers, who refused to hear my words; and they are gone after other gods to serve them; the house of Israel and the house of Judah have broken my covenant which I made with their fathers.

For according to the number of thy cities are thy gods, O Judah; and according to the number of the streets of Jerusalem have ye set up altars to the shameful thing, even altars to burn incense unto Baal.

And Jehovah saith, Because they have forsaken my law which I set before them, and have not obeyed my voice, neither walked therein; but have walked after the stubbornness of their own heart, and after the Baalim, which their fathers taught them.[1]

Worship of the Baals and other deities comes sweeping back. —

Will ye . . . burn incense unto Baal, and walk after other gods that ye have not known?[2]   Why have they provoked me to anger with their graven images and with foreign vanities?[3]   They shall spread them before the sun, and the moon, and all the host of heaven which they have loved, and which they have served, and after which they have walked, and have worshipped.[4]

This recognition of the gods of Canaan and the east does not at all mean abandoning orthodox faith in Jehovah; the prophets have introduced certain rather irreligious notions about honesty and purity in business and society being a vital part of religion.   All these things may well go by the board in favor of the older religion which trusted in Jehovah as the god of Israel who would not permit his people to be destroyed, and which properly recognized also the power and claims of the old Canaanite deities and of the gods of the great conquering peoples of the Euphrates and the Nile!

Once more religious conservatism triumphed, adding to itself such newer elements as were assimilable to its lower aspects. Among these is found Isaiah's teaching that Jehovah's temple could not be captured; this fitted well with the older ideas that Amos had denounced, and, in Jeremiah's time, it had become an accepted dogma.   Since it had been vindicated in Isaiah's day by the catastrophe and incontinent withdrawal of Sennacherib, it was now erected into a universal truth.   That which was a vital

---

[1] Jeremiah 11, 9-10, 13, 9 13, 14.   [2] 7 9.   [3] 8 19b.   [4] 8 2a.

teaching for one generation, within a century became a dogma, sacred and condemning as heresy the larger truth needed by the new generation.

Behold ye trust in lying words, that cannot profit. Will ye steal, murder, and commit adultery, and swear falsely, and burn incense unto Baal, and walk after other gods that ye have not known, and come and stand before me in this house, which is called by my name and say, We are delivered; that ye may do all these abominations? Is this house, which is called by my name, become a den of robbers in your eyes? Behold, even I have seen it, saith Jehovah.

But go ye now unto my place which was in Shiloh, where I caused my name to dwell at the first, and see what I did to it for the wickedness of my people Israel. And now, because ye have done all these works, saith Jehovah, and I spake unto you, rising up early and speaking, but ye heard not; and I called you, but ye answered not; therefore will I do unto the house which is called by my name, wherein ye trust, and unto the place which I gave to you and to your fathers, as I did to Shiloh. And I will cast you out of my sight, as I have cast out all your brethren, even the whole seed of Ephraim.[1]

As Amos had done, so this prophet appeals from present, established religious practice and doctrine to the purer days of the beginning of Israel's religion.

Thus saith Jehovah of hosts, the God of Israel: Add your burnt-offerings unto your sacrifices, and eat ye flesh. For I spake not unto your fathers, nor commanded them in the day that I brought them out of the land of Egypt, concerning burnt-offerings or sacrifices: but this thing I commanded them, saying, Hearken unto my voice, and I will be your God, and ye shall be my people; and walk ye in all the way that I command you, that it may be well with you. But they hearkened not, nor inclined their ear, but walked in their own counsels and in the stubbornness of their evil heart, and went backward, and not forward. Since the day that your fathers came forth out of the land of Egypt unto this day, I have sent unto you all my servants the prophets, daily rising up early and sending them: yet they hearkened not unto me, nor inclined their ear, but made their neck stiff: they did worse than their fathers.[2]

Something like this is ever the recourse of the prophet when temporary truths become erected into permanent dogmas, and

[1] Jeremiah 7 8-15.   [2] Jeremiah 7 21-26.

practices of worship become, through long custom, sacred ends in themselves — Paul appeals from Moses to the spiritual root of all Israel's religion, personal faith in Jehovah (Galatians 3 [1-22]); Luther from the authoritative church of his day to Paul; the prophets of to-day from Luther, Calvin, Augustine, and the rest to Christ and to the prophets of the Old Covenant. In this, the Christian prophet of every age may find himself at one in spirit with his Master who recognized the necessarily temporary character of particular laws and went back of them to that which was fundamental and universal (*e.g.* Matthew 19 [3-8]).[1]

Jeremiah's messages of doom cut him off from all human sympathy and companionship. Even the men of his own town, the little priestly city of Anathoth, conspired against his life, forbidding him to preach in the name of Jehovah.[2]

Seeing the imminence of terrible destruction, the prophet felt that he must not take a wife and have sons and daughters to die by pestilence or be consumed by sword and famine.[3] As living witness to the inevitable, speedy doom, Jeremiah must even denounce mourning with those who mourn or rejoicing with those who rejoice.[4]

In this period of his life, the compulsion seen in the prophet's early ministry, that drove him on against his will, leads to fierce inner struggles.

Righteous art thou, O Jehovah, when I contend with thee; yet would I reason the cause with thee: Wherefore doth the way of the wicked prosper? wherefore are all they at ease that deal very treacherously? Thou hast planted them, yea, they have taken root; they grow, yea, they bring forth fruit: thou art near in their mouth, and far from their heart. But thou, O Jehovah, knowest me; thou seest me, and triest my heart toward thee: pull them out like sheep for the slaughter, and prepare them for the day of slaughter.

How long shall the land mourn, and the herbs of the whole country wither? for the wickedness of them that dwell therein, the beasts are

---

[1] In our own day, the first-hand study of Israel's prophets and, far more than that, the new first-hand study of the life and teachings of Jesus, in their relation to the conditions of our age, is producing great rendings and tearings in theological conceptions and ecclesiastical practices.

[2] 11 [21].   [3] 16 [1-4].   [4] 16 [5-8].

consumed, and the birds; because they said, He shall not see our last end.

O Jehovah, thou hast persuaded me, and I was persuaded; thou art stronger than I, and hast prevailed: I am become a laughing-stock all the day, every one mocketh me.   For as often as I speak, I cry out; I cry violence and destruction! because the word of Jehovah is made a reproach unto me, and a derision, all the day.   And if I say I will not make mention of him, nor speak any more in his name, then there is in my heart as it were a burning fire shut up in my bones, and I am weary with forbearing, and I cannot contain.   For I have heard the defaming of many, terror on every side.   Denounce, and we will denounce him, say all my familiar friends, they that watch for my fall; peradventure he will be persuaded, and we shall prevail against him, and we shall take our revenge on him.   But Jehovah is with me as a mighty one and terrible: therefore my persecutors shall stumble, and they shall not prevail; they shall be utterly put to shame, because they have not dealt wisely, even with an everlasting dishonor which shall never be forgotten.   But, O Jehovah of hosts, that triest the righteous, and seest the heart and the mind, let me see thy vengeance on them; for unto thee have I revealed my cause.   Sing unto Jehovah, praise ye Jehovah; for he hath delivered the soul of the needy from the hand of evil-doers.

Cursed be the day wherein I was born; let not the day wherein my mother bare me be blessed.   Cursed be the man, who brought tidings to my father, saying, A man-child is born unto thee; making him very glad. And let that man be as the cities which Jehovah overthrew, and repented not; and let him hear a cry in the morning, and shouting at noon-time; because he slew me not from the womb; and so my mother would have been my grave, and her womb always great.   Wherefore came I forth out of the womb to see labor and sorrow, that my days should be consumed with shame?[1]

Through such wrestlings, the prophet came to a personal fellowship with God, beyond that which we see in any other hero of ancient Israel.   From his hours of despair he goes forth strong to meet his task and perform it, a task increasingly difficult which can be accomplished only as strength grows with need.

If thou hast run with the footmen, and they have wearied thee, then how canst thou contend with horses? and though in a land of peace thou art secure, yet how wilt thou do in the pride of the Jordan?   For even thy brethren, and the house of thy father, even they have dealt treacherously

[1] 12 [1-4], 20 [7-18].   Compare also 11 [20], 14 [10-13], 18 [19-23].

with thee; even they have cried aloud after thee: believe them not, though they speak fair words unto thee.[1]

We may not leave this period of Jeremiah's activity without some notice of the exultant taunt-song with which he greets Nebuchadrezzar's victory over Necho, in 604 B.C. Jeremiah immediately recognized Babylon as the power destined to rule the west, and saw in Necho's defeat the removal of the chief support of Jehoiakim's evil reign.

Set in line the buckler and shield and draw near to battle!
Harness the horses and mount, ye riders, and take your stand with your
    helmets!
Polish the lances, put on the coats of mail!

Why are they terrified and turning backward?
They flee in wild flight and look not back; terror on every side!
The swift cannot flee away nor the mighty warrior escape!
Northward beside the River Euphrates they have stumbled and fallen!

Who is this that riseth up like the Nile, whose waters toss themselves like
    the streams?
And he saith, I will rise up, I will cover the earth, I will destroy its in-
    habitants!
Go up, ye horses, and rage, ye chariots, let the mighty warriors go forth:
Cush and Put, armed with shields, and the Ludim who bend the bow!

But that day is Jehovah's day of vengeance, that he may avenge himself
    on his adversaries;
And the sword shall devour to satiety and shall drink its fill of their
    blood.
For Jehovah hath a sacrifice in the north-land beside the River Euphrates.

Go up to Gilead and take balm, O virgin daughter of Egypt!
In vain hast thou employed many medicines; there is no healing for
    thee.
Nations have heard thy wail, and the earth is full of thy outcry.
For hero hath stumbled against hero, they are fallen both of them to-
    gether![2]

[1] 12 5-6.
[2] 46 3-12. Translation of C. F. Kent in *Sermons, Epistles, and Apocalypses of Israel's Prophets*, p. 218.

The victory of Nebuchadrezzar at Carchemish receives interpretation also from the prophet Habakkuk, who must have spoken at about this time.   His tiny book opens with a cry, out of the violence and injustice that prevail in Judea.   "How long?" Like Micah 6 and 7, the oracle is constructed in the form of dramatic dialogue, at least as far as 2 5.[1]   When the prophet fails to get a satisfactory answer to the problem of the unpunished triumph of the wicked over those more righteous, he takes his stand upon his watch tower and waits for an answer.

In the Chaldeans he sees the instrument of Jehovah's punishment of his people, as, a century before, Isaiah had seen in the Assyrian the rod of Jehovah's hand.   Isaiah had noted that the proud Assyrian had thought himself gratifying his own lust when he was thus used, and Habakkuk, in 1–2 4, does not go beyond applying Isaiah's thought to the conquering power of his day. In 2 5–20, there is sure confidence that the Chaldean in his turn shall suffer just retribution.   This finds expression in a taunt-song against the one that has plundered many nations, beginning : —

> Woe to the proud and treacherous,
> The arrogant one who never has enough,
> Who makes his desire wide as Sheol,
> He is like death, unsatisfied,
> For he hath gathered to himself all the nations,
> And brought together to himself all peoples.
> Shall not these, all of them, take up a proverb against him.[2]

The noble psalm of faith which closes the book is generally counted a later production.

The death of Jehoiakim, some seven years after Nebuchadrezzar's victory, called out from Jeremiah a song of woe in which the people were forbidden to lament the king who had builded his house by unrighteousness and his chambers by injustice.[3] The Babylonian siege of Jerusalem, following three months later, gave Jeremiah occasion for laments which are now imbedded in the twelfth and thirteenth chapters of the book.   The prophet

---

[1] This may have been the entire original prophecy of Habakkuk.

[2] Translation of C. F. Kent, based on a revision of the corrupt Hebrew text.   [3] Jeremiah 22 13–23.

now assured Jehoiakim and the queen mother that their fate was certain and that they should not return from Babylonia.

After the first captivity had begun in 597, false hopes of speedy restoration for the captives were working injury to the community in Jerusalem and the one in Babylon as well, and Jeremiah directed his energies to counteracting this evil. With symbolic vision of the contrasted baskets of figs, one good, the other so bad that the figs could not be eaten, Jeremiah the teacher sought to impress the true situation.[1] Realizing as Jeremiah did that the future hope of the nation lay in its nobler elements that had been carried to Babylon, and confident that the captivity would be long, the far-seeing prophet strove to perpetuate the people in the distant land. He sent a letter to them, urging them to marry, rear families, and seek the peace of the city whither they had come.[2] False prophets promised early restoration; along that line of unpractical and superstitious faith lay the extinction of Judah. Jeremiah was forced to deliver an elaborate oracle against the teachers who flattered the people's hopes.[3]

One of the optimistic prophets, Hananiah, broke a wooden yoke which Jeremiah had put upon his own neck to symbolize coming captivity, declaring in Jehovah's name, "Even so will I break the yoke of Nebuchadrezzar king of Babylon." Replacing the yoke of wood with one of iron, Jeremiah pronounced doom on Hananiah, and declared that the test would be, as it had been with the prophets of old, whether the promised peace came. In opposition to all who would encourage rebellion, he announced that Jehovah had given all these lands to Nebuchadrezzar.

The situation was strikingly parallel to that of a century before when Isaiah strove to dissuade Hezekiah from revolt against Assyria. The statesman-prophet's sound wisdom was flouted now as then, and the mad revolt came. The king, too weak to resist the nobles, still respected Jeremiah's word and sent messengers to seek his counsel or prayer once and again; the prophet's assurance was always of the hopelessness of resistance to Babylon and the certainty of doom for all who did not surrender. The old *ignis-fatuus*, the expectation of help from Egypt, doubtless frustrated Jeremiah's counsels. Egypt actually sent out an

[1] Jeremiah 24.   [2] Jeremiah 29.   [3] Jeremiah 23 9-40.

army that forced the Chaldeans hastily to raise the siege; Jeremiah gave assurance that the besiegers would surely return and burn the city.

At this time of temporary relief, Jeremiah undertook to visit Anathoth, to receive his inheritance there. At the city gate he was arrested as a deserter, and the princes quickly judged him worthy of stripes and prison. Later he was cast into an empty cistern and left to starve in the mud at its bottom. Escaping this horrible fate through the intervention of a friend in the king's household, he was kept in less rigorous confinement, where the king continued to consult him, though he dared not follow the counsel given.

Jeremiah's uncle came to him in prison to sell him a family field in Anathoth. With all legal formality Jeremiah purchased the land, demonstrating his faith that, though destruction was at hand, houses and fields and vineyards should yet be bought in Judea.

With the fall of Jerusalem, the Babylonians learned what Jeremiah's attitude toward the war had been, and they gave him his choice of going to Babylon or remaining with those who were left in the land; he chose the latter course, but, a few months later, was carried down into Egypt, when the little company with whom he dwelt fled thither. This great prophet disappears from view in Egypt, after a public ministry of more than forty years.

Jeremiah's teaching from 597 to 586 yields little of poetic oracle or of striking truth for general application. The prophet was chiefly occupied during this trying period with immediate, practical ends, seeking to avert, as far as possible, the self-sought doom of his loved people and to preserve through wreck and ruin the remnants of the nation. That, out of this sombre time of chastened and unswerving service the prophet did suffer himself to take occasionally the long look ahead, we have seen in the redemption of the family field. The present with its almost hopeless tasks to be performed and its anguish of soul to be endured could not be all for one who believed in Jeremiah's God — "Houses and fields and vineyards shall yet again be bought in this land." Out of these gloomy years came, besides, something far greater than that hope; houses and fields and vineyards restored would not have seemed to him in itself a thing greatly to be desired; a transformed nation there must be to enjoy these blessings.

Jeremiah began his ministry before Josiah's reform; he saw the awful conditions left by Manasseh; then these were swept away by a reform which outwardly transformed the nation, only to be restored in the complete counter-reaction under Jehoiakim and his successors. The era offered a great school in the futility of law, though that law was the noblest ever written, though it put into working form the best ideals of the loftiest idealists. In his later years Jeremiah saw that there must be, not only restoration to a bountiful land, but transformation from within where life has its springs.

Behold, the days come, saith Jehovah, that I will make a new covenant with the house of Israel, and with the house of Judah; not according to the covenant that I made with their fathers in the day that I took them by the hand to bring them out of the land of Egypt; which my covenant they break, although I was a husband unto them, saith Jehovah. But this is the covenant that I will make with the house of Israel after those days, saith Jehovah: I will put my law in their inward parts, and in their heart will I write it; and I will be their God, and they shall be my people. And they shall teach no more every man his neighbor, and every man his brother, saying, Know Jehovah; for they shall all know me, from the least of them unto the greatest of them, saith Jehovah: for I will forgive their iniquity, and their sin will I remember no more.[1]

This passage, which is one of the culminating points of the Old Covenant thought, obviously suggested the name for the Christian religion and for its collection of sacred books — the New Covenant or Testament.

The tragic life of Jeremiah was one of the most significant in the history of humanity. Through anguish of soul Hosea first apprehended the unquenchable love of Jehovah for Israel, and it was through anguish that Jeremiah came into conscious fellowship with God, as no other of whom we have record before Christ. Not in wife nor child, in kindred nor nation, could his sensitive, loving heart be granted the joy and consolation of fellowship; bitterly he complained of his awful loneliness, but in this very complaint he found the universal heart and came to see the unseen.

[1] Jeremiah 31 [31-34].

In Jeremiah it is possible to watch the transition from a national to an individual religion. It would be difficult to say where else in literature one could better put the finger down to mark the beginning of the history of individualism. In Jeremiah's writings we find, then, the record of one of the most important advance steps in the history of literature as well as the history of religion.

The communal character of the earliest poetry of all peoples was emphasized in the early part of the present volume, which has recognized also that in the early prose of Israel we cannot speak of individual authors. In the early prophets, the point of view has been found to be generally tribal or national rather than, individual; on the nation was to fall the blessing or the judgment promised. In the book of Deuteronomy the point of view was largely the same in this respect. In Jeremiah we come to clear expression of the thought that the individual has standing in the sight of God.

In those days they shall say no more, The fathers have eaten sour grapes, and the children's teeth are set on edge. But every one shall die for his own iniquity: every man that eateth the sour grapes, his teeth shall be set on edge.[1]

It was Jeremiah's bitter experience of separation and weakness, driving him into closest personal communion with God, together with the imminent downfall of the nation, that gave a new sense of the individual. In the history of government, ethics, literature, or religion, it is recognized that we go far astray if we fail to see the universal law of the priority of tribal or communal consciousness to the distinctly individual. In the literature and religion of Israel, the mighty significance of the transition can easily be traced.

[1] Jeremiah 31 29-30.

CHAPTER XVI

(597 to 586 B.C.)

If it was matter of surprise that so much literature of Northern Israel survived the catastrophe of 722, it is more difficult to understand how so many of the writings of Judah were preserved at the time of the Babylonian captivity. It may be that some precious rolls, which later found their way back to Judea, were carried by those who had fled to Egypt; the story of Jeremiah's last preaching [1] must have been brought thence, and other matter may have been. Those who remained in Palestine may have preserved some writings; but Babylon now became the centre of literary activity, and it is evident that the devoted love which led the exiles to carry their precious books with them was the means of keeping from destruction the major part of the literature discussed in the previous chapters, together, we must suppose, with much that has since disappeared. Many writings undoubtedly perished in the confusion of the capture and subsequent burning of the city, and in the herding together of the exiles for their long, overland journey on foot. Possibly the official chronicles which had been kept from the days of David until this time were now destroyed; presumably only such rolls as were held most dear by individual owners were hugged close and carried those seven hundred miles.

In general, we can infer that the exiles carried with them their composite histories that dealt with traditions and events from Adam to the death of Solomon. Of these, our books of Samuel, the history of Solomon's reign, and the narratives of the Judges were probably separate rolls; while the narrative from the creation to the death of Joshua may have been treated as one book. They carried also a history of Northern Israel and one of Judah, cover-

[1] Jeremiah 44.

ing all the years of the divided kingdom; though these are now lost, a compiler in the exile used them. Collections of stories about Elijah and Elisha and concerning other prophets, used by the compiler of Kings, the little books of Amos, Hosea, Micah, Zephaniah, Nahum, and Habakkuk, books of the genuine prophecies of Isaiah and Jeremiah — all these must have been taken, not as a Bible, but as little rolls, each consisting of one book or succession of very short books. Perhaps most important of all in the minds of the exiles, was the law book which had been found in the Temple in the eighteenth year of Josiah and had been made the basis of the great reform led by that king. Certainly this book had a controlling influence on the writing of the exile and on the life of the people for a hundred and fifty years.

Besides these writings, we have seen reason to think that collections of songs from Northern Israel, now embodied in the Psalter, may have been among the treasures which survived all the vicissitudes of time (Chapter IX). In addition, there must have been Judean hymns as well; some composed perhaps as early as the tenth century were noted in Chapter III. Others were written at various periods during the three centuries and a half of Judean history that we have seen to be so rich in prose compositions and in the poetic oracles of the great prophets.[1]

Two poems that quite clearly belong to the age of the monarchy are the prayer for victory on behalf of the king about to go forth to war (Psalm 20) and the *Te Deum* on the king's return victorious (Psalm 21) : —

> Jehovah answer thee in the day of trouble;
> The name of the God of Jacob set thee up on high;
> Send thee help from the sanctuary,
> And strengthen thee out of Zion;
> Remember all thy offerings,
> And accept thy burnt-sacrifice;
> Grant thee thy heart's desire,

---

[1] Professor Briggs, *Psalms, Int. Crit. Com.*, 1906, finds some twenty-one psalms or parts of psalms that he assigns with varying confidence to the period between the division of the kingdom and the fall of Jerusalem. They are 2, 3, 19 $^{2-7}$, 20, 21, 23 (perhaps time of Solomon), 27 $^{1-6}$, 28, 36 $^{2-5}$, 45, 46, 54, 55?, 56, 58, 60 $^{3-7}$, $^{12b-14}$, 61, 62, 72 $^{1-7}$, $^{13-17a}$, 87, 110.

And fulfil all thy counsel.
We will triumph in thy salvation,
And in the name of our God we will set up our banners:
Jehovah fulfil all thy petitions.
Now know I that Jehovah saveth his anointed;
He will answer him from his holy heaven
With the saving strength of his right hand.
Some trust in chariots, and some in horses;
But we will make mention of the name of Jehovah our God.
They are bowed down and fallen;
But we are risen, and stand upright.
Save, Jehovah:
Let the King answer us when we call.

The king shall joy in thy strength, O Jehovah;
And in thy salvation how greatly shall he rejoice!
Thou hast given him his heart's desire,
And hast not withholden the request of his lips.
For thou meetest him with the blessings of goodness:
Thou settest a crown of fine gold on his head.
He asked life of thee, thou gavest it him,
Even length of days for ever and ever.
His glory is great in thy salvation:
Honor and majesty dost thou lay upon him.
For thou makest him most blessed for ever:
Thou makest him glad with joy in thy presence.
For the king trusteth in Jehovah;
And through the lovingkindness of the Most High he shall not be moved.
Thy hand will find out all thine enemies;
Thy right hand will find out those that hate thee.
Thou wilt make them as a fiery furnace in the time of thine anger:
Jehovah will swallow them up in his wrath,
And the fire shall devour them.
Their fruit wilt thou destroy from the earth,
And their seed from among the children of men.
For they intended evil against thee;
They conceived a device which they are not able to perform.
For thou wilt make them turn their back;
Thou wilt make ready with thy bowstrings against their face.
Be thou exalted, O Jehovah, in thy strength:
So will we sing and praise thy power.

The beautiful hymn praising the glory of God in the heavens (19 ¹⁻⁶) could consistently be the product of the last period of the monarchy, when the worship of the heavenly bodies themselves was so prominent among the faithless : —

> The heavens declare the glory of God ;
> And the firmament showeth his handiwork.
> Day unto day uttereth speech,
> And night unto night showeth knowledge.
> There is no speech nor language ;
> Their voice is not heard.
> Their line is gone out through all the earth.
> And their words to the end of the world.
> In them hath he set a tabernacle for the sun,
> Which is as a bridegroom coming out of his chamber,
> And rejoiceth as a strong man to run his course.
> His going forth is from the end of the heavens,
> And his circuit unto the ends of it ;
> And there is nothing hid from the heat thereof.

Associated in thought with this morning hymn is the morning prayer of the harassed leader who wakens to thoughts of Jehovah's protection : —

> Jehovah, how are mine adversaries increased !
> Many are there that rise up against me.
> Many there are that say of my soul,
> There is no help for him in God.
> But thou, O Jehovah, art a shield about me ;
> My glory and the lifter up of my head.
> I cry unto Jehovah with my voice,
> And he answereth me out of his holy hill.
> I laid me down and slept ;
> I awaked ; for Jehovah sustaineth me.
> I will not be afraid of ten thousands of the people
> That have set themselves against me round about.
> Arise, O Jehovah ; save me, O my God :
> For thou hast smitten all mine enemies upon the cheek bone ;
> Thou hast broken the teeth of the wicked.
> Salvation belongeth unto Jehovah :
> Thy blessing be upon thy people.

One of the noblest of the hymns which came from the days of
the monarchy is found in the prayer for a true king, apparently an
accession hymn, more appropriate for Josiah than for any other of
the kings of Judah.   Parts of this psalm imply later Messianic
hopes and must be omitted from the original, preëxilic ode.[1]

Give the king thy judgments, O God,
And thy righteousness unto the king's son.
He will judge thy people with righteousness,
And thy poor with justice.
The mountains shall bring peace to the people,
And the hills, in righteousness.
He will judge the poor of the people,
He will save the children of the needy,
And will break in pieces the oppressor.
They shall fear thee while the sun endureth,
And so long as the moon, throughout all generations.
He will come down like rain upon the mown grass,
As showers that water the earth.
In his days shall the righteous flourish,
And abundance of peace, till the moon be no more.
He will have pity on the poor and needy,
And the souls of the needy he will save.
He will redeem their soul from oppression and violence;
And precious will their blood be in his sight:
And they shall live; and to him shall be given of the gold of Sheba:
And men shall pray for him continually;
They shall bless him all the day long.
There shall be abundance of grain in the earth upon the top of the
    mountains;
The fruit thereof shall shake like Lebanon:
And they of the city shall flourish like grass of the earth.
His name shall endure for ever;
His name shall be continued as long as the sun:

The original book of songs that passed current under the name
of David, from which so many poems were embodied in the later
collections making up our Psalter, was not completed until post-
exilic times.   We have no means of knowing, indeed, how far
the early poems that were embodied in the collections lying back

[1] See Briggs, *Psalms, Int. Crit. Com., in loc.*

of the Book of Psalms were already grouped at the close of the monarchy.   The fact, however, that the early days of the kingdom produced collections of national hymns (see pp. 42–43) makes it highly probable that the preëxilic poems of the Book of Psalms were gathered into books of poems which were carried to Babylon along with the rolls that we can name and describe more precisely.

In addition to songs from the kingdom of Judah ultimately embodied in the Book of Psalms, other poems used by the compilers of the exile were carried to Babylon in some form.   One of these is appended to the history of David contained in Samuel. It is styled "the last words of David," but was composed at a much later date than the time of "Israel's sweet singer," perhaps during the reign of Hezekiah or Josiah.[1]

> Says David, son of Jesse,
> The man who was exalted,
> Of Jacob's God anointed,
> And Israel's sweet singer:
>
> "Through me spoke Yahweh's spirit,
> His word upon my tongue was;
> Thus spoke the God of Jacob,
> To me said Israel's rock:
>
> "'Who rules mankind in justice,
> Who in the fear of God reigns,
> Is like the light that breaks forth,
> The sun on cloudless morning.'
>
> "Is not my house with God so?
> He made with me a covenant,
> His watchcare has preserved me,
> What I wished has succeeded.
>
> "Like thorns the bad are cast off,
> They are not led by his hand.
> Who touches them must armed be,
> With spear of wood and iron." [2]

---

[1] Schmidt, *Messages of the Poets*, p. 370.   See also H. P. Smith, *Samuel, Int. Crit. Com.*, p. 381.

[2] Translation by Schmidt in *The Messages of the Poets.*

The "song of Moses" concerning Jehovah's just dealings with Israel very probably dates from Josiah's reign.[1] The opening stanzas as translated by Schmidt are: —

> Give ear, O heavens, I will speak;
> Listen, O earth, to my mouth's words!
> Let my instruction fall like rain,
> And like the dew my words drop down,
> Like showers on the tender grass,
> Like streams upon the withered herb.
>
> For Jehovah's name I will proclaim.
> O give ye honor to our God!
> A rock is he, perfect his work,
> For all his ways are right and true:
> A faithful God, in nothing false,
> He ever upright is and just.
>
> When the Most High scattered mankind,
> And parted wide the sons of men,
> And fixed for nations their abodes,
> In number as the sons of God,
> On Jehovah's lot fell Israel,
> Jacob became his heritage.
>
> He found him in the wilderness,
> A desert where no water was;
> He watched him, kept him, cared for him,
> As for the apple of his eye.
> As eagle that stirs up her nest,
> Flutters and stirs above her young,
>
> He spread abroad his wings, took him,
> And on his pinions held him high;
> He let him o'er high places ride,
> And let him eat fruit of the field;
> Let him suck honey from the cliff,
> And oil out of flinty rock.

Whether there were as yet any formal collections of the nation's gnomic wisdom from which the post-exilic books of aphorisms

---

[1] Driver, *Deuteronomy, Int. Crit. Com.*, p. 346 f.; Schmidt, *Messages of the Poets*, p. 336 f.

drew material is much more doubtful.   We have no clear evidence that Israel in the days of the monarchy made elaborate written collections of proverbs as she did of national songs; yet there is adequate reason to believe that aphoristic wisdom of form similar to that which makes up the great body of the post-exilic book of Proverbs is as old as the nation, and there may have been written collections of proverbs carried to Babylon at the beginning of the sixth century.   About the time of the end of the kingdom, "the wise" appear as a distinct class, along with priests and prophets.[1]

The exiles took with them a rich and varied literature on which they meditated deeply and to which we shall find them adding many new elements in far-off Babylonia.

[1] Jeremiah 18 18.

CHAPTER XVII

PROPHECY AND ELEGY IN THE EARLY YEARS OF EXILE

(592 to about 570 B.C.)

THE exile could not bring about any such sudden and complete break in the literary history of the nation as in its political life; yet the influence of this great national experience is immediately felt in the form and thought of the literature and ultimately works out changes that are revolutionary. The writings of Ezekiel afford interesting illustrations of the continuity of the literary life of the people and also of the modifying influences of the exile.

Ezekiel was a young priest carried to Babylon among the selected ten thousand deported in 597. Five years later, he began his public ministry as a prophet to the exiles who were settled by the Chebar in central Babylonia.[1] His message was at one with that which Jeremiah was delivering at the same time in Jerusalem. Its aim was to prepare the people for the crushing blow which the coming destruction of the trusted city and temple would inflict. Both in Jerusalem and Babylonia there were prophets who were stoutly maintaining the false faith that Jerusalem could not be captured and that the exile would be a very brief matter.[2] As Hananiah in Jerusalem had broken the wooden yoke from Jeremiah's shoulders,[3] so Shemiah in Babylonia was outraged because Jeremiah had sent word to the exiles that the captivity would be long. He wrote to the priest in charge of the Jerusalem temple that such a madman, who made himself a prophet, ought to be

---

[1] The Chebar has often been identified with the Habor of Mesopotamia, but the excavations conducted by the University of Pennsylvania at Nippur, in central Babylonia, have resulted in the identification of the canal Kabaru (the "great canal") which ran down through the heart of Babylonia. Hilprecht argues that the exiles were settled quite near to Nippur, not far from this canal. — *Explorations in Bible Lands during the Nineteenth Century*, pp. 411 ff.   [2] Jeremiah 29 8-9.   [3] p. 222.

put in the stocks.[1] Ezekiel was forced to make use of all the
vivid methods of objective teaching that his fertile genius could
devise to impress the futility of the hope of speedy return and the
certainty of the coming destruction of Jerusalem. He portrayed
the city on a tile and laid mimic siege against it, casting up a
mound, setting camps, and planting battering rams round about.
Forty days he lay on his side, each day for a year, the period which
the iniquity of the house of Judah should be borne. He ate polluted bread because Israel was to eat her bread unclean among
the nations; he carefully measured his food and drink, for thus
the besieged ones would be forced to do in the famine-stricken
city. Cutting off his own hair, burning, smiting, scattering it,
he indicated that a third of Jerusalem's inhabitants should perish
by famine and pestilence, a third by the sword, and a third should
be scattered to the winds, with a sword drawn out after them.[2]

Besides performing symbolic actions, Ezekiel described con-
cretely actual conditions as he saw them existing, or again, with
no less of vividness, the symbolic visions of his own soul. The
very temple which Jeremiah found the people trusting as a palladium, Ezekiel pictured as desecrated by the grossest animal
worship and nature worship.[3] In vision, he saw Jehovah departing from his polluted house.[4]

Ezekiel expanded and made more definite Jeremiah's doctrine
of individualism. The proverb, "The fathers have eaten sour
grapes and the children's teeth are set on edge" was popular in
Babylon,[5] as it was also in Judea.[6] To interpret the blow that
had fallen in 597 as a national judgment due to the sins of a former
generation was a natural application of the doctrine of the prophets,
a doctrine inadequate for the exigency of the present situation.
The earlier prophets had dealt with the nation; the end of the
nation has now begun and the individual must find his relation
to the God of justice. The transition to individualism, begun in
Jeremiah, is greatly furthered in Ezekiel : —

Yet say ye, Wherefore doth not the son bear the iniquity of the father?
When the son hath done that which is lawful and right, and hath kept all
my statutes, and hath done them, he shall surely live. The soul that

---

[1] Jeremiah 29 24-29.   [2] Ezekiel 4 and 5.   [3] Chapter 8.
[4] 11 22-23.   [5] 18 2.   [6] Jeremiah 31 29.

sinneth, it shall die: the son shall not bear the iniquity of the father, neither shall the father bear the iniquity of the son; the righteousness of the righteous shall be upon him, and the wickedness of the wicked shall be upon him.

But if the wicked turn from all his sins that he hath committed, and keep all my statutes, and do that which is lawful and right, he shall surely live, he shall not die. None of his transgressions that he hath committed shall be remembered against him: in his righteousness that he hath done he shall live. Have I any pleasure in the death of the wicked? saith the Lord Jehovah; and not rather that he should return from his way, and live? But when the righteous turneth away from his righteousness, and committeth iniquity, and doeth according to all the abominations that the wicked man doeth, shall he live? None of his righteous deeds that he hath done shall be remembered: in his trespass that he hath trespassed, and in his sin that he hath sinned, in them shall he die.[1]

Since the captives of 597 and their kindred left behind in Jerusalem were in communication, thought in one centre answered thought in the other. The prophets of false hope taught the same dangerous doctrine in each region, and the true prophets who saw the inevitable doom were one in doctrine, whether in Jerusalem or on the river Chebar. Ezekiel's methods, too, of recounted vision and symbolic action were the outgrowth of the methods that had long been used by the Judean prophets. Yet it is true that Ezekiel's symbolism, especially in his visions, developed into a form new and bewildering.

Isaiah had described his inaugural vision in symbols that are intelligible and beautiful in every age and land; but the imagery of Ezekiel's inaugural vision, while it fascinates those who love esoteric mysteries, repels most, normally constituted men and women of to-day.

And I looked, and, behold, a stormy wind came out of the north, a great cloud, with a fire infolding itself, and a brightness round about it, and out of the midst thereof as it were glowing metal, out of the midst of the fire. And out of the midst thereof came the likeness of four living creatures. And this was their appearance: They had the likeness of a man; and every one had four faces, and every one of them had four wings. And their feet were straight feet; and the sole of their feet was like the sole of

[1] Ezekiel 18 [19-24].

a calf's foot; and they sparkled like burnished brass.   And they had the
hands of a man under their wings on their four sides; and they four had
their faces and their wings thus: their wings were joined one to another;
they turned not when they went; they went every one straight forward.
As for the likeness of their faces, they had the face of a man; and they four
had the face of a lion on the right side; and they four had the face of an ox
on the left side; they four had also the face of an eagle. . . .

And above the firmament that was over their heads was the likeness
of a throne, as the appearance of a sapphire stone; and upon the likeness
of the throne was a likeness as the appearance of a man upon it above.
And I saw as it were glowing metal, as the appearance of fire within
it round about, from the appearance of his loins and upward; and from the
appearance of his loins and downward I saw as it were the appearance
of fire, and there was brightness round about him. As the appearance of
the bow that is in the cloud in the day of rain, so was the appearance
of the brightness round about.   This was the appearance of the likeness of
the glory of Jehovah.   And when I saw it, I fell upon my face, and I heard
a voice of one that spake.

And he said unto me, Son of man, stand upon thy feet, and I will
speak with thee.   And the Spirit entered into me when he spake unto
me, and set me upon my feet; and I heard him that spake unto me.
And he said unto me, Son of man, I send thee to the children of Israel, to
nations that are rebellious, which have rebelled against me: they and
their fathers have transgressed against me even unto this very day.   And
the children are impudent and stiff-hearted: I do send thee unto them;
and thou shalt say unto them, Thus saith the Lord Jehovah.   And they,
whether they will hear, or whether they will forbear (for they are a rebellious house), yet shall know that there hath been a prophet among them.
And thou, son of man, be not afraid of them, neither be afraid of their
words, though briers and thorns are with thee, and thou dost dwell among
scorpions; be not afraid of their words, nor be dismayed at their looks
though they are a rebellious house.   And thou shalt speak my words unto
them, whether they will hear, or whether they will forbear; for they are
most rebellious. . . .

Then the Spirit lifted me up, and I heard behind me the voice of a great
rushing, saying, Blessed be the glory of Jehovah from his place.   And
I heard the noise of the wings of the living creatures as they touched one
another, and the noise of the wheels beside them, even the noise of a great
rushing.   So the Spirit lifted me up, and took me away; and I went in
bitterness, in the heat of my spirit; and the hand of Jehovah was strong
upon me.   Then I came to them of the captivity at Tel-abib, that dwelt

by the river Chebar, and to where they dwelt; and I sat there over-whelmed among them seven days.[1]

Aside from the grotesque combination of faces, wheels, wings, eyes, burning fire, the style is repetitious and prosaic in the giving of the commission. The earlier prophets had thought in the more universal language of the hills and valleys, the clouds and rains, the fruitful fields and pastures of their varied landscape, or in the hardly less universal terms of the homely arts of the household or the daily toil of the farmer and shepherd. Why does Ezekiel, who is so similar to them in his message and his method of teaching, adopt this outlandish imagery?

Five years have now passed since the prophet and his fellow exiles lost their last glimpse of the Syrian mountains and came to live on the monotonous plain of Babylonia where a princess from the north was once so lorn for a glimpse of a hill that her royal spouse constructed for her that wonder of the ancient world, a park with artificial hills, the "hanging gardens of Babylon." On the unending plain of Babylonia, with its rank crops of grain growing wherever the great sluggish canals brought their irrigating moisture; on the banks of one of these ditches, never more hearing the music of mountain torrent or looking off across the deep, broad valley to the red wall of Moab, or up to white-capped Hermon, Ezekiel and his fellow exiles had for five long years seen nought but the stars above and the stupendous works of men.

The American excavations at Nippur on the Chebar canal have revealed the ruins of the great temple of Bel and other structures with imposing sculptured figures, on which Ezekiel and his hearers may have looked. The pictorial imagination of the Hebrew prophet is filled now with the imagery of Babylonia. He seizes upon the very symbols, composite figures, part man, part beast, part bird, that the Babylonians used in their palaces and temples. Perhaps we should say these have filled his imagination until in a night of intense conviction, they appear in his ecstatic vision in bewildering confusion and new combinations. From all this, however, there comes no mere fantastic dream; rather the prophet of conquered Israel sees the symbols of the religion whose devotees

[1] Ezekiel 1 4-10, 1 26-2 7, 3 12-15.

have conquered, all united in a construction that speaks of life, power, intelligence, swift and purposeful movement, serving as the throne and chariot of the God of defeated Judea, and bringing him to his exiled follower to direct and strengthen for a great task.

The mass of the exiles thought of Jehovah as dwelling in Judea and in his temple. Soon Jerusalem will fall, and then all the world will know that Bel and Marduk are mightier than Jehovah. All this Ezekiel understands full well, but with the "audacious certitude of faith" that ever controls the true prophet, he sees his God sitting enthroned above all such great symbolic figures as inspired the awe and reverence of mighty Babylon; he sees him present in Babylon itself.

Every Hebrew prophet lived intensely in his immediate surroundings and spoke to his generation in the imagery with which he and they were daily familiar; but the spirit of the true prophet rose free above those surroundings, for he saw over and through all the eternal presence. The picturing was never an end in his word, but only a means to find entrance through the hard forehead to the stiff heart.

In Ezekiel's painstaking accuracy as to dates and details, we have perhaps the mark of this prophet's priestly training; in larger measure, the influence of Babylonian culture. With that commercial people the date of a document was of large concern, and accurate systems of dating were early developed. To the spirit of earlier Israel this had been very foreign. Amos might date his message three years before the earthquake, but from what point was the earthquake dated?

The symbolism of Ezekiel, his exact and repetitious style, and some of his leading ideas become paramount influences in the post-exilic literature. Ezekiel is indeed a most significant transition figure in the literary history of Israel. With roots struck deep in the past he was yet intensely alive to the present surroundings and future needs of his people.

At the time of the final siege of Jerusalem, Ezekiel's wife dies, yet the prophet refrains from all the outward acts of mourning, something almost inconceivable in the east. Through such extreme action, he becomes, as Isaiah in captive garb had been, a living prophecy of the stunning grief that is to fall upon Judah.[1]

With the capture of Jerusalem the whole tenor of Ezekiel's message is changed. The period of inactivity that lasted until the news of the city's fall reached Babylon may have served to prepare the prophet for the new task now before him. The portion of the book of Ezekiel that contains the oracles of the new period begins with a stern self-examination of the prophet's grave responsibility. Ezekiel does not hesitate to apply his doctrine of individual responsibility to himself as the watchman upon whom the blood of the city rests if he perform not his duty.

And the word of Jehovah came unto me, saying, Son of man, speak to the children of thy people, and say unto them, When I bring the sword upon a land, and the people of the land take a man from among them, and set him for their watchman; if, when he seeth the sword come upon the land, he blow the trumpet, and warn the people; then whosoever heareth the sound of the trumpet, and taketh not warning, if the sword come, and take him away, his blood shall be upon his own head. He heard the sound of the trumpet, and took not warning; his blood shall be upon him; whereas if he had taken warning, he would have delivered his soul. But if the watchman see the sword come, and blow not the trumpet, and the people be not warned, and the sword come, and take any person from among them; he is taken away in his iniquity, but his blood will I require at the watchman's hand.

So thou, son of man, I have set thee a watchman unto the house of Israel; therefore hear the word at my mouth, and give them warning from me. When I say unto the wicked, O wicked man, thou shalt surely die, and thou dost not speak to warn the wicked from his way; that wicked man shall die in his iniquity, but his blood will I require at thy hand. Nevertheless, if thou warn the wicked of his way to turn from it, and he turn not from his way; he shall die in his iniquity, but thou hast delivered thy soul.[2]

After this preface our prophet turns to meet the need of those who are crushed, feeling that they cannot live under the judgment which has fallen upon them; he turns to assure them that Jehovah has no pleasure in the death of the wicked, but desires rather that they turn from their evil ways and live. Previously Ezekiel's message has been one of doom, and this has been necessary

---

[1] 24 15-24. [2] 33 1-9.

to prepare the people for the blow that was coming, but now when they are crushed under the stroke and are ready to accuse Jehovah of cruel delight in punishment, the prophet must find thoughts of hope.   Weak despair is as fatal now as was vain hope before.

Ezekiel now finds himself a popular preacher; he has been vindicated and the false prophets, we may surmise, silenced.   He is the talk of the town, they flock to hear him, they enjoy his discourse, but they do not his words.

And as for thee, son of man, the children of thy people talk of thee by the walls and in the doors of the houses, and speak one to another, every one to his brother, saying, Come, I pray you, and hear what is the word that cometh forth from Jehovah.   And they come unto thee as the people cometh, and they sit before thee as my people, and they hear thy words, but do them not; for with their mouth they show much love, but their heart goeth after their gain.   And, lo, thou art unto them as a very lovely song of one that hath a pleasant voice, and can play well on an instrument; for they hear thy words, but they do them not.[1]

Still undismayed the prophet preaches.   Through him Jehovah promises to gather his sheep out of all places whither they have been scattered, to feed them upon the mountains of Israel by the watercourses, himself becoming their shepherd.

In the vision of the valley filled with dry bones, Ezekiel addresses himself again to those who have given up in despair, who say "Our bones are dried up, and our hope is lost; we are clean cut off."   Again, by uniting two sticks, he represents figuratively a promised reunion between Judah and Northern Israel, with one Davidic king ruling.

The prophecy of King Gog, who with the hordes from the uttermost parts of the north is to attack Judah, gives Ezekiel's peculiar, fantastic, yet realistic imagination full play.   The strange picture which the prophet here develops of a great gathering of the distant nations against Jehovah's people to be cut off with terrible slaughter just when victory seems certain, may have its suggestion far back in the days when Isaiah promised such fate to the incoming hordes of Assyria, but in Ezekiel the picture becomes generalized to

[1] 33 30-32.

include any distant and terrible nations and to mark Jehovah's ultimate vindication of his power. In this general form, the vision of Ezekiel is the prototype of the many apocalypses that follow; by the beginning of the Christian era the apocalypse seems almost the only form of literature in vogue in Palestine. If Isaiah's picture of Assyria's advance and downfall gave form to the hope, Ezekiel's firm conviction that Jehovah must win back his lost prestige gave it substance. This conception comes to expression again and again in chapters 33–39.[1]

Chapters 40 to 48 contain plans for the rebuilt temple, the reëstablished worship, and the reapportioned land. The temple proper is evidently to be like the old temple of Solomon, destroyed by Nebuchadrezzar, but its outer courts and gates are to be constructed on a scale quite unknown to the preëxilic temple. The worship, too, is to be marked by certain refinements and developments unknown to the law of Deuteronomy and other preëxilic literature. The land from the border of Damascus northward beside Hamath, in the Lebanon region, and south to Kadesh, the centre of the ancient wilderness sojourn, is to be divided into twelve horizontal bands from the east side to the west side, each the portion of a tribe. Seven of the divisions are north of Jerusalem and five south. In the centre lies the sanctuary, with the land of priests and Levites and the prince's portion. In this final vision of the restored Israel, the priest Ezekiel gives free rein to himself. The great preëxilic prophets had minimized or denounced ritual; Ezekiel, although he shares something of their ethical insight, finds the climax of his hopes in a more highly developed priestly organization of life than had been dreamt in the days of the monarchy. In this line of thought, too, he becomes a controlling force upon post-exilic Judaism which, a century and a half later, enters upon its era of almost complete legalism.

Some of Ezekiel's imagery in his prophecies after 586 is beautiful. Supremely so is his picture of the Divine shepherd with the selfish shepherds who have tended the flock of Israel and have permitted the fat sheep to shoulder away the lean and weak.

[1] 36 23–36, 37 28, 38 23.

R

And the word of Jehovah came unto me, saying, Son of man, prophesy against the shepherds of Israel, prophesy, and say unto them, even to the shepherds, Thus saith the Lord Jehovah: Woe unto the shepherds of Israel that do feed themselves! Should not the shepherds feed the sheep? Ye eat the fat, and ye clothe you with the wool, ye kill the fatlings; but ye feed not the sheep. The diseased have ye not strengthened, neither have ye healed that which was sick, neither have ye bound up that which was broken, neither have ye brought back that which was driven away, neither have ye sought that which was lost; but with force and with rigor have ye ruled over them. And they were scattered, because there was no shepherd; and they became food to all the beasts of the field, and were scattered. My sheep wandered through all the mountains, and upon every high hill; yea, my sheep were scattered upon all the face of the earth; and there was none that did search or seek after them. . . .

For thus saith the Lord Jehovah: Behold, I myself, even I, will search for my sheep, and will seek them out. As a shepherd seeketh out his flock in the day that he is among his sheep that are scattered abroad, so will I seek out my sheep; and I will deliver them out of all places whither they have been scattered in the cloudy and dark day. And I will bring them out from the peoples, and gather them from the countries, and will bring them into their own land; and I will feed them upon the mountains of Israel, by the watercourses, and in all the inhabited places of the country. I will feed them with good pasture; and upon the mountains of the height of Israel shall their fold be: there shall they lie down in a good fold; and on fat pasture shall they feed upon the mountains of Israel. I myself will be the shepherd of my sheep, and I will cause them to lie down, saith the Lord Jehovah. I will seek that which was lost, and will bring back that which was driven away, and will bind up that which was broken, and will strengthen that which was sick: but the fat and the strong I will destroy; I will feed them in justice.

And as for you, O my flock, thus saith the Lord Jehovah: Behold, I judge between sheep and sheep, the rams and the he-goats. Seemeth it a small thing unto you to have fed upon the good pasture, but ye must tread down with your feet the residue of your pasture? and to have drunk of the clear waters, but ye must foul the residue with your feet? And as for my sheep, they eat that which ye have trodden with your feet, and they drink that which ye have fouled with your feet.

Therefore thus saith the Lord Jehovah unto them: Behold, I, even I, will judge between the fat sheep and the lean sheep. Because ye thrust with side and with shoulder, and push all the diseased with your horns, till ye have scattered them abroad; therefore will I save my flock, and they shall no more be a prey; and I will judge between sheep and sheep. And I will set up one shepherd over them, and he shall feed them, even my servant David; he shall feed them, and he shall be their shepherd. And I, Jehovah, will be their God, and my servant David prince among them; I, Jehovah, have spoken it.[1]

The picture of the prophet as watchman is most effective; it truly expresses vital thought and in a way that grips the memory; yet it is in sharpest contrast to Isaiah's imagery. In Isaiah illustrations came tumbling over each other, fifteen or sixteen different ones in a short chapter, three or four in a verse. When he did permit himself to carry out one illustration at length, as in the case of the ship laboring in the storm, all was spontaneous action and sudden transition to some new aspect of the scene. Ezekiel works out deliberately his illustration of the watchman through nine verses and uses this to introduce an address that contains not one illustration or bit of figurative language. In the main, the address is a series of general statements. In this respect, too, it is in sharpest contrast to the method of the early prophets who almost never made a generalization, but put everything into specific, concrete pictures. Once in this address, Ezekiel gives an example or two of specific sins (33 [15]), and once, by attributing words to the people, he gives a little human touch that shows why he was preaching this sermon; now that Jehovah's judgment had fallen, it seemed to the people to have come unjustly, as we have seen elsewhere.

In chapter 36, the address to the mountains, rivers, and valleys of Israel gives some picturesqueness, though the semi-personification is carried out much more elaborately than in the earlier prophets. It is generally true of Ezekiel that he elaborates and becomes labored when he essays any figure of speech. He seems to say to himself, "Go to now, and let us speak in a figure," and when he has once found a good comparison, he can hardly let go. Occasionally a figurative expression seems almost unconscious; such an one is, "I will take away the stony heart out of your flesh."

In the present arrangement of the book of Ezekiel, there stands between the group of prophecies delivered before the fall of Jerusalem and those just considered, a collection of oracles con-

[1] 34 [1-6, 11-24].

cerning foreign nations — Ammon, Moab, Edom, Philistia, Tyre, Sidon, Egypt. In distant Babylonia, the alert prophet learned of the treatment of Judah by its vengeful, jealous neighbors and maintained keen interest in the fates of Phœnicia and Egypt. His taunting dirges over Tyre and over the Egyptian king are especially interesting to the student of literature. Rudyard Kipling took no more satisfaction in exhibiting his technical knowledge in "The Ship that Found Herself" than Ezekiel in bringing his knowledge of geography and commerce into the description of the ship of state that foundered. This is true even though verses 9b to 25a may be no part of the dirge. The fact that the figure of the ship disappears in these verses and that the characteristic elegiac metre is also wanting makes it probable that originally the dirge did not contain this s ction. With this omitted we have a sarcastic lament over the anticipated wreck of Tyre in which the qina metre [1] may be seen to excellent advantage. Tyre is at the time of writing supreme in all Phœnicia; hence the men of the other cities, Sidon, Arvad, and Byblos, may well be represented as her rowers and calkers.

Tyre, thou saidst: A ship am I; perfect in beauty.
In the heart of the sea is thy bound ; thy builders perfected thy beauty.
Of cypress from Hermon they made for thee, all thy planks.
A cedar from Lebanon they took, a mast to form.
Of lofty oaks from Bashan, they fashioned thy oars;
Thy deck, of ivory with boxwood, from the Cyprian isles.
Fine linen with broidery from Egypt was thy canvas.
Violet and purple from the coasts of Greece, were thy hangings.
The men of Sidon and Arvad, were thy oarsmen.
Thy own skilful ones, Tyre, were in thee; they were thy pilots.
The elders of Byblos were in thee, menders of thy rents;
And thou wast filled and greatly laden, in the heart of the seas.
Onto the high seas they brought thee, those rowing thee.
The east wind shattered thee, in the heart of the waters.
Thy wealth and wares, thy merchandise, thy mariners and sailors,
Menders of thy rents, thy merchants, and all thy warriors
Shall fall into the heart of the sea, on the day of thy fall.
At the sound of the cry of thy pilots, thy rowers (?) shall tremble;
And shall leave their ships, all who grasp an oar.

[1] See p. 32.

Mariners, all sailors of the sea, on the land shall they stand,
And shall utter their voice over thee, and bitterly cry,
And dust shall cast on their heads, shall roll in ashes,
Shall make a baldness for thee, and sackcloth gird on,
For thee weep in bitterness of soul, mourning bitterly,
And shall take up a dirge over thee, and lament over thee:
Who was lofty as Tyre, in the midst of the sea?
When thy wares came from the seas, thou didst supply peoples.
By abundance of wealth and goods, thou madest rich earth's kings.
Now art thou shattered in the sea, in depths of waters.
Thy wares and all thy people, sank in thy midst.
All dwellers on the coasts are awestruck at thee,
And their kings are greatly horrified, their faces are pallid.
The merchants of the peoples are shocked at thee; thou art a destruc-
    tion,
And shalt be nought forever.[1]

The lament over Egypt is of greater literary interest. Both the conception and the construction of this primitive "Inferno" are notable. The refrain is tantalizing. Read the poem and you will catch its cadence every few lines; take the printed text and try to underscore this refrain at each recurrence and you are curiously baffled in trying to determine which clauses to include. Possibly some of the irregularity may be due to the corruption of the text; this varies greatly in the Hebrew and the Greek and is highly unsatisfactory in each. The original form of the dirge may have run somewhat as follows: —

Than whom art thou more beautiful? go down and be laid with the
    uncircumcised.
Among the sword-slain shall they fall, to the sword is she given.
Mighty warriors shall speak to him, with his helpers, from out Sheol:
They are gone down, they lie, the uncircumcised, slain of the sword.

There is Asshur and all her host, about her grave;
All of them slain, fallen by the sword,
Whose graves are placed in the uttermost pit,
And her host is about her grave.
All of them slain, fallen by the sword,
Who caused terror in the land of the living.

[1] Ezekiel 27 [3b-9a], [25b-36]. For emendations of the text see especially Bertholet, *Das Buch Hesekial, Kurzer Hand-Commentar* and Kittel, *Bib. Heb.*

There is Elam and all her host, about her grave.
All of them slain, fallen by the sword,
Who went down uncircumcised to the netherworld,
Who caused terror in the land of the living,
And they bear their shame with those who go down to the pit.[1]

There is Mesech-Tubal and all her host about her grave,
All of them uncircumcised, sword-slain,
For their terror was put in the land of the living;
And they lie not with the fallen heroes of old,
Who went down to Sheol with their weapons of war,
And laid their swords beneath their heads,
And their shields upon their bones;
For the terror of their might was in the land of the living.
Thou too in the midst of the uncircumcised shalt lie,
With the slain of the sword.

There is Edom, her kings and all her princes,
Who are laid in their might with the sword-slain.
They with the uncircumcised shall lie,
And with those who go down to the pit.

There are the princes of the north and all the Zidonians,
Who went down slain in the terror of their might,
And lie uncircumcised with the sword-slain.
And they bear their shame with those who go down to the pit.

Then shall Pharaoh see and be comforted for all his host.
Oracle of the Lord Jehovah.
For he caused his terror in the land of the living,
And he shall be laid in the midst of the uncircumcised,
With the sword-slain,
Even Pharaoh and all his company.
Oracle of the Lord Yahweh.[2]

While Ezekiel sang, with a prophet's confidence, anticipatory dirges over Tyre and Pharaoh, other poets were uttering heart-broken laments over Jerusalem. Traditionally these are ascribed to the prophet Jeremiah. It is conceivable that he may have composed one or more of the dirges, although our knowledge of

[1] Verse 25 omitted; so Toy and Bertholet.   Septuagint omits all but one clause.   [2] Ezekiel 32 19-32.

Jeremiah's personality and literary style, gathered from the writings that are certainly his, does not favor this theory. It is almost impossible to believe that Jeremiah wrote the fifth lament with its outcry "Our fathers have sinned and are not, and we have borne their iniquities," for this is contradictory to the great doctrine that Jeremiah first enunciated in sharp opposition to those who held that they were suffering for their fathers' sins.[1] The author of the fourth lament (verse 17) apparently identifies himself with those who looked for help from Egypt, of whom Jeremiah was never one. In 2 ⁹, the statement that the prophets of the daughter of Zion find no vision from Jehovah sounds strange in the mouth of the prophet Jeremiah; while the closing verses of Lamentations 1 and 3 seem out of harmony with Jeremiah's ideas concerning the Chaldeans as Jehovah's instrument.

The book of Lamentations exhibits the Hebrew elegy in its perfection of artistic development. The typical elegiac metre is realized with a uniformity that one rarely finds in Hebrew verses as they have come down to us. The verse-structure is felt even in a translation that makes no effort to reproduce the metrical effect of the original. In addition to their rigid metrical form, the first four poems are acrostics. A few lines of each in a translation that seeks to reproduce this feature will serve to illustrate the form: —

Alas! how doth the city solitary, that was full of people!
> how is she become as a widow, she that was great among the nations,
> the princess among the provinces, how is she become tributary!

By night she weepeth, the tears are on her cheeks,
> among all her lovers she hath none left to comfort her;
> all her friends have dealt treacherously with her, they are become
> her enemies.

Thus the poem goes on through the twenty-two letters of the Hebrew alphabet. The second is of similar structure, but in the third the three lines of each group begin with the same letter: —

Am I not the man that have seen affliction by the rod of his wrath?
Aye, He hath brought me into darkness, not into light;
Against me only turneth He His hand all the day long.

[1] Jeremiah 31 ²⁹⁻³⁰; cf. p. 225.

Broken of Him are my bones, my flesh and my skin hath He wasted away;
Builded hath He against me; He hath compassed me with gall and
    travail,
Brought me into dark places, as they that be dead of old.

The fourth lament is arranged in distichs beginning with the
successive letters: —

Alas, how is the gold become dim, how is the most fine gold changed!
    the stones of the sanctuary are poured out in the top of every street!
Behold the sons of Sion, the precious ones, comparable to fine gold!
    how are they esteemed as earthen pitchers, the work of the hands of the
        potter![1]

The fifth dirge is written in twenty-two distichs, like the fourth,
but the lines are not alphabetical.

In these elegies, it is clear that we do not have the free, un-
hampered verse of the prophets or of the earlier days of Hebrew
song; we find, rather, the apparent spontaneity of art that has
attained mastery of its particular form so that it is not hampered
by the form, however rigid this may be. The terminology, as
well as the structure, has become somewhat conventionalized. In
2, for example, we hear constantly of the daughter of Judah, the
daughter of Zion, the virgin daughter of Zion. The figure is that
met in Amos's little elegy two hundred years before. Such
conventional phraseology is generally characteristic of lyric poetry.
That the conventionalities of form and phraseology were thoroughly
mastered will be obvious to one who reads with this in mind
2 [8-10, 12, 14, 15][2]

Jehovah hath purposed to destroy the wall of the daughter of Zion;
He hath stretched out the line, he hath not withdrawn his hand from
    destroying:
And he hath made the rampart and wall to lament; they languish together.

___

[1] Translations taken from *The Psalms Chronologically Arranged*, by
Four Friends, pp. 421 ff.

[2] Woodberry notes (*Appreciation of Literature*, p. 30) that the imagery
of lyric poetry has these elements of permanence; the nightingale, the
serenade, the enclosed garden, the Eden isle are images and situations
charged with associations of long use; "they are, in fact, a ritual of love
service, and possess a ceremonial beauty and solemnity; they are parts
of ancient poetic worship. They are like a fixed musical scale on which
the emotion which is the imageless burden of song, rises and falls."

Her gates are sunk into the ground ; he hath destroyed and broken her bars:
Her king and her princes are among the nations where the law is not ;
Yea, her prophets find no vision from Jehovah.
The elders of the daughter of Zion sit upon the ground, they keep silence ;
They have cast up dust upon their heads ; they have girded themselves
    with sackcloth :
The virgins of Jerusalem hang down their heads to the ground.
They say to their mothers, Where is grain and wine ?
When they swoon as the wounded in the streets of the city,
When their soul is poured out into their mothers' bosom.
Thy prophets have seen for thee false and foolish visions ;
And they have not uncovered thine iniquity, to bring back thy captivity,
But have seen for thee false oracles and causes of banishment.
All that pass by clap their hands at thee ;
They hiss and wag their head at the daughter of Jerusalem, saying,
Is this the city that men called The perfection of beauty, The joy of the
    whole earth ?

The writer pictures the capture of the city, the grief of the people,
the concrete cause of their ruin, the joy and taunts of their enemies
almost as vividly as Isaiah could have done in his utterly free and
varied literary form.   One may not say as much for the spontaneity
of the preceding poem, yet the varied imagery throughout even this
one compares not unfavorably with that of the earlier compositions
which were not poured into any such rigid mould.   We marvel at
the artistic perfection which the elegy attained in ancient Israel.

It is commonly noted that the lyric temper tends to sadness ;
and Cheyne, a Biblical scholar of literary culture, exclaims, "Is
there another such book in the whole world — such an 'almost
unalloyed expression of unrestrained anguish and utter, unconsolable desolation'?"[1]   The writer of the article Poetry[2] in the
ninth edition of the *Encyclopædia Britannica*, placing the Hebrew
lyric above the Greek lyric in its combination of " unconscious
power with unconscious grace," holds that the "Great Lyric"
must be an outpouring of the soul not toward man, but toward
God.   We cannot attribute the "unconsolable desolation" of the
poems of Lamentations to the mere personal grief of a man who
has seen affliction, or to patriotic sorrow for the destruction of
Jerusalem, coupled with sympathy for exiled countrymen.   As

[1] Jeremiah, *His Life and Times*, p. 181.   [2] Theodore Watts.

the Hebrew lyric of joy attained its greatest heights only in the
rapturous outpouring of the poet's soul to his God; the Hebrew
song of mourning attained its greatest perfection, not in sorrow
for the dead, but in anguish when the wrath of God was poured
out upon the sin of His people.

It may be that not all the poems of Lamentations were composed
in the early years of the exile; but all except the third seem quite
clearly to have the conditions of this period as their background,
and no important reasons appear for regarding 2 and 4, at least,
as of any later date.

Whether the brief oracle of Obadiah was occasioned by the
conduct of the Edomites at the capture of Jerusalem in 586 or
by the circumstances of some later time is not wholly clear. At
the time of the exile, we know that the Edomites took advantage
of the depopulation of Judea to extend their territory northward;
Ezekiel speaks of "all Idumea which have appointed my land
into their possession." [1] It may well be that the picture given in
Obadiah describes the conduct of the Edomites in 586 B.C.

For the violence done to thy brother Jacob, shame shall cover thee,
and thou shalt be cut off for ever. In the day that thou stoodest on the
other side, in the day that strangers carried away his substance, and foreigners entered into his gates, and cast lots upon Jerusalem, even thou
wast as one of them. But look not thou on the day of thy brother in the
day of his disaster, and rejoice not over the children of Judah in the day
of their destruction; neither speak proudly in the day of distress. Enter
not into the gate of my people in the day of their calamity; yea, look
not thou on their affliction in the day of their calamity, neither lay ye
hands on their substance in the day of their calamity. And stand thou
not in the crossway, to cut off those of his that escape; and deliver not
up those of his that remain in the day of distress. [2]

Despite its brevity, Obadiah is certainly a composite writing;
the verses preceding those given above contain an older oracle
against Edom that has no special reference to the circumstances
of Obadiah's time. [3] The closing verses of Obadiah give a glorious
outlook for the future of Jerusalem.

[1] 36 5.   [2] Obadiah 10–14.
[3] Essentially the same oracle is given at an earlier date in Jeremiah
49 14–16, 9–10a, 7.   That Obadiah does not quote from Jeremiah seems
clear from the fact that he has the material in the better order. Both
prophets quote an earlier prophecy.

CHAPTER XVIII

PROPHETIC PRINCIPLES APPLIED TO HISTORY

(*About 600 to 550 B.C.*)

Israel's narrative writing during the two centuries from the time of the united kingdom to the period of Amos, produced the fresh and beautiful stories of Saul and David, of the Judges, of Moses, of the Patriarchs, and of pre-patriarchal times, of Israel's wars with Syria, and of the deeds of Elijah and other early prophets. Much of this material is so imbued with the spirit of Israel's prophets that some of the documents are commonly called prophetic histories. The Joseph narratives, for example, show that before the days of Amos and Isaiah, Israel's God was conceived in terms both ethical and international; for Joseph to sin against his Egyptian master was to sin against God,[1] and God was thought of as using even the evil purposes of man to bring about beneficent ends.[2]

Our study has showed that narrative prose writing was not stopped by the coming of the great era of prophetic literature, yet the first great age of historical prose writing had reached its fruition before 750 B.C., and that which followed in the next century was only an aftermath. The fresh creative genius of Israel was now occupied with present crises and was expressing itself in the varied forms of the prophetic oracles or, when public speech was forcibly checked, was busied in formulating its great principles into working laws. Thus the new prophetic movement and the experiences of Manasseh's reactionary reign occasioned the great code of Deuteronomy; again, Deuteronomy and the experience of the exile occasioned the second great era of historical writing.

The leading ideas of Deuteronomy seemed to receive absolute, divine sanction by the fact of the exile. Israel's disloyalty had

---

[1] Genesis 39 9.   [2] Genesis 50 20.

251

led to the consequences repeatedly urged in Deuteronomy. The requirements of the law could not be carried out in the exile as they were in Josiah's reign, hence the vital spirit of the nation's creative thought turned to the past where it was possible to study the out-working of the Deuteronomic principles.

The two great principles that underlay Josiah's reform were aspects of the doctrine of absolute loyalty to Jehovah alone. One of these principles was that Israel's prosperity and continuance in Canaan depended upon such loyalty. The other was that such loyalty demanded the destruction of the high places with all their accompaniments and the centralization of public worship in the Jerusalem temple. The hero stories of the age of struggle with Canaanite and Philistine afforded ample material for emphasiz-ing the first. The stories of this age, as preserved in the north and south, had already been woven into one narrative. Whether they formed a separate roll or had been treated up to this time as merely a continuation of the conquest narrative, they were now taken as a distinct literary unit and were given an elaborate editing. The stories themselves were full of loyalty to Jehovah and of faith because of his deliverances from the many enemies in Canaan and round about. What better examples of the truth of Deuteronomy's doctrine could be found than the old narratives of this age of vicissitudes? It needed only to point the moral, and all must see. So the old pictures of frequent distress from enemies and deliverance by national heroes were framed all to match, and a general frame constructed for the whole, giving a unitary impression to all the collection.

And the children of Israel again did that which was evil in the sight of Jehovah: and Jehovah strengthened Eglon the king of Moab against Israel, because they had done that which was evil in the sight of Jehovah. And he gathered unto him the children of Ammon and Amalek; and he went and smote Israel, and they possessed the city of palm-trees. And the children of Israel served Eglon the king of Moab eighteen years.

But when the children of Israel cried unto Jehovah, Jehovah raised them up a saviour, Ehud the son of Gera, the Benjamite, a man left-handed. And the children of Israel sent tribute by him unto Eglon the king of Moab. And Ehud made him a sword which had two edges, a cubit in length; and he girded it under his raiment upon his right thigh. And he offered the tribute unto Eglon king of Moab: now Eglon was a very fat man. And when he had made an end of offering the tribute, he sent away the people that bare the tribute.   But he himself turned back from the quarries that were by Gilgal, and said, I have a secret errand unto thee, O king. And he said, Keep silence.   And all that stood by him went out from him.   And Ehud came unto him; and he was sitting by himself alone in the cool upper room.   And Ehud said, I have a message from God unto thee.   And he arose out of his seat.   And Ehud put forth his left hand, and took the sword from his right thigh, and thrust it into his body: and the haft also went in after the blade; and the fat closed upon the blade, for he drew not the sword out of his body; and it came out behind. Then Ehud went forth into the porch, and shut the doors of the upper room upon him, and locked them.

Now when he was gone out, his servants came; and they saw, and, behold, the doors of the upper room were locked; and they said, Surely he is covering his feet in the upper chamber.   And they tarried till they were ashamed; and, behold, he opened not the doors of the upper room: therefore they took the key, and opened them; and, behold, their lord was fallen down dead on the earth.

And Ehud escaped while they tarried, and passed beyond the quarries, and escaped unto Seirah.   And it came to pass, when he was come, that he blew a trumpet in the hill-country of Ephraim; and the children of Israel went down with him from the hill-country, and he before them. And he said unto them, Follow after me; for Jehovah hath delivered your enemies the Moabites into your hand.   And they went down after him, and took the fords of the Jordan against the Moabites, and suffered not a man to pass over.   And they smote of Moab at that time about ten thousand men, every lusty man, and every man of valor; and there escaped not a man.   So Moab was subdued that day under the hand of Israel.   *And the land had rest fourscore years.*

And after him was Shamgar the son of Anath, who smote of the Philistines six hundred men with an ox-goad: and he also saved Israel.[1]

And the children of Israel again did that which was evil in the sight of Jehovah, when Ehud was dead.   And Jehovah sold them into the hand of Jabin king of Canaan, that reigned in Hazor; the captain of whose host was Sisera, who dwelt in Harosheth of the Gentiles. And the children of Israel cried unto Jehovah: for he had nine hundred chariots of iron; and twenty years he mightily oppressed the children of Israel.

*   *   *   *   *   *   *   *

And the land had rest forty years.[2]

[1] Judges 3 [12-31].   [2] 4 [1-3], 5 [31b].

These examples may serve to illustrate the kind of editorial treatment that is given also to the stories of Gideon-Jerubbaal, Jephthah, and Samson. Fortunately the editors did little to these stories from Israel's golden age of narrative except to give them their frame — a frame of wood, we are tempted to call it.

The story of Othniel is no story at all, but is wholly made up of the characteristic phrases of the editors. The same is true of the six so-called minor judges, concerning whom no details are given.[1] Whether these were added by a later hand to bring the number to twelve or were in the sources, we cannot tell.

The general introduction prefixed to the collection of stories is found in chapters 2 [6]–3 [6]. The heart of this is 2 [11-19].

And the children of Israel did that which was evil in the sight of Jehovah, and served the Baalim; and they forsook Jehovah, the God of their fathers, who brought them out of the land of Egypt, and followed other gods, of the gods of the peoples that were round about them, and bowed themselves down unto them : and they provoked Jehovah to anger. And they forsook Jehovah, and served Baal and the Ashtaroth. And the anger of Jehovah was kindled against Israel, and he delivered them into the hands of spoilers that despoiled them; and he sold them into the hands of their enemies round about, so that they could not any longer stand before their enemies. Whithersoever they went out, the hand of Jehovah was against them for evil, as Jehovah had spoken, and as Jehovah had sworn unto them : and they were sore distressed.

And Jehovah raised up judges, who saved them out of the hand of those that despoiled them. And yet they hearkened not unto their judges; for they played the harlot after other gods, and bowed themselves down unto them : they turned aside quickly out of the way wherein their fathers walked, obeying the commandments of Jehovah; but they did not so. And when Jehovah raised them up judges, then Jehovah was with the judge, and saved them out of the hand of their enemies all the days of the judge: for it repented Jehovah because of their groaning by reason of them that oppressed them and vexed them. But it came to pass, when the judge was dead, that they turned back, and dealt more corruptly than their fathers, in following other gods to serve them, and to bow down unto them; they ceased not from their doings, nor from their stubborn way.

To the Deuteronomic book of Judges that was compiled during the exile, later hands added from old sources the brief summary

[1] Shamgar, Tola, Jair, Ibzan, Elon, Abdon.

of the conquest, 1 1–2 5, and the two appended narratives, chapters 17–21.   These fall without the general plan of the editors of the book.   They furnish, however, very early narratives of great interest and value.

The composite history from Adam to the conquest of the east-Jordan territory, the period of history contained in the present books of Genesis, Exodus, and Numbers, was given only very slight touches by the exilic editors of the Deuteronomic school.

The book of Deuteronomy itself received additions of historical material which fitted it into the history at the close of the east-Jordan conquest.   The most notable are the historical retrospect, in chapters 1 1–4 40, and the account of the death of Moses and the estimate of him as a prophet, in chapter 34.   In this material, as in the remainder of the book, dependence upon the great northern and southern Israelite history for knowledge of the past is evident.

With the beginning of the story of the conquest of the land in the first chapter of Joshua, the work of the exilic editors becomes everywhere noticeable.   The chapter "is constructed almost entirely of phrases borrowed from Deuteronomy"[1] and indeed throughout the book the hand of the editor is manifest to one familiar with the distinctive phraseology and thought of Deuteronomy.   This is especially the case in the first twelve chapters. The book of Joshua in its present form was not, however, the work of the Deuteronomic editors.   Like Genesis, Exodus, and Numbers, its completion belongs to the third great era of historical composition.

Why the Deuteronomic editors did not treat the book of Samuel as they did the stories of the Judges, we can only conjecture. Possibly it was because the subject-matter did not lend itself so well to the enforcement of one specific, Deuteronomic lesson; possibly it was because it already expressed very well their general interpretation of history.   In this portion of the national history, they merely made additions or modifications here and there to emphasize a little more clearly their thought of its significance. The denunciation of Eli, in 1 Samuel 2, is a passage that exhibits their characteristic touch.

[1] Driver, *Intro. Lit. Old Test.*, p. 105, Edition of 1910.

And there came a man of God unto Eli, and said unto him, Thus saith Jehovah, Did I reveal myself unto the house of thy father, when they were in Egypt in bondage to Pharaoh's house? and did I choose him out of all the tribes of Israel to be my priest, to go up unto mine altar, to burn incense, to wear an ephod before me? and did I give unto the house of thy father all the offerings of the children of Israel made by fire? Wherefore kick ye at my sacrifice and at mine offering, which I have commanded in my habitation, and honorest thy sons above me, to make yourselves fat with the chiefest of all the offerings of Israel my people? Therefore Jehovah, the God of Israel, saith, I said indeed that thy house, and the house of thy father, should walk before me for ever: but now Jehovah saith, Be it far from me; for them that honor me I will honor, and they that despise me shall be lightly esteemed. Behold, the days come, that I will cut off thine arm, and the arm of thy father's house, that there shall not be an old man in thy house.[1]

The editors terminated the main narrative of David's reign with the list of his officers given in 2 Samuel 20, and appended to this some at least of the miscellaneous material constituting chapters 21–24. This appended matter itself gives interesting evidence of gradual accumulation, since the stories of the famine and the pestilence in chapters 21 and 24, that evidently were taken from some common, early source, are cut apart by the insertion of two poems and a list of David's heroes.

The history of the kingdom from Solomon to the exile furnished opportunity for more abundant and more varied illustration of the Deuteronomic principles than even the stories of the Judges. The dependence of national prosperity upon absolute loyalty to Jehovah was demonstrated more impressively in the division of the kingdom and the final downfall of its two parts than in the vacillations and vicissitudes of the early struggle for the land. To this the later era added opportunity to emphasize the principle of loyalty manifested in the centralization of worship.

The exilic editors did not have at hand a composite history of the divided kingdom as of the earlier ages; they must themselves compile this great and complex work. In comparison with this task their undertakings hitherto considered were simple indeed. Perhaps the compilation and interpretation of the history which

[1] 2 27-31.

resulted in the book of Kings was the work of many laborers, during a half-century or more. There are traces of two stages in the editing, one antedating the fall of Jerusalem, and the other carrying us beyond the middle of the exile. Only in minute details can these stages be distinguished, and we therefore take up Kings simply as a literary product of the Deuteronomic age, which begins before the fall of Jerusalem. The work as a whole must have been completed soon after 561, the date of the last event recorded; only the slightest traces of any later editing have been noted. From the exile onward the Jews had Deuteronomy, Judges, Samuel, and Kings in essentially their present form.

The history of the composite authorship and gradual growth of the Pentateuch, Joshua, Judges, and Samuel has been deciphered only by the united effort of many trained eyes; but in Kings the evidence is open to all. At the close of Solomon's reign, we read: Now the rest of the acts of Solomon, and all that he did, and his wisdom, are they not written in the book of the acts of Solomon? We have found bits of poetry ascribed to earlier books of poems, but we have not met direct references to prose histories such as the book of the acts of Solomon must have been. At the death of Solomon's son, we read: Now the rest of the acts of Rehoboam, and all that he did, are they not written in the book of the chronicles of the kings of Judah? To this same book of chronicles [1] reference is made at the close of nearly every Judean reign until the death of Jehoiakim in 597 B.C.

It is in the time of David that we first hear of an official scribe as a member of the court. From this time forward we need not doubt that more or less complete official annals were kept in Israel, as they were among the kindred Babylonians and Assyrians. Whether the books of the acts of days of Solomon and of the kings of Judah were these official annals or not, we do not know with certainty. The probability seems to be that they were not, since these books are cited for some things that might not have been included in state records; it is somewhat difficult to see, too, how the compilers of Kings would have had access to the government documents. All we can say is that the editors had some sort of a history of Solomon's reign and of the Judean kings who followed

[1] Literally, "acts of days" = daily record of events.

S

him, which has since been lost, and which contained much material not in our Kings — Now the *rest* of the acts, are they not written?

For the kings of Northern Israel similar reference is constantly made to the book of the chronicles of the kings of Israel. We do not know just what the relation of this book was to that from which we found a few extensive extracts in the latter part of 1 Kings and opening of 2 Kings.[1] Those were such early, vivid stories as Ahab's defeat of the drunken Ben-hadad and Jehu's rebellion. This material may have been included along with that from other sources in the "acts of days." The stories of Elijah and Elisha must have existed, in part at least, in separate books from which the editors of our Kings selected copious extracts. Stories in which other prophets are the central figures were also inwoven with the principal sources.

The narrative of the reign of Solomon in 1 Kings 1–11 is an interesting piece of composition. The first two chapters are taken from the early history of David's court and family life which makes up the greater part of 2 Samuel. The remaining chapters are not placed chronologically, but are grouped about the central theme of Solomon's building operations, the whole being arranged topically.

The book of the acts of Solomon was compiled, perhaps, not very far from the time of the great Judean history of antiquity. The chronicles of the kings of Israel may have been completed soon after 722. The chronicles of the kings of Judah cannot have been ended before 597, to which point it carried the history.

The final chapter concerning Solomon's reign is old in its kernel, but large additions were made by the editors which give the color and tone to the whole. The religious interpretation of history characteristic of the Deuteronomic age is prominent. Solomon is faithless to Jehovah, worships other deities, adversaries are raised up to punish him.[2] The downfall of Northern Israel gives the editors occasion for a protracted pointing of the moral.

[1] Chapter VI.

[2] As the section stands, this interpretation is so superimposed on the original narrative that one who was an adversary "all Solomon's days" (11 [25]) appears as raised up by God to punish the King for the sin of his old age (11 [4]).

And it was so, because the children of Israel had sinned against Jehovah their God, who brought them up out of the land of Egypt from under the hand of Pharaoh king of Egypt, and had feared other gods, and walked in the statutes of the nations, whom Jehovah cast out from before the children of Israel, and of the kings of Israel, which they made. And the children of Israel did secretly things that were not right against Jehovah their God: and they built them high places in all their cities, from the tower of the watchmen to the fortified city; and they set them up pillars and Asherim upon every high hill, and under every green tree; and there they burnt incense in all the high places, as did the nations whom Jehovah carried away before them; and they wrought wicked things to provoke Jehovah to anger; and they served idols, whereof Jehovah had said unto them, Ye shall not do this thing. Yet Jehovah testified unto Israel, and unto Judah, by every prophet, and every seer, saying, Turn ye from your evil ways, and keep my commandments and my statutes, according to all the law which I commanded your fathers, and which I sent to you by my servants the prophets. Notwithstanding, they would not hear, but hardened their neck, like to the neck of their fathers, who believed not in Jehovah their God. And they rejected his statutes, and his covenant that he made with their fathers, and his testimonies which he testified unto them; and they followed vanity, and became vain, and went after the nations that were round about them, concerning whom Jehovah had charged them that they should not do like them. And they forsook all the commandments of Jehovah their God, and made them molten images, even two calves, and made an Asherah, and worshipped all the host of heaven, and served Baal. And they caused their sons and their daughters to pass through the fire, and used divination and enchantments, and sold themselves to do that which was evil in the sight of Jehovah, to provoke him to anger. Therefore Jehovah was very angry with Israel, and removed them out of his sight: there was none left but the tribe of Judah only.[1]

It is not only where such striking events call for interpretation that the compiler's hand is noticeable; for the entire period of the divided kingdom the editors have inwoven the history after a very careful system. The account of each reign opens and closes with regular formulas which give the chronological relation of the reign to the corresponding reign in the other kingdom and pass judgment on each king. In the case of Northern Israel, this judgment is without exception unfavorable. From the stand-

[1] 2 Kings 17 7-18.

point of the Deuteronomic law of the central sanctuary, the great
sin of Jeroboam was the establishment of places of worship outside
of Jerusalem.   In this respect each king of Israel followed the.sin
of Jeroboam, the son of Nebat.   To a few kings of Judah qualified
approbation is given, limited by the fact that the high places were
not taken away.   In only two cases is this limitation omitted,
those of Hezekiah and Josiah.   The estimate of all the kings is
made on purely religious grounds and is determined by the law of
the central sanctuary.   Thus the Deuteronomic editors put their
stamp upon the history of the kingdom from Solomon's reign
forward, as completely as they did upon the age of the Judges.
They left the book of Kings as the chiefest monument of their
zeal.   Prophetic principles formulated into law, and burned into
the souls of earnest thinkers by the devastation of city and temple,
gave new meaning to the national history and led to the second
great stage of historical writing in Israel.

In our own day the study of sociology and economics has given
historians a new point of view from which they are reëxamining
the story of the past and emphasizing the hitherto neglected factors.
So the prophets of the eighth century B.C. and their successors in
the seventh century gave a new point of view for the interpretation of Israel's history.   In each age the new light tends to give,
for a time, a one-sided view, capable of recognizing only one explanation of all things.   The Deuteronomic editors had a new
insight into the meaning of history, but their interpretation obscured some of the truth of the old, natural narratives which had
had no hard-and-fast interpretation to give.

The language and style of Deuteronomy, as well as the thought,
colored all that the historians of this age touched.   Very much
of the general impression made by the prose of the Old Testament
is due to this epoch.   While the story-telling charm of the earlier
age has been lost, earnestness of thought and deep conviction give
a solemn rhythm to all that is written.   Even some repetitiousness
is without wearisomeness where the reach of the thought is such
that frequent reiteration is necessary.   As in earlier ages, so in
this, the Old Testament style is found perfectly adapted to the
thought and feeling.   The era of "national inexperience" that
found its expression in the swift-told tale of heroic adventure is

gone forever.   The naïve stories of that earlier age win the child and delight all whose life still courses lustily.   In the second great era of Israel's historical writing, the stern strength of men who know defeat, but not despair, who know how to fail without self-excuse, who look back with tense gaze, determined to understand and profit by mistakes, grips and holds the reader of matured conscience.

CHAPTER XIX

SONGS AND ORACLES OF THE RESTORATION

(About 550 to 450 B.C.)

In Babylonia, where the historians of Israel were interpreting the story of their nation in terms of the philosophy of Deuteronomy, political confusion suddenly arose. Following the death of Nebuchadrezzar in 561, three kings ruled in rapid succession and a fourth had already seized the throne, within less than seven years after Nebuchadrezzar's death. For the time, Babylon maintained her great empire, so that the new king was able to dictate who should reign in distant Tyre; but dangers were threatening. The alliance which Nebuchadrezzar had consistently maintained with the Medes was now broken, and this people was crowding down upon Babylon in Mesopotamia, much as the Assyrians had done nine hundred years before. A rebellion against the Medes in the province of Anshan, in northern Elam, resulted in the downfall of the Median king Astyages and gave the rebellious Persian prince, Cyrus of Anshan, the rule of the Medo-Persian empire of which he became the founder. The Babylonian king, Nabonidus, welcomed the conquest of Media as a divine intervention; but soon the upstart Cyrus was threatening Babylon, as Astyages had done. An alliance between Lydia, Sparta the head of the Greek states, and Babylon led Cyrus quickly to his great western campaign, in which he conquered Lydia before the allies could aid.

Ezekiel's voice of hope had been stilled for a quarter-century, but the spirit of prophecy needed only some sign among the nations to call forth anew its song of doom and cheer. Now some unnamed prophet-poet sang: —

Upon a treeless mountain lift up a signal, raise a cry to them,
Wave the hand that they may enter the princely gates.
I myself have given command to my consecrated ones, to execute my
    wrath,

I have also summoned my heroes, my proudly exultant ones.
Hark, a tumult on the mountains, as of a mighty multitude !
Hark, an uproar of kingdoms, of gathered nations !
It is Jehovah of hosts mustering the martial hosts.

They are coming from a distant land, from the end of heaven,
Jehovah and his instruments of wrath, to destroy the whole earth.
Wail, for Jehovah's day is at hand ; as destruction from the Almighty
 Destroyer it comes.
Therefore all hands hang down helpless,
Therefore every human heart doth melt, and men are dismayed.
Pains and throes seize them ; like a woman in travail they writhe ;
Astounded they gaze at each other ; their faces glow like flames.

Behold Jehovah cometh, pitiless, with fury and burning anger,
To make the earth a desolation, and to destroy the sinners thereon.
For the heavens and its Orions cease to shed their beams,
The sun is darkened at his rising, and the moon gives no brilliant light.
I will punish the earth for its wickedness, and the wicked for their iniquity,
I will still the arrogance of the proud, and lay low the presumption of
 tyrants.
I will make mortals rarer than gold, and men than the fine gold of Ophir.

Therefore I will make heaven tremble, and the earth shall shake in its
 place,
Because of the fury of Jehovah of hosts, and in the fury of his burning
 anger.
And then like a hunted gazelle, or a sheep with none to fold them,
They will turn each to his own people, and flee each to his own land ;
Whoever is found will be thrust through, and whoever is caught will fall
 by the sword,
And their children shall be dashed to pieces before their eyes.
Their houses shall be plundered and their wives shall be ravished.

Behold, I stir up against them the Medes,
Who consider not silver, and take no pleasure in gold,
(They lay hold on) bow (and spear, they are cruel),
(They break in pieces all) the young men, (and the maidens) shall be
 dashed in pieces.
On children they will look with no pity, they have no compassion on the
 fruit of the womb,
And Babylon, the most beautiful of kingdoms, the proud glory of the
 Chaldeans shall be,
As when God overthrew Sodom and Gomorrah.

It shall be uninhabited forever, and tenantless age after age;
No nomad shall pitch there his tent, nor shepherds let their flocks lie down
  there,
But wild cats shall lie down here, and their houses shall be full of jackals;
Ostriches shall dwell there, and satyrs shall dance there,
Howling beasts shall cry to each other in its castles, and wolves in its
  revelling halls;
Its time is near at hand, its day shall not be extended.[1]

It was probably the same prophet who sang the mocking dirge
over Babylon that recalls so vividly Ezekiel's lament over Egypt.[2]

> Ah! stilled is the tyrant,
> And stilled is the fury!
> Broke hath Jehovah the rod of the wicked,
> Sceptre of despots:
> Stroke of (the) peoples with passion,
> Stroke unremitting,
> Treading in wrath (the) nations,
> Trampling unceasing.
> Quiet, at rest, is the whole earth,
> They break into singing;
> Even the pines are jubilant for thee,
> Lebanon's cedars!
> "Since thou liest low, cometh not up
> Feller against us."
>
> Sheol from under shuddereth at thee
> To meet thine arrival,
> Stirring up for thee the shades,
> All great-goats of earth!
> Lifteth erect from their thrones
> All kings of peoples.
> *All of them answer and say to thee, —*
> "Thou, too, made flaccid like us,
> To us hast been levelled!
> Hurled to Sheol is the pride of thee,
> Clang of the harps of thee;
> Under thee strewn are (the) maggots,
> Thy coverlet worms."

[1] Isaiah 13 2–22. Translation from Kent, *Sermons, Epistles, and Apocalypses of Israel's Prophets*, pp. 316 ff.   [2] Page 246.

How art thou fallen from heaven
   Daystar, son of the dawn;
(How) art thou hewn down to earth,
   Hurtler at nations.
And thou, thou didst say in thine heart,
   "The heavens will I scale,
Far up to the stars of God
   Lift high my throne,
And sit on the mount of assembly,
   Far back of the north,
I will climb on the heights of (the) cloud,
   I will match the Most High!"
Ah: to Sheol thou art hurled,
   Far back of the pit!

Who see thee at thee are gazing;
   Upon thee they muse:
Is this the man that staggered the earth,
   Shaker of kingdoms?
Setting the world like the desert,
   Its cities he tore down;
Its prisoners he loosed not
   (Each of them) homeward.
All kings of peoples, yes all,
   Are lying in their state;
But thou! thou art flung from thy grave,
   Like a stick that is loathsome.

Beshrouded with slain, the pierced of the sword,
   Like a corpse that is trampled.
They that go down to the stones of a crypt,
   Shall not be with them in burial.
For thy land thou hast ruined,
   Thy people hast slaughtered.
Shall not be mentioned for aye
   Seed of the wicked!
Set for his children a shambles,
   For guilt of their fathers!
They shall not rise nor inherit (the) earth,
   Nor fill the face of the world with cities.

But I will arise upon them,
   Sayeth Jehovah of hosts;

> And I will cut off from Babel
>> Record and remnant,
> And scion and seed,
>> Saith Jehovah:
> Yea, I will make it the bittern's heritage,
>> Marshes of water!
> And I will sweep it with sweeps of destruction,
>> Sayeth Jehovah of hosts.[1]

The impassioned prophecy against Babylon in Jeremiah 50–51, in which the Medes are the instrument of doom on the city, was composed by some other poet at about the same time as the oracles in Isaiah 13 and 14. "The burden of the wilderness of the sea" (Isaiah 21 [1-10]) was perhaps also occasioned by the expected attack of the Medo-Persian power. In the prophetic poems called "burdens," there is often a weird effect; as "whirlwinds in the south sweep through," so they seem to come "from the wilderness, from a terrible land." Suggestion and mystery rather than definite statement, characterize them. The great mass of the exiles, like the mass of people in any age, saw the wealth, power, and magnificence of Babylon and were awed by the splendor of her religious ceremonies. The reigning king was peculiarly devoted to the ancient gods of Babylon; much of his energy was devoted to restoring their old-time shrines and forms of worship. In Babylon and in other cities of the realm his ambitions in this direction were carried out on a magnificent scale. To the gods who had given glory to Babylonia thousands of years before Israel had covenanted with Jehovah at Sinai, Nabonidus trusted for aid against the threatening dangers. In these and in the immense strength of his fortifications, no doubt his confidence seemed well grounded to Jewish exiles without the vision of their prophet poets.

It may have been after Babylon had fallen, although it is commonly believed to have been while Cyrus was still in the north and west that the wonderful songs of faith and cheer in

---

[1] Isaiah 14 [4-23]. Translation from G. A. Smith, *Isaiah*, *Expositor's Bible*, I, p. 413 ff. The metre is the same in this and the preceding selection; Dr. Kent prints the long broken lines as single lines and Dr. Smith, as two lines.

Isaiah 40–48 were first sung.[1] The great theme is given at the outset : —

Comfort ye, comfort ye my people, saith your God.
Speak ye comfortably to Jerusalem ; and cry unto her,
That her warfare is accomplished, that her iniquity is pardoned,
That she hath received of Jehovah's hand double for all her sins.[2]

Then a voice is heard, a messenger in the wilderness, which separates the exiles from home : A great, easy highway is being built to make the return possible for weary feet. The voice that commands the road through the wilderness, commands again with the one word "Cry," and one answers, "What shall I cry ? " "Human pride and power quickly pass, but God's promise shall be accomplished." On the timeless wings of song, we pass from the separating wilderness to the hills of Judah and hear Jerusalem and the cities of Judea bidden to welcome back the God whom Ezekiel had seen departing from the polluted and doomed city. What sort of a god is their god ? Listen : —

Who hath measured the waters in the hollow of his hand,
And meted out heaven with the span,
And comprehended the dust of the earth in a measure,
And weighed the mountains in scales,
And the hills in a balance ?

Who hath directed the Spirit of Jehovah,
Or who being his counsellor hath taught him ?
With whom took he counsel, and who instructed him,'
And taught him in the path of justice, and taught him knowledge,
And showed to him the way of understanding ?
Behold, the nations are as a drop of a bucket,
And are accounted as the small dust of the balance :
Behold, he taketh up the isles as a very little thing.
And Lebanon is not sufficient to burn,
Nor the beasts thereof sufficient for a burnt offering.
All the nations are as nothing before him,
As less than nothing, and vanity.[3]

---

[1] For the view that these are to be dated after 538, see Kent, *Sermons, Epistles, and Apocalypses of Israel's Prophets*, pp. 27–29, 336.

[2] Isaiah 40 [1-2].   [3] Isaiah 40 [12-17].

Contrast the other gods : —

> To whom then will ye liken me,
> That I should be equal to him ? saith the Holy One.
> Lift up your eyes, and see
> Who hath created these,
> That bringeth out their host by number;
> He calleth them all by name.[1]

This is lyric poetry, but it has the qualities and power of the drama. It is like the prelude of an opera; it almost sings itself, voice answering voice. The chapters following give a succession of lyrics, all so unified in theme and, to some extent, progressive in thought, that the whole of 40 to 48 can almost be called one dramatic lyric.

The identification of the personality of the prophet with God is here so complete that any perfectly clear differentiation of speakers is impossible. Throughout chapter 40, however, God is spoken of in the third person, while clearly He is himself speaking at the opening of the next chapter. The scene is like that at the opening of Micah 6. There the prophet summoned the mountains and hills to form a majestic court before which Jehovah should plead his cause with his people; then Jehovah himself spoke.[2] Here it is Jehovah who bids the islands sit in silence and the people to come near to trial.

Had the Greek unerring instinct for form and proportion in building or statue? The poets of Israel were equally unerring in their soul-union with nature. Imagine summoning vast prairies or awesome deserts to sit as court for God and his people in judgment! But the mountains and the islands! — these, spite of their greatness, have individuality and personality.

Turning back from form to thought, we notice that, while the prelude chapter struck the different chords that give the entire theme, the situation is not before us till Jehovah begins his plea for the trust of his people: —

> Who hath raised up one from the east,
> Whom he calleth in righteousness to his foot?
> He giveth nations before him,

[1] Isaiah 40 25-26a.   [2] Micah 6 1-8.

> And maketh him rule over kings;
> He giveth them as the dust of his sword,
> As the driven stubble to his bow.
> He pursueth them and passes on safely,
> Even by a way that he hath not gone with his feet.
> Who hath wrought and done it,
> Calling the generations from the beginning?
> I Jehovah, the first,
> And with the last, I am he.[1]

The Babylonian exiles needed no commentary to enable them to recognize the one from the east before whom the nations had been driven stubble. Already Cyrus had pursued the king of Lydia to his capital, the very end of the earth to the ancient Oriental. Well did the islands of the Mediterranean and Ægean fear when they saw it; fifty years more and a successor of Cyrus will not stop at the coast of Asia Minor. As it is in Babylon, so the poet sees it among the distant peoples united against Cyrus; they hastened to create more images of the gods, to gain help against the invader whom no human power could check. "But thou, Israel, art my servant whom I have chosen"; in all this panic fear of the nations there is only hope for thee. Next, the prophet seems to speak a few lines in his own person, explaining the purpose of God in it all : —

> That they may see and know,
> And consider, and understand together,
> That the hand of Jehovah hath done this,
> And the Holy One of Israel hath created it.[2]

The people cannot believe, so the poet represents Jehovah as saying, "Produce your cause," and the prophet himself goes on, "Let them show us what shall happen." Then Jehovah himself again : —

> Behold, ye are of nothing, and your work is of nought.

The following songs reiterate, elaborate, and make specific. There is not only to be a broad, easy highway from Babylon to Judea, but God shall lead the blind and shall make darkness light before them.[3] The nothingness of other gods is repeatedly pictured by contrast with the might and majesty of Jehovah and

[1] 41 2-4.   [2] Isaiah 41 20.   [3] 42 16.

by realistic descriptions of the making of idols and carrying their images about in religious procession.[1] The downfall of Babylon which was not specifically mentioned in the opening chapters is made very definite and vivid as the poems advance: —

> Thus saith Jehovah,
> Your Redeemer, the Holy One of Israel:
> For your sake I have sent to Babylon,
> And I will bring down all of them as fugitives.[2]

> Down! and sit in the dust, O virgin,
>   Daughter of Babel!
> Sit on the ground, with no throne,
>   Daughter of Kashdim!
> For not again shall they call thee
>   Tender and Dainty.
> Take to thee millstones, and grind out the meal,
> Put back thy veil, strip off the garment,
> Make bare the leg, wade through the rivers;
> Bare be thy nakedness, yea, be beholden thy shame!
>   Vengeance I take, and strike treaty with none.

> *   *   *   *   *   *   *

> And thou saidst, For ever I shall be mistress,
> Till thou hast set not these things to thy heart,
>   Nor thought of their issue.

> Therefore now hear this, Voluptuous,
>   Sitting self-confident:
> Thou, who saith in her heart, "I am: there is none else.
> I shall not sit a widow, nor know want of children."
> Surely shall come to thee both of these, sudden, the same day,
>   Childlessness, widowhood!
> To their full come upon thee, spite of the mass of thy spells,
> Spite of the wealth of thy charms — to the full!

> And thou wast bold in thine evil; thou saidst,
>   "None doth see me."
> Thy wisdom and knowledge — they have led thee astray,
> Till thou hast said in thine heart, "I am: there is none else."

---

[1] 46 1.   [2] 43 14.

Yet there shall come on thee Evil,
    Thou know'st not to charm it.
 And there shall fall on thee Havoc,
    Thou canst not avert it.
And there shall come on thee suddenly,
    Unawares, Ruin.
Stand forth, I pray, with thy charms, with the wealth of thy spells —
With which thou hast wearied thyself from thy youth up —
    If so thou be able to profit,
    If so to strike terror !
 Thou art sick with the mass of thy counsels :
    Let them stand up and save thee —
Mappers of heaven, Planet-observers, Tellers at new moons —
    From what must befall thee !

Behold, they are grown like the straw !
    Fire hath consumed them ;
Nay, they save not their life
    From the hand of the flame !
— 'Tis no fuel for warmth,
    Fire to sit down at ! —
Thus are they grown to thee, they who did weary thee,
    Traders of thine from thy youth up ;
    Each as he could pass have they fled ;
        None is thy saviour ! [1]

At the conclusion of the group of poems, there is a ringing cry to go forth from Babylon, for, in the prophet's vision, the people of Jehovah are already free to return. [2]

In these poems and those which immediately follow in the book of Isaiah, the culmination of the prophetic idea of God is reached. No previous writing gives such clear and sweeping declarations of the one God of all the earth ; creator and preserver.   Toward these conceptions, the inspired teachers of Israel had been reaching in the midst of a world and a people which believed that each region or tribe had its own god, who must be especially honored

---

[1] 47 1-3, 7-15. Translation of G. A. Smith, *Isaiah, Expositor's Bible*, II, p. 195 ff.

[2] If this section of the book of Isaiah dates from the time after the fall of Babylon in 538, the freedom to return is literal.

in that region or whose glory was inextricably bound up with the military success and prosperity of that people. In following the writings of the prophets in chronological order, the gradual development of this stupendous conception is clearly seen — one God, a personal being, creator and preserver. Only through the effects of the struggle of nations, only through the destruction of the temple and temple-city was it possible for Israel to rise to a conception of a God who was not limited to one part of the earth's surface and largely to one people. While the prophets struggled to guide their little people amid the overwhelming waves of the great tides of nations in commotion, prophet added to prophet some new vision of the great pilot; only when Israel had lived for a generation in the midst of the splendors of the Babylonian religion was it possible by contrast to set forth the uniqueness of the one God.

Chapters 49 to 55 form a new group of oracles, in various ways distinct from 40 to 48. There are no further allusions to Cyrus, and the contrasting of Jehovah with the idol-gods has also disappeared. In general, the poems of this group are less original and spontaneous than the preceding ones. They probably come from a time after a beginning had been made in the restoration of Jerusalem. Two of the best songs of the group are those beginning: "Awake, awake, put on strength, O arm of Jehovah," and "Ho, every one that thirsteth, come ye to the waters."[1]

A unifying link in the two groups is the succession of poems concerning Jehovah's servant. If these were an original part of the collection, then 40 to 55 must almost certainly have formed one collection. Many critics, however, find in the servant passages the parts of one poem worked into the text by a later hand, after two distinct collections of prophecies (40–48, 49–55) had been united; in them we find one theme, with progress and culmination of thought. In Isaiah 40 to 48 the prophetic conception of God reaches its climax, and, in this poem, the prophetic conception of man culminates; so that 40 to 55 taken together give two summits in the central thoughts of the Old Testament literature — God and man.

As Israel's thought advances, man is considered in his twofold

[1] 51 9–52 12, 55.

relation — to God and to his fellow-man and, in the ideal servant, this twofold treatment reaches its highest point. If one draws a composite portrait from the successive passages,[1] it will be found to contain at least the following traits: To the eye that looks for physical beauty and external pomp, nothing will appear, for his visage and form are marred more than any man, and he has no comeliness nor beauty. He is despised and esteemed not. In his suffering, he is thought to be one smitten of God and is forced to endure punishment and insult. Instead of regal self-assertion and loud display, there will be quiet gentleness and meekness; he shall not cause his voice to be heard in the street; he shall be before his persecutors dumb, as a victim led to the slaughter; he shall not even break the weakest staff nor put out the dimmest light. His worth will be wholly of a moral type. He shall inaugurate justice; there shall be in him no violence nor deceit, and by his knowledge he shall justify many. His powers will be at the service of others, for his skill of speech will be to help the weary. He will endure for the sake of others; in their behalf he will be mighty. He will not stop until he establishes judgment in the world. He will bring light to the Gentiles, open the eyes of the blind, and bring out prisoners. His mouth will be like a sharp sword. He will be ready to hearken to Jehovah, absolute faith in whom will make his face like flint.

Whoever the writer had in mind in this strange, composite picture, whether some one of the past or the future, or only a personification of the genius of the nation, we have here insight into deep facts of human life. Hawthorne found in our common sin the bond that unites soul to soul. It is rather a pessimistic interpretation of life, but there is truth in it. Browning, struggling ever with the question "why ill should hap to man," found in our common pain that which develops the highest human qualities of sympathy toward man and gratitude toward God. The poet of the sixth century before Christ saw the fact, he did not seek to explain it, — saw the universal fact that he who comes close to God and seeks to do his will in service to man will be misunderstood, deemed smitten of God, despised and rejected of men. The history of civilization — the martyrs of philosophy, science,

[1] 42 1-9, 49 1-13, 50 4-11, 52 13-53 12.

T

political liberty, as well as of religion, declare that the ancient poet saw the deep things of life as they are. The great servants of God, whether their service has been in the cause of advancing knowledge or righteousness, have been and still must be despised and rejected of men, men of sorrows and acquainted with grief. In the lower realms of life, animal and human, we may find the law of tooth and claw; in the higher realms, the law of the soul an offering for sin prevails. This law unites man to man and man to God. The truth seen by the author of the *Marble Faun* is a very small part of the truth; the truth seen by the prophet-poet of the sixth century B.C. and by the philosopher-poet of the nineteenth century after Christ complement each other and carry us far as human eye has yet reached into the eternal mystery of life as it is at its centre and circumference. The scientist may talk of the struggle for life and the struggle for the life of others; the theologian may talk of the vicarious principle; they are scientific names for the facts that the poets have seen.[1]

The poets of the Restoration possessed all the gifts of the greatest of their race for expressing their thought in appropriate imagery, in concrete pictures, and in bold personifications. Yielding ourselves to their changing mood, we feel the transitory character of human life in the fading flower and grass; we see the tender plant springing up, even the marvel of a root out of dry ground, the rain and snow coming from heaven, making earth bud and bring forth seed for the sower and bread for the eater. We watch the fir and myrtle grow up instead of the thorn and brier, or we are led by springs of water. We look upon Lebanon's height with her beasts; we hear the waves of the sea roaring; our gaze is directed to the starry heavens; we mount with wings as eagles;

---

[1] In some one of his writings, Henry E. Krehbiel has called attention to the fact that the idea of German poetry is that "salvation comes to humanity through the self-sacrificing love of woman." The poet of ancient Israel saw the law in its more universal terms. Parallels between the poem of the *Suffering Servant* and Psalm 22, beginning "My God, my God, why hast thou forsaken me?" are often noted. Although the Psalm comes from the Restoration period and is of essentially the same age as the *Suffering Servant*, it lacks the insight of that great poem, failing to show the necessary connection between its night of suffering and the glorious future. See Kirkpatrick, *The Psalms*, p. 114.

our thought soars to the height of the heavens above the earth. Jehovah is pictured as measuring the waters in the hollow of his hand and weighing the mountains in scales, stretching out the heavens as a curtain and spreading them as a tent to dwell in, or as making a way in the sea. He is again, a rock, the only rock. Still giving ourselves to their guidance, we watch the laborers at work, the carpenter and smith, the shepherd feeding his flock; we see the sheep shearing and the lamb led to the slaughter, the potter treading the clay or fashioning it as he wills, the refiner of precious metal at his work. We note the instrument of threshing, the hunter's snare, the antelope caught in the net, the bruised reed and smoking flax, the polished shaft of the archer in its quiver, the moth that destroys a garment or the garment that grows old. We are led to picture a man struggling through a deep, swift stream. Israel is now a divorced woman, now the wife of Jehovah, now one who has been sold into slavery for no price. Jehovah's wrath is a draught in a cup. Those who seek satisfaction in idolatrous worship are feeders upon ashes. The curious might almost make a complete study of the arts and industries and all the circumstances of the daily life of the age from the pictures given in these poetic oracles. One does not feel, however, any such conscious display of knowledge as in Ezekiel; we are again with true poets who think in pictures instinctively.

Among the most graphic of the pictures from life that appear on the pages of these prophets are the sarcastic descriptions of idol manufacture and worship : —

> To whom then will ye liken God,
> And what likeness place beside him?
> An image! a craftsman cast it,
> And a smelter overlays it with gold.
> Each one helps the other and says to his fellow, Be courageous!
> So the craftsman encourages the smelter,
> The smoother with the hammer him who smites the anvil,
> Saying of the plating, It is good;
> And he fastens it securely with nails.
> He who is too poor to do this
> Chooses a tree that is not decayed,

Seeks for himself a skilled craftsman,
To set up an image that shall not totter.[1]

The smith prepares it on the coals.
With hammers he fashions it,
He forges it with his strong arm,
He becomes hungry also and has no strength,
He drinks no water and is faint.
The carpenter stretches out a line,
Traces it in outline with a stylus,
Shapes it with scraping tools and a compass,
And makes it like a human figure,
Like the beauty of a man, to dwell in a house!

One cuts down cedar trees for his use,
And chooses a cypress or oak,
He lets it grow up among the trees of the forest,
Or plants a pine, and the rain makes it grow.
So it becomes fuel for man,
And he takes some therefrom and warms himself,
He also sets it ablaze and bakes bread,
Yea, he makes a god and worships it!
Makes an image and bows before it!

Half of it he burns in the fire,
And upon its coals he roasts flesh!
He eats the roast and is satisfied!
He warms himself and says, Aha!
I am warm and see the glow.
The rest of it he makes into a god,
He bows down to his image and worships it,
And prays to it and says:
Deliver me, for thou art my god!

They have no knowledge nor discernment,
For their eyes are besmeared past seeing,
And their minds past comprehending.
And he takes it not to heart,
Nor is there any knowledge or sense to say:

[1] 40 18-20, 41 6-7. Translation and arrangement from Kent, *Sermons, Epistles, and Apocalypses of the Prophets*, p. 338.

> Half of it I have burned in the fire,
> I have also baked bread upon the coals,
> I have roasted flesh and have eaten;
> And the rest of it shall make an abomination,
> To a block of wood shall I bow down?[1]

The poet's own personality is elusive throughout. He is often styled "The Great Unknown"; we do not even know, as we have seen, whether the songs are all from one poet or from more.

After the conquest of Asia Minor, Cyrus turned his attention to the regions eastward of his empire, and it was not until 538 that he moved directly on Babylon. Internal dissensions had, by this time, paved the way for easy conquest. There was some fighting done on the northern borders of the country, but once victorious here, Cyrus's forces were able to enter the capital without a struggle. In accord with his general policy of recognizing the religion of conquered peoples and permitting those who had been deported to return and rebuild their devastated homes, Cyrus permitted the rebuilding of Jerusalem and the return of exiles. In the course of the next eighteen years some few leading men went from Babylon to Jerusalem. Sheshbazzar of the seed-royal went as governor and probably a considerable company with him. By 520, Sheshbazzar had been succeeded as local governor by Zerubbabel, a grandson of Jehoiachin; Joshua the chief priest had also gone up from Babylon. Doubtless each of these brought followers with him. When the rebuilding of the temple was begun in 520, others had come from Babylon bringing a contribution of silver and gold; but there was no considerable return of exiles from Babylon for many years. From Egypt and other regions near Judea, doubtless many fugitives had come back before 538. The reëstablishment of some sort of order under Sheshbazzar must have attracted many more from neighboring districts. Soon homes began to rise among the desolate ruins of Jerusalem, so that in 520 the people were living in ceiled houses, though the temple still lay in hopeless ruin, as it had been left sixty-six years before.

---

[1] 44 12–19. Translation from Kent, *Sermons, Epistles, and Apocalypses,* pp. 350–351.

At this juncture, one who had inherited something of the spirit of the earlier prophets appeared to rouse Zerubbabel, Joshua, and the people to the great task of rebuilding the temple. The scanty crops that had been given, he interpreted as due to neglect of this primal duty. Three weeks after his first stimulating address, work was begun; but soon the magnitude of the task proved most discouraging. Again the prophet spoke: —

Who is left among you that saw this house in its former glory? and how do ye see it now? is it not in your eyes as nothing? Yet now be strong, O Zerubbabel, saith Jehovah; and be strong, O Joshua, son of Jehozadak, the high priest; and be strong, all ye people of the land, saith Jehovah, and work: for I am with you, saith Jehovah of hosts, according to the word that I covenanted with you when ye came out of Egypt, and my Spirit abode among you: fear ye not. For thus saith Jehovah of hosts: Yet once, it is a little while, and I will shake the heavens, and the earth, and the sea, and the dry land; and I will shake all nations; and the precious things of all nations shall come; and I will fill this house with glory, saith Jehovah of hosts. The silver is mine, and the gold is mine, saith Jehovah of hosts. The latter glory of this house shall be greater than the former, saith Jehovah of hosts; and in this place will I give peace, saith Jehovah of hosts.[1]

Soon this brave preacher, Haggai, was supported by Zechariah, who addressed the people in Jehovah's name, warning them by the fate of their fathers and the certainty of Jehovah's word. Thus, through the warning and encouragement of these two prophets, the work of building the temple went forward. Haggai's last message was given just three months after the building was begun; Zechariah continued his prophetic work at least two years longer.

A greater contrast than that exhibited in the oracles of Haggai and Zechariah cannot be imagined. Haggai speaks as a practical man who sees the immediate thing to be done and goes about it in the most direct way. Of vision and symbol, he is innocent, and of deep moral and spiritual insight almost equally devoid. He believes in the time-honored doctrine that material prosperity depends on faithfulness to Jehovah. Such faithfulness can be manifested simply by rebuilding; do this, and Jehovah will bless. The passage quoted above in which the shaking of the heavens

[1] Haggai 2 3-9.

and the earth is promised, approaches more nearly to the rhetorical power and poetic form of the earlier prophets than any other from Haggai's lips.   Zechariah, on the other hand, had been a student of Ezekiel's prophecies and was little behind his master in the imagery of symbolic vision.   Angelic horsemen, horns cut down, a man with a rod measuring Jerusalem, the high-priest clothed in filthy garments and accused by the Adversary, a golden lamp fed with oil from two olive trees, a great roll of a book flying through the air, a woman placed in an ephah and carried to Babylon, chariots with many colored horses, all these appear in Zechariah's strange visions.   All convey some message needed by the community in its weakness and discouragement.   In part, the visions speak of world-conditions favorable for the great effort, and of future peace and glory for the city; in part, they tell of sin expiated by the years of devastation, sin borne away to Babylon.   Ezekiel's teaching, too, that henceforth the curse of sin shall fall upon the sinner and not on the community as a whole is reimpressed.

The visions are followed by a symbolic act of crowning the living Davidic representative.[1] Like Ezekiel, Zechariah could turn from the symbolism of vision and act to simple exhortation or promise.   In such case, he repeats the old message of the early writing prophets — the message of justice, mercy, and truth, rather than ceremonial.

Speak unto all the people of the land, and to the priests, saying, When ye fasted and mourned in the fifth and in the seventh month, even these seventy years, did ye at all fast unto me, even to me?   And when ye eat, and when ye drink, do not ye eat for yourselves, and drink for yourselves? Should ye not hear the words which Jehovah cried by the former prophets, when Jerusalem was inhabited and in prosperity, and the cities thereof round about her, and the South and the lowland were inhabited?

And the word of Jehovah came unto Zechariah, saying, Thus hath Jehovah of hosts spoken, saying, Execute true judgment, and show kindness and compassion every man to his brother; and oppress not the widow, nor the fatherless, the sojourner, nor the poor; and let none of you devise evil against his brother in your heart.[2]

[1] 6 9-15.   For discussion of this passage, see G. A. Smith, *Book of the Twelve Prophets*, Vol. II, p. 309.

[2] Zechariah 7 5-10.

Most of Zechariah's writing is in prose form, but at times he breaks forth into song, as when he appeals to the exiles to return from Babylon : —

> Hoy, Hoy, flee from the land of the north,
> > Oracle of Jehovah;
> For from the four winds of heaven I gather you,
> > Oracle of Jehovah.
> Hoy, escape to Zion, thou that dwellest in Babylon,
> For thus sayeth Jehovah of hosts,
> The one touching you, toucheth apple of my eye.
> Lo, I am about to shake my hand over them,
> And they shall be spoil to their servants.
> And ye shall know that Jehovah of hosts sent me.[1]

The work of rebuilding the temple was completed two years after the last recorded word of Zechariah. It was after this work was accomplished that a poet whose voice is that of "the great unknown" heard in Isaiah 40–55 sings of Jerusalem's glory. Whether it is the same prophet or one of kindred spirit we cannot say. His first hymn begins: —

> Arise, shine; for thy light is come,
> And the glory of Jehovah is risen upon thee.
> For, behold, darkness shall cover the earth,
> And gross darkness the peoples;
> But Jehovah will arise upon thee,
> And his glory shall be seen upon thee.
> And nations shall come to thy light,
> And kings to the brightness of thy rising.[2]

The concluding lines of this lyric are peculiarly beautiful : —

> I will also make thy officers peace,
> And thine exactors righteousness.
> Violence shall no more be heard in thy land,
> Desolation nor destruction within thy borders;
> But thou shalt call thy walls Salvation,
> And thy gates Praise.

[1] Zechariah 2 6-9. Translation based on a revised text; emendations suggested chiefly by Septuagint readings.
[2] Isaiah 60 1-3.

The sun shall be no more thy light by day;
Neither for brightness shall the moon give light for thee:
But Jehovah will be unto thee an everlasting light,
And thy God thy glory.
Thy sun shall no more go down,
Neither shall thy moon withdraw itself;
For Jehovah will be thine everlasting light,
And the days of thy mourning shall be ended.
Thy people also shall be all righteous;
They shall inherit the land forever,
The branch of my planting,
The work of my hands, that I may be glorified.
The little one shall become a thousand,
And the small one a strong nation:
I, Jehovah, will hasten it in its time.[1]

The following poem opens with the supreme expression of the true mission of Jehovah's messenger. When he who was the perfect revelation of his Father would bring to the neighbors of his boyhood home an understanding of the mission which he had undertaken, it was these words he made his own.[2]

The Spirit of the Lord Jehovah is upon me;
Because Jehovah hath anointed me
To preach good tidings unto the meek;
He hath sent me to bind up the broken-hearted,
To proclaim liberty to the captives,
And the opening of the prison to them that are bound;
To proclaim the year of Jehovah's favor,
And the day of vengeance of our God;
To comfort all that mourn;
To appoint unto them that mourn in Zion,
To give unto them a garland for ashes,
The oil of joy for mourning,
The garment of praise for the spirit of heaviness;
That they may be called trees of righteousness,
The planting of Jehovah, that he may be glorified.[3]

To bring the message of comfort to the scattered and broken-hearted exiles of his race, to announce to them that the hour of

---

[1] Isaiah 60 [17b-22].   [2] Luke 4 [18].   [3] Isaiah 61 [1-3].

Jehovah's deliverance was at hand, to turn their mourning into rejoicing, were precisely the ends which the wonderful prophet of restoration was striving to attain; but they were ends which only a greater than he could achieve.

The remaining prophecies of Isaiah 56–66 are of uncertain date and authorship. Some of them may even date from the years after the rebuilding of the walls by Nehemiah, in the middle of the fifth century. Some seem to come from the years of discouragement that followed upon the high hopes of the earlier restoration with its rebuilding of the temple.

Noble thoughts nobly expressed appear in these chapters again and again, shining all the more brilliantly because of the dark background. The old, prophetic demand for justice that rang out so clear in the eighth century is reiterated: Thus saith Jehovah, Keep ye justice and do righteousness; for my salvation is near to come, and my righteousness to be revealed.[1] For I, Jehovah, love justice, I hate robbery with iniquity; and I will give them their recompense in truth, and I will make an everlasting covenant with them.[2]

The profound truth that moral wrong separates from God is heard once more: —

> Lo, Jehovah's hand is not shortened to deliver,
> Nor is his ear too dull to hear;
> But your guilt has become a barrier
> Between you and your God.
> And your sins have hidden his face from you,
> For your hands are defiled with blood,
> And your fingers with guilt.
> Your lips speak falsehood;
> Your tongue mutters wrong.[3]

The description of the true service which Jehovah would have reaches a climax in Isaiah 58: —

> Is such the fast that I have chosen?
> The day for a man to afflict his soul?
> Is it to bow down his head as a rush,
> And to spread sackcloth and ashes under him?

---

[1] Isaiah 56 1.   [2] Isaiah 61 8.   [3] Isaiah 59 1-3.

Wilt thou call this a fast,
And an acceptable day to Jehovah?
Is not this the fast that I have chosen:
To loose the bonds of wickedness,
To undo the bands of the yoke,
And to let the oppressed go free,
And that ye break every yoke?
Is it not to deal thy bread to the hungry,
And that thou bring the poor that are cast out to thy house?
When thou seest the naked that thou cover him;
And that thou hide not thyself from thine own flesh?
Then shall thy light break forth as the morning,
And thy healing shall spring forth speedily;
And thy righteousness shall go before thee;
The glory of Jehovah shall be thy rearward.
Then shalt thou call, and Jehovah will answer;
Thou shalt cry, and he will say, here I am.[1]

To this message of Israel's prophets, reiterated in varying form from the days before the fall of Northern Israel till the restoration of Judah, no word can be added until Jesus himself shall picture the final day of testing: —

Then shall the King say unto them on his right hand, Come, ye blessed of my Father, inherit the kingdom prepared for you from the foundation of the world: for I was hungry, and ye gave me to eat; I was thirsty, and ye gave me drink; I was a stranger, and ye took me in; naked, and ye clothed me; I was sick, and ye visited me; I was in prison, and ye came unto me. Then shall the righteous answer him, saying, Lord, when saw we thee hungry, and fed thee? or athirst, and gave thee drink? And when saw we thee a stranger, and took thee in? or naked, and clothed thee? And when saw we thee sick, or in prison, and came unto thee? And the King shall answer and say unto them, Verily I say unto you, Inasmuch as ye did it unto one of these my brethren, even these least, ye did it unto me.[2]

The Restoration period was rich in songs that have found place in the book of Psalms.

By the rivers of Babylon,
There we sat down, yea, we wept,
When we remembered Zion[3]

[1] Isaiah 58 5-8.   [2] Matthew 25 34-40.   [3] Psalm 137 1.

gives expression to a luxury of retrospective grief and leads on to terrible imprecation upon the enemies of 586. A large number of psalms that picture harassment by petty enemies find their best setting in the years before Nehemiah built the walls (444 B.C.) and enabled the city to defend itself.   Such an one is Psalm 9–10, originally one poem.   A part of this is: —

> I will give thanks unto Jehovah with my whole heart;
> I will show forth all thy marvellous works.
> I will be glad and exult in thee;
> I will sing praise to thy name, O thou Most High.
> When mine enemies turn back,
> They stumble and perish at thy presence.
> For thou hast maintained my right and my cause;
> Jehovah also will be a high tower for the oppressed,
> A high tower in times of trouble;
> And they that know thy name will put their trust in thee;
> For thou, Jehovah, hast not forsaken them that seek thee.
> Have mercy upon me, O Jehovah;
> Behold my affliction which I suffer of them that hate me,
> Thou that liftest me up from the gates of death;
> That I may show forth all thy praise.
> In the gates of the daughter of Zion.
> I will rejoice in thy salvation.
> Arise, O Jehovah; let not man prevail:
> Let the nations be judged in thy sight.
> Put them in fear, O Jehovah:
> Let the nations know themselves to be but men.[1]

Some penitential prayers are among the more beautiful songs of this era.   Psalm 6 may be the oldest of these.

> O Jehovah, rebuke me not in thine anger,
> Neither chasten me in thy hot displeasure.
> Have mercy upon me, O Jehovah; for I am withered away:
> O Jehovah, heal me; for my bones are troubled.
> My soul also is sore troubled:
> And thou, O Jehovah, how long?
> Return, O Jehovah, deliver my soul:
> Save me for thy lovingkindness' sake.

[1] Psalm 9 1–4, 9–10, 13–14, 19–20.

For in death there is no remembrance of thee:
In Sheol who shall give thee thanks?
I am weary with my groaning;
Every night make I my bed to swim;
I water my couch with my tears.
Mine eye wasteth away because of grief;
It waxeth old because of all mine adversaries.
Depart from me, all ye workers of iniquity;
For Jehovah hath heard the voice of my weeping.
Jehovah hath heard my supplication;
Jehovah will receive my prayer.
All mine enemies shall be put to shame and sore troubled:
They shall turn back, they shall be put to shame suddenly.

The adversaries who appear within this psalm are foes within the
community.   More beautiful in its thought is

Blessed is he whose transgression is forgiven,
Whose sin is covered.
Blessed is the man unto whom Jehovah imputeth not iniquity.
And in whose spirit there is no guile.
When I kept silence, my bones wasted away
Through my groaning all the day long.
For day and night thy hand was heavy upon me:
My moisture was changed as with the drought of summer.
I acknowledged my sin unto thee,
And mine iniquity did I not hide:
I said, I will confess my transgressions unto Jehovah;
And thou forgavest the iniquity of my sin.
For this let every one that is godly pray unto thee in a time when thou
    mayest be found:
Surely when the great waters overflow they shall not reach unto him.[1]

Such poetic expressions indicate the deep sense of guilt that
rested upon the harassed community which rebuilt the temple,
but could not defend itself against jealous neighbors.   Zechariah's
visions, at the time of rebuilding, were in part addressed to the
task of convincing the people that Jehovah no longer imputed
iniquity.

The very beautiful and familiar penitential psalm 51, with its
prayer for the rebuilding of the walls of Jerusalem in order that

[1] Psalm 32 1-6.

worthy offerings may be made, comes from the time just before or during Nehemiah's work.   It begins: —

Have mercy upon me, O God, according to thy lovingkindness:
According to the multitude of thy tender mercies blot out my trans-
    gressions.
Wash me thoroughly from mine iniquity,
And cleanse me from my sin.
For I know my transgressions;
And my sin is ever before me.
Against thee, thee only, have I sinned,
And done that which is evil in thy sight;
That thou mayest be justified when thou speakest,
And be clear when thou judgest.

CHAPTER XX

(About 450 to 432 B.C.)

THE temple was brought to completion in 516 B.C., but the walls of Jerusalem, thrown down in 586, were not then restored. So the ancient stronghold lay open and unprotected, and the Judean community could not maintain itself separate from the mixed surrounding population. On the south the Edomites remained in possession of a part of the old territory of Judea; on the west the inhabitants of the Philistine plain were in close communication with the Judeans; on the north the mixed population, made up chiefly of the remnants of Israel and the various pagan peoples who had been forcibly settled among them two centuries before, were in constant business intercourse and were also sharing the worship of the new temple; even the Arabians on the east were in close touch. All these little peoples taken together made only a part of one of the great satrapies into which Darius divided the vast Persian Empire, and none of them could have a very distinct political or commercial life. Through the inevitable intermingling of the Judean community with these various neighbors, racial identity was rapidly being lost. The exiles in Babylon were under far more favorable conditions for the preservation of racial and religious integrity as well as for economic and social advancement. With the commercial adaptability of their race, they entered into the activity of Babylonia under the liberal conditions afforded by the Persian government.

The prophet Malachi, speaking when some seventy discouraging years had passed after the completion of the temple, gives a vivid picture from life of the general pessimism and religious scepticism that had followed upon the disappointment of the high hopes roused by the prophets of the closing years of exile and of the partial restoration. The people looked for the evidence of God's love in material prosperity. This was in accord with the ancient doctrine, so clearly presented in its national aspects in Deuteronomy and so forcibly emphasized in the Deuteronomic editing of the nation's history. Haggai, the practical man whose work was to get the immediate thing done, had pressed this doctrine to the extreme, in rousing the people to build. They had built the temple for God, three score years and ten had gone by, and where was Jehovah's shaking of the nations and filling this house with glory? If the silver and the gold were his to give, why did he not bestow them upon the people who had labored and sacrificed to build his house? With their low standard, it is no wonder that the people said, "Wherein hast thou loved us?" or "It is vain to serve God."[1]

Malachi could do little to prove that God did love, save to point back to very ancient history,[2] and to promise for the future.[3] He could, however, on very good ground, show the people that they did not deserve any more prosperity than they were enjoying.

Ye offer polluted bread upon mine altar. And ye say, Wherein have we polluted thee? In that ye say, The table of Jehovah is contemptible. And when ye offer the blind for sacrifice, it is no evil! and when ye offer the lame and sick, it is no evil! Present it now unto thy governor; will he be pleased with thee? or will he accept thy person? saith Jehovah of hosts.

Ye say also, Behold, what a weariness is it! and ye have snuffed at it, saith Jehovah of hosts; and ye have brought that which was taken by violence, and the lame, and the sick; thus ye bring the offering: should I accept this at your hand? saith Jehovah. But cursed be the deceiver, who hath in his flock a male, and voweth, and sacrificeth unto the Lord a blemished thing; for I am a great King, saith Jehovah of hosts, and my name is terrible among the Gentiles.[4]

Will a man rob God? yet ye rob me. But ye say, Wherein have we robbed thee? In tithes and offerings. Ye are cursed with the curse; for ye rob me, even this whole nation. Bring ye the whole tithe into the store-house, that there may be food in my house.[5]

They were worshipping after a fashion, but a very poor fashion, and, too, they were intermarrying with the heathen, divorcing their

---

[1] Malachi 1 [2], 3 [14].   [2] *Ibid.* 1 [3].   [3] *Ibid.* 1 [5].
[4] *Ibid.* 1 [7-8, 13-14].   [5] *Ibid.* 3 [8-10a].

Jewish wives in order to make favorable alliances.[1] Moral vices, such as the ancient prophets had so strenuously condemned, were naturally rife at a time when loyalty to Jehovah went no further than keeping up a wretched, perfunctory ritual.

And I will come near to you to judgment; and I will be a swift witness against the sorcerers, and against the adulterers, and against the false swearers, and against those that oppress the hireling in his wages, the widow, and the fatherless, and that turn aside the sojourner from his right, and fear not me, saith Jehovah of hosts.[2]

In a somewhat Socratic method, Malachi thus draws out the shortcomings of the people. He is not, however, able to see the weakness of the conception that material rewards should be proportionate to spiritual virtues, on which the scepticism and lax conduct rest. If Malachi had read the poem of the Suffering Servant, its truth had not reached him. His message is: —

Bring ye the whole tithe into the store-house, that there may be food in my house, and prove me now herewith, saith Jehovah of hosts, if I will not open you the windows of heaven, and pour you out a blessing, that there shall not be room enough to receive it. And I will rebuke the devourer for your sakes, and he shall not destroy the fruits of your ground; neither shall your vine cast its fruit before the time in the field, saith Jehovah of hosts. And all nations shall call you happy; for ye shall be a delightsome land, saith Jehovah of hosts.[3]

Toward the illumination of this doctrine of rewards, with its partial truth and partial error, Malachi has nothing to offer. From his viewpoint, the only hope is in the coming of a refiner and purifier who shall purge the people as gold and silver, that they may offer unto the Lord an offering in righteousness.[4] The only mitigation of the future judgment is that before the great and terrible day of the Lord come, there shall be one to warn as Elijah warned Ahab, lest Jehovah come and smite the earth with a curse.[5]

Malachi had learned something of the truth that had been new when the prophets who preceded him first taught it, but his mind was too completely dominated by mechanical, priestly con-

---

[1] Malachi 2 11-16.   [2] Ibid. 3 5.   [3] Ibid. 3 10-12.

[4] Ibid. 3 2-3.   [5] Ibid. 4 5-6

U

ceptions to follow them to the heights that they had attained. The priestly age so distinctly foreshadowed in Ezekiel is at hand.

The conditions indicated by Malachi are those which Nehemiah finds when he reaches Jerusalem in 444 B.C. The work which this great leader must undertake is the rebuilding of the city walls. To carry out any thoroughgoing reforms, the people must be able to separate their worship, and, to some extent, their entire life from the intermingling of pagan and semi-pagan neighbors. This done, it is possible to maintain a rigid observance of the Sabbath and to put an effectual stop to the mixing of the Jewish blood through foreign marriage. With the establishment of a regular poll tax for the support of the temple worship, the wretched condition of this worship pictured by Malachi could not recur. The reforms carried out by Nehemiah are directed toward exactly the conditions that Malachi deplored and which seemed to him curable only by the refiner's fire.

Nehemiah's work was epoch-making; without it the perpetuation of the Jew and Judaism in Palestine would have been impossible.[1] Its story is told by Nehemiah himself, in a notable memoir that is now embodied in the later book of Nehemiah as chapters 1–2, 4–7 ^{5a}, 12 $^{31-32, \, 37-40}$, 13 $^{4-30}$.[2] From both the historical and literary point of view this memoir is one of the most interesting documents of ancient Israel; historically, it is the first-hand testimony of the leader of an undertaking that made possible the Judaism which persisted from 400 B.C. until the coming of Jesus, and has persisted even to the present day; as a piece of narrative, it is the autobiographical writing of one of the men who have determined the course of history during many centuries.

The *Commentaries* of Cæsar give no more vivid pictures of strategy and struggle and do not reveal the writer himself as intimately as this diary of Nehemiah. The night ride of inspection gives a picture that forever holds the imagination : —

---

[1] In this discussion it is assumed that the work of Ezra is later than that of Nehemiah. See Chapter XXI, p. 307.

[2] In its present form, 13 $^{4-30}$ is probably recast by the editor of the present book. See Kent, *Israel's Historical and Biographical Narratives*, p. 362.

And I arose in the night, I and some few men with me; neither told I any man what my God put into my heart to do for Jerusalem; neither was there any beast with me, save the beast that I rode upon. And I went out by night by the valley gate, even toward the jackal's well, and to the dung gate, and viewed the walls of Jerusalem, which were broken down, and the gates thereof were consumed with fire. Then I went on to the fountain gate and to the king's pool; but there was no place for the beast that was under me to pass. Then went I up in the night by the brook, and viewed the wall; and I turned back, and entered by the valley gate, and so returned. And the rulers knew not whither I went, or what I did; neither had I as yet told it to the Jews, nor to the priests, nor to the nobles, nor to the rulers, nor to the rest that did the work. [1]

The story of the plots to secure possession of Nehemiah's person or to discredit him reveal the man most interestingly.

Now it came to pass, when it was reported to Sanballat and Tobiah, and to Geshem the Arabian, and unto the rest of our enemies, that I had builded the wall, and that there was no breach left therein (though even unto that time I had not set up the doors in the gates), that Sanballat and Geshem sent unto me saying, Come, let us meet together in one of the villages in the plain of Ono. But they thought to do me mischief. And I sent messengers unto them, saying, I am doing a great work, so that I cannot come down: why should the work cease, whilst I leave it, and come down to you? And they sent unto me four times after this sort; and I answered them after the same manner. Then sent Sanballat his servant unto me in like manner the fifth time with an open letter in his hand, wherein was written, It is reported among the nations, and Gashmu saith it, that thou and the Jews think to rebel; for which cause thou art building the wall: and thou wouldst be their king, according to these words. And thou hast also appointed prophets to preach of thee at Jerusalem, saying, There is a king in Judah: and now shall it be reported to the king according to these words. Come now therefore, and let us take counsel together. Then I sent unto him, saying, There are no such things done as thou sayest, but thou feignest them out of thine own heart. For they all would have made us afraid, saying, Their hands shall be weakened from the work, that it be not done. But now, O God, strengthen thou my hands.

And I went unto the house of Shemaiah the son of Delaiah the son of Mehetabel, who was shut up; and he said, Let us meet together in the

---

[1] Nehemiah 2 [12-16].

house of God, within the temple, and let us shut the doors of the temple : for they will come to slay thee; yea, in the night will they come to slay thee.   And I said, Should such a man as I flee? and who is there, that, being such as I, would go into the temple to save his life?   I will not go in.   And I discerned, and, lo, God had not sent him; but he pronounced this prophecy against me : and Tobiah and Sanballat had hired him.   For this cause was he hired, that I should be afraid, and do so, and sin, and that they might have matter for an evil report, that they might reproach me.   Remember, O my God, Tobiah and Sanballat according to these their works, and also the prophetess Noadiah, and the rest of the prophets, that would have put me in fear.[1]

Here as elsewhere the pervading impression is of the simplicity of the truly great man.   Shrewd to see the machinations of his enemies, in his own life he was simple and direct, moving along broad, straight lines.   The wealthy governor who needed not to collect the taxes of his little province for his own support; who yet entertained at his table day by day with regal generosity; the confidential, loved, and trusted officer of the ruler of the vastest and best governed empire the world had ever seen, shows us his heart with the simplicity of a child.

[1] Nehemiah 6 [1-14].

CHAPTER XXI

PRIESTLY IDEALS IN LAW AND HISTORY

(*About 450 to about 300 B.C.*)

THE composite history of the exodus and wilderness periods which the Jews carried with them to Babylon contained the brief law codes of Exodus 20–23 and 24, ascribed to the Sinai period. This history, as edited and expanded during the exile, contained also the Deuteronomic code, ascribed to the east-Jordan sojourn. These codes dealt in part with laws of sacrificial worship, but the priestly ritual, as a whole, was handed down mainly through the unbroken usage and tradition of the sanctuary, until the destruction of Jerusalem interrupted for seventy years the temple worship. Then the exiled priests were stimulated to commit to writing and so preserve for future generations the ceremonial practices of Jehovah's worship. The first fruits of this movement were the code of laws now constituting chapters 17 to 26 (perhaps 11 also) of Leviticus and Ezekiel's plan for the restored temple-worship. We have noted already (Chapter XVII) that Ezekiel introduced into his plan some elements unknown before the exile. In some respects his ideas seem to be an advance upon those of Leviticus 17–26, which, it is inferred, was probably codified chiefly between 597 and 586. The central idea of this first Leviticus code is indicated by the frequent repetition "Be ye holy, for I am Jehovah your God" and similar phrases, which have led to its designation, in modern times, as the "Law of Holiness." Some of the laws deal with general social relations, but the chief interest of the code is ritual purity. Doubtless these laws embody very ancient practice, but in some features they show development beyond those of Exodus 20–23 and Deuteronomy 12–26.

After the temple was rebuilt in 520–516 B.C., we have seen from contemporary evidence that worship was conducted in a wretched way down to the time of Nehemiah. Meanwhile the greater portion of the people remained in Babylonia, and the priestly portion of the community busied itself in codifying and further developing the law, against the day when there might come a more complete restoration. The result of their labors is seen in the remainder of Leviticus and many laws of kindred form and character in Exodus and Numbers.

The older combined history, even with its Deuteronomic editing, did not adequately present certain aspects of the history from the priestly point of view. The priests in Babylonia were, for example, greatly interested in preserving pure tribal blood and developed elaborate genealogies. As time passed by, therefore, the men who wrote the ritual laws, or others of kindred spirit, were moved to write a genealogical and historical outline into which the laws might be fitted, as those of the earlier codes were fitted into the history already existing. These men felt the great importance of preserving the sense of family and tribal identity and the national religious customs, such as the Sabbath, circumcision, and the sacrifices. Above all they would emphasize the covenant relation between Jehovah and Israel, the very basis of their religion, in distinction from the religions that regarded the gods as belonging to certain districts or tribes intrinsically, rather than by voluntary choice and mutual agreement. In briefly rewriting the history, they brought out the covenant idea and recorded the institution of the ritual practices, as it seemed to them these must have developed from the earliest times. Into this as a framework they fitted their law codes as given at Sinai, where they accounted the most elaborate ecclesiastical organization to have been established, quite contrary to the representation of the earlier histories.[1]

It is one of the easiest tasks of Old Testament criticism to dis-

---

[1] This recalls the phrase from later Rabbinic literature, "a law from Moses on Sinai." Under this caption were included parts of the oral law (as distinguished from the written or Old Testament code) which had previously not been definitely formulated or gathered in writing. This phrase for centuries was taken literally to mean that these oral laws were also given by Moses on Sinai. More critical study has suggested that it is but a projection in time back to Moses and to Sinai of such common customs and laws as had become binding after centuries of usage. The process is interesting as being parallel to the above.

tinguish this strand of narrative and legal material from the earlier documents with which it was eventually interwoven. Its language, style, interests, and theological conceptions separate it as widely from the earlier documents as a pre-Darwinian treatise on natural history is separated from a modern work on biology.

The new history opened with the systematic, lofty, and mature account of creation now found in Genesis 1–2 4a. It is this latest account that some scientists have sought to harmonize with modern cosmogony. Side by side with this latest narrative there stands in our Genesis (2 4ff) the picturesque story of creation taken from the early Judean history. No attempt is made to harmonize the latter with present-day science. In the one, the style is rigid and repetitious, but of majestic movement, while the thought is orderly and progressive. In the other the style is "free and flowing" without rigid, repetitious phrases; the arrangement is that of the story-teller who orders his material for its picturesque effect and cares little for exact chronological order.

In reading Genesis 1 and 2, one comes suddenly, in the latter part of verse 4 of chapter 2, into a new vocabulary.[1] It is no longer God but Jehovah God who acts; he no longer creates but makes and forms. The first story shows its interest by its culmination in the sanctifying of the seventh day; the second leads on to the temptation and fall. Perhaps the most striking difference of all is in the conception of God. In the first chapter he creates by fiat; he sees that his work is good and approves it, but there is no suggestion of a being who walks and talks among men. In the second story, he takes material, he shapes it, and breathes into it as though he were a physical being; his voice is heard, walking in the garden in the cool of the day, and altogether the conception is anthropomorphic and primitive.

The second narrative was considered in Chapter V as the opening of the great Judean history that was compiled in the ninth century B.C., not later than 800. The first chapter is from the opening of the priestly history compiled in the fifth century B.C. In the four centuries separating the two, lies all the work of the great prophets from Amos to the Great Unknown, who gradually

[1] The beginner in Hebrew who has learned to read quite freely in the vocabulary and style of chapter 1, comes up with a round turn.

developed the idea of God until he was at last conceived as creator and preserver of all the visible universe.

The priestly account of creation ends with the phrase "These are the generations of the heavens and the earth." We next meet a similar phrase in chapter 5[1], and immediately the student of the original finds himself in the familiar vocabulary of 1–2[4a], and the style suddenly becomes rigid and repetitious.

> This is the book of the generations of Adam. In the day that God created man, in the likeness of God made he him; male and female created he them, and blessed them, and called their name Adam, in the day when they were created. And Adam lived a hundred and thirty years, and begat a son in his own likeness, after his image; and called his name Seth: and the days of Adam after he begat Seth were eight hundred years; and he begat sons and daughters. And all the days that Adam lived were nine hundred and thirty years: and he died.
>
> And Seth lived a hundred and five years, and begat Enosh: and Seth lived after he begat Enosh eight hundred and seven years, and begat sons and daughters: and all the days of Seth were nine hundred and twelve years: and he died.
>
> And Enosh, lived ninety years, and begat Kenan: etc.[1]

The parallel genealogy of 4[16-25] that cannot retain a regular form for two verses, stands in striking contrast: —

> And Cain went out from the presence of Jehovah, and dwelt in the land of Nod, on the east of Eden. And Cain knew his wife; and she conceived, and bare Enoch: and he builded a city, and called the name of the city, after the name of his son, Enoch. And unto Enoch was born Irad: and Irad begat Mehujael; and Mehujael begat Methushael; and Methushael begat Lamech. And Lamech took unto him two wives: the name of the one was Adah, and the name of the other Zillah. And Adah bare Jabal: he was the father of such as dwell in tents and have cattle. And his brother's name was Jubal: he was the father of all such as handle the harp and pipe. And Zillah, she also bare Tubalcain, the forger of every cutting instrument of brass and iron: and the sister of Tubalcain was Naamah. And Lamech said unto his wives: —
>
> Adah and Zillah, hear my voice;
> Ye wives of Lamech, hearken unto my speech:

---

[1] Genesis 5[1-9].

> For I have slain a man for wounding me,
> And a young man for bruising me:
> If Cain shall be avenged seven-fold,
> Truly Lamech seventy and seven-fold.

And Adam knew his wife again; and she bare a son, and called his name Seth: For, said she, God hath appointed me another seed instead of Abel; for Cain slew him. And to Seth, to him also there was born a son; and he called his name Enosh. Then began men to call upon the name of Jehovah.[1]

The one belongs to the late priestly narrative, the other, to the early story narrative.

In chapters 6–9, the flood story, the two documents are closely interwoven. When they are separated, each gives a fairly complete and self-consistent story. In the priestly account, the time is given in exact terms, year, month, day, following the practice which appears in the prophets of the exile and restoration; in the other, the time is given in the round numbers seven and forty.[2] The late account leads up to the covenant with Noah, which plainly refers back to the account of creation, from the same document.

And God blessed Noah and his sons, and said unto them, Be fruitful, and multiply, and replenish the earth. And the fear of you and the dread of you shall be upon every beast of the earth, and upon every bird of the heavens; with all wherewith the ground teemeth, and all the fishes of the sea, into your hand are they delivered. Every moving thing that liveth shall be food for you; as the green herb have I given you all. But flesh with the life thereof, which is the blood thereof, shall ye not eat. And surely your blood, the blood of your lives, will I require; at the hand of every beast will I require it: and at the hand of man, even at the hand of every man's brother, will I require the life of man. Whoso sheddeth man's blood, by man shall his blood be shed: for in the image of God made he man. And you, be ye fruitful, and multiply; bring forth abundantly in the earth, and multiply therein.[3]

Chapter 10 begins "Now these are the generations of," and again there is a barren genealogy for a few verses (1–7) which is resumed in 20 and 22–32. This is continued in 11 [10 ff] and carries the race on to Abram.

[1] Genesis 4 [16-26].   [2] See Chapter V, pp. 72–74.   [3] Genesis 9 [1-7].

These are the generations of Shem. Shem was a hundred years old, and begat Arpachshad two years after the flood: and Shem lived after he begat Arpachshad five hundred years, and begat sons and daughters.

And Arpachshad lived five and thirty years, and begat Shelah: and Arpachshad lived after he begat Shelah four hundred and three years, and begat sons and daughters. . . .

And Terah lived seventy years, and begat Abram, Nahor, and Haran.

Now these are the generations of Terah. Terah begat Abram, Nahor, and Haran; and Haran begat Lot.[1]

Thus for pre-Abramic times, the late priests' history had the majestic story of creation and a systematic narrative of the flood. These were connected by a genealogy that reached from Adam to Noah, ten generations, and continued from Noah to Abram, ten generations; it also carried the side lines out for a few generations. The first story of the history culminated in the Sabbath, the second, in the covenant of meat eating with the proscription of blood.

Both of the narratives of pre-Abramic times existed in the Assyro-Babylonian literature, in far earlier and grossly polytheistic forms. The Babylonian flood story has already been read in comparison with that of the early prophetic history.[2] In the creation stories the closer parallelism is between the priestly account and the Babylonian story. A few lines from the latter will illustrate some resemblances with the Biblical account and emphasize the striking character of the differences. Bel-Marduk, champion of the forces of light and order, has overcome Tiamat, the personification of darkness and chaos, the "deep" (*tehom*) of Genesis 1.

And the lord stood upon Tiamat's hinder parts,
And with his merciless club he smashed her skull.
He cut through the channels of her blood,
And he made the North wind bear it away into secret places.
His fathers beheld, and they rejoiced and were glad;
Presents and gifts they brought unto him.
Then the lord rested, gazing upon her dead body,
While he divided the flesh of the . . . ,[3] and devised a cunning plan.

---

[1] Genesis 11 10-12, 26-27.   [2] See Chapter V, pp. 80–84.

[3] Perhaps "body."

He split her up like a flat fish into two halves;
One half of her he stablished as a covering for heaven.
He fixed a bolt, he stationed a watchman,
And bade them not to let her waters come forth.
He passed through the heavens, he surveyed the regions (thereof),

*   *   *   *   *   *   *   *

He (*i.e.* Marduk) made the stations for the great gods;
The stars their images, as the stars of the Zodiac, he fixed.
He ordained the year and into sections he divided it;
For the twelve months he fixed three stars.
After he had [. . .] the days of the year [. . .] images,
He founded the station of Nibir[1] to determine their bounds;
That none might err or go astray.[2]

In Genesis 12–16, only a few verses can be identified as belonging to the late priestly document.[3] They serve to make the briefest possible connections between that which has preceded and the account of the circumcision-covenant and the promise of the birth of Isaac which fill chapter 17. The birth of Isaac occupies three or four verses near the beginning of chapter 21,[4] but the story of Abraham's purchase of a burial-place for Sarah is the next considerable narrative.[5] This is a more living story than is usually found in the priestly history, although in comparison with the movement of the earlier stories in the prophetic documents it appears a little too prolonged and repetitious.[6] The death and burial of Abraham and the generations of Ishmael made up the next section of this document.[7]

[1] *I.e.* Jupiter.
[2] Translation from King, *The Seven Tablets of Creation*, Vol. I, pp. 75–79.
[3] 11 31–32, 12 4b–5, 13 6, 11b, 16 1a, 3, 15–16.   [4] Verses 2b–5.
[5] Chapter 23.
[6] The conventional mode of bargaining depicted, persists to-day among the Arabs wherever found. The Spectator described in *The Outlook*, a few years ago, an experience in an Arabic restaurant in New York City, that reproduced almost the words of Ephron. The restaurant keeper at first protested that he could not accept any money from his guest, and, when pressed, asked, "What is a luncheon worth eighty cents between me and thee?" And The Spectator hearkened to the modern Ephron and gave him the silver which he had named.
[7] 25 7–11a, 12–17.

The material from the creation to the death of Abraham may suffice to illustrate the general style and interest of the late priestly history. It appears as made up of genealogical framework that included narratives where something of legalistic interest was presented — the institution of the Sabbath, the covenants with Noah and Abraham, the securing of a legal tenure in Canaan. It is an institutional history with little interest in anything else. In marked contrast was the garrulous interest of the early Judean document in everything human. Names and customs, joys and sorrows of individuals, sin and its growing consequences, these and many other things of daily life and experience were all told in charming, simple story. That history was in the strictest sense literature; this is not, except as the term is stretched to include all the significant writings of a nation.

Throughout the remainder of the patriarchal age the traditional history contained little of interest to this document. The journeying and family of Jacob and his burial in Canaan received some attention, but the dramatic stories of Joseph are wholly due to the earlier Judean and Ephraimite histories. The following period, however, demanded greatest attention; the priestly history had its own narrative of the call of Moses, the plagues, and the crossing of the Red Sea, while the elaborate details concerning the tabernacle and the mathematical arrangement of the camp, in Exodus and Numbers, all come from the late historians who conceived of the most developed ritualistic arrangements as instituted by Moses. The earlier histories give a very different picture of the exodus and wilderness period; they are in general agreement with the pre-exilic prophets who regard the wilderness age as one of great simplicity in religious forms.[1]

The allotment of the land to the various tribes was described with great detail in the priestly history; this now constitutes the greater part of the latter half of Joshua. It represents a very late conception, assigning to the tribes land that never belonged to Israel until after David's conquests. Such, in brief outline, was the idealized national history composed in Babylonia after the exile, the first great product of a new school of historical writing.

[1] Amos 5 25, Jeremiah 7 22.

The precise date of the great, new, historico-legal document in relation to the work of Nehemiah is difficult to determine. It certainly was unknown in Palestine when Nehemiah arrived there in 444 B.C. Whether the law was promulgated by Ezra during Nehemiah's governorship is very doubtful. It was so conceived by the later compiler who inserted an account of this between the sections of Nehemiah's diary; but it is at least equally probable that the priestly history and law was not brought to Jerusalem until a few years later than Nehemiah's time. It is safe to say simply that not far from the year 400 B.C., Jerusalem was in possession of the priestly history and law combined in one document.

Then there existed two works on the history of antiquity, of which one contained, as its centre and standard, the law book Deuteronomy, and the other, the law book Leviticus. This condition could not last long. Soon the two histories must be worked into a harmony; this had been done with the two earlier histories, not long after the fall of Northern Israel, and with the chronicles of the kings of Israel and of the kings of Judah, during the exile; this would be done later with Matthew's collection of Christ's sayings and Mark's story of his deeds; this would be done in the second century A.D. in Tatian's Diatessaron, a compilation of all four gospels into a connected story of Christ; this would be done, as we have seen, by successive compilers with the early narratives of English history.

The priestly history and law represented the prevalent spirit of 400 B.C. far more closely than the prophetico-priestly history and law of the sixth century did, although the earlier was by no means to be discarded. The natural consequence was a compilation which took the priestly history as its basis and framework and fitted the fuller, earlier history into this scheme. The composite work forms our books of Genesis, Exodus, Leviticus, Numbers, and Joshua, often denominated, because of their unity of composition, the Hexateuch. The entire work was given its final stamp by the late priestly history that made the groundwork.

Only when the successive strata of the narrative and law are distinguished, is it possible to understand the development of the law, literature, and religion of Israel. In this great book is the stratum of the simple, childlike apprehension of God and life in the age of inexperience and boundless hope; in it is the interpretation that grew out of the vital preaching of the great prophets, first formulated in Deuteronomy and applied in the humility of defeat and exile; in it finally was the interpretation of life given by those who sought to make the chastened nation fit for the blessing of a holy God through perfect devotion in worship.

Estimating the documents from the point of view of their religious spirit, the earliest are styled prophetic, because they interpret life in terms of a moral God and moral forces. The next are called prophetico-priestly or prophetico-legalistic, since they aim to interpret prophetic principles into laws. The third group is the priestly or legalistic, in which the great prophetic principles have disappeared under the sway of priesthood. The two great elements of religion which persist and struggle to-day in the Jewish church and the Christian, the moral and the institutional, are remarkably combined in the Hexateuch. This composite work grew out of centuries of life and the most varied experiences; it is not strange that it fits into the varied needs of multitudes of individuals, of hundreds of generations.

At the close of the fifth century B.C., we at last have the books of Genesis, Exodus, Leviticus, Numbers, Deuteronomy, and Joshua in their final form. Forgetting for the moment the successive strata which tell the story of their growth, one may look upon them as a finished series of books and observe their general plan and scope: They form a remarkably clear, connected, and orderly group of narratives. The first eleven chapters of Genesis contain traditions of the beginnings of the human race; the view narrows from the race as a whole to the Semites, and then to the Hebraic branch of this race. The remainder of the book has the story of the beginnings of the chosen people. It opens with the separation of the Hebrew ancestors from their kindred in Mesopotamia, indicates their kinship with Edom, Moab, Ammon, and certain desert tribes, and includes the first sojourn in Palestine and the migration to Egypt. Exodus begins with the rapid increase of Jacob's descendants in Egypt and the attempts made to repress them. It carries the story through the deliverance from Egypt, the journey to Sinai, and the principal events at Sinai, ending with the completion of the tabernacle. Leviticus is included at this point as made up of laws given to Moses at Sinai. Numbers opens with Israel still at the foot of the mount of revelation, and includes the larger part of the wilderness life, bringing the narrative forward to the plains east of the Jordan, where a portion of Israel settles permanently. Deuteronomy is in the form of addresses delivered by Moses in the east-Jordan region and closes with the death of the great leader. Joshua takes up the history where it is left with the death of Moses and gives an account of the conquest of Palestine and its ideal allotment to the tribes. The farewell addresses of Joshua, his death and burial in the promised land, and the burial of the bones of Joseph brought up from Egypt, close this unique library of ancient, historical tradition.

The series of histories made up of Judges, Samuel, and Kings had been completed a century and a half earlier than the final composition of the Hexateuch [1] under the influence of the reign of Deuteronomy, and it was never compiled with any priestly history. Judges opens with a summary of the initial conquest of the land (1^1–2^5) and then takes up the struggles by which Israel made good her claims. Samuel begins near the close of the period of the Judges and, with Kings, gives the entire history of the monarchy from its rise to the Babylonian exile. The two series of histories show a slight overlapping at the opening of Judges, but, viewed together, they give a marvellously ordered narrative covering five centuries of national history and reaching back from these historical times to the more and more uncertain eras of tradition and legend.

As time passed, the development of priestly ideals and usages made the composition of a new history of Judah inevitable. The fourth century probably produced a "midrash" of the book of the kings of Israel and Judah.[2] This would be an expansion and modification of the books of Samuel and Kings bringing their narrative more into accord with the ideas of the later century. A writer, who worked not earlier than about 300 B.C., made use of this and of the earlier histories that have been preserved in

---

[1] See Chapter XVIII.
[2] 2 Chronicles 24 [27]; translated "commentary."

composing the ecclesiastical history of Judah which forms 1 and 2 Chronicles.

In the study of Israel's methods of historical composition the books of Chronicles are of great significance in showing both how exactly the historiographer embodied extracts from his sources and how freely he expanded or even corrected these where they failed to express his conceptions of the earlier ages.

Chronicles opens with nine chapters of genealogies extending from Adam down to the time of the writer. Following these, the history is begun at the death of Saul and extended to the exile. The affairs of Northern Israel are not included except as they concern Judah; this fact, together with the great emphasis upon everything connected with the temple, indicates the writer's range of interest. Whether they are taken directly from Samuel and Kings or through the medium of a midrash, many passages are in almost verbatim agreement with the earlier histories; others are condensed. Wherever the temple comes into the history, so much additional material is given that the possibility of access to some special temple history is suggested.

The earlier history had recognized that even the better kings of Judah, with the exception of Hezekiah and Josiah, made no attempt to do away with the high places. From the point of view of the Chronicler's age, this is inconceivable, and he states that these kings removed the high places, although the books of Kings state distinctly that they did not.[1] To him it is inconceivable, too, that soldiers should have been permitted to enter the temple in the revolution which overthrew Athaliah; he therefore substitutes the bands of ministering Levites.

And in the seventh year Jehoiada strengthened himself, and took the captains of hundreds, Azariah the son of Jeroham, and Ishmael the son of Jehohanan, and Azariah the son of Obed, and Maaseiah the son of Adaiah, and Elishaphat the the son of Zichri, into covenant with him. And they went about

And in the seventh year Jehoiada sent and fetched the captains over hundreds of the Carites and of the guard, and brought them to him into the house of Jehovah; and he made a covenant with them, and took an oath of them in the house of Jehovah, and showed them the king's son. And he commanded

[1] See, for example, 1 Kings 22 [43] and 2 Chronicles 17 [6].

in Judah, and gathered the Levites out of all the cities of Judah, and the heads of fathers' houses of Israel, and they came to Jerusalem. And all the assembly made a covenant with the king in the house of God. And he said unto them, Behold, the king's son shall reign, as Jehovah hath spoken concerning the sons of David. This is the thing that ye shall do: a third part of you, that come in on the sabbath, of the priests and of the Levites, shall be porters of the thresholds; and a third part shall be at the king's house; and a third part at the gate of the foundation: and all the people shall be in the courts of the house of Jehovah. But let none come into the house of Jehovah, save the priests, and they that minister of the Levites; they shall come in, for they are holy: but all the people shall keep the charge of Jehovah. And the Levites shall compass the king round about, every man with his weapons in his hand; and whosoever cometh into the house, let him be slain: and be ye with the king when he cometh in, and when he goeth out.

So the Levites and all Judah did according to all that Jehoiada the priest commanded: and they took every man his men, those that were to come in on the sabbath, with those that were to go out on the sabbath; for Jehoiada the priest dismissed not the courses. And Jehoiada the priest delivered to the captains of hundreds the spears,

them, saying, This is the thing that ye shall do: a third part of you, that come in on the sabbath, shall be keepers of the watch of the king's house; and a third part shall be at the gate Sur; and a third part at the gate behind the guard: so shall ye keep the watch of the house, and be a barrier. And the two companies of you, even all that go forth on the sabbath, shall keep the watch of the house of Jehovah about the king. And ye shall compass the king round about, every man with his weapons in his hand; and he that cometh within the ranks, let him be slain: and be ye with the king when he goeth out, and when he cometh in.

And the captains over hundreds did according to all that Jehoiada the priest commanded; and they took every man his men, those that were to come in on the sabbath, with those that were to go out on the sabbath, and came to Jehoiada the priest. And the priest delivered to the captains over hundreds the spears and shields that had been king David's, which were in the house of Jehovah. And the guard stood, every man with his weapons in his hand, from the right side of the house to the left side of the house, along by the altar and the house, by the king round about. Then he brought out the king's son, and put the crown upon him, and gave him the testimony; and they made him king, and anointed him; and they clapped and bucklers, and shields, that had been king David's, which were in the house of God. And he set all the people, every man with his weapon in his hand, from the right side of the house to the left side of the house along by the altar and the house, by the king round about. Then they brought out the king's son, and put the crown upon him, and gave him the testimony, and made him king: and Jehoiada and his sons anointed him; and they said, Long live the king.[1]

their hands, and said, Long live the king.[2]

In such ways the late priestly writer reveals the spirit and ideas of the age which followed the Nehemiah-Ezra reforms.

It was probably the same writer who composed the books of Ezra and Nehemiah. Here he had as sources Nehemiah's own memoir, an Aramaic document from which he embodied brief extracts without translating into Hebrew,[3] and a Hebrew narrative concerning Ezra. This material he arranged to tell the story, as he understood it, of the return from Babylon to Jerusalem, the rebuilding of the temple, and the work of Ezra and Nehemiah. In the composition his peculiar point of view is evident again and again; he cannot conceive that the despised people who remained in Judea rebuilt the city and temple. He pictures this as the work of a great company returning from Babylon immediately after Cyrus's conquest. He cannot conceive, either, that the layman Nehemiah instituted the reforms which resulted in the hierocratic Judaism of his day; he therefore has the scribe Ezra precede Nehemiah to Jerusalem and there carry out reforms that make impossible the work of Nehemiah as it is recorded so simply and naturally in his own diary. He has thus left knotty problems for the historian of Judaism; he has, however, preserved the priceless narrative from the memoir of Nehemiah and also material of some historical and literary value from the other documents named above.

---

[1] 2 Chronicles 23 1-11.   [2] 2 Kings 11 4-12.   [3] Ezra 4 7-23, 5 3-6 15.

Had any one soon after 300 B.C. ventured to compile Samuel and Kings with the Chronicler's work, he would have produced a history of the monarchy representing the same three stages that are found in the Hexateuch. Since this was never done, we have preserved separately a history of the monarchy from its rise to its downfall in Samuel-Kings and a partly parallel history of Judea from David to Ezra in Chronicles-Ezra-Nehemiah.

Looking back from 300 to the tenth century B.C., the historical writing of ancient Israel is seen divided quite distinctly into three great eras. The first extends from the beginning of connected prose writing, under the early monarchy, to a time shortly before the publication of Deuteronomy, approximately from 950 to 650 B.C. So far as extant materials show, it began in Southern Israel with the early Saul and David stories and later gathered into a connected narrative all available materials concerning earlier generations until Southern Israel had its great story of humanity from Adam to the monarchy. In Northern Israel, the first era began about one hundred years later, with nearly contemporaneous history, and extended the story back to Abraham. In its final stage, this great era compiled a history from the northern and southern documents. From this age come nearly all the charming stories of deep human interest which give supreme literary value to such books as Genesis, Exodus, Judges, and Samuel. Their moral ideals are crude, their theology is primitive, but they are instinct with a childlike consciousness of God and a wholesome moral sense.

The second great era of historical writing was the outgrowth of the Deuteronomic reform and the exile. It resulted in slight editorial additions to some portions of the earlier histories and in drastic reëditing of other parts, always from the point of view of a definite philosophy of history. This era produced, also, two new historical works, our books of Judges and Kings. Where the editors of this school touched heavily, either in interpretation of old narratives or in editing new compilations, literary charm languished. Since, however, these men wrote with deepest religious purpose, interpreting history out of experience, there is a certain solemn earnestness even in their monotonous repetition of phrase that gives dignity and almost eloquence, contributing its characteristic elements to the Old Testament narrative style.

The third great era of historical writing is still further removed from the æsthetic charm of the early narratives that pictured human life in its simple, universal elements and interests.   The Deuteronomists saw the national life whole, as a great drama working itself out under the fixed and formulated will of God, almost as inexorable as the Fate of the Greek tragedians; the late priestly historians saw the same national history schematized as the mechanical development of a system of ordinances and institutions.   In the working out of the latter scheme, not only has all human motive and agency disappeared and the consciousness of the immediate presence of God in the daily life of the individual vanished, but the tremendous moral convictions of the Deuteronomic editors have also gone.   History has become little more than the orderly development of the ceremonial practices and institutions of Israel.   Repetition of formulas, characteristic of the writing of the preceding age, has now gone to absolute extreme; yet, as has been said, this very repetition has at times an almost poetic effect, or at least gives a liturgical rhythm, that adds its distinctive element to the composite feeling of the Biblical style.

In each one of the narrative writings of Israel, there is harmony between form and thought, the result, in the final analysis, of sincerity.   Each type of writing is the true expression of the life of the age from which it emanates, for there is in the Old Testament narrative no "fine writing" in which the form obtrudes itself.   The writers were not seeking to produce literature; but to express life as it was in them, demanding to be heard and so, even schematized, institutional history rose at times into the realm of literature.

CHAPTER XXII

(432 to 332 B.C.)

In tracing the development of priestly ideals in law and history
through the composition of Chronicles-Ezra-Nehemiah, we were
brought down to a time after the close of Persian rule. We kept
our eyes fixed, however, upon one rather narrow path, and shall
err if we think of the time of priestly reform and the generations
immediately following as wholly occupied with the matters of
interest to the lawyers and priestly historians. It was an age
of story and song, as well as one of ritual law and history.

The book of Ruth, in its present form, was issued as a protest
against the cruel enforcement of separation, demanded by Nehemiah and Ezra. When Nehemiah chased from him the grandson
of the high priest who had married the daughter of Sanballat, the
young priest may have found it no great hardship to remain loyal
to his foreign wife and assume charge of the rival temple which his
wealthy and powerful father-in-law was able to construct for him
on Mt. Gerizim; but, in many cases, there must have been cruel
separation or bitter expatriation.

Ruth is the story of a day when the relations of Israel with her
neighbors were normal and free. At that ancient time, a man of
Bethlehem-judah might find refuge, with all his family, across
the Jordan, among the broad fields of Moab, when famine visited
the scanty soil of Judah's rocky hills. There the man's sons
might marry women of Moab, and the wives prove loving
daughters to the widowed mother, one of them so faithful in her
devoted love that she gladly faced separation from her own people,
with poverty and widowhood, rather than leave her Judean
mother-in-law. In the end the Moabitess found a true husband
in Judea, and her son's grandson became Israel's greatest king.

The scene is in the days of the judges, but these were in the distant past when the story was written; it begins "And it came to pass in days when the judges judged," and, when the writer comes to describe a legal transaction, he has to speak as an antiquarian explaining the incident in his narrative.

Now this was the custom in former time in Israel concerning redeeming and concerning exchanging, to confirm all things: a man drew off his shoe, and gave it to his neighbor; and this was the manner of attestation in Israel. So the near kinsman said unto Boaz, Buy it for thyself. And he drew off his shoe.[1]

In the east, practices scarcely change from millennium to millennium, yet taking off and handing the shoe as seal of a contract was evidently a forgotten custom. Without this direct internal evidence, a comparison of the whole tone of the story with the fierce and brutal conditions prevalent in the time of the judges would indicate that those days were in the far past.

The story suggests in its literary quality, as well as in its place of origin, the early Judean prose; it may have been treasured in Bethlehem-judah along with the stories of Bethlehemites now forming the appendix of Judges.[2] In its present form, however, it shows everywhere the influence of an idealizing process of which those "grim tales" are wholly innocent; "in Ruth the principal characters are amiable, God-fearing, courteous, unassuming." [3] With Nehemiah's diary and, from a later period, Maccabees, Ruth stands as a monument to the fact that the development of the mechanical, priestly type of narrative writing did not mean the extinction of Israel's gifts for story-telling. Whatever nucleus of the story may have come down from the distant past, we count the present book of Ruth a product of the age of priestly reform, albeit the work of one who was not in accord with the extreme measures of that reform. Without pointing the moral, the development of the tale shows where the writer's sympathies lie in the matter of foreign marriages and subtly draws the reader's sympathies, too. — Had not the noble Boaz married the altogether lovely Ruth, the story would have been most disappointing.

[1] 4 7–8.   [2] See Kent, *Beginnings of Hebrew History*, pp. 27–28.
[3] Driver, *Introduction to the Literature of the Old Testament* (1910), p. 456.

The unhappy controversy, out of which the book of Ruth sprang, is long past, but the book is ever recognized as "one of the best told and most beautiful stories in all literature." [1]   In the present time, when the writing of the short story has become almost a distinct profession, with a technical literature discussing its science and art, we find most of the tests for the proper structure of such stories fully met by the book of Ruth.   The short story is, we are told, "a series of nicely graded scenes or stages leading to a climax." "The conclusion is the solving of all problems, the termination of the narrative itself, and the artistic severing of all relations between narrator and reader."   "Simplicity, as well as brevity, contributes to the intensity of the conclusion."   It has not only unity of plot, but "unity of impression, which depends upon the story's *tone*." [2] These dicta, intended as general principles, might have been designed as descriptions of the story of Ruth.   In one point alone, this short story may perhaps fail to conform to present standards. The story is not clearly limited to the presentation of "a turning point in the life of a *single* character"; that Naomi is the real heroine in whose "magnetic personality" is found "the thread running through the whole, and binding the parts together" has been maintained. [3] Guy de Maupassant and others of his craft leave no doubt as to the central character in their stories.   In this early story, however, the attention is not unpleasantly distracted between Ruth and Naomi, for their lives and hopes are completely identified.   Certainly we could not choose which we would have less prominent and attractive.

To comment upon the beauty and effectiveness of the crucial scenes in Ruth would be superfluous. We recall them; the first is the occasion when Naomi seeks to send back her daughters-in-law, still young enough to begin a new life among their own people, while she, bereft of husband and sons, will return alone and ageing to her native town.   The writer shows us Ruth in a few undying words from her own lips, and we can imagine the strength and

---

[1] Jessup and Canby, *The Book of the Short Story*, p. 4.

[2] *The Short Story — Its Principles and Structure*, by E. M. Albright, pp. 70, 77–78, 80, 84.   The second of the quotations is taken by Albright from Barrett's book on the short story.

[3] Moulton, *Literary Study of the Bible*, p. 235.

fortitude of the older woman who would have deprived herself
of such a daughter.

And she said, Behold, thy sister-in-law is gone back unto her people,
and unto her god: return thou after thy sister-in-law. And Ruth said,
Entreat me not to leave thee, and to return from following after thee; for
whither thou goest, I will go; and where thou lodgest, I will lodge; thy
people shall be my people, and thy God my God; where thou diest, will
I die, and there will I be buried: Jehovah do so to me, and more also, if
aught but death part thee and me.[1]

Ten years have wrought a change in Naomi, who went out with
her husband and well-grown sons.   When she returns all the little
town is excited, but they scarcely recognize the desolate widow,
and they say, "Is this Naomi?"   She answers, "Call me not
Naomi" (delightfulness); "Call me Mara" (bitterness): in accordance with the ancient doctrine, she interprets her bereave-
ment as the testimony of God against her.

The story moves rapidly from significant incident to significant
incident.   In the next scene, we meet a delightful old phrase which
the revisers have left unchanged; "and *her hap was* to light on a
part of the field belonging to Boaz — it perfectly expresses the
Hebrew, too.   In the meeting with Boaz, from the modern point
of view, the conversation is stilted, but the human touch of the
narrator is not lacking in his quiet enumeration of the courtesies
of Boaz to the maiden, as he reached her the parched corn at the
meal-time and afterward directed his young men to let fall also
some of the handfuls of purpose for her.

The scene of Boaz at the gate of the little city is a vigorous one.
Here it is a case of sharp, decisive business dealings, and all is in
contrast to the earlier incidents in which the women have been
prominent.

The story is an idyl, picturing a different world from that of
the realistic, primitive narratives of the age of the judges.   Society
has advanced far from those rude days before such a story as that
of Ruth could even be conceived.   The old power of simple, vivid,
rapid narration is not dead, though much labored prose has been
written in the centuries since the early days of Israel's literature.

1] 15-17.

Our next tale was regularly copied by the ancient Jews on the scroll with the eleven short books of prophecy; but it is not a collection of visions, oracles, sermons, like the others; it is instead a story about a prophet.

There was one Jonah, son of Amittai, who lived before Amos and predicted the success of Jeroboam II.[1] There may have been a tradition that this prophet went on some sort of a foreign mission; it was certainly the custom of Israel's prophets to pronounce doom on foreign nations, though they usually did their threatening in their own land and for the warning or encouragement of their own people. As the story proceeds in the book of Jonah, the prophet was told to go and announce doom in the great capital of mighty and terrible Assyria, and he fled in another direction, to the most remote region he could think, where the God of Israel could not reach him. According to Jonah's later defence of himself, it was not because he feared to deliver the message, but because he knew God to be so compassionate that the doom would not be executed.

Throughout the book, the heathen appear to excellent advantage; the sailors, though in dire distress, labor manfully before they consent to put overboard the self-confessed cause of their danger, and it is with an earnest prayer to Jonah's God that they finally cast him out. At the preaching of Jonah, who at last goes perforce on his mission, all Nineveh speedily repents with fasting and works meet for repentance. Jonah behaves about as badly as possible from beginning to end of the story; to his primary disobedience, he adds absolutely heartless indignation because his prophecy is not carried out against the now repentant city. The object that he desired was the destruction of Nineveh, or, at any rate, the vindication of himself as a reliable predictor. To serve a compassionate God was most distasteful to him. Not only is the God of this book compassionate upon those who repent, he is patient with his pettish child and tries to teach him a lesson of mercy by the gourd, a lesson that shall help him to understand why God pities Nineveh.

Such are the contrasting character elements of the story. Is not the meaning of the whole clear, if we give it a moment's

[1] 2 Kings 14 25.

intelligent thought? The God of Israel cares for the gentiles; he does not take pleasure in the death of the wicked;[1] he would have all men everywhere to repent and be saved — but this last is New Testament thought and language! The simple fact is that this little book, which has been so cruelly despised and misunderstood, is one of the mountain peaks in Old Testament literature, gilded with the dawn of a new day; from its summit we catch a glimpse of the God in whom Jesus Christ believed and whom he revealed to men. Its outlook far surpasses that of Hosea, who so beautifully taught God's unquenchable love for Israel, his own wife, his own child. This narrative pictures forgiving, saving pity upon a city that Nahum well represented as a lion's den where the lion did tear in pieces enough for his whelps and strangled for his lionesses, and filled his caves with prey and his dens with ravin. One prophet saw only this in Nineveh, and his figurative words do not exaggerate what the Assyrian kings calmly tell of themselves in words and stone-carved pictures. The author of the book of Jonah saw in Nineveh a great city wherein were more than six score thousand persons who could not discern between their right hand and their left hand, on whom God had pity.

Is the book history? is it an ancient tradition developed into a story, largely imaginative? is it a parable or allegory? All three views have been maintained; one may hold either view that is found convincing, but if one loses sight of the conception of God that this book contains, he will never know to what sublime height the Old Testament thought rose. This is a culminating point in the central theme of Israel's ancient literature, the nature of God. In this book, we see the life of Israel rising triumphant in its hardest battle, its battle with self. National pride and exclusiveness are here humbled in the dust, and God is exalted to the loftiest height that man can conceive.

In its thought of God, the book of Jonah rises toward the level of the parable of the prodigal son, and it is most reasonably interpreted as a parable, or more strictly an allegory. Jonah is Israel in the allegory; one prophet had called his people a blind servant and messenger.[2] The water monster is Babylon swallowing Israel; to picture Israel's enemies as a water monster was a

---

[1] Ezekiel 33 [11].   [2] Isaiah 42 [19].

favorite practice,[1] and already, long before this book was written, the Babylonian exile had been figuratively described as a swallowing up and belching forth.

Nebuchadrezzar the king of Babylon hath devoured me, he hath crushed me, he hath made me an empty vessel, he hath, like a monster, swallowed me up, he hath filled his maw with my delicacies; he hath cast me out.

And I will execute judgment upon Bel in Babylon, and I will bring forth out of his mouth that which he hath swallowed up; and the nations shall not flow any more unto him: yea, the wall of Babylon shall fall.[2]

If this interpretation be correct, if Jonah represents the narrow, cruel attitude of Israel toward the gentiles, then the thought of the book has a further significance. Like Ruth it is a protest, but not directed toward any one manifestation of harsh exclusiveness; it rather strikes at the very centre of the narrowness, the pride, the cruel heartlessness of the religions and national life of later Judaism.

While legalism had become dominant among the leaders of the nation and was stifling among the people the truths for which the great prophets had stood, there were at least two men, — we may well hope that there were others who shared their spirit, — but there were at least two men who with true insight and great literary gifts were telling their beautiful stories of love and character that rose above little, national boundaries, and of a God who was compassionate father over all.

We place these books in a period that used to be included in "four centuries of silence" and hear heralds of the light still calling when "the night of legalism" was darkening. These heralds, the writers of Ruth and Jonah, promise the coming age seen centuries later by the Apostle Paul, in which there shall be neither Greek nor Jew, . . . barbarian, Scythian, bond, nor free.[3]

In the books of Ruth and Jonah, we listen to the voices of those who rose spirit-free out of the tightening bonds of ecclesiasticism. In the book of Joel we read the words of one who was a student of the ancient prophets and sought to apply their thought to his own

---

[1] Isaiah 26 21, 27 1, 51 9, 10.   [2] Jeremiah 51 34, 44.
[3] Colossians 3 11.

day; he was one who lacked their free, creative spirit, however, and so could not rise above the narrow standards of his age.

A devastating plague of locusts, such as brings stark famine to Palestine from time to time, seemed to Joel the oft-threatened day of Jehovah,[1] coming as destruction from the Almighty, a day of darkness and gloominess, a day of clouds and thick darkness,[2] but Joel does not call upon the people to amend their conduct toward one another, as the earlier prophets had done; he would instead have them exhibit true penitence in temple prayer. When the immediate calamity passes, and the former and latter rains assure the wheat and wine, Joel recalls that Jehovah's day has been promised as a day of destruction upon Israel's enemies following calamities to herself, and his imagination paints apocalyptic vision in flaming colors.

> And it shall come to pass afterward,
> That I will pour out my spirit upon all flesh;
> And your sons and your daughters shall prophesy,
> Your old men shall dream dreams,
> Your young men shall see visions:
> And also upon the servants and upon the handmaids
> In those days will I pour out my Spirit.
> And I will show wonders in the heavens and in the earth:
> Blood, and fire, and pillars of smoke.
> The sun shall be turned into darkness and the moon into blood,
> Before the great and terrible day of Jehovah cometh.[3]

I will gather all nations and will bring them down into the valley of Jehoshaphat;
And I will execute judgment upon them there for my people and for my heritage Israel,
Whom they have scattered among the nations; and they have parted my land.[4]

> Multitudes, multitudes, in the valley of decision!
> For the day of Jehovah is near in the valley of decision.
> > The sun and the moon are darkened,
> > And the stars withdraw their shining.
> > And Jehovah will roar from Zion,
> > And utter his voice from Jerusalem;

[1] Joel 1 15.   [2] Ibid. 2 2.   [3] Ibid. 2 28-31.   [4] Ibid. 3 2.

And the heavens and the earth shall shake;
But Jehovah will be a refuge unto his people,
And a stronghold to the children of Israel.
So shall ye know that I am Jehovah your God,
Dwelling in Zion my holy mountain;
Then shall Jerusalem be holy,
And there shall no strangers pass through her any more.[1]

The psalmody of ancient Israel is not an exception to the rule that "sadness prevails in the lyric and the lyrical temperament";[2] the wretched seventy-five years preceding the rebuilding of the walls called forth more songs than the following century of comparative peace and prosperity. In the midst of the grim and sombre writings characterizing the literature of Israel from the eighth century onward, it is a relief to come upon some songs of thanksgiving and joy that express the spirit of those who rejoiced in the new order. Psalm 30, if it refers to national restoration and not merely that of an individual, may well voice the feeling of this era.

I will extol thee, O Jehovah; for thou hast raised me up,
And hast not made my foes to rejoice over me.
O Jehovah, thou hast brought up my soul from Sheol;
Thou hast kept me alive, that I should not go down to the pit.
Sing praise unto Jehovah, O ye saints of his,
And give thanks to his holy memorial name.
Thou, Jehovah, of thy favor hadst made my mountain to stand strong:
Thou didst hide thy face; I was troubled.
I cried to thee, O Jehovah;
And unto Jehovah I made supplication:
What profit is there in my blood, when I go down to the pit?
Shall the dust praise thee? shall it declare thy truth?
Hear, O Jehovah, and have mercy upon me:
Jehovah, be thou my helper.
Thou hast turned for me my mourning into dancing;
Thou hast loosed my sackcloth, and girded me with gladness;
To the end that my glory may sing praise to thee, and not be silent.
O Jehovah my God, I will give thanks unto thee for ever.[3]

---

[1] Joel 3 [13-17].

[2] Woodberry, *The Appreciation of Literature*, p. 46.

[3] For omission of verses 2, 5, 6, see Briggs, *Psalms, in loc.*

The beautiful evening hymn (Psalm 8) shows familiarity with both the first and second chapters of Genesis and evidently comes from a time after the completion of the Hexateuch.

O Jehovah, our Lord,
How excellent is thy name in all the earth,
Who hast set thy glory upon the heavens!
Out of the mouth of babes and sucklings hast thou established strength,
Because of thine adversaries,
That thou mightest still the enemy and the avenger.
When I consider thy heavens, the work of thy fingers,
The moon and the stars, which thou hast ordained;
What is man, that thou art mindful of him?
And the son of man, that thou visitest him?
For thou hast made him but little lower than God,
And crownest him with glory and honor.
Thou makest him to have dominion over the works of thy hands;
Thou hast put all things under his feet:
All sheep and oxen,
Yea, and the beasts of the field,
The birds of the heavens, and the fish of the sea,
Whatsoever passeth through the paths of the seas.
O Jehovah, our Lord,
How excellent is thy name in all the earth!

Psalm 29, the song of the thunder storm, affords a fine example of the noble conception of nature as instinct with God, noted in a previous chapter. This offers an attractive modification of the ancient picture of Jehovah's approach from Sinai in the thunder clouds. The storm passes over the Judean hills from north to south. "His voice is heard in the pealing of the thunder above the storm clouds; the storm bursts, it shatters the cedars and shakes the mountains in the far north; the lightnings flash; the deserts to the far south with their affrighted denizens tremble; and over all resounds the chorus, Glory." "The seven times repeated *voice of the Lord* is like successive peals of thunder";[1] the Hebrew is *qol Yahweh*.

Ascribe unto Jehovah, O ye sons of the mighty,
Ascribe unto Jehovah glory and strength.

[1] Kirkpatrick, *The Book of Psalms*, p. 149.

Ascribe unto Jehovah the glory due unto his name;
Worship Jehovah in holy array.

The voice of Jehovah is upon the waters:
The God of glory thundereth,
Even Jehovah upon many waters.
The voice of Jehovah is powerful;
The voice of Jehovah is full of majesty.
The voice of Jehovah breaketh the cedars:
Yea, Jehovah breaketh in pieces the cedars of Lebanon.
He maketh them also to skip like a calf;
Lebanon and Sirion like a young wild-ox.
The voice of Jehovah cleaveth the flames of fire.
The voice of Jehovah shaketh the wilderness;
Jehovah shaketh the wilderness of Kadesh.
The voice of Jehovah maketh the hinds to calve,
And strippeth the forests bare:
And in his temple everything saith, Glory.

Jehovah sat as King at the Flood;
Yea, Jehovah sitteth as King for ever.
Jehovah will give strength unto his people;
Jehovah will bless his people with peace.

The happy era introduced by Nehemiah, in 444, was ended a century later, when Artaxerxes Ochus cruelly devastated Jerusalem. The experiences of the last dozen years of the Persian age are reflected in such a prayer as that of Psalm 102 $^{1-11}$, in which the poet still trusts God, though he has taken up and then cast away.

Hear my prayer, O Jehovah,
And let my cry come unto thee.
Hide not thy face from me in the day of my distress:
Incline thine ear unto me;
In the day when I call answer me speedily.
For my days consume away like smoke,
And my bones are burned as a firebrand.
My heart is smitten like grass, and withered;
For I forget to eat my bread.
By reason of the voice of my groaning
My bones cleave to my flesh.
I am like a pelican of the wilderness;

I am become as an owl of the waste places.
I watch, and am become like a sparrow
That is alone upon the housetop.
Mine enemies reproach me all the day;
They that are mad against me do curse by me.
For I have eaten ashes like bread,
And mingled my drink with weeping,
Because of thine indignation and thy wrath:
For thou hast taken me up, and cast me away.
My days are like a shadow that declineth;
And I am withered like grass.

Before the close of the Persian rule the little hymnal, Psalms 3–41, was probably compiled. This is a Yahwistic collection in which the proper name of Israel's God occurs nearly twenty times as often as the general name God (Elohim). Psalms 14 and 40 [13-17] occur, in practically duplicate form, in the second book of the Psalter, where they have undergone an editing characteristic of that book, which has generally substituted God for Jehovah.

All the psalms in the collection 3 to 41 are ascribed by their headings to David, except 10 and 33; of these 10 is properly a part of 9. Back of this book lay an earlier and larger collection of hymns which went by the name of *David* and which was later drawn upon largely in the composition of the second book of the Psalter. The Davidic prayer-book,[1] containing many hymns of the Persian age, must itself have been compiled not long before the collection 3 to 41.[2]

[1] See Psalm 72 [20].

[2] Whether the word "to," translated "of" in our English versions, was intended by the original editor who attached the headings of the Psalms ascribed *to* David to indicate authorship, or only the name of the well-known collection from which these hymns were taken, it is impossible to determine.

CHAPTER XXIII

THE GREAT MASTERPIECE, JOB

(Latter Part of Fourth Century B.C.)

THE book of Job is one of that group of five or six world poems that stand as universal expressions of the human spirit. The *Iliad*, the *Niebelungenlied*, the *Divina Comedia*, belong to no age or nation, yet each is a distinctive product of its own time and of the race that gave it birth; in any other age, or among any other peoples, neither could have arisen. Similarly, Job is a characteristic product of post-exilic Israel. Without the work of the earlier prophets, the Deuteronomic era, the soul agonies of Jeremiah, the downfall of the nation and its interpretation by the writers of the exile, the book of Job could not have been written.

Many students of Hebrew literature count this poem the immediate outgrowth of the exile; its relation to the whole development of Israel's literature suggests rather its composition in the latter part of the fourth century B.C., shortly before the end of the Persian rule, or soon after Alexander's conquest. The prologue and epilogue (1–2, 42 $^{7-17}$) may have formed an earlier prose story of Job, and some portions of the poem are best interpreted as later accretions.

The prologue moves rapidly, giving a series of distinct pictures: the ancient sheik, perfect, upright, and prosperous; the heavenly council; the first series of catastrophes. In the description of the last, one feels a formal, artificial structure somewhat like that of the late, priestly prose. The hero, his name, his home, his character, his misfortunes, are all introduced in the one chapter. The brief second chapter pictures: a second heavenly council; a new catastrophe; Job after the new misfortune has fallen upon him; the arrival of the three friends and their seven days' watch with Job.

This prologue offers a curious interpretation of human suffering. It presents a man perfect, upright, scrupulous in his piety; when his sons have had their birthday feasts, he rises early and performs sacrifices for them all, lest they have sinned in some way. Jehovah himself declares that there is none like him in all the earth, perfect, upright, fearing God, and turning away from evil. Upon this one comes loss of property, loss of family, and loathsome disease. The old stories of Israel had taught that it was sin which brought suffering upon humanity ; the prophets had developed the doctrine of a righteous God who rewarded virtue and punished sin in the nation and the individual; already the sages had formulated this idea into many a proverb. Here is a new conception ! Among the superhuman beings, the sons of God, who from time to time present themselves before Jehovah, is one called the Satan, "the Adversary." [1]   The same word occurs in 1 Samuel 29 [4] — The princes of the Philistines are afraid that David will be an adversary (satan). The word is first met as applied to a superhuman being in Zechariah 3 [1], where the high priest is clothed in the sins of the people with the Satan standing at his right hand to act as his adversary.[2]   In Zechariah there is no further explanation of the Satan's functions ; in Job it appears that this son of God goes to and fro in the earth as an adversary to man. He cannot believe that any man is really good, really loves goodness for its own sake ; "Does Job fear God for nought ?" is his sarcastic question, and when Job stands the first test, the satanic mind is not satisfied. The Satan, new as he is in the Biblical literature, is not the newest and strangest conception in this story ; a God who, to satisfy this evil-minded son of his, permits misery to come to a perfect and upright man, is the most astonishing element in the story. Is this the God of justice of whom Amos and Ezekiel spoke, or the God of love that Hosea and Jeremiah came to know ?

Job and the friends, it is to be remembered, knew nothing of any such reasons for the misfortunes ; the writer uses a kind of dramatic irony, putting the readers into possession of facts unknown to the actors in the tragedy that is to follow. Job, knowing of no reason for his misfortunes, accepts them with complete resignation — The Lord gave and the Lord hath taken away ; blessed be

---

[1] This is translated as a proper name in the English Bible, but in the Hebrew it has the definite article.

[2] To *be* or *act as adversary* is a denominative verb formed from *satan.*

the name of the Lord, is his word of submission.   When his wife
bids him to curse God and die, he answers, What? shall we
receive good at the hand of God, and shall we not receive evil?

The friends come from distant regions; they do not know Job,
so changed is he; in true oriental fashion, they lift up their voices
and weep and rend every one his mantle and sprinkle dust upon
their heads.   Then they sit in silence seven days and nights,
seeing Job's great grief. So the prologue, the prose narrative,
closes.

The poem begins with Job's curse or lament.   In a lyric of great
pathos Job asks, Why was I ever born?   Why died I not at birth?
Why can I not die now?   There is a strikingly similar passage in
the *Œdipus Coloneus.*

> Happiest beyond compare
> Never to taste of life;
> Happiest in order next,
> Being born, with quickest speed
> Thither again to turn
> From whence we came.

It is difficult to account for the change in Job from complete
resignation to bitter outcry, if the poem and prose prologue were
originally one and do not represent two different stories awkwardly
joined.   It would seem, however, that there must have been something before the poem to make it intelligible at all, and either one
of two explanations is suggested to account for the change : Job's
fortitude has given way under the stress and progress of his
disease; this is commonly held to have been elephantiasis, a form
of leprosy, horrible in its physical effects and, if possible, even
more terrible in its mental aspects; or Job is maddened by the
silent, accusing presence of his friends.   It becomes clear to the
reader, as the poem advances, that the friends interpret Job's
sufferings as the sure evidence of his sins; possibly he realized this
in the seven days and nights of silence and so was driven to desperate outcry.

To Eliphaz there is no excuse for Job's words; such giving way
to grief is quite unworthy of one who has been a counsellor and
upholder of others.   Job ought to be confessing his sin, instead of
complaining in this fashion.   In the sight of God, before whom no

man can be just, Job is no doubt a great sinner; trouble does not come without a cause, though it is true that man is born to trouble as naturally as the sparks fly upward. If I were in your place, Eliphaz says to Job, I would seek unto God and commit my cause unto him; then he goes off into ascription of lofty praise to God, promising great blessings to Job if he accepts correction and does not despise the chastening of the Almighty.

On the strength of 4^{12ff}, Eliphaz has sometimes been called a mystic.

> Now a thing was secretly brought to me,
> And mine ear received a whisper thereof.
> In thoughts from the visions of the night,
> When deep sleep falleth on men,
> Fear came upon me, and trembling,
> Which made all my bones to shake.
> Then a spirit passed before my face;
> The hair of my flesh stood up.
> It stood still, but I could not discern the appearance thereof;
> A form was before mine eyes:
> There was silence, and I heard a voice, saying,
> Shall mortal man be more just than God?
> Shall a man be more pure than his Maker?

Job's answer seems at first to have little reference to the words of Eliphaz, except as he admits that his words have been rash[1] because of his great calamity. He longs for death and has no hope for the future, his strength cannot last; he is ready to faint, and pity ought to be showed him.[2] The figure with which he describes his experience with his friends is an effective one in that land of streams which are dry in summer's heat.

> My brethren have dealt deceitfully as a brook,
> As the channel of brooks that pass away;
> Which are black by reason of the ice,
> And wherein the snow hideth itself:
> What time they wax warm, they vanish;
> When it is hot, they are consumed out of their place.[3]

Chapter 7 describes the horror of Job's sickness and, near the close, turns to bitter words toward the watcher of men.

[1] 6^3.   [2] 6^{14}.   [3] 6^{15-17}.

If I have sinned, what do I unto thee, O thou watcher of men?
Why hast thou set me as a mark for thee,
So that I am a burden to myself?
And why dost thou not pardon my transgression, and take away mine
    iniquity?
For now shall I lie down in the dust;
And thou wilt seek me diligently, but I shall not be.[1]

Bildad speaks much more bluntly than Eliphaz has done. He
is shocked at Job's impiety: Doth God pervert judgment? he
indignantly asks and then he makes a maddening suggestion.

If thy children have sinned against him,
And he hath delivered them into the hand of their transgression;

At the close he holds out hope to Job, though it may be in sarcasm.
On the ground especially of 8 [8ff], Bildad has been styled a tradi-
tionalist, in contrast to Eliphaz.

For inquire, I pray thee, of the former age,
And apply thyself to that which their fathers have searched out
(For we are but of yesterday, and know nothing,
Because our days upon earth are a shadow);
Shall not they teach thee, and tell thee,
And utter words out of their heart?

Job now feels the full injustice of his fate; his sufferings prove
him guilty of sin. If it is true that God blesses the righteous
and gives suffering to the wicked, then the man who has great
misfortune must be peculiarly wicked; this was suggested in the
words of Eliphaz and is made very clear by Bildad. — If thou
wert pure and upright; surely now he would awake for thee, and
make the habitation of thy righteousness prosperous; this is the
irrefutable wisdom of the generations. While Job sees the power
of God and describes it better than the friends can, it is that very
power which is proving him guilty; therefore Job concludes that
God destroys the perfect and the wicked. Since wickedness rules
in the world, it must be that God is responsible for it.

The earth is given into the hand of the wicked;
He covereth the faces of the judges thereof:
If it be not he, who then is it? [2]

[1] 6 [20-21].   [2] 9 [24].

At length, Job returns to the thought of the opening lament and then pleads for a little respite before he goes to the land of midnight darkness.

> Are not my days few? cease then,
> And let me alone, that I may take comfort a little,
> Before I go whence I shall not return,
> Even to the land of darkness and of the shadow of death;
> The land dark as midnight,
> The land of the shadow of death, without any order,
> And where the light is as midnight.[1]

Job's plea to God for mercy is pathetic indeed, but the third friend, Zophar, feels nothing of the pathos; he is hot on a theological controversy.

> Should not the multitude of words be answered?
> And should a man full of talk be justified?
> Should thy boastings make men hold their peace?
> And when thou mockest, shall no man make thee ashamed?
> For thou sayest, My doctrine is pure,
> And I am clean in thine eyes.[2]

He wishes that God would speak and show Job the secrets of wisdom, and he makes the direct charge that God is exacting of Job less than his iniquity deserves. How more could be exacted it is difficult to see; Job would welcome death. At the end, Zophar also holds out hope, if Job will reform.

The point of view of the friends is now clear. They have inherited the noble truths worked out by Israel's great prophets; they believe in a God of justice and mercy, and they are most ardent defenders of this belief. A vast mass of experience, in all ages, confirms the truth of the prophetic doctrine that sin brings suffering to the sinner, but Job has had an experience which has opened his eyes to the fact that justice does not prevail on the earth; it does not in his case, and, as he looks about, he sees that it does not in other cases.

In the reply that closes this cycle of the debate, Job is decidedly sarcastic at the beginning.

[1] 10 20-22.   [2] 11 2-4.

No doubt but ye are the people,
And wisdom shall die with you.
But I have understanding as well as you;
I am not inferior to you:
Yea, who knoweth not such things as these?[1]

The friends had *inherited* noble truths, and Job recognizes that they know nothing but traditional truth, with which he is quite as familiar as they. To repeat such dogma to one in his condition is but a mockery.

In the thought of him that is at ease there is contempt for misfortune;
It is ready for them whose foot slippeth.

Euripides, in his *Alcestis*, expressed similar truth.

'Tis easier to advise, than suffering to endure.

Then Job gives a flash-light picture of life as it really is, not as theory paints it.

The tents of robbers prosper,
And they that provoke God are secure;
Into whose hand God bringeth.[2]

You say wisdom is with the ancients, he cries; No, wisdom is with God, and *power*, too. Then he gives a splendid, terrible description of the power and wisdom of God manifest with injustice.

With aged men is wisdom,
And in length of days understanding.

With God is wisdom and might;
He hath counsel and understanding.
Behold, he breaketh down, and it cannot be built again;
He shutteth up a man, and there can be no opening.
Behold, he withholdeth the waters, and they dry up;
Again, he sendeth them out, and they overturn the earth.
With him is strength and wisdom;
The deceived and the deceiver are his.
He leadeth counsellors away stripped,
And judges maketh he fools.
He looseth the bond of kings,
And bindeth their loins with a girdle.

[1] 12 2–3.   [2] 12 6.

He leadeth priests away stripped,
And overthroweth the mighty.
He removeth the speech of the trusty,
And taketh away the understanding of the elders.
He poureth contempt upon princes,
And looseth the belt of the strong.
He uncovereth deep things out of darkness,
And bringeth out to light the shadow of death.
He increaseth the nations, and he destroyeth them:
He enlargeth the nations, and he leadeth them captive.
He taketh away understanding from the chiefs of the people of the earth,
And causeth them to wander in a wilderness where there is no way.
They grope in the dark without light;
And he maketh them to stagger like a drunken man.[1]

Job was face to face with the problem that has become so insistent in these latter days; power and wisdom we find in the wonderful evolution of which men talk so glibly, but where's the justice in the law of tooth and claw? Is not the survival of the fittest the right of mere might? Job is a very modern book; it brings time-honored theory to the test in the laboratory of life. He knows the theory just as well as his confident friends, and he knows that the facts do not harmonize with the theory. Job was at heart a scientist, and when the scientific test of loyalty to simple fact is applied, time-honored theories often come crashing down.

The thirteenth chapter opens: —

> Lo, mine eye hath seen all this,
> Mine ear hath heard and understood it.
> What ye know, the same do I know also:
> I am not inferior unto you.

> Surely I would speak to the Almighty,
> And I desire to reason with God.[2]

There we begin to get at the heart of Job; he must come face to face with God. To him, these men who repeat pious platitudes are forgers of lies, thinking to defend and please God with that which is contrary to fact.

[1] 12 12-25.   [2] 13 1-3.

> Hear now my reasoning,
> And hearken to the pleadings of my lips.
> Will ye speak unrighteously for God,
> And talk deceitfully for him?
> Will ye show partiality to him?
> Will ye contend for God?
> Is it good that he should search you out?
> Or as one deceiveth a man, will ye deceive him?[1]

He will start out on bold adventure, abandoning orthodox falsehood, and, taking his life in his hand, will face God and present his case before him.

> Wherefore should I take my flesh in my teeth,
> And put my life in my hand?
> Behold, he will slay me; I have no hope:
> Nevertheless I will maintain my ways before him.[2]

Then the human strength of the sick man fails; if only God would remove his hand from him, he could argue his case, man's life is so brief and at its end, oblivion! O that thou wouldst hide me in the grave till thy wrath is passed and then give me a hearing, is his prayer.

This line of thought brings Job to the great mystery of the ages — If a man die, shall he live again? If Job could believe in a life beyond the grave, he could wait all the days of his appointed time, but he cannot believe it — The water washes away the stones, and thou destroyest the hope of man. Not life, but oblivion is man's fate. Job sinks back in despair, and the first cycle of the debate is ended.

The discussion proceeds through two more cycles, in which the friends are able to add little to the strength of their position, though their accusations become more direct; Eliphaz charges that Job's own mouth condemns him and later accuses the sufferer of a long category of sins, such as one in his former position might have committed. Job's professed inability to find God is cleverly, though superficially, perverted into ground for accusing him of sinning, in the confidence that God could not see him. The blunt and brutal Bildad quite loses his temper because of Job's lack of

[1] 13 6-9.   [2] 13 14-15.

respect for him and his friends; it must be confessed that Job
gives some occasion in his scorn for the miserable comforters who
have nothing new to offer in his perplexity.

In the third cycle Bildad interjects a few words only and Zophar's name does not appear. This has often been interpreted as
an intentional indication that the friends have been silenced. It is
probable, however, that a part of chapter 27 was originally assigned
to Zophar, since the point of view is that of the friends; in the
mouth of Job, the words could only be sarcastic. It is possible
also that Bildad's speech was originally longer.[1] Without the
rather inartistically obvious method of indicating the silencing of
the friends by assigning a few words only to Bildad and omitting
Zophar, it is evident that they have no more to say.

In the second cycle, it appears that all Job really asks of his
friends is some comprehending sympathy, while he fights his lonesome battle of the soul. It is God with whom the hero of the poem
is really concerned; the fact that God is his enemy without cause,
rends Job's heart. Early in the second cycle, Job rises to the
assurance that in heaven his case is clear; apparently this high
faith lasts a moment only, and his thoughts turn to the grave as
his only hope. A little later, he returns to the conviction that he
must have a vindicator[2] in heaven and that ultimately he will see
God. This much is clear, though the close of verse 26 is ambigu-
ous; it may possibly mean, as the King James version has it, in
my flesh I shall see God, or it may mean, as in the Revised versions,
without my flesh. The latter is the preferable rendering, although
it expresses a hope for the future life of the spirit quite foreign to
Job's usual thought. Once more, in the third cycle, Job cries,

> O that I knew where I might find him!
> That I might come even to his seat!

and goes on to express his firm faith that then he would get a fair
hearing. Though he cannot find God,[3] Job is confident that the
hidden one knows the way he takes, and that, when he has been
tried, he shall come forth as gold.

---

[1] Barton tentatively reconstructs Bildad's third speech: 25 1-6, 24 17,
18, 5-8, 30 3-8, 24 21, 22, 19, 20, 24. *Job, The Bible for Home and School.*

[2] 19 25. *Vindicator* (See R. V. margin) represents the idea of *goel*
better than *redeemer.*   [3] 23 3-7.

The debate closes with the friends silenced, though not convinced; perhaps Job himself would never have come to see the error in the current theology without the bitter experience that forced him to a new point of view.

Following the section that may have been Zophar's missing speech (27 [7-11, 13-23]), there comes a remarkable poem upon the unsearchableness of wisdom.[1] This is not assigned to any one of the speakers and probably was inserted by some one who felt that it added a thought to the subject under discussion; it is no real help to the working out of the plan of the book, but in itself is a precious memorial of one type of Israel's poetry. In the next three chapters, Job speaks at length, contrasting his former honor with his present dishonored condition, telling how he had been accustomed to give sympathy to the wretched, and defending himself against the charges of sin. Suddenly he thinks, What is the use of this long defence? The Almighty does not hear me, and I am defending myself without knowledge as to the nature of the indictment.

The doctrine of rewards and penalties, which counted misfortune as the sure mark of guilt, introduced a deep note of tragedy into the life of many an earnest soul in ancient Israel, a tragedy that we can only imperfectly realize. It finds expression in the psalmist's prayer,

> Who can understand his errors;
> Cleanse thou me from secret faults.

The Babylonian penitential psalms reflect the same anxiety concerning sin, the nature of which is unknown to the guilty one.

Following Job's conclusion of the debate [2] come the speeches of Elihu, prefaced by a prose statement. Elihu has kept silent while those older than he spoke, but now he bursts forth in indignation against Job and the friends who have not been able to answer; he describes himself as full of words, and so he proves to be. Despite his swelling promises, he adds little to the points the three have made. The entire section, 32 to 36, is best interpreted as an interpolation rather than the work of the master who composed the main part of the book.

[1] Chapter 28.   [2] 31 [40].

Dropping out the Elihu section, immediately after Job finishes speaking Jehovah answers him out of the stormwind. It is the old, poetic conception of the God of Israel appearing in the storm cloud; he comes to speak of his wisdom and power as seen in the creation of the world and in the order and control of the mighty forces of nature. The poetry is fine, though the thought is that common to the Hebrew prophets and poets, at least of the post-exilic period.

> Where wast thou when I laid the foundations of the earth?
> Declare, if thou hast understanding.
> Who determined the measures thereof, if thou knowest?
> Or who stretched the line upon it?
> Whereupon were the foundations thereof fastened?
> Or who laid the corner-stone thereof,
> When the morning stars sang together,
> And all the sons of God shouted for joy?
>
> Or who shut up the sea with doors,
> When it brake forth, as if it had issued out of the womb;
> When I made clouds the garment thereof,
> And thick darkness a swaddling-band for it,
> And marked out for it my bound,
> And set bars and doors,
> And said, Hitherto shalt thou come, but no further;
> And here shall thy proud waves be stayed?[1]

When Jehovah is made to speak, later,[2] of his unsearchable wisdom and power as seen in animal life, it is to us less sublime and, at times, almost ludicrous, unless we recall that superficial observations upon the habits of the wild creatures seemed recondite wisdom among the ancients.

At length Job is called upon to answer this display of the divine wisdom, and he replies: —

> Behold, I am of small account; what shall I answer thee?
> I lay my hand upon my mouth.
> Once have I spoken, and I will not answer;
> Yea, twice, but I will proceed no further.[3]

[1] 38 4-11.   [2] 39.   [3] 40 4-5.

Jehovah now goes on still more completely to humble Job with further descriptions of his power as as seen in the semi-mythical behemoth and leviathan.   From our point of view, this seems on a much lower level than the preceding words of Jehovah; perhaps it was a climax to those who lived in an age that believed in the creatures described.[1]

Job answers in words that give the real conclusion of his long struggle.

> Then Job answered Jehovah, and said,
> I know that thou canst do all things,
> And that no purpose of thine can be restrained.
> Who is this that hideth counsel without knowledge?
> Therefore have I uttered that which I understood not,
> Things too wonderful for me, which I knew not.
> Hear, I beseech thee, and I will speak;
> I will demand of thee, and declare thou unto me.
> I had heard of thee by the hearing of the ear;
> But now mine eyes seeth thee:
> Wherefore I abhor myself,
> And repent in dust and ashes.[2]

Viewed as a philosophical discussion of the problem of suffering, the closing chapters of the poem do not advance beyond the discredited argument of the friends, that God is too exalted to be understood or questioned; but the book of Job is not primarily a philosophical discussion; it is a poem in its essence, as well as in form.   It has often been called a dramatic poem, and it can be acted.[3] To be sure, the action is chiefly in the prologue; in the long debate, there is no change of scene or characters.   In the early Greek dramas little happened on the stage, what had happened elsewhere being recounted to the audience. The lack of actors and action on the stage itself was largely supplied by the chorus which, with its constant movement and song, filled and gratified the eye and ear.   The Greek drama grew out of a combination of the rhythmic movements of sacrificial ceremonies with

---

[1] Many regard 40 15 to 41 34 as a later addition.   For a concise argument see Barton, *Job*, pp. 31–32.   [2] 42 1-6.

[3] It was performed at Smith College, some twenty years ago — a performance that attracted wide attention.

lyric, narrative poetry, and dialogue. With all possible concessions made, we can hardly call Job a drama. It does not have
even the action of religious ceremony or dance of any kind, and
the dialogue is slow, though splendidly wrought out. In fact,
the Semites did not develop a drama in the European sense.
Job has more affinity with the drama than with any other form
of European poetry, but we have already noted that Semitic
literature has its own forms, and it is useless to try and bring these
rigidly under our Greek categories.

The book has again been denominated an epic, *The Epic of the
Inner Life*.[1] As Homer and Vergil wrote of wars and wanderings,
deeds of martial heroes who strove and struggled with great
strength or cunning to win success in ways that delighted the
Greeks and Romans, so the author of Job wrote of a typical Jewish
hero whose warfare was within the soul and whose wanderings
were on the restless seas of religious doubt and hope. In literary
form, the poem is less like an epic than a drama, yet the suggestion
of its epic quality has greatly helped to an understanding of the
true import of the book.

The friends have some individuality, at least Eliphaz and Bildad
have, yet their chief service is to present current doctrine effectively and to goad Job on in his long struggle toward a God in
whom his soul can rest. Viewing the book as the story of Job's
inner life, one finds more progress in the cycles of speeches than
when these are considered as a debate.

The God in whom Job has been taught to believe, no longer
exists for him; Job does not question the existence of one who
rules over the affairs of men, but he does deny that there is one
who rules with justice. He even holds God responsible for the
injustice done by human judges. When Job realizes that the
friends are trying to please God by lying for him, the author gives
us our first clear view of his hero's higher faith in God; he cannot
believe that God loves a lie, even when it is told in his defence.
That came out in the last speech of the first cycle; in the second
cycle, this faith in truth which is the inalienable right of every fearless lover of truth, led Job to his fleeting, returning faith that the
justice of his cause was recorded in heaven; it led him also to his

---

[1] See the volume of this title by Professor J. F. Genung.

momentary glimpses beyond the dark grave. At first there was only a question — If a man die shall he live again? If only Job could believe in that future chance, he could endure everything here. It is a wonderful, prophetic glimpse from a time when a clear faith in personal immortality had not yet come to man. After the Christian faith came clear, men learned to endure, as Job knew that he could, with joyous strength, through seeing the unseen. Again the hope returned to Job, and no longer as a mere question; it became, for the moment, a confident assurance that, though worms might destroy this body, he would come face to face with God.

Through the centuries since Job was written, philosophers and, especially, poets have struggled with the problem of Job. Browning is full of it, and so are the great dramatists from Æschylus to modern times. Partial solutions that go beyond the philosophy of Job have been offered; the full answer is not yet. The poet of the *Suffering Servant*, indeed, went far deeper than the author of Job into the mystery of suffering.

As an argument, Job is negative; it demolishes absolutely the theory that righteousness on the one hand and health, wealth, and honor on the other are always proportional. Perhaps that is all the intellectual achievement that ought to be demanded of any one writer, but that accomplishment is not what makes the book a great poem. Job, like all true literature, is an interpretation of life — "Life is deeper and wider than any particular lesson to be learned from it; and just when we think that we have at last guessed its best meanings, it laughs in our face with some paradox which turns our solution into a new riddle."[1] Job mirrors the struggles of brave, true men and women to-day, as well as in the fourth century before Christ. It proves itself peculiarly the college students' book among the writings of ancient Israel, for it tells the story of their inner life when they, like Job, are willing to venture all for faith in truth.

The last eight verses of the prose epilogue mark a sad reaction from the great poem. They give back to Job just double all his former wealth and family and bring life down to the vulgar, account-book standards that the poem spurned and shattered.

[1] H. A. Beers, *Split Zephyr.*

This must be a part of the older story of Job, which the poet allowed to remain, or else, an unfortunate accretion. As the book stands, the first part of the epilogue puts a noble seal of approval on the lesson of the poem. Jehovah condemns the friends who have not spoken the thing that was right as his servant Job has; they are to offer sacrifices and Job is to pray for them that they may escape the consequences of their folly. Without this sanction of Job's words, the poem itself indicates firm faith that God, though his ways are past finding out, will reveal himself to the one who seeks and in a measure that will satisfy and leave the soul at rest.

CHAPTER XXIV

WISDOM LITERATURE IN THE GREEK AGE

Ecclesiastes, Proverbs, and Ecclesiasticus

(*332 to 168 B.C.*)

IN the year 332 B.C., Alexander passed through Syria on his
way to Egypt, and Judea, in common with the other districts of
Palestine, came under the Macedonian rule. We have treated
the book of Job as written at about this time; further aspects of
Job's problem were subsequently discussed in Ecclesiastes and The
Wisdom of Solomon.[1] These books show that one group of
Jewish sages, during the three centuries before Christ, was reflect-
ing deeply upon "the great ethical and religious question of the
world — the question of the justice of the divine government."
Another class of reflective thinkers ignored such profound problems
and occupied itself with the questions of practical, everyday
life, producing books of gnomic wisdom, Proverbs and Ecclesiasticus.[2] After considering Ecclesiastes,[3] we shall turn to the work
of the latter group.

In spite of the intellectual bafflement in which the book of Job
ended, that work marked, we saw, a great advance upon the point
of view of the current philosophy. It was a real gain to the cause
of truth to recognize the fact that the rewards sought by men are
not always given in direct proportion to the wisdom and virtue of
the seeker. The question of Ecclesiastes is the natural sequel:
Are the rewards sought worth while, when obtained? — "What

---

[1] The latter work is a product of the Judaism of Alexandria and, as
such, shows constantly the influence of familiarity with Greek thought.
It was written after the period of history included in the present volume,
probably during the first century B.C.

[2] See C. H. Toy, *Proverbs, Int. Crit. Com.*, pp. xxvi f.

[3] The name is the Greek attempt to translate Koheleth, which signifies
a collector of sentences or a preacher.

z   **337**

profit hath a man of all his labor wherein he laboreth under the sun?" In terms of modern philosophy, wisdom here undertakes a search for values.

To test the question raised, the writer assumes the personality of him who was Israel's type of fullest attainment in wealth, power, and wisdom. He does not, however, carry out this impersonation very rigidly; he speaks often from the standpoint of one living under the hopeless oppression of an Oriental despotism, where there is "one corrupt ruler above another, making appeal for redress useless."

Life is empty; that is the "opening conclusion" or the thesis, and the ground for this view is suggested in verse 3, the great question already quoted, What profit hath a man of all his labor? — Are the rewards of life worth having? The question is not far from the modern query, Is life worth living? The verses that follow indicate the basis of the question; the life of nature and the life of man are just a meaningless round. The thought is a familiar one in various philosophies; it is characteristic of the hopeless world view of India, and the Stoics had their theory of the cycles of events.[1] In Koheleth the thought is not elaborated into that of a system of cycles; it is simply the weary round. Men labor and labor, but the crooked cannot be made straight and that which is wanting cannot be numbered.

In his assumed rôle as the wise king in Jerusalem, the preacher tries to satiety the various things that seem good; first, it was wisdom, practical insight into life, but this brought only sorrow. From this grave pursuit he turned to mirth and found it mockery; next came sensuous indulgence, wine, under restraint such as Epicurus taught, by which the physical capacity to enjoy might be conserved. Then he tried that form of creative activity to which wealth to-day so often turns for recreation, the laying out of great estates with their mansions, orchards, gardens, and pools. A horde of slaves cared for all this, and flocks and herds dotted the landscape; indoors trained musicians whiled away the hours.

---

[1] Whether Ecclesiastes is tinged by contact with Greek philosophical thought has been much debated. It certainly was not influenced to any great extent. Similarities with Stoicism may be accounted for in the reverse order, since Zeno was a Semite.

So long as the novelty lasted and there were new things to do, pleasure was found in it all;[1] but that was temporary. When Koheleth looked at the work done, all was emptiness and vexation of spirit. Wisdom is better than folly, yet all that one has accumulated must be left to another, and who knows but that one may be a fool!

Chapter 3 contains the familiar poem on a time for everything, followed by the observation that, as matters now are, this theory does not seem to be working just yet, and followed, too, by a definite rejection of the hope of a future life as a solution.

I said in my heart, It is because of the sons of men, that God may prove them, and that they may see that they themselves are but as beasts. For that which befalleth the sons of men befalleth beasts; even one thing befalleth them: as the one dieth, so dieth the other; yea, they have all one breath; and man hath no preëminence above the beasts: for all is vanity. All go unto one place; all are of the dust, and all turn to dust again. Who knoweth the spirit of man, whether it goeth upward, and the spirit of the beast, whether it goeth downward to the earth?[2]

Thus the search for a satisfying object of life's effort has proved vain. There is nothing better than that a man should rejoice in his works; for that is his portion; for who shall bring him back to see what shall be after him?[3]

The remainder of the book seems less orderly in its arrangement than the first three chapters. There are groups of brief maxims which exhibit little connection with their context.[4] In general these are much like the disconnected aphorisms gathered in the book of Proverbs. At one point, however, the view seems in harmony with Job rather than with the writers of Proverbs.

All this have I seen in my days of vanity: there is a righteous man that perisheth in his righteousness, and there is a wicked man that prolongeth his life in his evil-doing.[5]

[1] Ecclesiastes 1 10.

[2] Ecclesiastes 3 18-21. The writer recently heard a distinguished biologist speak of the "modern discovery that man is an animal." In the words of the observer of 2000 years ago, "There is no new thing under the sun."   [3] Ecclesiastes 3 22.

[4] Such are 5 1-9, 7, 10 2-11 10. Some of the verses in these sections are probably glosses, while others were included by the original writer. See G. A. Barton, *Ecclesiastes, Int. Crit. Com., in loc.*   [5] Ecclesiastes 7 15.

Following this there is an interesting warning against extremes, suggesting Aristotle's doctrine of the mean.

Be not righteous overmuch; neither make thyself overwise: why shouldest thou destroy thyself? Be not overmuch wicked, neither be thou foolish: why shouldest thou die before thy time? It is good that thou shouldest take hold of this; yea, also from that withdraw not thy hand.[1]

Glancing at the more connected portions, we read of the oppressions that are done under the sun,[2] of the cares and deceitfulness of riches,[3] and of the hopelessness of gratifying human desire.[4] It is natural that the thought of oblivion in death should recur to the writer in the midst of such meditations,[5] though his spirit rebounds from the despair of contemplating the common event to the possibility of activity and some attainable happiness. The picture of the poor man who by his wisdom saved his city gives promise of something more hopeful, until the cynical turn comes — yet no man remembered that same poor man.[6]

Near the close of the book comes the impressive poem,

> Remember now thy creator in the days of thy youth.[7]

Of this Professor Genung writes : —

"Better than anything else except the opening exclamation, the Book of Koheleth is known, to ordinary readers, by the elaborately colored chapter on the decline of the vital powers; it is the acknowledged high-water mark of poetic utterance. One is reminded of the Ninth Symphony of Beethoven, wherein, the utmost resources of orchestra proving inadequate to his mighty musical conception, he must needs supplement wood and strings and brass by a chorus of living human voices. It is no longer a Hebrew wisdom couplet that we hear, but a majestic tide of world poetry. And when we consider what and how it culminates, we cannot call this access of larger diction and rhythm adventitious. It is like the melting of struggling discords into a grave and solemn yet restful harmony."[8]

Professor Schmidt treats 11[7] to 12[7] as a connected "Song of Youth and Age." He translates the portion from chapter 11 : —

[1] Ecclesiastes 7[16-18a].   [2] *Ibid.* 4[1-3].   [3] *Ibid.* 5[10-17], 6[1ff.]
[4] *Ibid.* 6[7-12].   [5] *Ibid.* 9[1-6].   [6] *Ibid.* 9[13-15].
[7] *Ibid.* 12[1-7].   [8] J. F. Genung, *Words of Koheleth.*

Sweet is the light, good to the eyes
It is to see the shining sun.
Though many be the years he lives,
Man should in all of them rejoice.

Rejoice, O young man, in thy youth,
Let thy heart cheer thee in thy prime,
Walk in the way thy fancy leads,
Follow what pleases best thine eyes.

Remove all worry from thy mind,
And from thy body banish pain;
For youth is but a passing breath,
Life's dayspring only vanity.

He continues the translation of chapter 12 : —

The days of evil will draw nigh,
The years in which no pleasure is,
When the sun's light to darkness turns,
And after rain the clouds appear.[1]

A few concluding comments end this book, which has strangely
attracted and repelled different natures.   Many of its sentiments
greatly shocked some orthodox owner of an early copy who inter-
polated frequent stereotyped scraps of pious wisdom that seem
quite out of harmony with their context.[2]   Haupt sums up the
impressions of the book upon different natures : —

"The Book of Ecclesiastes is unparalleled in the whole range of Biblical
literature.   Ernest Renan spoke of it as the only charming book that
was ever written by a Jew.   Heinrich Heine called it the Canticles of
Skepticism, while Franz Delitzsch thought it was entitled to the name of
the Canticles of the Fear of God.   From the earliest times down to the
present age, Ecclesiastes has attracted the attention of thinkers.   It was
a favorite book of Frederick the Great, who referred to it as a Mirror of
Princes." [3]

[1] N. Schmidt, *The Messages of the Poets*, pp. 380–381.
[2] Indeed, there were probably at least two such early interpolators,
one of whom wrote from the point of view of orthodox "wisdom" and the
other from that of pious Pharisaic tendencies.   See McNeile, in *Hastings'*
(one volume) *Bible Dictionary* and Barton, in *Int. Crit. Com.*, p. 43 ff.
[3] *The Book of Ecclesiastes.*

Professor Genung finds in the repeated injunction to eat and drink and enjoy good in all one's labor a thought highly characteristic of the late nineteenth century, a thought very similar to that which finds repeated expression in Kipling's *Day's Work*.

"Doubtless the discovery, in which every wise soul will echo Koheleth, that when a man gets what he works for, however glorious or remunerative, it turns out inevitably to be no reward at all, does not satisfy, was what put him on the track of this inquiry, 'What profit?' From this he comes to see that there is really nothing outside of life itself that can possibly be offered as payment, as a cash equivalent for it. If this holds good at all — and no experience can gainsay it — it must hold good in any and every sphere. It is not in the nature of things to put up the allotted work, the developed aptitude, the supreme interest and power of one's life, in the market for pay. If life cannot be its own reward, there is nothing else to barter for it." [1]

Driver's interpretation represents more closely the thought of the writer of the third century B.C. "Life under all its aspects is dissatisfying and disappointing; the best that can be done with it is to enjoy — not indeed in excess, but in a wise and well-considered moderation, and as a gift intended by God to be enjoyed — such pleasures as it brings with it." [2]

The limitations of Koheleth and of his point of view need little emphasis. The hope of the great prophets for an age of justice, peace, and prosperity had not been realized. The interpretation of life given in the poem of the *Suffering Servant* meant nothing to this writer, if he had ever read the poem; of altruism he knew very little. With all his testing he had not tried joy in the service of others. With his view of life, what was the use of trying to make things better? Life was all a hopeless round, generation after generation. Koheleth deliberately rejected the thought of a personal immortality, which some in his day were accepting and which has made life full of hope in sorrow for multitudes; he

[1] Genung, *Words of Koheleth*.
"The closing words of the above quotation give an admirable statement of the conclusion that a twentieth century thinker may well reach when meditating upon 'the discovery in which every wise soul will echo Koheleth.'" (H. T. Fowler, *Studies in the Wisdom Literature*, p. 94.)

[2] Driver, *Introduction to the Literature of the Old Testament*.

never dreamed of an increasing purpose which through the ages runs and which makes life a glorious upward struggle for the race. The selfish, prudential aspect of ancient Hebrew wisdom reached its inevitable goal in Ecclesiastes.

In summing up the writing of the Hebrew monarchy (Chapter XVI) it was recognized that aphoristic wisdom appeared early in the history of Israel's thought and that by Jeremiah's time "the wise" had come to form a class, grouped with the priests and prophets;[1] it was recognized also that there may have been written collections of gnomic wisdom before the close of the monarchy. Proverbial literature necessarily lacks definite historical allusions, so that it is even more difficult to trace its history in detail than that of the Psalms.

Like Psalms, the book of Proverbs gives internal indication that it was a gradual growth. It is made up of five principal sections; chapters 1–9 consist of a series of discourses in praise of wisdom and serve as an introduction to the book, 30 to 31 form a series of appendixes, and the core of the book is composed of three principal collections of aphorisms — 10–22[16], 22[17]–24[34],[2] 25–29. That these are distinct collections is indicated both by their editorial headings[3] and by their internal structure.

The first group contains 375 separate aphorisms, all but one of which are distichs.[4] They deal with many subjects and show no orderly grouping. In the second section, there are few two-member proverbs; the thought usually runs through four, five, six, or more lines. In the third collection distichs are again numerous, though in no such overwhelming proportion as in the first group. That these sections are themselves compiled from smaller collections is clear upon closer examination.[5] Thus the

---

[1] Jeremiah 18[18].

[2] 24[23–34], which forms an appendix to 22[17]–24[22], might be counted as a fourth collection; it has its own heading, "These also are sayings of the wise."   [3] 10[1], 22[17ff], 25[1].

[4] It is probable that the one tristich (19[7]) contains one half of what was originally the 376th proverb.

[5] Chapters 10–15 once formed a separate book of antitheses, and 16–22[16], a book characterized by synonymous and synthetic parallelism. Even within these subordinate groups, identical or equivalent couplets suggest smaller original collections.

book of Proverbs shows its marks of growth as a slowly increasing treasury of national wisdom.   The earliest elements in the book may represent hoary antiquity, but each of the principal divisions contains indications of post-exilic elements, and probably no one of them was fully collected until the Persian or early Greek times; the book as a whole seems to have been completed by the years 250 to 200 B.C.

One of the latest portions of the book is the series of discourses in praise of wisdom.   Its opening paragraph gives the heading for the entire book and indicates the purpose of the type of wisdom-writing represented in Proverbs.

> To know wisdom and instruction;
> To discern the words of understanding;
> To receive instruction in wise dealing,
> In righteousness and justice and equity;
> To give prudence to the simple,
> To the young man knowledge and discretion:
> That the wise man may hear, and increase in learning;
> And that the man of understanding may attain unto sound counsels:
> To understand a proverb, and a figure,
> The words of the wise, and their dark sayings.[1]

The sages loved to put their erudition into brief and sometimes hidden form; the love of riddles we can trace back to the days of the judges in the Samson stories.   Among early peoples generally, wisdom tends to assume proverbial form; gnomic poetry was prevalent among the early Greeks as well as with the children of the East.   When the multiplication of books becomes easy and thought grows more complex and ramified, the gnome gives place to prolonged, connected discourse.   All this concerns the form of reflective writing; the introductory paragraph suggests also the purpose.   Prudence and righteousness are here intermingled and even identified.   Such indentification is easy when the belief prevails in material rewards for moral and religious virtue.   The prophets held this belief on the ground of faith in God's justice; the wise men pointed out its working in the natural course of the everyday relationships of life, and warned their hearers of the physical consequences of sin.   Their appeal to self-interest has

[1] Proverbs 1 2-6.

its legitimate place and is not necessarily incompatible with virtue that reaches far beyond mere prudent respectability.

> A wise son maketh a glad father;
> But a foolish son is the heaviness of his mother.
> Hatred stirreth up strifes;
> But love covereth all transgressions.
> Keep thy heart with all diligence;
> For out of it are the issues of life.[1]

Such maxims show a certain consideration for others and an appreciation of inner righteousness.   Of self-sacrifice, however, the range of thought in the book of Proverbs takes no more account than Koheleth.   The higher law of reward, the law of finding life through losing, belongs to a sphere of existence that Israel's sages did not enter.[2]

In the opening discourse we see incidentally where the wise men were wont to teach.

> Wisdom crieth aloud in the street;
> She uttereth her voice in the broad places;
> She crieth in the chief place of concourse;
> At the entrance of the gates,
> In the city, she uttereth her words:[3]

Later the indication is even more explicit.

> Doth not wisdom cry,
> And understanding put forth her voice?
> On the top of high places by the way,
> Where the paths meet, she standeth;
> Beside the gates, at the entry of the city,
> At the coming in at the doors, she crieth aloud:[4]

The sages of Israel found men where they were congregated in the open air, and there taught them, as the philosophers of Greece were also accustomed to do.

Like the great teachers of Greece and like the earlier prophet-teachers of their own race, Israel's sages were not without poetic

---

[1] Proverbs 10 [1, 12], 4 [23].

[2] The later Rabbi quoted in the Talmud and the Supreme Teacher emphasized its significance.

[3] Proverbs 1 [20-21].   [4] *Ibid.* 8 [1-3].

gifts. They could "make the ear an eye" with imaginative, realistic, word-picture.

> My son, if sinners entice thee,
> Consent thou not.
> If they say, Come with us,
> Let us lay wait for blood;
> Let us lurk privily for the innocent without cause;
> Let us swallow them up alive as Sheol,
> And whole, as those that go down into the pit;
> We shall find all precious substance;
> We shall fill our houses with spoil;
> Thou shalt cast thy lot among us;
> We will all have one purse: [1]

With vivid personification of wisdom and folly they made their appeal and warning attractive: Wisdom standing beside the gates at the entry of the city, crieth aloud.

> Unto you, O men, I call;
> And my voice is to the sons of men.
> Counsel is mine, and sound knowledge:
> I am understanding; I have might.
> By me kings reign,
> And princes decree justice.
> By me princes rule,
> And nobles, even all the judges of the earth.
> I love them that love me;
> And those that seek me diligently shall find me.
> Riches and honor are with me;
> Yea, durable wealth and righteousness.
> My fruit is better than gold, yea, than fine gold;
> And my revenue than choice silver.
> Jehovah possessed me in the beginning of his way,
> Before his works of old.
> I was set up from everlasting, from the beginning,
> Before the earth was.
> When there were no depths, I was brought forth,
> When there were no fountains abounding with water.
> Before the mountains were settled,
> Before the hills was I brought forth;

[1] Proverbs 1 [10-14].

While as yet he had not made the earth, nor the fields,
Nor the beginning of the dust of the world.
When he established the heavens, I was there:
When he set a circle upon the face of the deep,
When he made firm the skies above,
When the fountains of the deep became strong,
When he gave to the sea its bound,
That the waters should not transgress his commandment,
When he marked out the foundations of the earth;
Then I was by him, as a master workman;
And I was daily his delight,
Rejoicing always before him,
Rejoicing in his habitable earth;
And my delight was with the sons of men.[1]

In the second section of the book[2] each principal part begins: —

A wise son maketh a glad father;
But a foolish son is the heaviness of his mother.
Treasures of wickedness profit nothing;
But righteousness delivereth from death.
Jehovah will not suffer the soul of the righteous to famish;
But he thrusteth away the desire of the wicked.
He becometh poor that worketh with a slack hand;
But the hand of the diligent maketh rich.
He that gathereth in summer is a wise son;
But he that sleepeth in harvest is a son that causeth shame.
Blessings are upon the head of the righteous;
But violence covereth the mouth of the wicked.
The memory of the righteous is blessed;
But the name of the wicked shall rot.[3]

The plans of the heart belong to man;
But the answer of the tongue is from Jehovah.
All the ways of a man are clean in his own eyes;
But Jehovah weigheth the spirits.
Commit thy works unto Jehovah.
And thy purposes shall be established.
Jehovah hath made everything for its own end;
Yea, even the wicked for the day of evil.
Every one that is proud in heart is an abomination to Jehovah:

[1] Proverbs 8 4, 14–19, 22–31.   [2] *Ibid.* 10–22 16.   [3] *Ibid.* 10 1–7.

> Though hand join in hand, he shall not be unpunished.
> By mercy and truth iniquity is atoned for;
> And by the fear of Jehovah men depart from evil.
> When a man's ways please Jehovah,
> He maketh even his enemies to be at peace with him.[1]

The third collection of aphorisms[2] is a supplement to the first principal collection, and it is difficult to see why the "sayings of the wise"[3] were inserted between the two groups of proverbs which are ascribed to Solomon.[4] This collection of miscellaneous wisdom shows a highly conventionalized development in the form of the sages' teaching. First there is an effective hortatory introduction in which synonymous couplets are combined in synthetic relation — a form of parallelism which prevails throughout the section. The introduction reads: —

> Incline thine ear, and hear the words of the wise,
> And apply thy heart unto my knowledge.
> For it is a pleasant thing if thou keep them within thee,
> If they be established together upon thy lips.
> That thy trust may be in Jehovah,
> I have made them known to thee this day, even to thee.
> Have not I written unto thee excellent things
> Of counsels and knowledge,
> To make thee know the certainty of the words of truth,
> That thou mayest carry back words of truth to them that send thee?[5]

---

[1] Proverbs 16 [1-7].   [2] Chapters 25–29.   [3] *Ibid.* 22 [17-24].

[4] Solomon stood in much the same relation to Israel's philosophical literature that David did to the nation's psalmody. His contemporaries were deeply impressed by his wisdom; the one definite example preserved in early tradition, his judgment between the two mothers, shows a kind of shrewdness that would strongly appeal to simple-minded people. The story of the Queen of Sheba has it that Solomon was able to answer all her *riddles* (the same Hebrew word that is used in Proverbs 1 [6]), and a probably late tradition ascribes to him 3000 proverbs and 1005 songs, specifying that he spoke of plants and animals. Ancient proverb makers frequently used the habits of plants and animals to illustrate their teachings, but this practice is not characteristic of the sayings ascribed to Solomon in Proverbs. In the book of Proverbs, it is impossible to select any specific word as Solomon's, though some of his sayings may well be included.   [5] Proverbs 22 [17-21].

The sayings themselves begin : —

> Rob not the poor, because he is poor;
> Neither oppress the afflicted in the gate:
> For Jehovah will plead their cause,
> And despoil of life those that despoil them.

> Make no friendship with a man that is given to anger;
> And with a wrathful man thou shalt not go :
> Lest thou learn his ways,
> And get a snare to thy soul.

> Be thou not one of them that strike hands,
> Or of them that are sureties for debts.
> If thou hast not wherewith to pay,
> Why should he take away thy bed from under thee? [1]

Here and in the following collection there have been preserved some quaint poems on manners and morals. Especially delightful is : —

THE FIELD OF THE SLUGGARD

> I went by the field of the sluggard,
> And by the vineyard of the man void of understanding;
> And, lo, it was all grown over with thorns,
> The face thereof was covered with nettles,
> And the stone wall thereof was broken down.
> Then I beheld, and considered well;
> I saw, and received instruction :
> Yet a little sleep, a little slumber,
> A little folding of the hands to sleep;
> So shall thy poverty come as a robber,
> And thy want as an armed man. [2]

The same general theme occurs in the companion poems of chapter 6 and 27.

> Go to the ant, thou sluggard;
> Consider her ways, and be wise :
> Which having no chief,
> Overseer, or ruler,
> Provideth her bread in the summer,
> And gathereth her food in the harvest.

---

[1] Proverbs 22 22–27.   [2] *Ibid.* 24 30–34.

> How long wilt thou sleep, O sluggard?
> When wilt thou arise out of thy sleep?
> Yet a little sleep, a little slumber,
> A little folding of the hands to sleep:
> So shall thy poverty come as a robber,
> And thy want as an armed man.[1]

Be thou diligent to know the state of thy flocks,
And look well to thy herds:
For riches are not for ever;
And doth the crown endure unto all generations?
The hay is carried, and the tender grass showeth itself,
And the herbs of the mountains are gathered in.
The lambs are for thy clothing,
And the goats are the price of the field;
And there will be goats' milk enough for thy food, for the food of thy
    household,
And maintenance for thy maidens.[2]

In the second collection also there occurs the poem on

THE WINEBIBBER

Who hath woe? who hath sorrow? who hath contentions?
Who hath complaining? who hath wounds without cause?
Who hath redness of eyes?
They that tarry long at the wine;
They that go to seek out mixed wine.
Look not thou upon the wine when it is red,
When it sparkleth in the cup,
When it goeth down smoothly:
At the last it biteth like a serpent,
And stingeth like an adder.
Thine eyes shall behold strange things,
And thy heart shall utter perverse things.
Yea, thou shalt be as he that lieth down in the midst of the sea,
Or as he that lieth upon the top of a mast.
They have stricken me, shalt thou say, and I was not hurt;
They have beaten me, and I felt it not:
When shall I awake? I will seek it yet again.[3]

[1] Proverbs 6 [6-11].   [2] *Ibid.* [23-27].
[3] Proverbs 23 [29-35]. This song may be commended to the advocates of
realism in contrast to the mendacious praises of wine that are usually sung.

The appended chapters[1] contain some curious fragments of wisdom literature. At the beginning, Agur the son of Jakeh is sarcastic toward those who, like the friends of Job, claim knowledge of God's ways.

> Surely I am more brutish than any man,
> And have not the understanding of a man;
> And I have not learned wisdom,
> Neither have I the knowledge of the Holy One.
> Who hath ascended up into heaven, and descended?
> Who hath gathered the wind in his fists?
> Who hath bound the waters in his garment?
> Who hath established all the ends of the earth?
> What is his name, and what is his son's name, if thou knowest?[2]

The prayer that may be Agur's[3] is marked by homely wisdom advocating the doctrine of the mean in nobler example than in the instance noted in Ecclesiastes.[4]

> Two things have I asked of thee;
> Deny me them not before I die:
> Remove far from me falsehood and lies;
> Give me neither poverty nor riches;
> Feed me with the food that is needful for me:
> Lest I be full, and deny thee, and say, Who is Jehovah?
> Or lest I be poor, and steal,
> And use profanely the name of my God.[5]

The curious tetrads of this first appendix[6] suggest the form of Amos: —

> For three transgressions of Damascus,
> Yea for four, etc.
>
> There are three things which are too wonderful for me,
> Yea, four which I know not.[7]

The form was no doubt an ancient, conventional mode of expressing effectively an indefinite number; a modification occurs in Proverbs 6[16].

> There are six things which Jehovah hateth;
> Yea, seven which are an abomination unto him.

---

[1] Proverbs 30–31.

[2] *Ibid.* 30 [2-4].

[3] We cannot be certain whether the editor intended to ascribe the entire chapter to Agur.

[4] See p. 339.

[5] Proverbs 30 [7-9].

[6] *Ibid.* 30 [15b-31].

[7] *Ibid.* 30 [18].

The purpose was partly at least mnemonic,[1] though in Amos the familiar form was used for rhetorical purposes.

The words ascribed to Lemuel, a King, as taught him by his mother [2] offer negative and positive advice for those in positions of authority. The positive injunctions are fine !

> Open thy mouth for the dumb,
> In the cause of all such as are left desolate.
> Open thy mouth, judge righteously,
> And minister justice to the poor and needy.[3]

The negative are no less significant in their demand that the King must avoid lust and intemperance which pervert just judgment.

> Give not thy strength unto women,
> Nor thy ways to that which destroyeth kings.
> It is not for kings, O Lemuel, it is not for kings to drink wine;
> Nor for princes to say, Where is strong drink?
> Lest they drink, and forget the law,
> And pervert the justice due to any that is afflicted.[4]

The book of proverbs closes with an alphabetic ode in praise of the ideal housewife.[5]   Cheyne writes in regard to it: —

"It is very interesting to see the ideal of womanhood formed by a late Hebrew poet.   Activity appears to him the one great feminine virtue — not, however, the activity which is entirely devoted to trifling details, for the ideal woman 'is like the ships of the merchant; from far she brings her food.'   Nor is she a stranger to sympathetic impulses: 'she holds out her hand . . . to the afflicted, and stretcheth forth her hands to the needy.' . . .   Nor must we forget 'one of the most beautiful features of the portrait': 'she opens her mouth with wisdom, and a law of kindness is on her tongue.'"[6]

During the greater part of the third century before Christ, when the book of Proverbs was growing into its final form, Judea

---

[1] The Jewish pupil learned natural history or moral precepts by devices similar to those by which we fix the number of days in the successive months: —

> Thirty days hath September,
> April, June, and November; etc.

[2] Proverbs 31 [1-9].   [3] Ibid. 31 [8-9].   [4] Ibid. 31 [3-5].
[5] Ibid. 31 [10-31].   [6] Job and Solomon.

was subject to the Ptolemies of Egypt. The Seleucid rulers of Antioch made frequent efforts to secure control of the land but did not meet with permanent success until 198, when Antiochus III ("The Great") attached all Palestine to the Kingdom of Syria. The next few years were peaceful and happy ones for the Jewish community; it was at this time, between 198 and 175 B.C., that Jesus ben-Sirach wrote "somewhat pertaining to instruction and wisdom; in order that those who love learning and are addicted to these things might make progress much more by living according to the law."[1] The book that he produced was translated into Greek by his grandson, while living in Egypt, and came to be included among the sacred books of the Alexandrian Jews;[2] it has come down to us under the name Ecclesiasticus.[3]

The general observations of Ben-Sirach do not concern themselves with problems more perplexing than the best way to get along smoothly and honestly in the world as it is.

> My son, go on with thy business in meekness;
> So shalt thou be beloved of an acceptable man.
> The greater thou art, humble thyself the more,
> And thou shalt find favour before the Lord.
> For great is the potency of the Lord,
> And he is glorified of them that are lowly.
> Seek not things that are too hard for thee,
> And search not out things that are above thy strength.
> The things that have been commanded thee, think thereupon;
> For thou hast no need of the things that are secret.
> Be not over busy in thy superfluous works;
> For more things are shewed unto thee than men can understand.[4]
>
> Be not hasty in thy tongue,
> And in thy deeds slack and remiss.
> Be not as a lion in thy house,
> Nor fanciful among thy servants.

[1] Prologue written in Egypt by the grandson of Ben-Sirach, soon after 132 B.C.

[2] It is thus one of the books of the Old Testament Apocrypha; *i.e.* those books that were included in the Greek translation of the Scriptures, but excluded from the Hebrew canon.

[3] That is, suitable to be read in churches.

[4] Ecclesiasticus 3[17-23]. This and the following extracts are taken from the British revised version of the Apocrypha.

2 A

Let not thine hand be stretched out to receive, and closed when
    thou shouldest repay.[1]

Set not thine heart upon unrighteous gains;
For thou shalt profit nothing in the day of calamity,
Winnow not with every wind,
And walk not in every path:
Thus doeth the sinner that hath a double tongue.
Be steadfast in thy understanding;
And let thy word be one.
Be swift to hear;
And with patience make thine answer.
If thou hast understanding, answer thy neighbour;
And if not, let thy hand be upon thy mouth.
Glory and dishonour is in talk:
And the tongue of a man is his fall.
Be not called a whisperer;
And lie not in wait with thy tongue:
For upon the thief there is shame,
And an evil condemnation upon him that hath a double tongue.[2]

Sweet words will multiply a man's friends;
And a fair-speaking tongue will multiply courtesies.
Let those that are at peace with thee be many;
But thy counsellors one of a thousand.
If thou wouldst get thee a friend, get him by proving,
And be not in haste to trust him.
For there is a friend that is so for his own occasion;
And he will not continue in the day of thy affliction.
And there is a friend that turneth to enmity,
And he will discover strife to thy reproach.[3]

If a mighty man invite thee, be retiring,
And so much the more will he invite thee.
Press not upon him, lest thou be thrust back;
And stand not far off, lest thou be forgotten.[4]

From this writer's incidental allusions it is possible to form a
vivid picture of the conditions of Jewish life in the opening years
of the second century before our era. The various handicrafts
of the time are described at some length in chapter 38: —

[1] Ecclesiasticus 4 [29-31].   [2] *Ibid.* 5 [8-14].
[3] *Ibid.* 6 [5-9].   [4] *Ibid.* 13 [9-10].

The wisdom of the scribe cometh by opportunity of leisure;
And he that hath little business shall become wise.
How shall he become wise that holdeth the plough,
That glorieth in the shaft of the goad,
That driveth oxen, and is occupied in their labours,
And whose discourse is of the stock of bulls?
He will set his heart upon turning his furrows;
And his wakefulness is to give his heifers their fodder.
So is every artificer and workmaster,
That passeth his time by night as by day;
They that cut gravings of signets,
And his diligence is to make great variety;
He will set his heart to preserve likeness in his protraiture,
And will be wakeful to finish his work.
So is the smith sitting by the anvil,
And considering the unwrought iron:
The vapour of the fire will waste his flesh;
And in the heat of the furnace will he wrestle with his work:
The noise of the hammer will be ever in his ear,
And his eyes are upon the pattern of the vessel;
He will set his heart upon perfecting his works,
And he will be wakeful to adorn them perfectly.
So is the potter sitting at his work,
And turning the wheel about with his feet,
Who is alway anxiously set at his work.
And all his handywork is by number;
He will fashion the clay with his arm.
And will bend its strength in front of his feet;
He will apply his heart to finish the glazing;
And he will be wakeful to make clean the furnace.[1]

Ben-Sirach goes on to recognize the useful and necessary function of skilled artisans in the body politic: —

All these put their trust in their hands;
And each becometh wise in his own work.
Without these shall not a city be inhabited,
And men shall not sojourn nor walk up and down therein.[2]

He speaks with the superiority of the intellectual aristocrat: —

---

[1] Ecclesiasticus 38 [24-30].   [2] *Ibid.* 38 [31-32].

And in the assembly they shall not mount on high;
They shall not sit on the seat of the judge,
And they shall not understand the covenant of judgment:
Neither shall they declare instruction and judgment;
And where parables are they shall not be found.
But they will maintain the fabric of the world;
And in the handywork of their craft is their prayer.

Not so he that hath applied his soul,
And meditateth in the law of the Most High;
He will seek out the wisdom of all the ancients,
And will be occupied in prophecies.
He will keep the discourse of the men of renown,
And will enter in amidst the subtilties of parables.
He will seek out the hidden meaning of proverbs,
And be conversant in the dark sayings of parables.
He will serve among great men,
And appear before him that ruleth:
He will travel through the land of strange nations;
For he hath tried good things and evil among men.
He will apply his heart to resort early to the Lord that made him,
And will make supplication before the Most High,
And will open his mouth in prayer,
And will make supplication for his sins.[1]

Earlier in the same chapter, the honorable service of the physician is discussed at length.

> Honour a physician according to thy need of him with the honours
>   due unto him:
> For verily the Lord hath created him.
> The skill of the physician shall lift up his head;
> And in the sight of great men he shall be admired.
> The Lord created medicines out of the earth;
> And a prudent man will have no disgust at them.[2]

The function of the apothecary is closely associated with that of the physician.

---

[1] Ecclesiasticus 38 ³³–39 ⁵.

[2] *Ibid.* 38 ¹, ³⁻⁴. The idea, still **regnant in the early nineteenth century**
A.D., that the more nauseous the concoction the more efficient, must
have prevailed in that day.

> With these will the apothecary make a confection;
> And his works shall not be brought to an end;
> And from him is peace upon the face of the earth.[1]

This paragraph ends with a quirk, suggesting that, after all, the physician is a necessary evil in a wicked world.

> He that sinneth before his Maker,
> Let him fall into the hands of the physician.[2]

The disrepute of mercantile pursuits that prevailed in the economic thought of Europe down to a recent date is suggested in Ben-Sirach.

> A merchant shall hardly keep himself from wrong doing;
> And a huckster shall not be acquitted of sin.[3]

The inherent difficulty of free social intercourse between those differing widely in wealth, a difficulty that political equality has proved powerless to overcome, is interestingly set forth.

Take not up a burden above thy strength;
And have no fellowship with one that is mightier and richer than thyself.
What fellowship shall the earthen pot have with the kettle?
This shall smite, and that shall be dashed in pieces.

Hath he had need of thee? then he will deceive thee,
And smile upon thee, and give thee hope:
He will speak thee fair, and say, What needst thou?
And he will shame thee by his meats,
Until he have made thee bare twice or thrice,
And at the last he will laugh thee to scorn:
Afterward will he see thee, and will forsake thee,
And shake his head at thee.[4]

Corruption and bribery add their factitious element in creating advantages for the rich and putting the poor at disadvantage.

> Contend not with a mighty man,
> Lest haply thou fall into his hands.
> Strive not with a rich man, lest haply he overweigh thee:
> For gold hath destroyed many,
> And turned aside the hearts of kings.[5]

---

[1] Ecclesiasticus 38 [8].   [2] *Ibid.* 38 [15].
[3] *Ibid.* 26 [29].   [4] *Ibid.* 13 [2, 6-7].   [5] *Ibid.* 8 [1-2].

All these and many other aspects of the intimate life of the age are open to one who cares to view them through the shrewd and kindly eyes of Ben-Sirach.

The book is a natural sequel to the great gnomic anthology, Proverbs; throughout, the same theory of rewards prevails and the same motives of self-interest are urged. At times, counsel seems prompted by generous thought of others, but usually consideration of personal advantage enters before the paragraph is finished. Generally the connection of thought extends through several couplets, or a considerable section, as in the "sayings of the wise" and the appendixes in the book of Proverbs; occasionally we come upon terse aphorisms like those in the Solomonic sections of Proverbs. One would need to be very familiar with the contents of the earlier writing to distinguish some sections of Ecclesiasticus from the book of Proverbs. Even the numerical form of proverb appears.

> Of three things my heart was afraid;
> And concerning the fourth kind I made supplication:
> The slander of a city, and the assembly of a multitude, and a false
>   accusation:
> All these are more grievous than death.[1]

Beginning with chapter 44, there is a long section in praise of famous men, quite different from anything in earlier books. The list commences with Enoch who "pleased the Lord and was translated" and proceeds on its unimpassioned way through Noah, Abraham, and their successors. After this comes a brief conclusion for the book (50 $^{27-29}$), followed by an appended " prayer of Jesus the son of Sirach," which proves a psalm of thanksgiving. At its conclusion, the writer tells how in his youth he prayed for wisdom, before the temple, and appeals to the unlearned to draw near

> And lodge in the house of instruction.

[1] Ecclesiasticus 26 [5].

CHAPTER XXV

Song of Songs and Psalms

(332 to 168 B.C.)

In strongest contrast to the didactic gnomes and songs of the sages, who flourished in the Greek age of Jewish history, is the love-lyric of the same era. Fortunately for our knowledge of Jewish literature, the fanciful interpretation given to early writings among the Jews at the close of the first century A.D. led them to regard the Song of Songs as an allegory representing the love of God and Israel. With such interpretation this book, in 90 A.D., secured final recognition in the third division of the Hebrew canon, and thus escaped the oblivion which it could so easily have found along with the other love songs of ancient Israel.

Post-exilic Judaism, which gradually selected that portion of the nation's literature forming the canon, was not primarily interested in ancient literature as literature. The Psalter might preserve a royal marriage hymn,[1] but its character as the temple hymnal excluded from its treasures most lyrics of human love. Isaiah might sing in the gay measure of the love songs familiar to his hearers and catch their dull ears for his parable of doom; but the love song was never finished. David's lament might preserve noblest expression of ideal love between man and man, or the poem in praise of a worthy woman[2] give admirable description of the wife approved by an aged philosopher, but song's great prompter through the ages, the rapturous love of youth and maid, was almost excluded from the poetry preserved by ancient Israel.

The treasured prose was richer in this element. The narrative of one who served seven years for his bride, "and they seemed

---

[1] Psalm 45, see p. 136.   [2] Proverbs, 31 [1-9].

unto him but a few days for the love he had to her"; the story of David and Abigail with its own deep, strong charm; that of Ruth and Boaz are unexcelled in any literature. Apart from the Song of Songs then, true human love finds some measure of just recognition in the extant literature; this book lifts the curtain high enough to let us see what the love songs of the folk were like.

Thus far literary interpretation may go to-day without much dispute; it is when we try to say whether the Song of Songs is one connected poem or not, that we find interpreters dividing. For a time after unnatural interpretations had been abandoned, the book was regarded as a collection of separate love songs; then the view prevailed that the whole formed a dramatic poem, with two principal characters, Solomon and a beautiful rustic maiden from northern Israel who had been brought to the King's harem. This theory failed to solve the poem and it was seen that there must be another leading character recognized, a rustic lover to whom the maiden had plighted her troth and to whom her heart was so true that the splendors of the court had no charms for her. In the presence of the King she was sad and abstracted, thinking, when he praised her charms, only of the absent lover; of him she dreamed by night and mused by day. At length, Solomon gave up in despair and let the faithful one return in her virgin purity to her shepherd lover in the north.

This theory won strong advocates, but meets great difficulties. At one time in the middle of the poem, it seems as though the rural lover were with the heroine; this cannot be, except as it represents her imaginings, and there is much besides that requires most ingenious explanation to fit any such theory. If this poem were truly a drama, it would be the one example preserved of ancient Semitic dramatic art, otherwise unknown.

The dramatic theory was succeeded by another interpretation which for a time seemed destined to possess the field. The German consul at Damascus, J. G. Wetzstein, called attention to the fact that among Arabs east of the Jordan and Lebanons there are still songs quite similar to parts of this book, connected with an interesting custom of the peasants. When a wedding occurs, on the marriage evening the bride displays her grace and agility, by the light of the leaping flames of a fire, brandishing a sword in

one hand and holding a handkerchief in the other, while she
dances. She is accompanied by a double chorus of men and
women, and the praise of her beauty of form and dress is sung with
a frank simplicity that would offend occidental standards of taste.
Such a chorus would be Song of Songs 7 $^{1-6}$.

> How beautiful are thy feet in sandals, O prince's daughter!
> Thy rounded thighs are like jewels,
> The work of the hands of a skilful workman.
> Thy body is like a round goblet,
> Wherein no mingled wine is wanting:
> Thy waist is like a heap of wheat
> Set about with lilies.
> Thy two breasts are like two fawns
> That are twins of a roe.
> Thy neck is like the tower of ivory;
> Thine eyes as the pools in Heshbon,
> By the gates of Bathrabbim;
> Thy nose is like the tower of Lebanon
> Which looketh toward Damascus.
> Thy head upon thee is like Carmel,
> And the hair of thy head like purple;
> The king is held captive in the tresses thereof.
> How fair and how pleasant art thou,
> O love, for delights!

For a week after marriage the festivities go forward; the bride
and groom are addressed as queen and king and are served by their
village friends. The first morning they go in royal procession to
the threshing floor where the king and queen are placed upon a
raised platform furnished with cushions; a song such as that of
3 $^{6-11}$ might describe the procession to the threshing floor, or might
be used on the previous day, when the bridegroom came up to the
wedding.

> Who is this that cometh up from the wilderness
> Like pillars of smoke,
> Perfumed with myrrh and frankincense,
> With all powders of the merchant?
> Behold, it is the litter of Solomon;
> Threescore mighty men are about it,
> Of the mighty men of Israel.

> They all handle the sword, and are expert in war:
> Every man hath his sword upon his thigh,
> Because of fear in the night.
> King Solomon made himself a palanquin
> Of the wood of Lebanon.
> He made the pillars thereof of silver,
> The bottom thereof of gold, the seat of it of purple,
> The midst thereof being paved with love,
> From the daughters of Jerusalem.
> Go forth, O ye daughters of Zion, and behold king Solomon,
> With the crown wherewith his mother hath crowned him
> In the day of his espousals,
> And in the day of the gladness of his heart.

Arrived at the threshing floor, the morning after the wedding, the groom may sing the praises of his bride as in 4 [1-4]: —

> Behold, thou art fair, my love; behold, thou art fair;
> Thine eyes are as doves behind thy veil.
> Thy hair is as a flock of goats,
> That lie along the side of mount Gilead.
> Thy teeth are like a flock of ewes that are newly shorn,
> Which are come up from the washing,
> Whereof every one hath twins,
> And none is bereaved among them.
> Thy lips are like a thread of scarlet,
> And thy mouth is comely.
> Thy temples are like a piece of a pomegranate
> Behind thy veil.
> Thy neck is like the tower of David
> Builded for an armory,
> Whereon there hang a thousand bucklers,
> All the shields of the mighty men.

She may sing in praise of him such an encomium as: —

> My beloved is white and ruddy,
> The chiefest among ten thousand.
> His head is as the most fine gold;
> His locks are bushy, and black as a raven.
> His eyes are like doves beside the water-brooks,
> Washed with milk, and fitly set.
> His cheeks are as a bed of spices,

As banks of sweet herbs:
His lips are as lilies, dropping liquid myrrh.
His hands are as rings of gold set with beryl:
His body is as ivory work overlaid with sapphires.
His legs are as pillars of marble, set upon sockets of fine gold:
His aspect is like Lebanon, excellent as the cedars.
His mouth is most sweet;
Yea, he is altogether lovely.
This is my beloved, and this is my friend.[1]

The theory as worked out and given currency, especially by Budde, was that in the Song of Songs we have a collection of the songs used in connection with such festivities, assumed to have prevailed anciently in Judea, as they now do east of the Jordan. The songs of our book are confessedly not in the order of the festivities and an editorial hand must be assumed, putting in portions here and there and giving some connection to the whole.[2]

While parts of the book may be made up of folk-songs arising in connection with some such customs as those described, the whole has a greater unity than seems compatible with this explanation of its origin. As the advocates of the dramatic theory saw, it tells a story, although with no such rigid dramatic structure as they worked out. It is not, then, in its present form, a collection of poems to be sung in connection with the festivities of the marriage week; rather a succession of lyrics that, albeit with some obscurity, tell a fairly intelligible tale of true love that is faithful despite the proffer of worldly splendor, and that ultimately is consummated in a happy marriage with the rustic lover; with him, near the close, the maiden is seen coming up from the wilderness.

Who is this that cometh up from the wilderness,
Leaning upon her beloved?

Under the apple-tree I awakened thee:
There thy mother was in travail with thee,
There was she in travail that brought thee forth.

Set me as a seal upon thy heart,

[1] Song of Songs 5 10–16a.

[2] The writer indicated his own leaning toward this view in a book review published in *The American Journal of Theology*, in January, 1903; to-day the theory does not satisfy him.

> As a seal upon thine arm:
> For love is strong as death;
> Jealousy is cruel as Sheol;
> The flashes thereof are flashes of fire,
> A very flame of Jehovah.
> Many waters cannot quench love,
> Neither can floods drown it:
> If a man would give all the substance of his house for love,
> He would utterly be contemned.[1]

This "matchless panegyric upon true love" is the real climax of the poem; the reflections which follow serve to bring the song to rest on the homely earth; just at the close, however, the lover calls upon his bride to sing, and she responds playfully with a quatrain similar to that with which she had adjured him to flee for safety in their hour of trouble.[2] Only now it is "hasten" instead of "turn" and "balsam mountains" rather than "cleft river."

> Hasten, my love,
>   As hastens gazelle,
> Or the chief stag
>   On balsam scented heights.[3]

Thus ends the book which Herder styled "Solomon's songs of love, the oldest and sweetest of the East."

Whether the psalms ascribed to the sons of Korah and to Asaph were, in their nucleus, collections made at the great sanctuaries of northern Israel [4] or whether they were, as most suppose, post-exilic, Levitical collections, they were known as separate hymnals in the early part of the Greek age and were used during this era, along with many psalms from the Davidic book, to form a large hymnal, differing from that compiled in the Persian age (Psalms 2–41). The new book (Psalms 42–83) shows its unifying editing by the overwhelming use of the general name for God instead of the specific name of Israel's God. Some hymns were included that were already in the collection 2–41, but with frequent substitution of Elohim for Yahweh.[5] At some subsequent date, Psalms 84–89,

---

[1] Song of Songs 8 [5-7].   [2] 2 [17].   [3] Translating rather freely 8 [14].
[4] See pp. 133 f.   [5] Cf. 53 with 14.

chiefly taken from the Korahite collection, were added at the close of this Elohist group, but without similar editing.[1]

Psalm 1, so like the book of Proverbs in its gnomic and didactic character, is best assigned to the Greek age, and it may have been placed in its present position soon after its composition, so that we may think of Psalms 1–89 as standing in essentially their present order and form during the era now under consideration. Most of the individual psalms in this composite book were written before Alexander's conquest and therefore belong to the literature of earlier times.[2]

One of the finest products of Israel's literature in the Greek age was a new book of religious poems, the Pilgrim Psalter (Psalms 120–134).[3] This is now generally regarded as a collection of songs used by the pilgrims who journeyed up to Jerusalem for the great annual feasts, though certain of the poems may have had other circumstances in view before they were adapted to this use.

To select some, rather than others, of these charming lyrics as examples of Israel's religious poetry seems almost invidious. Among the most inspiring are 121 to 126; in these we are led up the mountain side, into Jerusalem and the temple, and are compelled to let our gaze sweep round about the summits of the everlasting hills and upward to the heavens where Jehovah sits enthroned.

Throughout this little psalter, the power and grace of Israel's lyric is seen in its perfection. Ordinary parallelism, with its constant return upon itself, cannot express the rising tide of feeling and the rhythm becomes of the ascending type, in which the second line reiterates the thought briefly, and then adds a new element that lifts the soul still higher. So marked is this feature, that some have thought the term "ascents" descriptive of the rhythm rather than of the use of the songs in the pilgrimages.

---

[1] The editorial note at the close of Psalm 72, "The Prayers of David the Son of Jesse are ended," indicates that Psalm 86 of the appendix and other Psalms ascribed to David in the later collection of 90–150 were unknown to the editor. So far as Psalms 2–41 and 42–83 are concerned, the prayers of David were ended.

[2] As such, many have been discussed in chapters IX, XVI, and XXII.

[3] Psalm 139, like some in the group 1–89, may be Maccabean and added later to the collection.

121

I will lift up mine eyes unto the mountains:
From whence shall my help come?
My help cometh from Jehovah,
Who made heaven and earth.
He will not suffer thy foot to be moved:
He that keepeth thee will not slumber.
Behold, he that keepeth Israel
Will neither slumber nor sleep.
Jehovah is thy keeper:
Jehovah is thy shade upon thy right hand.
The sun shall not smite thee by day,
Nor the moon by night.
Jehovah will keep thee from all evil;
He will keep thy soul.
Jehovah will keep thy going out and thy coming in
From this time forth and for evermore.

122

I was glad when they said unto me,
Let us go unto the house of Jehovah.
Our feet are standing
Within thy gates, O Jerusalem,
Jerusalem, that art builded
As a city that is compact together;
Whither the tribes go up, even the tribes of Jehovah,
For an ordinance for Israel,
To give thanks unto the name of Jehovah.
For there are set thrones for judgment,
The thrones of the house of David.
Pray for the peace of Jerusalem:
They shall prosper that love thee.
Peace be within thy walls,
And prosperity within thy palaces.
For my brethren and companions' sakes,
I will now say, Peace be within thee.
For the sake of the house of Jehovah our God
I will seek thy good.

123

Unto thee do I lift up mine eyes,
O thou that sittest in the heavens

Behold, as the eyes of servants look unto the hand of their master,
As the eyes of a maid unto the hand of her mistress;
So our eyes look unto Jehovah our God,
Until he have mercy upon us.
Have mercy upon us, O Jehovah, have mercy upon us;
For we are exceedingly filled with contempt.
Our soul is exceedingly filled
With the scoffing of those that are at ease,
And with the contempt of the proud.

124

If it had not been Jehovah who was on our side,
Let Israel now say,
If it had not been Jehovah who was on our side,
When men rose up against us;
Then they had swallowed us up alive,
When their wrath was kindled against us:
Then the waters had overwhelmed us,
The stream had gone over our soul;
Then the proud waters had gone over our soul.
Blessed be Jehovah,
Who hath not given us as a prey to their teeth.
Our soul is escaped as a bird out of the snare of the fowlers:
The snare is broken, and we are escaped.
Our help is in the name of Jehovah,
Who made heaven and earth.

125

They that trust in Jehovah
Are as mount Zion, which cannot be moved, but abideth forever.
As the mountains are round about Jerusalem,
So Jehovah is round about his people
From this time forth and for evermore.
For the sceptre of wickedness shall not rest upon the lot of the righteous;
That the righteous put not forth their hands unto iniquity.
Do good, O Jehovah, unto those that are good,
And to them that are upright in their hearts.
But as for such as turn aside unto their crooked ways,
Jehovah will lead them forth with the workers of iniquity.
Peace be upon Israel.

126

When Jehovah brought back those that returned to Zion,
We were like unto them that dream.
Then was our mouth filled with laughter,
And our tongue with singing:
Then said they among the nations,
Jehovah hath done great things for them.
Jehovah hath done great things for us,
Whereof we are glad.
Turn again our captivity, O Jehovah.
As the streams in the South.
They that sow in tears shall reap in joy.
He that goeth forth and weepeth, bearing seed for sowing,
Shall doubtless come again with joy, bringing his sheaves with him.

Another wonderful collection of hymns that was mainly written in the Greek age is the *Hallel* or Praise group. In later Jewish liturgy, Psalms 113 to 118 formed the Hallel used at the great festivals,[1] but we need not suppose that the original collection was limited to these six. Little groups of similar character are scattered through the Psalter from 104 to 150; a large number of these begin or end with Hallelujah, Praise ye Yah (Jehovah).[2]

The members of the group 104–107 stand in interesting sequence; the first glorifies Jehovah's work in creation; it begins:—

Bless Jehovah, O my soul.
O Jehovah my God, thou art very great;
Thou art clothed with honor and majesty:
Who coverest thyself with light as with a garment;
Who stretchest out the heavens like a curtain;
Who layeth the beams of his chambers in the waters;
Who maketh the clouds his chariot;
Who walketh upon the wings of the wind;
Who maketh winds his messengers;

[1] Since 115–118 are sung after the Passover meal, it is probable that they were "the hymn sung by our Lord and His disciples before they left the upper chamber," Kirkpatrick, *Psalms*, p. 677.

[2] Briggs includes in the Hallels the four groups 104–107, 111–117, 135–136, 146–150, though regarding 147 and 149 as written after 168 B.C. and so not in the original collection. He also excludes 118 and 116 "regarded as Hallels in later usage." *Int. Crit. Com., Psalms*, I, p. lxxviii.

Flames of fire his ministers;
Who laid the foundations of the earth,
That it should not be moved forever.
Thou coveredst it with the deep as with a vesture;
The waters stood above the mountains.
At thy rebuke they fled;
At the voice of thy thunder they hasted away
(The mountains rose, the valleys sank down)
Unto the place which thou hadst founded for them.[1]

The second tells of God's dealings with Abraham, Isaac, and Jacob,
of Joseph's and Israel's descent into Egypt, of Moses, the plagues,
and escape.   Here is as close an approach to narrative poetry as
the Old Testament knows; a few lines are: —

And he called for a famine upon the land;
He brake the whole staff of bread.
He sent a man before them;
Joseph was sold for a servant:
His feet they hurt with fetters:
He was laid in chains of iron,
Until the time that his word came to pass,
The word of Jehovah tried him.
The king sent and loosed him;
Even the ruler of peoples, and let him go free.
He made him lord of his house,
And ruler of all his substance;
To bind his princes at his pleasure,
And teach his elders wisdom.
Israel also came into Egypt;
And Jacob sojourned in the land of Ham.
And he increased his people greatly,
And made them stronger than their adversaries.
He turned their heart to hate his people,
To deal subtly with his servants.
He sent Moses his servant,
And Aaron whom he had chosen.
They set among them his signs,
And wonders in the land of Ham.
He sent darkness, and made it dark;
And they rebelled not against his words.[2]

[1] Psalm 104[1-8].   [2] *Ibid.* 105[16-28].

2 B

Psalm 106 carries the story from the passage of the Red Sea through the wilderness and on to the mingling of foreign worship in Canaan, the events all being interpreted as examples of rebelliousness and deliverance.   The next continues the theme of deliverance from perils with the restoration from the exile in the foreground.

> O give thanks unto Jehovah; for he is good;
> For his lovingkindness endureth forever.
> Let the redeemed of Jehovah say so,
> Whom he hath redeemed from the hand of the adversary,
> And gathered out of the lands,
> From the east and from the west,
> From the north and from the south.
> They wandered in the wilderness in a desert way;
> They found no city of habitation.
> Hungry and thirsty,
> Their soul fainted in them.
> Then they cried unto Jehovah in their trouble,
> And he delivered them out of their distresses,
> He led them also by a straight way,
> That they might go to a city of habitation.
> Oh that men would praise Jehovah for his lovingkindness,
> And for his wonderful works to the children of men!
> For he satisfieth the longing soul,
> And the hungry soul he filleth with good.[1]

The next little group, 111–117, opens with two alphabetic poems, each consisting of a hallelujah and twenty-two lines.   The fact that the opening hallelujah stands apart from the acrostic structure suggests that it may have been added for liturgical use to these two songs which, apart from this, are quite in the wisdom vein.

> Praise ye Jehovah.
> Blessed is the man that feareth Jehovah,
> That delighteth greatly in his commandments.
> His seed shall be mighty upon earth:
> The generation of the upright shall be blessed.
> Wealth and riches are in his house;
> And his righteousness endureth forever.
> Unto the upright there ariseth light in the darkness:

[1] Psalm 107 [1-9].

He is gracious, and merciful, and righteous.
Well is it with the man that dealeth graciously and lendeth;
He shall maintain his cause in judgment.[1]

Of the two Hallels (113–114) that, in the later Passover ritual,
are sung before the supper, the appropriateness of 114 is obvious.

When Israel went forth out of Egypt,
The house of Jacob from a people of strange language;
Judah became his sanctuary,
Israel his dominion.
The sea saw it, and fled;
The Jordan was driven back.
The mountains skipped like rams,
The little hills like lambs.
What aileth thee, O thou sea, that thou fleest?
Thou Jordan, that thou turnest back?
Ye mountains, that ye skip like rams;
Ye little hills, like lambs?
Tremble, thou earth, at the presence of the Lord,
At the presence of the God of Jacob,
Who turned the rock into a pool of water,
The flint into a fountain of waters.

The opening of 115 that follows the supper is especially noble
in its thought of glory for Jehovah.

Not unto us, O Jehovah, not unto us,
But unto thy name give glory,
For thy lovingkindness, and for thy truth's sake.
Wherefore should the nations say,
Where is now their God?
But our God is in the heavens:
He hath done whatsoever he pleased.[2]

The cry, "Where is now their God?" followed later in the poem
by sarcastic description of helpless idol gods, echoes thought that
grew out of the Babylonian exile, but applies almost equally well
to the Egyptian deliverance.

Of this group, 117, a mere quatrain with a hallelujah, is a very
perfect psalm of praise.

---

[1] Psalm 112 [1-5].   [2] *Ibid.* 115 [1-3].

> Oh praise Jehovah, all ye nations;
> Laud him, all ye peoples.
> For his lovingkindness is great toward us;
> And the truth of Jehovah endureth forever.
> Praise ye Jehovah.

Psalm 136 gives a good example of the monotony of repetition that may develop under the influence of liturgical use. If, however, the main theme was sung by a solo voice and the trimeter refrain,

> Since his mercy's eternal,

was given by the chorus, as a response to each line, the effect must have been very impressive. If the refrain be omitted in reading, the remainder will be found a poem suggesting in theme the group 104–107.

> Oh give thanks unto Jehovah; for he is good;
> Oh give thanks unto the God of gods;
> Oh give thanks unto the Lord of lords;
> To him who alone doeth great wonders;
> To him that by understanding made the heavens;
> To him that spread forth the earth above the waters;
> To him that made great lights;
> The sun to rule by day;
> The moon and stars to rule by night;
> To him that smote Egypt in their first-born;
> And brought out Israel from among them;
> With a strong hand, and with an outstretched arm;
> To him that divided the Red Sea in sunder;
> And made Israel to pass through the midst of it;
> But overthrew Pharaoh and his host in the Red Sea;
> To him that led his people through the wilderness;
> To him that smote great kings;
> And slew famous kings;
> Sihon king of the Amorites;
> And Og king of Bashan;
> And gave their land for a heritage;
> Even a heritage unto Israel his servant;
> Who remembered us in our low estate;
> And hath delivered us from our adversaries;
> Who giveth food to all flesh;
> Oh give thanks unto the God of heaven.

146 to 150 form a group of doxologies, some of which were written before the close of the Greek age, and, presumably, formed a part of the original Hallel Psalter.

With the Pilgrim and Hallel collections as chief sources, the third great division of the present book of Psalms, 90–150, was formed by the insertion of many individual hymns which are without any special headings to indicate their source, a dozen ascribed to David,[1] and one bearing the name of Moses.[2] This last great group discernible in the evolution of the Psalter may have been collected, in the main, before the close of the Greek age, or it may have been the compilation of an editor living in Maccabean times. A number of individual psalms are assigned, with greater or less probability, to the Maccabean era, and .t is impossible to say whether these were inserted after our book of Psalms was practically completed or whether the book as a whole was compiled only in the Maccabean age. In either case, the Pilgrim Psalter and most of the Hallels, forming a large part of the third great section of our book, were collected before 168 B.C., and it is not at all improbable that the three great groups, 1–41, 42–89, 90–150, stood much as they now do and that the book of Psalms was substantially completed in the Greek age. The division of the second and third groups, resulting in the present pentateuchal structure of the book of Psalms, is arbitrary and to be counted one of the latest elements in the long history of the book.

In the Psalter, viewed as a whole, all phases of Israel's thought, developed by her prophets, priests, and sages, find beautiful expression. Since the greater part of these lyrics were written or revised and expanded in the later centuries of the Old Testament era, they represent the prophetic and priestly thought in their developed and spiritualized form. It is not strange, therefore, that all types of religious consciousness, through the centuries, find something in the book of Psalms to meet the deep needs of the soul.

One element alone in the life of post-exilic Israel which has frequent and intense expression in these lyrics continually perplexes those who have entered into the highest thought of Israel's teachers; it is the bitter cry for vengeance upon enemies. Against

[1] 103, 108–110, 138–145. [2] 90.

just such a spirit as this we have found the writer of Jonah protesting and, generations before the book of Psalms was completed, the poem of the Suffering Servant had presented a very different ideal of life.   Still the common consciousness of Israel cried out for vengeance upon those who compassed her about with hatred and fought against her without a cause,[1] and the nation's great hymnal more truly reflects that common consciousness than the writings of such supreme seers as the author of Jonah or of the Suffering Servant.

Similar limitation is seen in what may be called the wisdom psalms.   Here we have the common dogma of the sages, that long life, wealth, and family are the necessary reward of him who feareth Jehovah, rather than the deeper insight of the author of Job.   This aspect of the psalms fails to give the same perplexity as the imprecatory element, since the common Christian consciousness has not yet risen to the level of Job and the Great Teacher in its thought of rewards and penalties.

When the limitations have been recognized, the fact remains that the generations bear irrefutable testimony to the undying truth and worth of this unique anthology, in fulfilling the highest mission of song.   Post-exilic Judaism had advanced far above and beyond that early Israel which collected the songs of *The Wars of Yahweh*, or the Psalter could not have become the great, recognized, national treasury of song.

[1] See Psalm 109 [3], etc.

CHAPTER XXVI

LITERATURE OF THE EARLY MACCABEAN ERA

(168 to about 135 B.C.)

WHEN Palestine was incorporated in the Syrian kingdom by
Antiochus the Great (198 B.C.),[1] the influence of the degenerated
Greek civilization of Antioch became dominant in Jerusalem; the
Judaism that had survived Babylonian exile seemed doomed to
disintegrate under the pervasive influence of Greek athletics,
theatres, and gay religious festivals. Antiochus Epiphanes, who
succeeded to the Syrian throne, was not satisfied with the progress
Hellenistic civilization was making among his Jewish subjects
and determined to root out completely all the rites and usages
which made in any way an heterogeneous element in his
kingdom. He forbade the observance of Sabbath and circumcision, ordered all copies of the Law burned, and all Jews to worship
the Greek gods; horrible torture and death were the only alter-
natives. The temple was polluted by vile orgies of the Syrian
soldiers, and an altar of Zeus, the "abomination of desolation,"
set upon the great altar of Jehovah, with swine's flesh used in
sacrifice.

Such measures could have but one result; they kindled into
life all the loyalty to the law that had been developed under the
Nehemiah-Ezra reform. The roll of martyrs became long and
glorious; many fled to the caves of the wilderness, where a thousand were found and killed unresisting on a Sabbath day. Then
the fires leaped forth in the Maccabean revolt, begun (168 B.C.)
by an aged priest Mattathias and continued by his sons, at first
under the leadership of Judas called Maccabeus. This son of
Mattathias proved himself, not only one of the most devoted
patriots, but one of the cleverest strategists of military history.
With his growing band of heroic followers, he entrapped and cut

[1] See p. 351 f.

to pieces army after army sent to put down the revolt. Now he caught the enemy in a narrow defile where predominant numbers were of no avail; again, when their forces were divided attempting a night surprise in the mountains, his whole band swept down upon their unsuspecting camp in the open plain. The story, told with majestic simplicity two generations later, in 1 Maccabees, is one of the most thrilling of history. By December, 165 B.C., Judas was able to cleanse the polluted precincts of the temple and restore the daily worship of Jehovah, never again to be inter-. mitted till the priests fell, calmly conducting sacrifices at the altar, while their temple burned, in 70 A.D.

Religious liberty secured, many of the more fanatical religionists deserted Judas, failing to understand the necessity of political independence. Four years later, with diminished forces, the great leader met his death in hopeless battle. The Maccabean brothers carried forward the struggle, until, through keen diplomacy, taking advantage of the strifes of the many claimants to the Syrian throne, they obtained recognition of independence, twenty years after the death of Judas. The Maccabean state retained independence till the coming of Pompey in 63 B.C. The death of the last of the brothers of Judas Maccabeus in 135 B.C. marks the point to which we carry our survey of the history.

That the struggle and victories of the Maccabees called forth lyrics of prayer and praise from faithful worshippers of Jehovah, we cannot question; some of these, as noted in the previous chapter, are believed to have found entrance into the book of Psalms. If that collection had not been already edited as a whole, we should expect to find more songs from the Maccabean age included. Beautiful psalms written in the next century, and traditionally ascribed to Solomon, form a separate collection that was never included in the national hymnal.[1]

Out of the darkness of Antiochus's persecution came such cries for vengeance and deliverance as Psalm 79.[2]

[1] An excellent English edition of this later product of Israel's psalmody, edited by Ryle and James, is published by the Cambridge University Press and, in America, by Macmillan and Company, under the title "Psalms of the Pharisees, or Psalms of Solomon."

[2] While the nucleus of this psalm is probably earlier, it was expanded to meet the conditions of the later era.

O God, the nations are come into thine inheritance;
Thy holy temple have they defiled;
They have laid Jerusalem in heaps.
The dead bodies of thy servants have they given to be food unto the birds
    of the heavens,
The flesh of thy saints unto the beasts of the earth.
Their blood have they shed like water round about Jerusalem;
And there was none to bury them.
We are become a reproach to our neighbors,
A scoffing and derision to them that are round about us.
How long, O Jehovah? wilt thou be angry forever?
Shall thy jealousy burn like fire?
Pour out thy wrath upon the nations that know thee not,
And upon the kingdoms that call not upon thy name.
For they have devoured Jacob,
And laid waste his habitation.
Remember not against us the iniquities of our forefathers:
Let thy tender mercies speedily meet us;
For we are brought very low.
Help us, O God of our salvation, for the glory of thy name;
And deliver us, and forgive our sins, for thy name's sake.
Wherefore should the nations say, Where is their God?
Let the avenging of the blood of thy servants which is shed
Be known among the nations in our sight.
Let the sighing of the prisoner come before thee:
According to the greatness of thy power preserve thou those that are
    appointed to death;
And render unto our neighbors sevenfold into their bosom
Their reproach, wherewith they have reproached thee, O Lord.
So we thy people and sheep of thy pasture
Will give thee thanks for ever:
We will show forth thy praise to all generations.

When victory had come to Judas, there were outpourings of praise.

      Rejoice in Jehovah, O ye righteous:
      Praise is comely for the upright.
      Give thanks unto Jehovah with the harp:
      Sing praises unto him with the psaltery of ten strings.
      Sing unto him a new song;
      Play skilfully with a loud noise.

> For the word of Jehovah is right;
> And all his work is done in faithfulness.
> He loveth righteousness and justice:
> The earth is full of the lovingkindness of Jehovah.
> By the word of Jehovah were the heavens made,
> And all the host of them by the breath of his mouth.
> He gathereth the waters of the sea together as a heap:
> He layeth up the deeps in storehouses.
> Let all the earth fear Jehovah:
> Let all the inhabitants of the world stand in awe of him.[1]

The most characteristic literature growing out of the persecution and struggle for freedom were the great apocalypses Daniel and Enoch 83–90. The growth of apocalypse[2] is one of the most distinctive and interesting phases of Israel's literary history.

Apocalypse is a direct outgrowth of prophecy, a branch whose appearance announces the dwindling or death of the parent stem.[3] The new branch is first clearly seen in Ezekiel where two great characteristics of the fully developed apocalypse are prominent: fantastic symbolism and the picture of a great day when the nations shall be gathered against Israel and when, in his people's last extremity, Jehovah will destroy their enemies and vindicate his power.[4] This conception could not develop as a mere monopodial branch of prophecy, for the prophetic and apocalyptic conception of life are eternally contradictory. One conceives the hope of the future as an inward transformation, bringing nation and individual into willing harmony with God; the other trusts in a manifestation of external power to destroy the wicked and leave the righteous.

From Ezekiel's time forward the apocalyptic elements of prophecy increase. Zechariah adopts Ezekiel's symbolism, while

[1] Psalm 33 seems best assigned to this time. The opening lines are given above.

[2] Translated into Latin-English by "revelation," and meaning etymologically *uncovering*.

[3] It offers an example of sympodial branching, by which the "branch virtually becomes the trunk, and the real trunk or ascending portion is reduced to a mere twig, or may ultimately fail of support altogether and disappear through atrophy." — Ward, *Pure Sociology*, p. 72.

[4] Ezekiel 38–39.

retaining much of the genuine spirit of prophecy; Joel takes both the form and thought, converting the older prophetic symbol of peace into a call to war, and picturing the nations as gathered together against Israel, to be cut down by Jehovah, for his people's deliverance and his own vindication.

Proclaim ye this among the nations; prepare war; stir up the mighty men; let all the men of war draw near, let them come up. Beat your plowshares into swords, and your pruning-hooks into spears; let the weak say, I am strong. Haste ye, and come, all ye nations round about, and gather yourselves together: thither cause thy mighty ones to come down, O Jehovah. Let the nations bestir themselves, and come up to the valley of Jehoshaphat; for there will I sit to judge all the nations round about. Put ye in the sickle; for the harvest is ripe: come, tread ye; for the winepress is full, the vats overflow; for their wickedness is great. Multitudes, multitudes in the valley of decision! for the day of Jehovah is near in the valley of decision. The sun and the moon are darkened, and the stars withdraw their shining. And Jehovah will roar from Zion, and utter his voice from Jerusalem; and the heavens and the earth shall shake: but Jehovah will be a refuge unto his people, and a stronghold to the children of Israel. So shall ye know that I am Jehovah your God, dwelling in Zion my holy mountain: then shall Jerusalem be holy, and there shall no strangers pass through her any more.[1]

Joel cannot conceive a day when Egypt and Assyria shall worship with Israel; for him the peace and perpetuity of Jerusalem demand the desolation of her neighbors. Though true prophecy had not fully disappeared in the fourth century B.C., the spirit of apocalypse was fast becoming ascendant.

The late oracles appended to Zechariah (chapters 9–14, especially 12–14) show still further development of apocalyptic tendencies.

Behold, a day of Jehovah cometh, when thy spoil shall be divided in the midst of thee. For I will gather all nations against Jerusalem to battle; and the city shall be taken, and the houses rifled, and the women ravished; and half of the city shall go forth into captivity, and the residue of the people shall not be cut off from the city. Then shall Jehovah go forth, and fight against those nations, as when he fought in the day of battle. And his feet shall stand in that day upon the mount of Olives, which is before Jerusalem on the east; and the mount of Olives shall be

---

[1] Joel 3 9-17.

cleft in the midst thereof toward the east and toward the west, and there shall be a very great valley ; and half of the mountain shall remove toward the north, and half of it toward the south. And ye shall flee by the valley of my mountains; for the valley of the mountains shall reach unto Azel;[1] yea, ye shall flee, like as ye fled from before the earthquake in the days of Uzziah king of Judah; and Jehovah my God shall come, and all the holy ones with thee. And it shall come to pass in that day, that there shall not be light; the bright ones shall withdraw themselves: but it shall be one day which is known unto Jehovah; not day, and not night; but it shall come to pass, that at evening time there shall be light. And it shall come to pass in that day, that living waters shall go out from Jerusalem; half of them toward the eastern sea, and half of them toward the western sea: in summer and in winter shall it be.

And Jehovah shall be King over all the earth: in that day shall Jehovah be one, and his name one. All the land shall be made like the Arabah, from Geba to Rimmon south of Jerusalem; and she shall be lifted up, and shall dwell in her place, from Benjamin's gate unto the place of the first gate, unto the corner gate, and from the tower of Hananel unto the king's winepresses. And men shall dwell therein, and there shall be no more curse; but Jerusalem shall dwell safely.

* * * * * * * *

And it shall come to pass, that every one that is left of all the nations that came against Jerusalem shall go up from year to year to worship the King, Jehovah of hosts, and to keep the feast of tabernacles. And it shall be, that whoso of all the families of the earth goeth not up unto Jerusalem to worship the King, Jehovah of hosts, upon them there shall be no rain. And if the family of Egypt go not up, and come not, neither shall it be upon them; there shall be the plague wherewith Jehovah will smite the nations that go not up to keep the feast of tabernacles. This shall be the punishment of Egypt, and the punishment of all the nations that go not up to keep the feast of tabernacles. In that day shall there be upon the bells of the horses, HOLY UNTO JEHOVAH; and the pots in Jehovah's house shall be like the bowls before the altar. Yea, every pot in Jerusalem and in Judah shall be holy unto Jehovah of hosts; and all they that sacrifice shall come and take of them, and boil therein: and in that day there shall be no more a Canaanite in the house of Jehovah of hosts.[2]

The vision culminates in worship, *ritually* pure; priest and apocalyptist now express the nation's ideals and they two are

---

[1] Probably a place near Jerusalem.   [2] Zechariah 14 1-11 16-21.

closely kindred, since each conceives the hope of humanity to rest in some power imposed from without, rather than in the power of transforming love.

Two aspects of later apocalyptic literature are wanting in Ezekiel, Joel, and Zechariah 9-14: putting the vision into the mouth of some ancient worthy [1] and telling the history of the past, with more or less of accuracy and detail, down to the time of the writer. The favorite mouthpiece in the second and first centuries B.C. became Enoch, "the seventh from Adam." Under his name a number of visions have come down to us. Most of these were anciently edited into one volume, divided into 108 chapters.[2] Chapters 1-36 were written during the latter part of the Greek age, before the persecutions of Antiochus Epiphanes. The writer sets himself the task of justifying the ways of God, maintaining that the righteous will not always suffer and the wicked prosper. The opening is "The words of the blessing of Enoch, wherewith he blessed the elect and righteous, who will be living in the day of tribulation, when all the wicked and godless are to be removed." The presence of evil in the world is attributed to the events recorded in Genesis 6 [1-4]; although the offspring of the fallen watchers perished in the flood, their spirits persisted as demons and perpetuated wickedness.

The next section of the book of Enoch (83-90) was written in the midst of the Maccabean struggle and deals much more in detail with national history. This book, for it is a separate book, is divided into two main parts, the former of which treats of the first world judgment, the Flood, and the latter of the history from Adam to the final judgment. The writer's theology agrees with that of 1-36 in attributing the corruption of man to the fallen angels. The calamities that have befallen Israel are attributed to seventy shepherds or angels who have proved faithless to their trust, instead of pasturing Israel.

The book begins: "And now, my son Methuselah, I will show thee all my visions which I have seen, recounting (them) before

[1] This suggests the mode of the ancient oracular poetry ; see p. 41.

[2] Chapters 1-36 and 83-90, written before 135 B.C., fall within the scope of the present volume. This Book of Enoch is published in English, with introduction and notes, at the Clarendon Press, Oxford, edited by R. H. Charles.

thee. Two visions I saw before I took a wife, and the one was quite unlike the other: on the first occasion when I was learning to write, on the second, before I took thy mother, I saw a terrible vision, and concerning them I prayed to the Lord. I had laid me down in the house of my grandfather Malâlêl, when I saw in a vision how the heaven collapsed and was borne off and fell to the earth. And when it fell to the earth I saw how the earth was swallowed up in a great abyss, and mountains hung suspended on mountains and hills sank down on hills, and high trees were rent from their stems and hurled down and sunk in the abyss. And thereupon utterance came into my mouth, and I lifted up my voice to cry aloud, and said: 'The earth is destroyed.' And my grandfather Malâlêl waked me as I lay near him, and said unto me: 'Why dost thou cry aloud, my son, and why dost thou thus make lamentation?' Then I recounted to him the whole vision which I had seen, and he said unto me: 'What thou hast seen, my son, is terrible, and thy dream-vision is of grave moment as to the sin of all sin of the earth: it must sink into the abyss and be destroyed with a great destruction. And now, my son, arise and make petition to the Lord of glory, since thou art a believer, that a remnant may remain on the earth. My son, all this will come from heaven upon the earth, and there will be violent destruction upon earth.'"

The second vision, beginning with chapter 85, pictures the history of humanity under the symbols of domestic animals and beasts and birds of prey. The first parents and their children are domestic cattle; the fallen angels are fallen stars, their offspring elephants, camels, and asses. There come forth from heaven four beings like white men who bind the fallen stars in the abyss of the earth. One of the heavenly beings secretly instructs a white bull who builds a great vessel in which he and three bulls are saved from the flood: Only one of the three was white, like the one who builded; of the other two, one was red as blood and the other black, and these two gendered "lions, tigers, dogs, wolves, . . . falcons, vultures, . . . and ravens." So the story goes forward, the chosen line represented by white bulls and, in later generations, by sheep, while their enemies are creatures of prey.

When at last the outlook is blackest and the "sheep were devoured by the dogs and eagles and kites" "and the sheep became few," "lambs were borne by those white sheep, and they began to open their eyes and to see, and to cry to the sheep. But the sheep did not cry to them and did not hear what they said to them, but were exceedingly deaf, and their eyes were exceedingly and forcibly blinded. And I saw in the vision how the ravens flew upon those lambs and took one of those lambs, and dashed the sheep in pieces and devoured them. And I saw till horns grew upon those lambs, and the ravens cast down their horns; and I saw till a great horn of one of those sheep branched forth, and their eyes were opened. And it looked at them and their eyes opened, and it cried to the sheep and the rams saw it and all ran to it. And notwithstanding all this, those eagles and vultures and ravens and kites still kept tearing the sheep and swooping down upon them and devouring them : still the sheep took no action, but the rams lamented and cried out. And those ravens fought and battled with it and sought to destroy his horn, but they had no power over it. And I saw them till the shepherds and eagles and those vultures and kites came, and they cried to the ravens that they should break the horn of that ram, and they battled and fought with it, and it battled with them and cried that his succour should come unto him. And I saw till that man who wrote down the names of the shepherds and carried (them) up unto the presence of the Lord of the sheep came, and he helped that ram and showed it everything, that he had come down to help it. And I saw till a great sword was given to the sheep and the sheep proceeded against all the beasts of the field to slay them, and all the beasts and the birds of the heaven fled before their face."

With these victories of the "great horn," Judas Maccabeus, the world's history, as we know it, ends and the great judgment is ushered in; "and I saw till a throne was erected in the pleasant land and the Lord of the sheep sat himself thereon, and that other took the sealed books and opened them before the Lord of the sheep."

The writer knows nothing of the death of Judas in 161 B.C. and of the tribulations through which the Maccabees finally secured political independence. He is familiar with the early success of Judas and counts this rebellion the beginning of the end of all Israel's sufferings. In Enoch 83–90 we have a great, typical apocalypse, written between 168 and 161 B.C., probably before the rededication of the temple in 165.

In the same interval of three years, between 168 and 165, the book of Daniel was written. Earlier stories concerning an ancient, righteous man, Daniel, were current. These were used as illustrations of Jehovah's care for those who were faithful to him; they tell of the steadfastness of the young Jewish captive and his three friends, in keeping themselves from defilement with food consecrated to heathen deities; they narrate the marvellous deliverance of the three who refuse to worship the golden image set up by Nebuchadrezzar, and of Daniel when he is cast into the lion's den for praying to his God. Mingled with these stories of faithfulness are accounts of Daniel's God-given wisdom in the interpretation of vision and dream.

Nebuchadrezzar's dream of the great image forms the only strictly apocalyptic section in the first half of the book. In this vision, history down to the time of the writer is recorded in symbolic form, as foreseen by one of earlier times; the history terminates with God's judgment upon the world powers and the establishment of his own kingdom. The remaining narratives of chapters 1–6, Nebuchadrezzar's dream of the tree and the handwriting on the wall, seem designed to enforce the thought of God's rule over the kingdoms of the earth.

If we had only the first six chapters of Daniel, it might not be possible to determine with certainty the succession of kingdoms included in the world view of the image vision, although the closing words of chapters 5 and 6 indicate that the writer thought of a kingdom of the Medes as intervening between that of Babylonia and that of Cyrus the Persian. This suggests that Media, Persia, and Greece were typified by the silver, brass, and iron, the division of Alexander's kingdom being suggested by the legs and feet. This identification of the successive kingdoms is confirmed by the visions of chapters 7–12.

Chapter 8 gives the clearest indication of the writer's historical horizon. In this section, the two horns of the ram, the higher of which came up last, are definitely said to be the kings of Media and Persia, and the great horn on the rough he-goat is named as the first king of Greece who cast down the ram to the ground. The four horns that spring up in place of the great horn are the four divisions of Alexander's kingdom. The little horn, that came forth from one of these and took away the continual burnt offering and cast down the place of the sanctuary,[1] is most clearly Antiochus Epiphanes. The restoration of the sanctuary[2] and the death of Antiochus[3] are foreseen, but beyond these the vision does not extend.

The outlook is the same in chapter 11 as in 8; the section tells of the Persian invasion of Greece, of Alexander and the division of his kingdom, of the conflicts between the Ptolemies and Seleucids, and especially of Antiochus Epiphanes and his persecution.[4] In this vision too, the historical survey terminates with the anticipated death of Antiochus.[5] The little horn of chapter 7, who wears out the saints of the Most High and thinks to change the times and the law, must also be Antiochus, and the four kingdoms, those already indicated in the image vision. The coming of the little horn marks the beginning of the end, for now the Ancient of Days sits in judgment and destroys the beast.

The vision of the seventy weeks, in chapter 9, is the most baffling of the book, but it too seems to terminate in Maccabean times; the division into 7 + 62 + 1 weeks of years is most naturally explained as representing the time from Jeremiah's prophecy of seventy years to the edict of Cyrus permitting the rebuilding; then from the rebuilding to the murder of the high priest in 171 B.C.; finally the period of persecution in the midst of which comes the desecration of the temple.

For the afflicted sufferers under the persecution of Antiochus, every element of the book would have its inspiring message. They are told, in effect, that God has permitted the succession of great powers to rule over his people, from Nebuchadrezzar to Antiochus, and that this subjection is about to end and the rule of the saints of the Most High to be established.

Daniel and Enoch 83–90 are two of the greatest of the apocalypses; their study only anticipates the ascendency of this type

---

[1] Daniel 8 [9-12].   [2] Ibid. 8 [13-14].   [3] Ibid. 8 [25].
[4] Ibid. 11 [21ff].   [5] Ibid. 11 [45].

2 c

of writing attained in the two centuries before and after Christ. In this unique literary form the unquenchable faith of Israel was embodied by a multitude of writers, until the form was adopted by Christianity in the book of Revelation, where the old apocalyptic conceptions were expanded to include the risen Messiah in heaven, about to come and establish his reign on earth.

Consideration of the later development of apocalypse has led us, for the moment, far beyond the limits of time properly included within the present volume.   One other book coming from the times of the first generation of Maccabees, or very shortly after, remains to be considered.   Esther is a story that seeks to account for the origin of the late Jewish feast of Purim and, unintentionally, witnesses to the bitter hatred engendered in the souls of the harassed people.   Almost the only noble or ennobling element in the book is the devotion of Esther to the cause of her people, as she ventures her life, saying: so will I go in unto the king, which is not according to the law; and if I perish, I perish.[1]

One's estimate of the book as a skilful piece of narrative writing will be much higher than its evaluation spiritually and ethically. The story as such is orderly, clear, interesting, and progressive, leading on well to the culmination in the establishment of the feast and Mordecai's charge to observe it, for which the whole is told. The writer accomplishes his purpose in so effective a manner that to-day "manuscripts of the Book of Esther are more numerous than of any other portion of the Old Testament."[2]   If the charm of Israel's early stories is lacking and some of their spontaneity and wonderful selection of the most effective elements are not found in this comparatively late story, the gift of vivid, effective narration has not been lost during the Greek age;   to this both Daniel and Esther testify.   Despite its hortatory purpose, the book of Esther contains a succession of scenes no less striking than the one of the banquet, and culminating in an exhortation, the more effective because indirect.

So the king and Haman came to banquet with Esther the queen.   And the king said again unto Esther on the second day at the banquet of wine, What is thy petition, queen Esther? and it shall be granted thee:

[1] Esther 4 16.   [2] Paton, *Esther*, in *Int. Crit. Com.*

and what is thy request? even to the half of the kingdom it shall be performed. Then Esther the queen answered and said, If I have found favor in thy sight, O king, and if it please the king, let my life be given me at my petition, and my people at my request: for we are sold, I and my people, to be destroyed, to be slain, and to perish. But if we had been sold for bondmen and bondwomen, I had held my peace, although the adversary could not have compensated for the king's damage. Then spake the king Ahasuerus and said unto Esther the queen, Who is he, and where is he, that durst presume in his heart to do so? And Esther said, An adversary and an enemy, even this wicked Haman. Then Haman was afraid before the king and the queen. And the king arose in his wrath from the banquet of wine and went into the palace garden: and Haman stood up to make request for his life to Esther the queen; for he saw that there was evil determined against him by the king.[1]

With the book of Esther, our study has included all the extant writings of ancient Israel down to the latest that received recognition in the Hebrew canon. No Hebrew book outside of the canon antedating 200 B.C. has been preserved. From the early part of the second century B.C. forward many extra-canonical writings exist, though commonly not in the Hebrew language. We have included those written during the period under survey, in order to make our study of the literature of ancient Israel as complete as possible down to the death of Simon Maccabeus.

[1] Esther 7 1-7.

INDEX